Interpretive Guide
to the
Millon Clinical Multiaxial Inventory

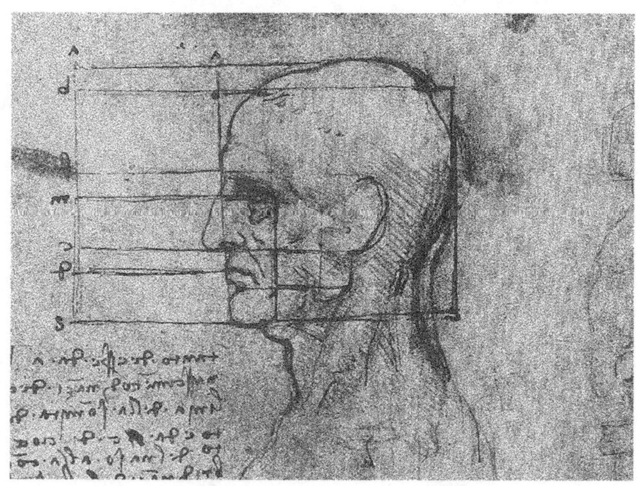

Interpretive Guide *to the* Millon Clinical Multiaxial Inventory

THIRD EDITION

JAMES P. CHOCA

AMERICAN PSYCHOLOGICAL ASSOCIATION

WASHINGTON, DC

Published by
American Psychological Association
750 First Street, NE
Washington, DC 20002
www.apa.org

To order
APA Order Department
P.O. Box 92984
Washington, DC 20090-2984

Tel: (800) 374-2721; Direct: (202) 336-5510
Fax: (202) 336-5502; TDD/TTY: (202) 336-6123
Online: www.apa.org/books/
E-mail: order@apa.org

In the U.K., Europe, Africa, and the Middle East, copies may be ordered from
American Psychological Association
3 Henrietta Street
Covent Garden, London
WC2E 8LU England

Typeset in Futura and New Baskerville by World Composition Services, Inc., Sterling, VA

Printer: Sheridan Books, Inc., Ann Arbor, MI
Cover Designer: Minker Design, Bethesda, MD
Technical/Production Editor: Rosemary Moulton

Library of Congress Cataloging-in-Publication Data

Choca, James, 1945–
Interpretive guide to the Millon Clinical Multiaxial Inventory / James P. Choca.—3rd ed.
p. cm.
Includes bibliographical references and index.
ISBN 1-59147-040-4 (alk. paper)
1. Millon Clinical Multiaxial Inventory. 2. Personality disorders—Diagnosis. I. Title.

RC473.M47C48 2004
616.89′075—dc22 2004004236

British Library Cataloguing-in-Publication Data
A CIP record is available from the British Library.

Printed in the United States of America
Third Edition

This book is dedicated to Theodore Millon,
to the memory of Robert Meagher, and to all
those whose names appear in the reference list.
It is their insight, creativity, understanding,
and dedication that are celebrated in these pages.

Contents

Foreword

Theodore Millon

The pleasure I had in reading and then writing the foreword to the first edition of this book has been extended and reinforced in my reading of this third edition, a deservedly well-received interpretive guide to the Millon Clinical Multiaxial Inventory (MCMI). Professor Choca's exemplary text further illustrates his skill for epitomizing complex ideas without trivializing them. His detailed exposition of the MCMI–III is comprehensive in scope and conscientious in its attention to matters of use to both practicing clinician and graduate student. I know of no other book that so thoroughly and so compactly sets out the essentials of this widely used clinical inventory. As I did in my first foreword, I would like to sketch briefly some of the events that gave rise to the initial development of the MCMI.

A year or two after the publication in 1969 of my *Modern Psychopathology* text, I began to receive letters and phone calls from graduate students who read the book and thought it provided ideas that could aid them in formulating their dissertations. Most inquired about the availability of an "operational" measure they could use to assess or diagnose the pathologies of personality that were generated by the text's theoretical model. Regretfully, I said that there was no such tool available. Nevertheless, I encouraged them to pursue whatever lines of interest they may have had in the subject. Some were sufficiently motivated to state that they would attempt to develop their own "Millon" instrument as part of the dissertation enterprise.

As the number of these potential Millon progenies grew into their teens, my concern grew proportionately regarding both the diversity and the adequacy of these representations of the theory. To establish a measure of instrumental uniformity for future investigators, as well as to ensure at least a modicum of psychometric quality among tools that ostensibly reflected the theory's constructs, I was prompted (perhaps "driven" is a more accurate word) to consider undertaking the test-construction task with a research supervision group composed of psychologists- and psychiatrists-in-training during their internship and residency periods. All had read *Modern Psychopathology* and found the proposal of working together to develop instruments that might identify and quantify the text's personality constructs to be both worthy and challenging.

About 11 or 12 of us were involved in that first phase. Some were asked to analyze the possibilities of identifying new indexes from well-established projective tests, such as the Rorschach and the Thematic Apperception Test; others were to investigate whether we could compose relevant scales from existing objective inventories, such as the Sixteen Factor Personality Questionnaire (16PF; Cattell, 1986) and the Minnesota Multiphasic Personality Inventory (MMPI; Hathaway & McKinley, 1967). Another group examined the potential inherent in developing a new and original structured interview. After 4 or 5 months of weekly discussions, the group concluded that entirely new instruments would be required if we were to represent the full scope of the theory, especially its diverse and then-novel pathological personality patterns. Naively, we assumed that the construction tasks could be completed in about 18 months, a time period that would allow several members of the group to participate on a continuing basis. Despite the fact that we "postponed" developing the interview schedule, the "more limited" task of the inventory itself took almost 7 years to complete.

The initial form of the clinical instrument we developed was titled the Millon–Illinois Self-Report Inventory. At this early phase Jim Choca became acquainted with the test-construction project, although he was quite knowledgeable at the time about the theory and its personality derivations. He has remained one among a small group of early adherents who not only has followed the development of the test but also has continued to contribute to its further progress; one fruit of this involvement is this, the third edition of his MCMI interpretive guide. In this volume, Choca again demonstrates that useful efforts at personality assessment are neither impertinent nor grandiose fantasies of an inchoate science. Nevertheless, it must be said that psychodiagnostic procedures in the past contained more than their share of mystique. Not only were assessments often an exercise in oracular craft and intuitive artistry, but they typically were clothed in obscure and esoteric jargon. However, change in the character of personality theory and assessment began to brew in the late 1960s. Slow though these advances may have been, there were clear signs that new ideas would begin to emerge. Thus, projective techniques, such as the Rorschach, began to be analyzed quantitatively and were increasingly anchored to the empirical domain. The objective inventories, such as the 16PF and MMPI, were increasingly interpreted in terms of configural profiles. No longer judged as independent scales, these formerly segmented self-report instruments were being analyzed integratively, possessing their clinical utility primarily as gestalt composites.

The insistence that interpretation be "objective"—that is, anchored solely to empirical correlates—gave way to clinical syntheses, including the inferred "dynamics" of the once maligned projectives. The newest of tools moved increasingly toward composite pictures (i.e., "whole" personalities). Personality formulations were no longer conceived of as random sets or discrete attributes (i.e., scales) that must be individually deduced and then pieced together, but as integrated configurations from the start. The MCMI represents this trend toward integrated personality profiles, going a step further than most assessment techniques by including *all* of the *Diagnostic and Statistical Manual* (4th ed.; *DSM–IV;* American Psychiatric Association, 1994) personality disorders in a single inventory. Not to be overlooked are the sound psychometric ways in which newer tools have been constructed. Thus, the MCMI has sought explicitly to wed the empirical and quantitative features of the structured objective inventories with the inferential and intuitive qualities that characterize the projective techniques. It is this bridging of the quantitative, intuitive, and integrative that Choca has also made special in his book.

We should not overlook the very seminal status given the personality syndromes in the *DSM.* With the advent of the third and fourth editions of this official classification, personality disorders not only gained a place of consequence among syndromal categories but also became central to its multiaxial schema. The logic for assigning personality its own special status was viewed as more than a matter of differentiating syndromes of a more acute and dramatic form from those of a longstanding and prosaic character. More relevant to this partitioning decision was the assertion that personality serves usefully as a foundation, an essentially permanent substrate from which clinicians can better grasp the significance and meaning of their patients' more transient and florid disorders. In the *DSM–IV,* then, personality disorders not only possess a nosological status of prominence in their own right but also are given a contextual role that makes them fundamental to the understanding and interpretation of all other psychopathologies. Here, again, Choca has provided readers with an opportunity to examine the various ways in which the MCMI–III demonstrates the interrelationships between Axis I and Axis II.

As Choca has noted in this book, he has taken a few positions that differ from my own formulations; in many respects, a number of his alternatives remain truer to my early notions than I have. In fact, his work has led me to reevaluate some of my own "deviations"; for example, I have considered that several of the MCMI personality "disorders" scales may be better conceived as personality "styles." Prompted by his views on the matter, I have begun to write in this most recent decade about the importance of tying the notion of "normal" personality styles to their extensions into personality "disorders." Unfortunately, the foreword to a book is not the place to expand on themes of this nature. To be brief, however, I have always judged it best to orient different inventories that bear my name to different populations. Thus, the MCMI–III is oriented toward matters of import among adult mental health patients; the MACI centers attention on adolescent clinical populations; the recent MBMD focuses on patients whose primary ailments are of a medical or physical nature; and the Millon Index of Personality Styles (MIPS; T. Millon, Weiss, Millon, & Davis, 1994) is geared to "normals," or nonclinical clients. The forthcoming M-PACI is directed toward problematic youngsters in the 9- to 12-year-old range; the MCCI currently being developed is designed for troubled college students; and two instruments are in the research phase for industrial and organizational assessment purposes, namely the MIJS and the MHRI.

There are numerous additions and clarifications in this third edition that deserve special note. Especially valuable is the very extensive bibliography, which lists available references for the practicing clinician and the research investigator as well as for the student exploring sources for a course paper, master's thesis, or doctoral dissertation. This literature is referenced in the text, providing thereby as complete a coverage of MCMI-related studies as can be found anywhere. More than writing just an MCMI "beginner's book," of which there are now several available, Choca willingly undertook a thoughtful exposition of numerous advanced issues—for example, such worthy psychometric topics as base-rate calculations of prevalence scores and positive predictive power. Not inclined to whitewash the test only with praise, Choca does not stint on including critiques of the instrument or its guiding theory. Notable also is his willingness in an assessment book to engage in a discussion of the important topic of therapy, detailing key themes that illustrate the utility of the inventory as a guide for planning various treatment interventions.

Among the text's value to many readers will be an implicit one—namely, the growing appeal of the MCMI's theoretical and research fertility.

The inventory should be seen as more than just another tool in the diagnostician's assessment kit. It can provide clinicians with a theoretical schema for mastering the realm of personality pathology, a means for understanding the processes that underlie their patients' overtly dysfunctional behaviors, thoughts, and feelings. Moreover, the openness of the guiding theory, as Choca discusses it, not only illuminates a patient's personal life but also encourages investigators to tap into numerous research variables that together form the MCMI's generative and multidimensional model.

In closing, let me congratulate Professor Choca on being the first and best to provide the psychological profession with a full and rich text on the instrument. Other MCMI volumes are available, but few are as informed and extensive as his. In this edition, he has taken an even more commanding position than before as the premier expositor of the Millon Clinical Multiaxial Inventory.

Acknowledgments

I would like to thank all of those who have theorized about or researched the fields of personology and psychometrics. Most predominant on that list, of course, is Theodore Millon. Dr. Millon's well-conceptualized personality prototypes gave the field of personology a new and exciting beginning. His personal encouragement and the support that my work has received from him have given further impetus to my enthusiasm about personology and psychological measurement.

This book contains the contributions of many other individuals. None of my projects would have been possible without the statistical and computer programming expertise of Dan Garside. The help of Diana Zak in transcribing my dictations and checking over the manuscript was invaluable.

I am very indebted to Edward Rossini, director of the School of Psychology at Roosevelt University, who has supported my projects and shared research and diagnostic interests for years. Other psychologists who have helped me with research projects have included Robert Craig, Susan Dudish-Poulsen, Michael Helford, Kennise Herring, Steven Kvaal, Linda Laatsch, Gerald O'Keefe, Don Nelson, Luke Shanley, Steven Strack, and Eric Van Denburg. I appreciate the contributions of faculty and staff of the School of Psychology such as Judith Dygdon, Steven Meyers, Rosemary Moran, Jeri Morris, Linda Santos, Jonathan Smith, Martin Weinstein, and Edward Wygonik. The literature search was partly done by research assistants funded by Roosevelt University, Alix Sieradzki, David Barreto, and Lydia Richardson.

Finally, I would like to thank the staff of the Books Department of the American Psychological Association, particularly Acquisitions Editor Susan Reynolds, Development Editor Kristine Enderle, and Production Editor Rosemary Moulton.

Interpretive Guide *to the* Millon Clinical Multiaxial Inventory

Introduction

This book was written to help students and professionals in the mental health fields, particularly psychologists, understand and interpret the Millon Clinical Multiaxial Inventory (MCMI). To appreciate all sections of this book, readers will need to be acquainted with the basic concepts in the field of psychological testing and statistics. Knowledge of psychopathology and the fourth edition of the *Diagnostic and Statistical Manual of Mental Disorders* (*DSM–IV;* American Psychiatric Association, 1994), the psychiatric classification system, would also be helpful.

The MCMI is available in three versions: the original, the second edition (MCMI–II), and the most current edition, the MCMI–III. The original version was referred to as the MCMI by the literature of that era but will be called the MCMI–I in this book. Throughout this work, the label *MCMI* is used when the issue discussed applies to any version of the test. Otherwise, the particular version of the test (MCMI–I, MCMI–II, or the MCMI–III) will be noted.

This edition of the *Interpretive Guide* has been updated with the material that has become available since the publication of the second edition. In response to feedback, this third edition covers the basics more carefully. In that way, it is hoped that readers who are not knowledgeable about certain areas (e.g., psychometric concepts) may have an easier time following the material presented. Finally, discussion of MCMI–I and MCMI–II studies that addressed issues related to those previous versions of the test was taken out or greatly abbreviated, because those versions of the test are no longer current.

In spite of the fact that many MCMI–I and MCMI–II studies were taken out for this edition of the *Interpretive Guide,* a great number of such studies are still included. Chapter 5, for instance, kept studies dealing with the Validity and Modifier Indices of the MCMI–II, because those scales have basically stayed the same for the MCMI–III. Studies describing clinical syndromes on the basis of MCMI scores are still offered in chapter 7 because such studies speak of relationships between clinical constructs that go beyond the particular version of the test. For instance, studies showing that there are alcoholics with a narcissistic–histrionic personality as well as alcoholics with a negativistic–borderline personality offer valuable information, and it should not matter that the information was obtained with a previous version of the MCMI. Finally, studies examining the relationship between the MCMI and other instruments were retained in chapter 8. Although the MCMI–III is substantially different from the previous versions (see chap. 1, this volume, for more details), the corresponding scales of the MCMIs are very highly correlated (see chap. 8). It would be expected, as a result, that relationships that existed between an instrument and a previous version of the MCMI would endure with the MCMI–III.

This *Interpretive Guide* is divided into 11 chapters. Chapter 1 provides an overview of how the MCMI was designed and organized. A brief description of the kinds of items used for each of the clinical scales also is included in that chapter. In chapter 2, the basics of personality style theory and the model that provides the theoretical underpinning for the MCMI–III are discussed. Chapter 3 reviews the processes used to standardize the MCMI–III. In chapters 4 and 5, extraneous variables that may affect the validity of the instrument are explored, in terms of both individual variables (chap. 4) and the response sets used by the person taking the test (chap. 5).

The book goes on to share my ideas about how the MCMI–III can be used in the assessment of personality styles (chap. 6) and provides narratives for many of those styles. The use of the test in the assessment of personality disorders and clinical syndromes is discussed in chapter 7. Chapter 8 explores the use of the MCMI with other psychological tests, and chapter 9 reviews what is known about the MCMI and psychotherapy.

Thus, chapters 1 through 9 were designed to provide the foundation the reader needs to interpret the MCMI in an informed manner and make appropriate recommendations. Having covered that background, the book continues with chapter 10, which maps out the interpretive logic. The four cases offered in chapter 11 are meant to make the entire process come alive with real clinical examples.

Throughout this book I have attempted to integrate Millon's theory, the MCMI, and the data that countless researchers have accumulated using this instrument. I have personally favored the MCMI since it came into existence. The MCMI findings I obtained through the years have undoubtedly contributed in a very substantial way to the evaluations of the patients

I have seen. In our field, however, there are no perfect tools. It should be obvious that we can perform a better diagnostic job if we are aware of the limitations of our instruments, as well as their strengths. In that spirit, I have tried to give MCMI critics their do and integrate their work with the work that supports the MCMI.

In addition to those objectives, it has been my goal to write a book that is well organized and explains clearly, in a readable manner, what are often difficult concepts and complex issues. As my reader, you now become the most important person, since you are the ultimate judge of the success I have had in meeting my objectives. Although the book is dedicated to my sources, it is meant for you, and it is my hope that it meets your needs and expectations.

Part I

Design, Development, and Operating Characteristics of the MCMI

Overview of the MCMI

This chapter provides an overview of the third edition of the Millon Clinical Multiaxial Inventory (MCMI–III; Millon, 1994a). After a brief introduction to the instrument, the chapter presents common uses of the test, as well as who may be an appropriate examinee, and the advantages of using the MCMI–III. A discussion of the administration and scoring of the inventory precedes a review of the test scales. Also discussed is whether the MCMI–III measures the emotional state of the individual or more permanent attributes. Finally, the chapter closes with a preview of the logic and steps used in interpreting MCMI–III protocols and the use of the Pearson Assessment automated report.

Introduction to the MCMI–III

The MCMI–III is a 175-item, true–false self-report psychological inventory intended to be used with emotionally disturbed patients. The MCMI is one of the most popular instruments of its kind (Belter & Piotrowski, 1999; Camera, Nathan, & Puente, 1998; Piotrowski & Keller, 1989; Piotrowski & Lubin, 1989, 1990; Watkins, Campbell, Nieberding, & Hallmark, 1995). Its use is commonly taught in clinical psychology training programs (Childs & Eyde, 1999). Forty percent of internship sites in the United States want their interns to come in with a good working knowledge of this instrument (Clemence & Handler, 2001). In spite of concern about a recent decline in the number of MCMI publications (Craig & Olson, 2002), the list of references in this book attests to the quantity of research that has been published with the instrument. The inventory is used in countries outside of the United States and has been translated into several other languages (H. J. Jackson, Rudd, Gazis, & Edwards, 1991; Luteijn, 1990; Montag & Comrey, 1987; Mortensen & Simonsen, 1990; Simonsen & Mortensen, 1990; Vereycken, Vertommen, & Corveleyn, 2002).

The MCMI offers automated interpretations especially designed for correctional settings (Millon, Davis, & Millon, 1998). The test is well suited for screening offenders in need of mental health interventions (Retzlaff, Stoner, & Kleinsasser, 2002). The instrument is used in forensic evaluations (Borum & Grisso, 1995; Craig, 1999b; Dyer, 1997, 1999; McCann & Dyer, 1996; Schutte, 2001), in the evaluation of custody litigants (Ackerman & Ackerman, 1996; Halon, 2001; Lampel, 1999), in the assessment of individuals filing for disability or compensation (Repko & Cooper, 1985; Retzlaff & Cicerello, 1995), and in the evaluation of military personnel (Rudd & Orman, 1996; Vereycken et al., 2002). In the recent past only two personality tests (the Minnesota Multiphasic Personality Inventory [MMPI] and the Rorschach) have been the subject of more publications than the MCMI (Butcher & Rouse, 1996; Ritzler, 1996). In contrast to the empirical-keying method used for the MMPI (Hathaway & McKinley, 1967), the MCMI items were chosen on a theoretical basis, following the concepts and ideas developed by Millon.

In keeping with the current psychiatric nosology, the MCMI is partly categorical in nature: It has different scales to measure different prototypes (e.g., the dependent personality) that are conceptually different from other entities (e.g., the narcissistic personality). It avoids some of the drawbacks of a categorical system (see Widiger, 1992) by offering dimensional scores for each of the prototypes. In other words, although cutoff scores and different scales allow the classification of the examinee as having or not having a particular attribute, the inventory still permits measurement of the level or strength of any of the attributes.

The MCMI–I has 20 clinical scales, the MCMI–II has 22, and the MCMI–III has 24. The scales are clustered into four groups: personality style scales, severe personality scales, clinical syndrome scales, and severe clinical syndrome scales. All versions of the test have an adjustment factor and a validity scale. The MCMI–II and the MCMI–III have two other scales measuring examinee response tendencies.

This chapter discusses the use of the MCMI, the type of individual who may be an appropriate examinee, and the advantages of this test over similar instruments. How the test is administered and scored is covered next; in the latter sections the focus is on the literature about the test, rather than on the actual scoring details. The reader is referred to the test manual for the scoring procedure (Millon, 1994a). A review of the scales and the types of items that the different scales contain is then offered. The chapter concludes by presenting the logic that is followed in interpreting MCMI results.

Uses of the MCMI

One way in which the MCMI can be used is for clinical decision making, or the identification of individuals who have or do not have a particular psychological attribute. For instance, the MCMI–I was used to predict which individuals would be recommended for discharge from the U.S. Air Force (Butters, Retzlaff, & Gibertini, 1986; Retzlaff & Deatherage, 1993) and which incarcerated felons would drop out of an educational program (Ahrens, Evans, & Barnett, 1990).

The fact that the MCMI weighted scores are tied to the base rate of a particular attribute potentially makes this instrument more useful than others for selecting individuals with that attribute. In an article that has become a classic in the psychometric literature, Meehl and Rosen (1955) highlighted the importance of examining local prevalences when a test is used to place examinees into diagnostic groups. Consider, for instance, a psychiatric ward in an upper-middle-class neighborhood in which 95% of the patients have been diagnosed with major depression. Knowing that statistic, we could assign any patient in that ward to the depressed group and be correct 95% of the time, without having any information about the individual. If a depression scale were used for diagnosing depression in such a setting, it would be very difficult for this scale to do better than chance. Clinicians can calculate the gain the scale would offer by determining the positive predictive power of the scale in their specific situation.[1] If the gain

[1] The positive predictive power (PPP) can be calculated through the following equation:

$$PPP = (P \times Sn)/(P \times Sn) + (1 - P)(1 - Sp)$$

where P is the local prevalence, Sn is the sensitivity of the scale from the test manual, and Sp is the specificity of the scale (Gibertini, Brandenburg, & Retzlaff, 1986). Applying this equation to the example given above, we would obtain a PPP of .98:

$$PPP = (.95 \times .57)/(.95 \times .57) + (1 - .95)(1 - .73) = .98$$

Because we would be able to guess correctly 95% of the time by assuming that all patients in the ward were depressed, the scale would help us improve our decision effectiveness by only 3% ([.98 – .95] × 100) and may not be worth the bother. In a more heterogeneous setting, where the prevalence of depression is 30%, the PPP would be .48, and the gain we would achieve by using the Major Depression is not sufficient, it may be possible to improve the test performance using the bootstrap methodology (see the Operating Characteristics of a Test section in chap. 3). Although in some settings the gain may still not be enough to warrant the use of the test, the MCMI can usually improve diagnostic accuracy enough to make the testing worthwhile.

The MCMI has been used to describe the psychological characteristics of a sample (e.g., Bryer, 1990). When the sample is made up of individuals with a common psychological attribute or clinical diagnosis (e.g., alcohol abusers), the findings can be generalized to speak for that particular group of people. The many studies that exemplify this use are covered throughout this book. The MCMI is even more commonly used to obtain information about a particular individual. The chapters that follow review many such attempts, as well as how the information obtained can be used in therapy.

Wakefield and Underwager (1993) warned against the uninformed use of the MCMI in a forensic setting. When used properly, however, the test also can be helpful in the courts. In their book on forensic assessments with the Millon inventories, McCann and Dyer (1996) reviewed applications of the MCMI in case law and criminal and civil cases. In addition to numerous instructive examples, their book discussed the role of the mental health professional as an expert witness and the process of preparing for testimony. Shorter reviews of forensic applications are also available (Dyer, 1997; McCann, 2002).

The MCMI was designed to measure personality traits and psychopathology. If the question of interest does not involve directly one of these two areas, the use of this test probably is inappropriate. Consider, for instance, a situation in which one desires to learn about an individual's marital stability. Because neither personality traits nor psychopathology addresses directly the issue of marital longevity, a diagnostician in this situation would be better off using other instruments.

The Appropriate Examinee

Some minimal requirements have to be met before the test can be administered meaningfully. The examinee has to be old enough to fit the norms

scale would be a more enticing 18%. More generally, the higher the prevalence of an attribute in a particular population, the less the statistical gain one would achieve by using any instrument.

of the test and has to have enough intellectual and emotional capacity to make sense of the test items. Although most of the items, at least in the case of the MCMI–II, require only fourth- or fifth-grade reading skills, individuals with less than 8 years of education may find the test too difficult to take it meaningfully (Schinka & Borum, 1993).

As a self-report questionnaire, the MCMI is likely to be most productive and revealing when the examinee is reasonably intelligent, has no difficulty understanding the items, knows himself or herself well enough to answer the questions accurately, and is willing to share what he or she knows openly and nondefensively. In other words, the ideal examinee is one who can become an active collaborator in the diagnostic process and who has the necessary skills to effectively contribute to this enterprise. Unfortunately, clinicians often are called on to test people who are not optimal examinees and who, for whatever reason, do not meet all of these requirements. The less ideal the examinee is, of course, the less meaningful the results are bound to be. In extreme cases, such results should be seen as invalid and should be disregarded.

Although Millon (e.g., 1982b, 1983, 1987, 1994a) has repeatedly warned against the use of the inventory with nonpsychiatric individuals, psychologists have often disregarded that instruction and have used the test with emotionally healthy people (e.g., Boyle & Le Déan, 2000; Elliott, Jackson, Layfield, & Kendall, 1996; A. R. King, 1998; Repko & Cooper, 1985; Watson & Sinha, 1995; Wierzbicki, 1997; Wierzbicki & Gorman, 1995). Millon's argument has been that the test was designed for, and standardized with, a psychiatric population and that the test norms may not be valid if the examinee does not fit the standardizing group. Going a step further, Moreland (1992) suggested that the clinical group with which the test is used must be similar to that used to standardize the test.

We have taken issue with that viewpoint (Choca, Shanley, et al., 1992). The major argument in favor of the restriction is the principle that psychological tests should be used only with individuals resembling the norming population. On a test of manual dexterity, for instance, it is obviously inappropriate to compute the standard score of an 80-year-old individual using norms for adolescents. However, the principle can and should be disregarded when there is a good reason to do so. Neuropsychologists routinely use the Wechsler Adult Intelligence Scale (WAIS–III; Wechsler, 1997), a test standardized with individuals who had not suffered brain damage, to measure the effects of brain damage. In this case, the purpose of the testing is to compare the examinee with a population who may be different, at least in terms of brain functioning, from that individual.

Thus, there is nothing intrinsically wrong with using a test standardized with one population to evaluate individuals from another population, as long as the clinician keeps in mind the group to which the examinee is being compared. In spite of this argument, Millon's concerns (1982b, 1983, 1987, 1994a) should not be taken lightly. Several of the properties of the inventory make the scores obtained by the nonpsychiatric examinee difficult to interpret.

One problem in interpreting the scores of a nonpsychiatric examinee is that it is difficult to know what to expect. Should the nonpsychiatric individual be expected to score lower or higher than the psychiatric population? The answer to this question depends on one's reasoning.

One way of looking at the question is to note that the weighted score used by the test, the Base Rate (BR) score, is anchored on the prevalence of particular attributes in the psychiatric population (see chap. 3, this volume). In theory, and from a purely statistical standpoint, the test would be expected to overdiagnose problems with the nonpsychiatric examinee. The reason is that the cutoff score for the different scales is set to mark a proportion of the population consistent with the prevalence of the characteristic in the psychiatric sample. Choosing the same proportion in a nonpsychiatric sample, in which the prevalence of the trait is much lower, would theoretically lead to having too many individuals score above the cutoff point.

Looking at the issue from an item–content point of view, however, would lead to the opposite expectation. In our response to Wetzler (1990), we argued that the severity of the items, tailored as they are for individuals with emotional problems, may mean that these items would not be endorsed by less disturbed individuals (Choca, Shanley, et al., 1992). The lack of endorsement would then result in an underdiagnosis of psychological attributes. Thus, from this vantage point, scores below the cutoff may still be revealing meaningful information in the case of a nonpsychiatric individual. A BR score of 35 or below clearly would be indicative of an absence of the attribute being measured because that score was used as the anchor point for the average in the nonpsychiatric sample. However, the clinician would have no scientific way of determining what to interpret among the scores that fall above a BR score of 35.

An additional problem with Millon's stance is the issue of what constitutes a psychiatric patient. The chronically psychotic individual who has multiple admissions to psychiatric wards obviously is a psychiatric patient, but what about a college student who uses the counseling service at the university when he is feeling depressed because his girlfriend left him? Is he a psychiatric patient? What about the high-functioning woman who has become anxious and uncomfortable while having to compete in a male-dominated law firm? In spite of the specific criteria used by the *DSM–IV*, our nosology does not draw a clear line between normality and psychopathology (Kendall, 1983; Sabshin, 1989). Moreover, in some cases the referral question is precisely whether or not the individual has a diagnosable psychiatric disorder. If it were inappropriate to use an instrument designed for psychiatric patients, there would be no instrument we could use in this situation.

Another issue is whether the inventory is so geared toward severe psychopathology that it cannot provide any useful measures for nonpsychiatric individuals. Comparing healthy university students with a general community sample, Boyle and Le Déan (2000) answered this particular question. They reported that "virtually all of the MCMI–III scales differed significantly between these two non-clinical groups, suggesting (contrary to Millon's assertion) that this multidimensional instrument may be useful for assessing non-clinical samples" (p. 787).

After consideration of all of these issues, it would seem permissible to use the MCMI with people who are not emotionally disturbed. Even more than usual, however, this practice requires well-informed interpretations. For instance, almost all examinees will have an elevated score on at least one of the basic personality scales, and such a finding should not be taken to mean that the individual has a personality disorder (see chap. 6, this volume, for further discussion). However, healthy examinees would be expected to have no elevations on any of the severe personality scales or clinical syndrome scales. If such elevations do occur, the diagnostician must search for further evidence of psychopathology in the history, or in other test results, before making a diagnosis. The user also will have to make other appropriate adjustments. The narratives, for instance, would typically have to be altered: Instead of talking about "obsessions" and "compulsions," one may discuss the examinee's orderly nature and preference for well-established behavior patterns.

Advantages of the MCMI

The choice of the MCMI over another self-report inventory is a matter partly of personal preference and partly of the professional's competence in interpreting the test protocol. There are, however, good arguments for encouraging clinicians to choose this instrument instead of others.

In my opinion, the main advantage the MCMI has over its main competitor, the MMPI–2 (Butcher, Dahlstrom, Graham, Tellegen, & Kaemmer,

1989), is that it is especially designed to measure personality traits (Axis II of the *DSM–IV*). The MCMI has an underlying theory, is much shorter, and is just as valid and reliable as the MMPI. Table 1.1 compares the two instruments on a variety of issues. Some practitioners have used both the MCMI and the MMPI and have discussed how the two tests complement each other (see chap. 8, this volume). However, these tests are more commonly considered to be similar enough that one is chosen over the other.

Compared with other instruments designed to measure personality traits (e.g., the NEO Personality Inventory [NEO–PI; Costa & McCrae, 1985]), the MCMI is a clinical inventory. It conceptualizes personality in the way clinicians think, using prototypes that have been part of the clinical literature for years. There is no doubt that a dependent personality disorder can be partially described in terms of primary traits such as conscientiousness or lack of openness to experience. However, to the clinician, the dependent personality prototype involves more than the sum of such primary traits. The same way that the term *water* is much more meaningful to the average person than "two molecules of hydrogen and an oxygen molecule," the five-factor model description of the dependent personality seems too convoluted and unduly complicated. Again, this may be a question of what the clinician understands best or is most comfortable with.

The MCMI is routinely used by itself, as a screening instrument, or as part of a test battery. When the test is part of a battery, the referral question and history can be used to determine what other tests should be included. A typical battery to evaluate emotional problems may include more specialized self-report questionnaires (e.g., the Eating Disorders Inventory [EDI–2; Garner, 1991]) and projective tests such as the Rorschach (Rorschach, 1921) and the Thematic Apperception Test (TAT; Murray, 1943). The author has routinely used the MCMI as part of a neuropsychological battery designed to evaluate brain dysfunction. In that case, the MCMI can help the clinician to see if, in addition to the intellectual dysfunction, the patient may be emotionally disturbed (see chap. 7, this volume).

Administration

The MCMI typically is administered with a well-designed form sold by Pearson Assessments (P.O. Box 1416, Minneapolis, MN 55440). Examinees answer the items on the same form on which the items are presented. A reusable booklet is also available that requires the examinee to answer the questions on a separate sheet. Examinees with intellectual difficulties have

Table 1.1

Comparison of the Millon Clinical Multiaxial Inventory (MCMI) and the Minnesota Multiphasic Personality Inventory (MMPI)

MMPI	MCMI
It has a long history and a great deal of literature.	It is relatively new and modern.
It is old and often based on obsolete diagnostic categories (e.g., psychasthenia).	The present version lacks literature.
It was developed with a solid empirical basis.	It was developed with a theoretical foundation.
Its development lacked a theoretical foundation, and as a result, the test does not have much cohesion. This leads to poor reliability coefficients and undoubtedly lowers the test's validity.	Development lacked an empirical basis: The empirical efforts made for the MCMI–I were mostly abandoned for later versions. It is supposedly based on Millon's theory, but it does not reflect the polarities proposed by his current theory, so that it is completely derived neither from Millon's theory nor from the *DSM–IV*.
It is thorough, having questions in all important areas.	It is short, using questions in an effective manner.
It is too long: It has too many items that have nothing to do with modern depictions of psychopathology.	It is too short: 175 items make up 27 scales (6.48 items per scale).
The *T* score is familiar and meaningful.	The Base Rate score has been usefully tied to prevalence.
The *T* score is unsound: It has been altered for uniformity, and it does not offer a measure of the prevalence of the disorder.	The Base Rate score is unsound: It is unfamiliar and complicated, it does not allow the user to calculate a percentile ranking, and it is adjusted multiple times in an unscientific manner.
It is well established and stable.	It is modern and responsive to new developments.
It has become too fixed and unalterable: Development of the present version took 7 years and changed three items.	It is too volatile and unstable: Items have been revamped after every decade without empirical basis for changes.
Full scoring involves too many templates and scales.	Scoring is too complicated and cumbersome.

more difficulty with this format than with the nonreusable form. However, the size of the print on the nonreusable form is smaller and harder to read for people with poor eyesight.

Examinees should complete the inventory by themselves in a comfortable setting; the room should be well lit and reasonably quiet. The examiner should explain the procedure well and should use the first few items to ensure that the examinee has understood the instructions. Audiotaped and computer presentations of the items are also available through Pearson Assessments (see address in previous paragraph).

The best practice is to have the examinee complete the inventory with the examiner in close proximity. This procedure allows the examinee to ask any questions as issues arise and allows the control necessary to ensure that the test is completed in a serious and meaningful manner. Depending on the examinee and the setting, this best practice may not need to be followed. In the case of a conscientious examinee invested in obtaining valid results from the evaluation, the test could even be sent home to be completed at the examinee's convenience. As Craig (1999b) pointed out, however, the best practice needs to be followed in forensic work. Sending the test home with the examinee, for instance, would violate the "chain of custody" requirement. In that case, the examiner could not testify that the test was completed by the examinee without help from anyone else.

Although the test was designed as a self-report inventory, it has been used successfully to have one person describe another individual. In that case, the agreement between the scores obtained by the person and those generated by others tends to be higher on scales measuring overt traits (e.g., Schizoid, Narcissistic, Compulsive, Hypomanic, Drug Abuse) and lower on scales dealing with personal feelings (Wheeler & Schwarz, 1989).

One issue that comes up repeatedly during the administration of the MCMI is the examinee's difficulty in deciding whether the item is mostly true or false. Some examinees object to statements that have the word *always* or *never* in them, pointing out that such statements are invariably an exaggeration and, strictly speaking, could never be true or false. In such cases, the author is likely to agree with the examinee, but then to encourage him or her to decide whether it is "mostly" true or false and to mark the form accordingly. Some of the substance abuse items raise questions among nonsubstance abusers because they seem to imply that the person has a substance abuse problem, regardless of the answer given. In those cases, the author tries to reassure the examinee that, for instance, admitting "success" in drinking a minimal amount of alcohol does not imply that drinking was a problem at one time. With any other question that the examinee may have, the examiner should encourage the examinee to complete the inventory in the most accurate way possible without ever suggesting what the answer should be. Examinees should be encouraged to answer all items, and if some are blank at the end, the examinee should be encouraged to read the items again and try to give an answer.

Scoring

Once a completed MCMI protocol has been obtained, the test must be scored. For the MCMI–I, the raw scores are obtained by simply counting the number of items for a given scale that were marked in a given direction. In the case of the MCMI–II, an item adds 1, 2, or 3 points toward the raw score of a particular scale, depending on how central to the concept of that particular clinical entity the item is thought to be.

Although the practice of differential raw score weights makes sense from a theoretical viewpoint, it has been criticized by several investigators. It has been argued that the weights add to the complexity of scoring without improving performance of the test (Retzlaff, Sheehan, & Lorr, 1990; Streiner, Goldberg, & Miller, 1993). Streiner and Miller (1989) demonstrated mathematically that the differential weighting could not have a significant effect. Retzlaff (1991) showed that the scores obtained with and without the weighting correlated at .97 or above on almost all scales and that the practice does not reduce the item overlap matrix enough to warrant its continued use. In response to these issues, the item weights were reduced to 2 points for the prototypical items and 1 point for nonprototypical items in the third edition of the test (Millon, 1994a).

The MCMI–II and the MCMI–III have been keyed so that most of the items have to be endorsed as true to count on the scale for which they were designed. This dependence on the true-keyed items for the calculation of raw scale scores has been noted as a potential problem. In a series of studies, Strack and his colleagues showed that the examinee's tendency to endorse items as true is a response bias, akin to what is measured by the Disclosure index, and that it strongly affects scale scores (Strack, 1991a; Strack, Lorr, & Campbell, 1990; Strack, Lorr, Campbell, & Lamnin, 1992).

The raw score for any of the three versions can be computed manually with the scoring templates sold by Pearson Assessments. The user can process the data through one of the systems offered by Pearson Assessments: The test blank can be mailed to the company in Minneapolis for scoring, or it can be processed on a personal computer using Pearson Assessments software and decoding equipment. In all cases, the user must purchase the appropriate materials or services from Pearson Assessments before scoring the test.

Once the raw scores are computed, they have to be converted into a standardized score. The MCMI uses different conversion tables for gender. The standard score used by the MCMI is the BR score. The BR score was developed in lieu of the *T* score often used by other tests and has been praised as a significant psychometric advance (Wetzler, 1990).

One problem with the *T* score used by other tests is that the endorsement pattern of the different psychiatric scales is not distributed normally. Consider the hypothetical scale distributions presented in Figure 1.1. When a cutoff line for elevated scores is drawn across all three of the curves (the vertical line on Figure 1.1), the line will be marking different percentiles of the sample for each of the scales (the areas under the curves to the right of the vertical line). A *T* score of 80 on the Depression scale of the original MMPI, for instance, may be associated with a different percentile rank than

Figure 1.1

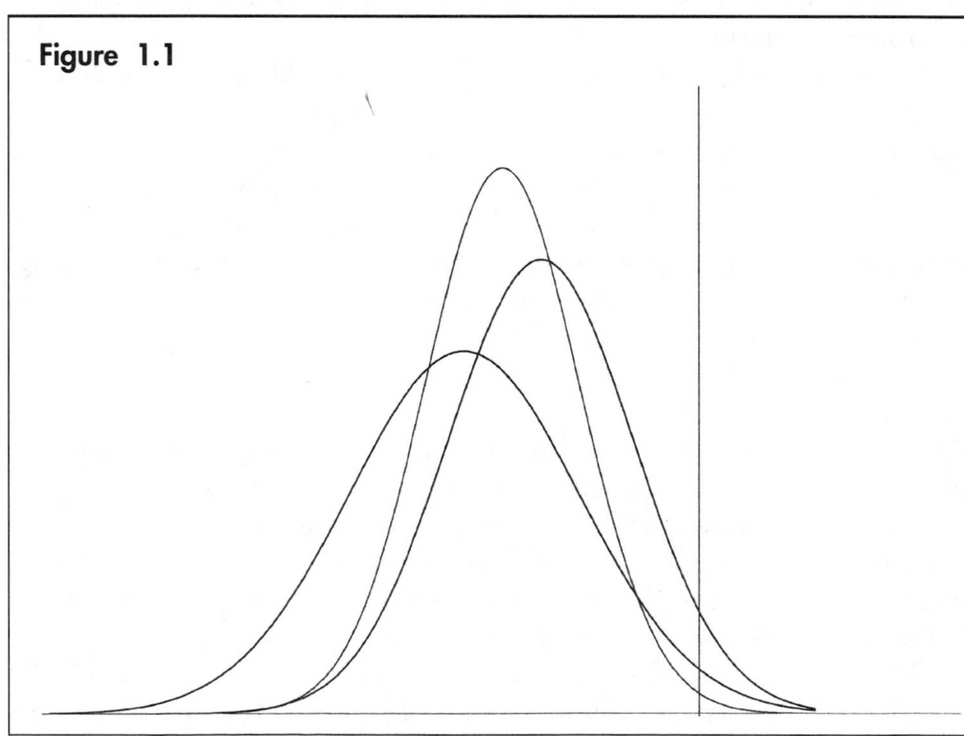

Hypothetical *T* score distributions of three different scales.

the same *T* score on the Schizophrenic scale. This effect is undesirable because it prevents the consistent statistical meaning of a particular *T* score elevation across the different scales.

Another problem with the *T* score is that it does not take into account the prevalence of the attribute being measured. The *T* score basically reflects how the examinee compares with the members of the standardizing population. On the original MMPI, the mean was 50 and the standard deviation was 10; therefore, the usual cutoff score of 70 is 2 standard deviations above the mean and defines 2% of the population. This 2% almost never corresponds to the prevalence rate of a particular disorder and introduces an automatic error. For instance, one third of psychiatric patients are thought to have a dependent personality (style or disorder); using a *T* score cutoff of 70 when testing for a dependent personality can be expected to return 2% of the sample and to miss the great majority of the true cases.

Both of the aforementioned problems led to the use of standardized scores for the MCMI that anchor cutoff scores to the prevalence of a particular disorder or trait in the psychiatric population, the BR score. The BR score was designed to indicate the probability that a particular examinee is similar to the group of psychiatric patients who were thought to have a particular trait or disorder. This measure obviously is different from one that indicates how far away from the mean of the population an examinee is on a particular trait (the *T* score of the MMPI). Thus, the standardized scores of these two tests (the MMPI and the MCMI) were specifically designed to give different information.

Millon anchored the BR scores on four different points: A BR score of 35 was defined as the median score for the normal or nonpsychiatric population, a BR score of 60 was set as the median for psychiatric patients, a BR score of 75 served as the anchor point for the definite presence of the particular characteristic being measured, and a BR score of 85 was defined as the point at which the characteristic in question is the predominant characteristic for the individual.

The BR score takes into account the prevalence of the particular characteristic in the population. As Meehl and Rosen (1955) indicated, the BR score involves an adjustment to the cutoff point to maximize correct classification by considering the effect of the prevalence of the attribute on the frequency of true positives and false positives. Thus, psychiatric disorders with high base rates will need lower cutoff points, and psychiatric disorders with low base rates will need relatively higher cutoff points (Millon, 1977). It has been argued that using a weighted score that takes into account prevalence improves the effectiveness of the diagnostic system (Finn, 1982;

Meehl & Rosen, 1955; Widiger, Hurt, Frances, Clarkin, & Gilmore, 1984; Widiger & Kelso, 1983). In fact, Duthie and Vincent (1986) demonstrated that the hit rate of the Diagnostic Inventory of Personality and Symptoms jumped from 44% to 70% when BR scores were used instead of *T* scores.

One can think of the BR score as indicating the probability that the examinee has the particular characteristics being measured rather than the simple position that he or she occupies in the normal distribution. As a result, a low BR score does not indicate anything about the examinee, as opposed to a low *T* score, which implies an absence of the characteristic being measured. That aspect of the BR score simplifies the process of interpreting the scores because the user needs to attend only to the elevations obtained, and the low scores can be disregarded.

Some critics of the MCMI have noted that in spite of its advantages, the BR score poses substantial problems. It is likely, for instance, that many practitioners will want to use the MCMI with hospitalized patients, and others may want to use it for outpatient screening (Hess, 1985). There is the possibility that two such different patient samples with potentially different base rates, when subjected to the same cutoff scores, would produce classification accuracy rates that are substantially different from those in the test manual. In such cases, the cutoff scores included in the test manual will not result in optimally accurate diagnoses (Butcher & Owen, 1978). Meehl and Rosen (1955) cautioned against the use of "inflexible cutting scores" for any psychometric device. Widiger (1985) suggested that "the MCMI would be improved by employing alternative cutoff points that varied according to the local base rate" (p. 987). Clinicians have long been urged to systematically collect local clinic prevalence data that then could be used in estimating pretest probabilities (Meehl & Rosen, 1955).

Even though the use of local norms would theoretically improve the hit rate, they are seldom if ever used. There are several reasons for this. First, the practitioner would have to go through the trouble and expense of collecting the necessary data. Secondly, the practice would create a confusing picture in that identical test protocols would lead to different weighted scores depending on the local population.

Returning to the scoring of the MCMI, after the BR score is computed for each scale, these scores are adjusted to take into consideration the examinee's response set or answering biases. The MCMI–I adjusted the BR score of some of the scales in accordance to a "weight factor" designed to indicate whether the examinee was likely to deny emotional traits or inflate them. Some scores also were adjusted when particular personality scales were predominantly elevated; this adjustment was based on the assumption that some personality styles include a tendency to exaggerate or minimize the presence of emotional problems.

In addition to both of these adjustments, the MCMI–II introduced adjustments for examinees appearing to be depressed or anxious, adjustments based on the results obtained on the Desirability and Debasement scales of the inventory, and adjustments for examinees who were in an inpatient psychiatric unit at the time they completed the test. Similar adjustments have been made for the MCMI–III. (For more information on how the adjustments are made, see the manual of the version that is being used.)

The adjustment of the BR scores has been controversial. Strack (1991b), for instance, noted that the system is "elaborate" and "confusing" (p. 3) and worried about scales that are corrected "up to four or five times" (p. 4); the fact that "one cannot ascertain how the specific correction weights were derived, nor evaluate their clinical utility" also concerned him (p. 4). The adjustments obscure the issue of where the respondent actually falls with regard to the norms on any of the adjusted scales (Choca, Shanley, et al., 1992).

Arguing against the adjustments from precisely the opposite point of view, H. R. Miller, Goldberg, and Streiner (1993) demonstrated that the MCMI–II generated virtually identical profiles using corrected and uncorrected BR scores. It also was apparent that the 3-point code-types (i.e., the highest three scale elevations) typically were the same, regardless of whether the corrections were applied. These researchers argued that the modification of the BR scores complicated the scoring and interpretation of the inventory without adding to its usefulness.

Scales of the MCMI–III

In the sections that follow, the scales of the MCMI–III are clustered into six groups: the Validity scale, the Modifying indexes, the personality style scales, the severe personality scales, the clinical syndrome scales, and the severe clinical syndrome scales. The last two groups are designed to tap the Axis I disorders of the *DSM–IV.*

In the rest of this section, I offer my own characterization of the kinds of items that are included in the different scales. Through the years, the labels used for the different scales have changed in the Millon instruments. Those label changes occasionally create some confusion. The different names that a scale might have had are noted in this chapter; subsequently, only the current name is given (written in italics in ensuing sections).

Although this book uses only one name for the sake of simplicity and consistency, the reader should be aware that the original sources cited might have referred to particular scales by a previous name.

Validity Scale

The *Validity scale* (Scale V) contains three or four items (depending on the version of the test) that are so absurd that all of them should be marked false by any examinee able to appropriately read and understand the items. An example of a validity item is Item 157 of the MCMI–III, which reads, "I have not seen a car in the last 10 years."

Modifying Indices

Millon (1987) noted that some examinees approach a self-report inventory with a response set that alters the clinical picture that will emerge from the test. For conscious or unconscious reasons, certain individuals are inclined to put their best foot forward and to deny characteristics that are not socially desirable. On the opposite side, there are people invested in portraying themselves as more severely dysfunctional than they actually are. The three Modifying indices were designed to assess such response sets and to flag those individuals who are unwilling or unable to appropriately read, understand, and complete the inventory. Millon called these scales "modifying indices" because they are used to adjust the weighted scores of some of the clinical scales.

The first modifying index, the *Disclosure index* (Scale X), is not a scale in the usual sense of the word, but a composite score computed from the personality scales. Theoretically, this index is made up of traits that are, to some degree, neutral in terms of their social desirability, providing a measure of how readily the individual owns any psychological attribute. Although the notion that the items used are neutral has been questioned (Piersma, 1989a), the index is still thought to provide a measure of the openness with which the test is taken. This index has been shown to be higher with psychiatric patients when compared with nonclinical examinees (Boyle & Le Déan, 2000). The latter finding probably reflects the more frequent endorsement of items by psychiatric patients rather than their necessarily being more open than the healthier groups.

The *Desirability index* (Scale Y) measures the tendency to portray oneself in a good light. Items that make the examinee look confident or gregarious and allege a regard for authority and a respect for the rules of society are the most prominent. Other items would indicate that the examinee is efficient and organized, avoids confrontation, has a moralistic but fun-loving attitude, experiences elevated moods, and denies the presence of alcohol abuse. As a group, psychiatric patients score lower on this index than the nonclinical population (Boyle & Le Déan, 2000).

The *Debasement index* (Scale Z), conversely, was designed to tap an attempt to look bad on the inventory. The most prominent items speak of feeling physically and emotionally empty, having low self-esteem, and becoming angry or tearful at the slightest provocation. Feelings of being unwanted and disliked may be present, along with possible self-destructive behaviors, feeling tense, being uncomfortable around others, or feeling guilty and depressed. Slightly less important are erratic moods, a desire to hurt people, a suspicious attitude, and mental confusion. As expected, psychiatric patients as a group score higher on this scale than do nonclinical individuals (Boyle & Le Déan, 2000).

Personality Style Scales

The first of the personality scales is the *Schizoid scale* (Scale 1). The main factor measured by this scale on the MCMI–II was that of social isolation (Choca, Retzlaff, Strack, Mouton, & Van Denburg, 1996; Stewart, Hyer, Retzlaff, & Ofman, 1995). Another important aspect may be passivity and lack of energy (Stewart et al., 1995).

The *Avoidant scale* (Scale 2A) measures a style that, like the Schizoid scale, is marked by social detachment. Avoidant individuals, however, face an approach–avoidance conflict: They would like to relate to others but feel such apprehension in social settings that they avoid interpersonal situations to decrease their anxiety. The items of this scale loaded onto two factors on the MCMI–II. The first of these factors reflects introversion and social isolation, and the second seems to tap an aimless and empty feeling (Choca, Retzlaff, et al., 1996; Stewart et al., 1995).

The *Depressive Personality scale* (Scale 2B) involves a tendency to have a pessimistic outlook on life. Individuals with elevations on this scale exhibit a melancholic mood and are unlikely to experience much pleasure in life. Similar individuals often harbor a chronic sense of loss and feel hopeless about the prospect of experiencing much pleasure in life. They typically have a low opinion of themselves. This scale was added to the MCMI–III because of Millon's belief that the pessimistic life outlook measured by the scale represents a prevalent personality. This personality, however, is not accepted as a personality disorder by the *DSM–IV.* Moreover, as S. E. Davis and Hays (1997) have shown, the depressive outlook the scale measures has a significant amount of overlap with the Major Depression scale. Despite the redundancy, the Depressive Personality scale was shown to make an independent contribution to the diagnosis of depression as a clinical syndrome (S. E. Davis & Hays, 1997).

The next two scales represent personality styles characterized by a need for strong relationships with people who are supportive and reassuring. The items of the *Dependent,* Submissive, Cooperative, or Passive–Dependent scale (Scale 3) underscore submissiveness, agreeableness, sociability (Choca, Retzlaff, et al., 1996; Stewart et al., 1995), and self-depreciation (Stewart et al., 1995). The most obvious features found in the *Histrionic scale* (Scale 4) for the MCMI–II were extraversion (Choca, Retzlaff, et al., 1996; Stewart et al., 1995), agreeableness, and behavioral acting-out (Choca, Retzlaff, et al., 1996). Predominant elevations on this scale are associated with an inclination to assess life events positively (Leaf, Ellis, DiGiuseppe, Mass, & Alington, 1991).

A positive view of life events also characterizes the next two scales (Leaf, Ellis, et al., 1991), the styles that Millon referred to as the "independent" styles. The personality styles that these scales were designed to measure are characterized by self-sufficiency in the person's relationships with others. Extraversion, a feeling of being special or unique (Choca, Retzlaff, et al., 1996; Stewart et al., 1995), and interpersonal arrogance (Choca, Retzlaff, et al., 1996) are the highlights of the *Narcissistic,* Confident, or Passive–Independent scale (Scale 5) of the MCMI–II.

The underlying theme of the antisocial style in Millon's system is the view of the world as a competitive place. The items of the *Antisocial,* Forceful, Competitive, or Active–Independent scale (Scale 6A) load onto factors reflecting behavioral acting-out, social mistrust (Choca, Retzlaff, et al., 1996; Stewart et al., 1995), and social independence (Choca, Retzlaff, et al., 1996).

The *Aggressive* or Sadistic scale (Scale 6B) is probably a more pathological variant of the antisocial personality style. This scale was designed to measure a tendency for an individual to be at least aggressive if not hostile in his or her interactions with others. An elevation on this scale describes an individual who tends to emphasize the ability to remain independent and who is not inclined to do what others tell him or her to do. Competitive by nature, such an individual may be seen as behaving in a callous manner in the struggle to get ahead of everyone else. He or she is likely to be distrusting, to question the motives that others may have for their actions, and to assume that one has to be vigilant and on guard to protect oneself. Projection is typically used as a defense, so that individuals obtaining elevations on this scale would be inclined to blame others for anything that goes wrong. Such a person is likely to be interpersonally "touchy": Excitable and irritable, he or she may have a history of treating others in a rough or mean manner and of angrily "flying off the handle" whenever he or she is confronted or opposed. Factorial studies with the MCMI–II characterize the scale as tapping emotional acting-out (Choca, Retzlaff, et al., 1996), strong-willed determination and social independence (Choca, Retzlaff, et al., 1996; Stewart et al., 1995), and defensive aggression (Stewart et al., 1995).

Factors found for the MCMI–II version of the *Compulsive scale* (Scale 7) included conscientiousness, restraint, affective stability, interpersonal ambivalence, closeness to experience, irritable intolerance, and a sense of virtuosity (Choca, Retzlaff, et al., 1996; McCann, 1992; Stewart et al., 1995). Predominant elevations on this scale have been found to be associated with fewer negative reactions to life events and have been taken, as a result, as a psychological asset (Leaf, Ellis, et al., 1991).

Finally, the *Negativistic scale* (Scale 8A) demonstrates an intense dislike of being controlled and a resentful attitude toward authority. Factors found with the MCMI–II have included neurotic moodiness (Choca, Retzlaff, et al., 1996), disagreeableness (Choca, Retzlaff, et al., 1996; Stewart et al., 1995), and emotional impulsiveness (Stewart et al., 1995). At least in the case of the MCMI–I, this scale appears to be related to perfectionism (Broday, 1988).

The *Self-Defeating scale* (Scale 8B), however, is considered to be a more pathological variant of the negativistic personality style. Judging from the items contained on this scale, individuals obtaining elevated scores usually have a poor self-image and believe that they need the help of others to make ends meet. Their self-images typically are so poor that they are uncomfortable when they are treated nicely and seem to seek out situations in which they will be hurt or rejected. It is as if they have come to expect mistreatment and routinely have, almost by design, the type of interpersonal interactions that would be expected to bring about the abuse. The resentment that these people harbor plays a role in bringing about negative interpersonal interactions.

Even though such individuals are inclined to put themselves down, some of the items deal with the likelihood that they also will devalue others. Other items relate to demonstrations of resentment in an insulting or even hostile way and the derivation of some pleasure from humiliating others. This tendency can be expected to create ill will from others, which then activates their own resentment in an angry, frustrating vicious cycle. Three factors have been found for the MCMI–II items: Dysthymia, Self-Abasement, and Agreeableness (Choca, Retzlaff, et al., 1996; Stewart et al., 1995). Hyer, Davis, Woods, Albrecht, and Boudewyns (1992) reported an association between elevations on this scale and a history of suicidal gestures, premature termination of treatment, a tendency to endorse more psychopathology, and a lower adjustment potential.

Severe Personality Scales

The three severe personality scales represent intrinsically more pathological syndromes than do the scales discussed previously. Considered possibly a pathological variant of the schizoid and avoidant personality styles, the *Schizotypal scale* (Scale S) was designed to measure a fear of human contact, suspicion and mistrust of others, and a preference for a life of passive isolation with few real relationships. Predominant among the items are those dealing with being somewhat eccentric and having habits that others may find peculiar. Judging from other items, individuals having elevations on this scale may have a rich fantasy life and mix their own personal idiosyncrasies with other material in their conversations. They may appear anxious and apprehensive or may demonstrate a flattening of affect. Finally, they may have feelings of depersonalization, feelings of emptiness, or ideas of reference. Paranoia, Introversion, and Aimless Lassitude have been found to be factors of the MCMI–II version of this scale (Choca, Retzlaff, et al., 1996).

The *Borderline scale* (Scale C), originally labeled the Cycloid or Cyclothymic scale, was designed to measure a pervasive pattern of instability in terms of moods, interpersonal relationships, and self-image. Elevations on this scale indicate that examinees typically respond in an impulsive and overemotional way and that their affective responses tend to be labile, at times showing apathy and numbness and at other times demonstrating an excessive amount of intensity or involvement. Sadness, hopelessness, and aimlessness may be underlying a more obvious emotional response. Such individuals may have significant problems with authority and resent any control placed on them. They can be aggressive, angry, or even cruel and are plagued by destructive ideas, which may be directed at themselves or others. The anger may be displaced temporarily by bothersome feelings of guilt or remorse. Their self-image also may be problematic because there are items relating to feeling worthless, being encumbered by self-doubt, and feeling used by others. For the MCMI–II, the items of this scale have been grouped into four factors: Depression, Behavioral Acting-Out, Submissive Dependency, and Hostile Dominance (Choca, Retzlaff, et al., 1996). There are indications that this scale, at least with the MCMI–I, tends to be elevated for any individual who has a personality disorder regardless of the type (Divac-Jovanovic, Svrakic, & Lecic-Tosevski, 1993). If so, elevations of this scale could indicate the presence of a personality disorder.

Because the conceptualization of the borderline syndrome in the literature is a "booming confusion" (Blatt & Auerbach, 1988, p. 199), it requires a few additional comments. Blatt and Auerbach provided a framework for making sense of the many ways in which borderline patients have been characterized. They argued that there are several syndromes for which this label has been used. When used in the sense of borderline schizophrenia, the term describes an "unstable" condition marked by "social role dysfunction, eccentricity, social withdrawal, attenuated psychotic symptoms, and multiple, bizarre, neurotic symptoms" (Blatt & Auerbach, 1988, p. 199). Under stressful conditions, these patients may develop a temporary psychotic state. It would seem that this type of "borderline schizophrenia" does not fit the *DSM–IV* conceptualization of the borderline patient and may be better labeled a schizotypal personality disorder. On the MCMI, perhaps an elevation of the Schizotypal scale should be expected. Accompanying that elevation, one may find elevations on the scales that measure social detachment—the Schizoid and the Avoidant—and possibly in the psychotic scales if the patient takes the test during a period of regression.

Blatt and Auerbach (1988) discussed another definition of the borderline patient that refers to a "relatively stable character pathology" (p. 199), which they called the "anaclitic" type, is characterized by "profound feelings of dependence and loneliness, fears of abandonment, and great affective lability in response to rejection or object loss" (Blatt & Auerbach, 1988, p. 199). This "anaclitic" borderline is the type described by the *DSM–IV* criteria. Although the Borderline scale of the MCMI–I was not originally designed to measure the borderline syndrome as it is known today, the MCMI–II and MCMI–III versions were substantially revised; the latter appears to be much more consistent with the *DSM–IV* criteria.

Basically, the *DSM–IV* borderline patient is an impulsive and emotionally labile person. Because these attributes also are an important aspect of several personality styles, an elevation on at least one of the basic personality style scales is to be expected. In fact, many of the theoreticians who have written on the topic of the borderline disorder (e.g., Kernberg, 1975) have distinguished between different styles of borderline patients, such as the hysterical or the narcissistic borderline. Stone (1980) offered a three-dimensional diagnostic cube that allows the categorization of several of the Millon personality styles at the borderline "psychostructural level" (p. 36). In the author's experience, individuals meeting criteria for the *DSM–IV* borderline personality disorder are likely to have elevated scores on either the Histrionic or the Negativistic scale of the MCMI–III.

As always, distinguishing between the different personality styles can add much to an understanding of patients' basic inclinations. For instance, much of the mood fluctuations and instability exhibited by histrionic borderline patients are likely to be designed to get attention. Therefore, helping the patients understand and deal with the attentional needs can be expected to be therapeutic. By contrast, negativistic borderline patients can be expected to benefit from exploring how they deal with their anger; the impulsive acting-out in that case often can be best understood as angry disappointments in relating to others.

Returning to the review of the scales, a suspicious and mistrustful attitude and a feeling of superiority are the most pronounced features measured by the *Paranoid scale* (Scale P). Other important factors deal with resenting authority and criticism, being insensitive to other people, and feeling emotionally and physically unconnected. Individuals with elevations on this scale may express a fear of losing autonomy and may be highly resistant to attempts by others to control their lives. A tendency to be perfectionistic and well organized, to be moralistic, to have little patience, and to be short-tempered may be present, along with a somewhat competitive attitude. The three factors that seem to make up most of this scale in the MCMI–II include Paranoia, Resentful Irritability, and Hostile Brashness (Choca, Retzlaff, et al., 1996).

Clinical Syndrome Scales

The clinical syndrome scales were designed to measure symptoms that are superimposed on the personality style. Typically, these symptoms are more closely associated with the patient's presenting complaints than are the personality styles and lead to Axis I *DSM–IV* diagnoses. The MCMI sets aside a different group of three scales to represent the severe clinical syndromes (discussed in the next section).

An elevation on the *Anxiety Disorder scale* (Scale A) is related to apprehension, phobic reactions, indecisiveness, tension, restlessness, and physical discomforts associated with tension. Other items deal with feeling confused, having a perceived inability to "do things right," and having diminished self-confidence. Adding in a lesser way to this scale are feelings of being unwanted and unappreciated, having a tendency to break into tears or become angry for no apparent reason, being dependent on someone else, and feeling depressed. This scale has been praised as "the most sensitive of the MCMI scales as a measure of psychological distress and disturbance" (Smith, Carroll, & Fuller, 1988, p. 172).

The *Somatoform Disorder scale* (Scale H) is characterized by complaints of fatigue, weakness, tension, jumpiness, inordinate sweating, aches, pains, and physical discomforts. To a lesser degree, the scale contains items dealing with a lack of self-confidence, being dependent on others, feeling mentally confused and unable to sort out one's thoughts, being easily provoked to the point of tears, having difficulty sleeping, and needing to be the center of attention.

The *Bipolar: Manic scale* or *Hypomania scale* (Scale N) was designed to measure restlessness, overactivity, elevated moods, pressured speech, impulsiveness, and irritability. Other contributing items deal with being gregarious and seeking attention, experiencing intense emotions, demonstrating jumpy and erratic behavior and moods, feeling superior to others, and being psychologically insensitive. A few items referring to a heightened sensitivity to sounds and a tendency toward alcohol abuse also are present.

An apathetic and dejected mood, feelings of discouragement, feelings of guilt or futility, and a lack of personal initiative are the cardinal issues reflected by the items of the *Dysthymia scale* (Scale D). Physical and emotional exhaustion, difficulty sleeping, low self-confidence, and self-destructive thoughts or actions also may be present, along with a tendency to break into tears or become angry at the slightest provocation. Judging by the items included, a distrust of others and a somewhat perfectionistic attitude also may be present.

The *Alcohol Dependence scale* (Scale B) is characterized by a history of excessive drinking that has produced problems in both home and work situations. Items dealing with diminished self-confidence and impulsivity also are evident, as is an aversion to being controlled and feeling tense, tired, sweaty, lonely, empty, and hopeless. A wish to be sociable and the experience of guilt feelings or mood swings affect this scale in a lesser way, as does respect for authority and lack of trust.

Similarly, the *Drug Dependence scale* (Scale T) is characterized by a history of drug use pronounced enough to cause difficulties in either home or work situations. Items highlight impulsivity, a tendency to hurt oneself or others, a propensity to use others, a resentment of authority, and an aversion to being controlled. Other contributing issues include being suspicious, having unexplained mood swings, feeling guilty and remorseful, professing to having no clear-cut goals and feeling aimless, being angry, feeling jumpy or tense, having low self-esteem, and behaving competitively.

The *Posttraumatic Stress Disorder scale* (Scale R) is new to the MCMI–III. This scale assesses the experience of a traumatic life situation and symptoms resulting from that experience, such as anxieties and nightmares.

Severe Clinical Syndrome Scales

Millon segregated the last three clinical syndrome scales into another group, this one of psychotic disorders. The first of these scales is the *Thought Disorder scale* (Scale SS). This scale was designed to select individuals suffering from confusion and disorganization of the thought processes, inappropriate affect, and unsystematized delusions or hallucinations. Contributing items also question the examinee about being suspicious and mistrustful, desiring isolation, feeling concern about being used by others, and experiencing sensations of physical or mental imbalance. Low self-esteem, a desire to hurt oneself and others, feelings of being unwanted and disliked, emotional constriction, and ideas of reference also are factors affecting this scale. Finally, a tendency to be rigid in one's thinking may be present.

In addition to the Bipolar: Manic and the Dysthymia scales described earlier, the MCMI contains a *Major Depression scale* (Scale CC) that measures a more severe affective disorder. Such a disorder would be characterized by a depressed mood of such magnitude that it prevents the individual from functioning. This depressed mood may be accompanied by difficulty sleeping, feelings of hopelessness, fear of the future, agitation, and psychomotor retardation. Other features include feeling physically drained, becoming angry or tearful with little provocation, feeling unworthy or undeserving, engaging in self-destructive behaviors, being socially withdrawn or too sexually inhibited, feeling tense, and experiencing diminished self-confidence or confusion.

Finally, the *Delusional Disorder scale* (Scale PP) assesses the presence of irrational ideas, particularly persecutory or grandiose ones. Feelings of superiority and fears of being used by others are markedly noticeable. Minor items that add to this particular scale include being moralistic, believing that some unknown entity is able to interfere with one's life, feeling emotionally detached, being rigid, feeling confused, and being somewhat perfectionistic.

Test Form

The MCMI–III is sold in two different forms, one meant for computer scoring and the other a reusable booklet designed for manual scoring. The form meant for computer scoring is more user-friendly in that the answers are given right next to the item text.

Blount and her colleagues asked people in Great Britain to rate the MCMI–III and three other questionnaires with regard to their user properties (Blount, Evans, Birch, Warren, & Norton, 2002). In spite of the fact that the MCMI–III is relatively short for a personality inventory, it was criticized for being excessively long. Other criticisms included poor wording of the items and the presence of vague items. Participants objected to items that posed more than one issue or that appeared irrelevant to the examinee (e.g., "I flew across the Atlantic 30 times last year"). The forced choice nature of the true–false format was also noted as objectionable. The MCMI–III was seen as the worst of the instruments included.

State Versus Trait

The MCMI theoretically measures fairly permanent attributes or traits as well as temporary states, such as a depressed mood. Some support for such theoretical expectations can be found in that the test–retest reliability tends to be higher for the personality scales than for the scales measuring clinical syndromes (see chap. 3, this volume). However, the test results are so colored by the feelings and perceptions of the examinee at the time of testing that it should be seen only as a reflection of the person at that time. Especially when the individual is acutely disturbed or feeling much different from his or her usual self, the results are likely to be much different from the results obtained on other occasions. As Piersma (1989a) warned, the possibility of such changes has to be constantly borne in mind.

Logic and Steps in MCMI Interpretation

Several logical sequential steps in interpreting an MCMI profile are typically followed (Craig, 1993b; Millon, 1994a; Van Denburg & Choca, 1997). These steps are as follows:

1. Examine the issue of the validity and defensiveness.
2. Review the responses obtained on notable specific items of the test.
3. Characterize the individual's basic personality style.
4. Evaluate, with both MCMI and historical data, the level of functionality of the personality style.

5. Describe the clinical syndrome or Axis I symptoms that the person appears to be experiencing.
6. Integrate all of the information in a holistic formulation of the individual.
7. Develop appropriate recommendations.

To accomplish this, both the theory and the research that is available about the instrument should be taken into account. The value of data from other sources, including historical information about the examinee and the results obtained through other psychological instruments, cannot be overemphasized.

These steps will be thoroughly reviewed in chapter 10, with illustrations and examples to train the reader in the interpretative process. The entire book, however, was designed to prepare the reader to carry out the interpretative task in an informed and competent fashion. Thus, information about the examination of invalidity and defensiveness (Step 1) is discussed in chapter 5. The use of item analysis (Step 2) is reviewed as a psychometric issue in chapter 3; notable items are offered as part of the interpretation of clinical syndromes in chapter 7. Chapter 6 covers the descriptions of personality styles (Step 3). The issue of how to distinguish between personality styles and personality disorders (Step 4) is discussed in chapter 2 in the review of personality theory; other materials that are relevant to that issue are included in discussions of personality styles (chap. 6) and personality disorders (chap. 7). The evaluation of clinical syndromes (Step 5) is covered in chapter 7. Help with the integration of results from other instruments (Step 6) can be obtained in chapter 8. The basis for treatment recommendations can be found in chapter 9. After the interpretative logic is reviewed in chapter 10, the entire diagnostic process is illustrated through the cases offered in chapter 11.

Pearson Assessment Automated Report

Many MCMI users score and interpret the test using the Pearson Assessment automated report system (Pearson Assessments, P.O. Box 1416, Minneapolis, MN 55440). A great deal of effort has gone into developing the reports, including questionnaires that required clinicians to compare different narrative styles. There is also a choice of narratives depending on the setting in which the test is being used, undoubtedly making the report even more appropriate. Nevertheless, the report should be seen as a computerized aid for the clinician and should not be taken at face value uncritically.

For one thing, the raw score of the Validity scale is not obvious if it is 0 or 1, and the program will offer a narrative interpretation in those cases. As will be discussed in chapters 5 and 9, some records with a Validity score of 1 should be seen as invalid and should not be interpreted. The issue cannot be resolved without questioning the examinee about the manner in which he or she took the test and will demand a subsequent clinical judgment. On the other hand, there may be protocols that are interpretable even though the usual rules would classify them as invalid (see section on clinical interpretations of invalid profiles in chap. 9).

The automated program will assume that if a personality scale is elevated, the examinee suffers from a personality disorder. This book will argue against making that assumption without solid historical evidence (see chaps. 6 and 9, this volume). This is another area in which a careful clinical judgment is necessary.

Finally, automated reports present more of a risk to clinicians of accepting the conclusions offered in them without making the necessary effort to check them against clinical observations and history. All of the caveats presented at the beginning of this chapter should be kept in mind at all times, especially when the automated system is being used.

2 Personality Theory

The MCMI is not tied to any of the traditional schools of psychology and can be used by clinicians having highly different views. The reasons for this eclecticism are that the test itself was designed to measure fairly covert traits or symptoms and that it does not have items dealing with etiology. Because the different schools of psychology are distinguished mostly by the causative factors they propose, a clinical tool that does not measure etiology will tend to be acceptable to a wider range of professionals.

This is not to say that the MCMI does not have a theoretical basis. Millon's theoretical writings have covered a wide gamut. He has hypothesized how personality traits may relate to one another (Millon, 1969, 1973, 1981, 1996; Millon & Davis, 1996; Millon & Millon, 1974), what the etiology of particular personality styles may be (Millon, 1969, 1973, 1990, 1996), and even how the adaptive potential of the personality style may fit into evolutionary theory (Millon, 1990, 1996; Millon & Davis, 1996). As opposed to the empirically derived Minnesota Multiphasic Personality Inventory (MMPI), the structure of the test obviously is tied to a way of viewing the individual.

Much of the strength of the MCMI is that it provides a measure of the individual's personality style. It is important, as a result, for the reader to have an appreciation for how the individual's personality enhances an understanding of that individual. This chapter will offer an introduction to basic psychodynamics and personality theory and a brief historical perspective of such theories. The discussion will move on to Millon's theory and its critics. The chapter will close with the distinction between normal and abnormal personality and the placement of the individual's personality in a social perspective.

Basic Psychodynamics

Endler and Edwards (1988) suggested that personality issues are best understood from a systemic, or interactional, view. From this perspective, as the individual relates to his or her environment, a certain amount of conflict often occurs (see Figure 2.1). Dohrendwend and Dohrendwend (1981) showed that stressful life situations typically have significant effects on any individual's well-being. Different individuals, however, react differently to a particular life stressor, depending on the psychological meaning that the specific event may have for them (Endler & Magnusson, 1976). A threshold can be postulated that varies from one person to the next, below which the friction is tolerated and causes no further difficulties even if it is experienced as tension or discomfort.

To avoid the discomfort resulting from friction between a person and his or her environment, the individual uses defense mechanisms. To the extent that these defenses lower the level of tension and do not cause

Figure 2.1

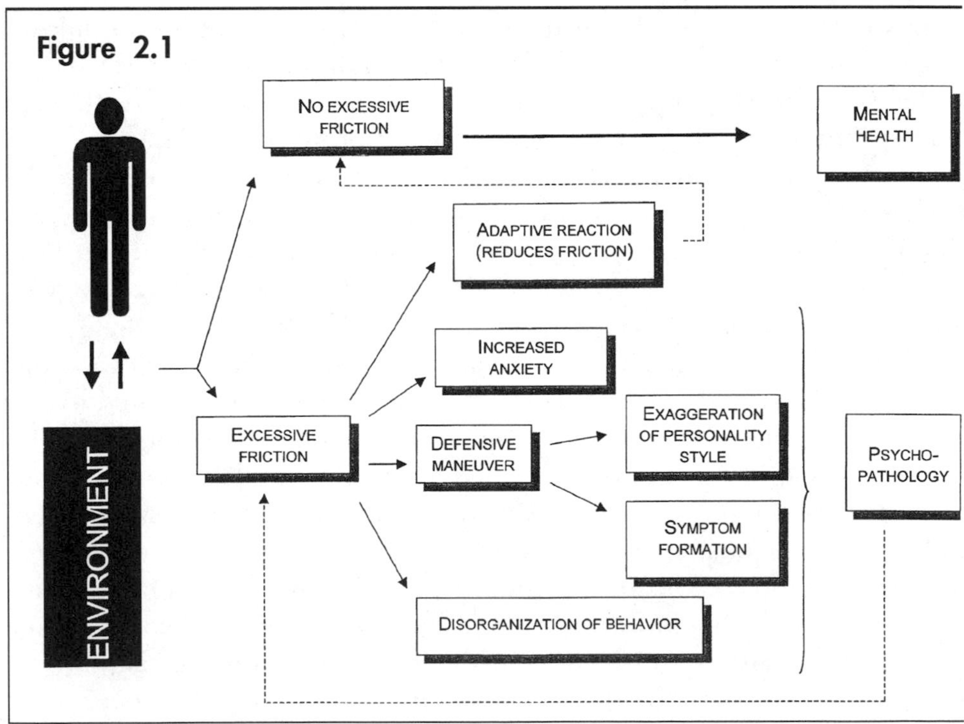

Basic psychodynamics.

additional problems, they are adaptive and allow the person to function better than he or she would without such mechanisms. When excessive, however, either the tension or the defenses can become a problem that the individual has to face, in addition to whatever difficulty was originally causing the friction. By then, either the friction or the defensive structure has become maladaptive and can be thought to be psychopathological.

Much of the friction that is generated between an individual and the environment is attributable to incompatibility. Consider, for instance, a person who has a great need to please others and has a tendency to be uncomfortable in situations in which decisions have to be made without consultation with others. As an entry-level employee, he or she may be placed under the tutelage of an older, more knowledgeable individual who is willing to teach the "tricks of the trade." Under this supervisor's mentorship, the employee performs well: The situation represents a good fit, and this good fit benefits this hypothetical worker, his or her supervisor, and the company.

Such a treasured employee eventually will be promoted to head a particular section of the company. Depending on the circumstances, the compatibility may drastically decrease. If this individual is not given much guidance in the new position and is expected to exert authority over disgruntled or problematic employees, he or she may be poorly equipped to do the job and may start experiencing a great deal of tension, unhappiness, or even psychopathology.

Although it may occur often enough, the good-fit scenario is not the most typical situation that can be discussed with regard to the compatibility between an individual and the environment. Most people are not lucky enough to have such a perfect fit with their surroundings that there is no friction. On the other hand, when the goodness of fit is awful, most individuals escape the situation altogether. As a result, in the great majority of the cases that one comes across, the fit between the individual and the environment includes complementary areas as well as difficulties.

To understand the relationship between an individual and the environment, one must consider many elements. Aspects of the environment, for instance, have to be understood, including the social and occupational situations in which the person may be involved. There also are many aspects that the individual brings into this equation, including his or her stage in life and abilities, expectations, and goals. This book aims to make the reader more aware of the contribution of yet another factor: the individual's personality style.

Personality Theory

By the term *personality style*, we mean the psychological essence of the person, regardless of pathology or ability to cope. The definition offered by the revised third edition of the *Diagnostic and Statistical Manual of Mental Disorders (DSM–III–R)*[1] is an "enduring" pattern of "perceiving, relating to, and thinking about the environment and oneself" that is "exhibited in a wide range of important social and personal contexts" (American Psychiatric Association, 1987, p. 335). In other words, a personality style is the set of lifelong assumptions that the person holds about the self and the world, along with the typical ways of thinking and feeling and the behavioral patterns associated with those assumptions. Personality traits are thought to be more egosyntonic and stable than the symptoms of a clinical syndrome, even if such expectation does not always hold (see Bronisch & Klerman, 1991, for contradictory evidence).

The aspect emphasized in this definition is that the personality style involves lifelong *assumptions* about oneself and others. This particular quality is what best sets the personality style apart from most other clinical constructs. From the basic assumptions people have about themselves and the world emerge patterns of thinking, ways of feeling, and typical behaviors that are compatible with those assumptions. For example, people who see themselves as being less capable than other people usually feel inadequate and behave in a cooperative and submissive manner.

The personality style also can be seen as a conglomerate of personality traits that tend to cluster together (Buss, 1989). As is the case with most human attributes, personality traits are not always distributed in a way that makes logical sense or that is internally consistent. One may encounter a disorganized, overemotional, and easily distractible individual who nevertheless keeps an impeccable office in which every file is labeled and every piece of paper is in the right place. There may be an inadequate–dependent man who becomes a tyrant at home after he has had a few drinks. These are, however, the exceptions rather than the rule. Most individuals who are orderly also are careful, clean, meticulous, disciplined, and punctual. It is the clusters of traits that go together that we refer to as a personality style.

[1] The *DSM–III–R* wording is offered here because the definition used with the *DSM–IV* makes Axis II sound more pathological and is, as a result, less helpful in the discussion of personality styles.

There are personality theorists who hold to a "situation-specific" rather than "trait" conceptualization of the personality (e.g., Mischel, 1968, 1973). As Buss (1989) argued, however, the debate over the relative power of the situation (or experimental manipulation) and the traits is unproductive; what needs to be studied is the way that traits and situations interact to produce a particular feeling or behavior.

Personality styles include the defenses that are typically used in coping with objectionable aspects of reality. However, the concept of personality styles goes beyond the definition of a defense mechanism. Although some relationship exists between personality styles and defenses, the correlations are not high (Whyne-Berman & McCann, 1995).

The way they are conceived here, personality styles are nonpathological entities. As Benjamin (1993) suggested, it is the song we sing through life, a song that may have many different renditions while retaining the same melody. Personality styles involve assumptions about life that are intrinsically neutral and that invariably have more than a grain of truth in their depiction of reality. For instance, an individual who comes to assume that he or she is more capable or appealing than others can obviously validate that assumption by emphasizing his or her positive attributes and the deficiencies or limitations of others. The fact that a person has some positive attributes, and that other people are less fortunate in some ways, is true of absolutely every human being but is emphasized only by those who have come to view themselves as superior.

Generally this book assumes that no personality style is necessarily better than any other. This assumption is not totally true. Both Millon (1981) and the fourth edition of the *Diagnostic and Statistical Manual of Mental Disorders* (*DSM–IV*; American Psychiatric Association, 1994) discussed personality styles that are presumed to be more adaptive. The healthy correlates of histrionic, narcissistic, and compulsive inclinations have been repeatedly shown (Boyle & Le Déan, 2000; Butters, Retzlaff, & Gibertini, 1986; Leaf, Alington, Ellis, DiGiuseppe, & Mass, 1992; Leaf, Alington, Mass, DiGiuseppe, & Ellis, 1991; Leaf, DiGiuseppe, et al., 1990; Leaf, Ellis, DiGiuseppe, Mass, & Alington, 1991; McAllister, Baker, Mannes, Stewart, & Sutherland, 2002; Nakao et al., 1992; Petrovic et al., 2002; Piersma & Boes, 1997b; Retzlaff & Deatherage, 1993; Rudd & Orman, 1996; Strack, Lorr, & Campbell, 1989). Individuals without psychiatric problems, for instance, typically score higher on histrionic and narcissistic scales (Strack et al., 1989). In fact, Baumeister (1989) has argued for a curvilinear relationship between positive self-regard and mental health where a small positive distortion is optimal. According to this theory, individuals who have too realistic a view are too hesitant and may be subject to depression; those who distort more than the optimal may have an inflated self-view and function poorly. McAllister and colleagues (2002) showed that the Narcissistic and Histrionic scales of the MCMI–III can be used to measure that optimal margin of illusion and are positive indicators as a result. The college performance of students is highly correlated with compulsive personality features (A. R. King, 1998).

Examining the issue from the point of view of liabilities, A. R. King (1998) established a tie between antisocial and negativistic personality features, poor class attendance, and academic performance deficits. Several studies have shown that psychiatric patients typically score higher than nonpsychiatric individuals on the schizoid, avoidant, and negativistic scales (Rudd & Orman, 1996; Strack et al., 1989). A negativistic personality makeup has been associated with poor adjustment (Retzlaff & Deatherage, 1993) and is typically accompanied by the presence of more problems than any of the other seven basic personality styles (Chick, Martin, Nevels, & Cotton, 1994). There even is evidence that the treatment response of patients with the "healthier" personality disorders is considerably better than the response of patients with the more dysfunctional personality types (Vaglum et al., 1990).

The research design issues raised by those investigations are so complex that it makes the question difficult to research.[2] Moreover, even if there is some advantage to particular personality styles, it is undeniable that well-functioning people can be found with any one of the trait clusters that we refer to as personality styles. Conversely, groups of very dysfunctional psychiatric patients have been found to have personality styles that are thought to be healthier (e.g., Craig & Olson, 1990).

[2] The attempt to show that different personality styles may be associated with different types of clinical syndromes (Axis I psychopathology), or with the severity of those syndromes, does not really answer the question of whether different personality styles are more or less functional in and of themselves. It is also of little value to compare individuals with different personality styles without taking into account the severity of their particular style, because extreme and inflexible styles—regardless of the type—can be expected to be less functional than those that are less extreme or more flexible. To answer the question one would have to, for instance, match individuals with different personality styles on the basis of the severity of their style, without taking into account their level of adjustment. Then, one would have to find a way to measure success or adjustment that is not biased against one or more of the personality styles. Self-report measures would not be acceptable because they can be expected to lead to narcissists, for instance, seeing themselves as more successful than dependent individuals. Similarly, many markers of success in Western society are related to traits like self-confidence; another element one would like to avoid in such a project is a circular definition between success or adjustment and narcissism. Further complicating the task is the fact that most personality styles represent a combination of

In any event, this book assumes that every personality style will give its bearer advantages and disadvantages. The orderly and disciplined individual, for example, will tend to perform better when the task demands meticulousness and careful attention to detail. Alternately, this individual may have difficulty with change or with situations in which a particular way of behaving cannot be rehearsed beforehand. In other words, the same character traits that can help a person become a good accountant may be a liability if the person wanted to become a stunt car driver.

Unfortunately, none of the ways of defining a personality style will allow a clear and unequivocal differentiation of this construct from other clinical entities (Hirschfeld, 1993). One must be aware that these definitions represent human attempts to conceive reality, not reality itself (Schwartz, Wiggins, & Norko, 1989). There is actually no clear-cut distinction between the personality style and the other psychological aspects of the individual. Widiger (1989) pointed out that the boundaries between personality styles and clinical syndromes are often unclear. The borderline personality disorder, for instance, is characterized partly by mood instability resembling affective disorders; the schizoid, avoidant, and schizotypal personalities have much in common with schizophrenia. When all is said and done, a clinician needs to develop an intuitive feeling for where to draw the line between what will be considered a personality style and what may be better conceived as abilities, psychopathology, motivated behavior, or other human attributes. The idea of personality styles is, at best, a conceptual framework that can be used to understand the vicissitudes of human nature rather than a tangible entity that one may be able to see in an indisputable manner.

The conceptualization of personality styles is further complicated by two facts. First, the relative dominance of the personality traits forming the personality style changes from one individual to another. As Widiger (1992) pointed out, there are different ways in which individuals may accumulate enough characterizing traits (or *DSM–IV* criteria) to be considered to have a particular personality. The fact that one histrionic individual may be uncomfortable when he or she is not the center of attention could make that person appear different from another histrionic individual who may not be uncomfortable in such circumstances. Second, most individuals have a mixture of elements in their personality, a fact that further complicates

more than one of the "pure" styles, so that the number of different groups necessary to do the work with accuracy becomes astronomical.

the clinical picture. A histrionic–narcissistic person may appear much different from a histrionic–dependent or a histrionic–negativistic individual. Millon (2002) noted that the recognized personality entities are nomothetic or group-based hypothetical prototypes and that clinicians must recognize the idiographic or individual characteristics of patients.

Not all of the recognized personality disorders can be depathologized easily into describing a personality style. For example, the borderline personality disorder involves a pattern of unstable relationships accompanied by an identity disturbance, impulsive acting-out, self-damaging acts, mood instability, a chronic sense of boredom or emptiness, inappropriate intense anger, and possible paranoid ideation or dissociative symptoms (American Psychiatric Association, 1994). It is difficult to conceive the core of this disorder as resulting from a basic assumption of life (Clarkin, Widiger, Frances, Hurt, & Gilmore, 1983). Moreover, this disorder has been seen theoretically as resulting from a failure of integration in the basic personality (Dorr, Barley, Gard, & Webb, 1983; Kernberg, 1975). Thus, in contrast to the personality styles in which some advantages can be seen for individuals having that particular style, the borderline pattern seems intrinsically problematic and disadvantageous.

If the premise is accepted that some of the personality disorder prototypes cannot be applied to define normal individuals, then it becomes a matter of judgment whether a recognized personality pattern has enough good qualities that it should be considered a personality style. In his original writings, Millon (1969) recognized the eight personality styles that are recognized in this book. This book will accept the borderline, paranoid, and schizotypal personality disorders as personality disorders, but not as patterns of behavior that are ever found in individuals who do not have an emotional disorder.

Historical Perspective

Primitive descriptions of personality styles can be traced back to the ancient Greeks. In his book *The Sacred Disease,* Hippocrates (460–357 B.C./1950) proposed that there were four "humors" in the human body and that the balance of these humors led to the person being either quiet, depressed, and oblivious or excited, noisy, and mischievous. It is of interest that even Hippocrates' etiologic concepts have survived the passage of time: Researchers are still proposing biochemical explanations for personality characteristics (for a review of psychobiological models, see Claridge, 1994).

Several founding fathers in the field of psychopathology wrote about particular personality styles. Freud and Abraham, for example, described the "oral–receptive character," which was the precursor of the dependent personality style (Abraham, 1924/1927). W. Reich (1949), another early psychoanalyst, also addressed the vicissitudes of character formation and the consistent patterning of defenses within a given personality. Perhaps the first person to emphasize the role of the underlying personality as a general aspect of all human beings was Adler (1956). The Adlerian approach is to describe the client's lifestyle on the basis of his or her history, attempting to conceptualize what makes that person tick. After a thorough evaluation of a client, a man may be described as being angry at his mother for abandoning him when he was a year old and as dedicating his life to finding women who have problems with commitment so that they can be punished for their disloyalty. Done in this manner, the person's lifestyle has the potential for being true to the uniqueness and individuality of the human being, because such a description would not apply to many other individuals.

The Adlerian approach, however, can be problematic in several ways. The issue of the validity and reliability in such a diagnostic system seems paramount: The odds that another clinician would arrive at the same statement regarding a person's lifestyle are extremely low. In fact, it is possible that the same clinician, on seeing the patient on a different occasion, may arrive at a somewhat different conceptualization of the person's psychological essence. There also is the issue of how much of the conceptualized lifestyle is a product of what the client actually is presenting, as opposed to being an imaginative fabrication on the clinician's part or a countertransference of the clinician's psychological issues.

Thus, in spite of the appeal of the Adlerian system, the concept of personality style cannot be used effectively without a model or system. In allowing the clinician to classify or group individuals, such a model would offer great advantages: One then can compare or contrast one person with another or apply data collected from a group of individuals (e.g., histrionics) to a single person who is thought to be a member of that group.

Any time a system of classification is developed, one must accept that individuals need to be bent to fit the model and that the sense of uniqueness that the individual presents must be forfeited to some degree. If clinicians were unwilling to do so, they would have to resign themselves to having little to say about the individual in addition to what the person says about himself or herself.

One method that has been used to develop a valid and reliable system for personality styles strives to be the most empirical. Building upon Allport and Odbert's (1936) search for terms that describe personality in the English language, Cattell (1946, 1965) factor analyzed all such words. His work led to 16 primary dimensions and culminated in the creation of the Sixteen Personality Factor Questionnaire (16PF) and its revision (Cattell, 1986). Cattell's approach obviously enjoys a scientific purity and psychometric simplicity that are difficult to match. More recently, McCrae and Costa (1985, 1986) revived the factorial approach and used it to develop their own questionnaire (Costa & McCrae, 1985). Costa and McCrae's five-factor model has received wide recognition and support (e.g., Wiggins & Pincus, 1989).

One problem with the factorial approach is that in spite of its obvious empirical and scientific basis, the approach has led to a striking lack of consensus among the researchers. Krug and Laughlin (1977) factor analyzed Catell's Clinical Analysis Questionnaire and found 9 higher order factors. The 3 factors that Costa and McCrae started with eventually expanded to 5. Working with patient samples, Harkness and McNulty (1994) found a different set of 5 factors. Cloninger's model calls for 7 factors (Cloninger, 1987; Cloninger & Svrakic, 1994). There are Eysenck's (1947, 1994) 2- and 3-factor models, Tellegen's (1985) 3-factor model, Siever and Davis's (1991) 4-factor model, and the 18 factors that Livesley and colleagues found (Livesley, Jackson, & Schroeder, 1989, 1992).

In cases where the factorial research was done with normal samples, the question about the appropriateness of using such a model with emotionally disturbed individuals has been raised. This has been a prominent issue with the five-factor model (Ben-Porath & Waller, 1992a, 1992b; see also Costa & McCrae, 1992a, 1992b). In spite of a noteworthy attempt to make the system more appealing to clinicians (Costa & Widiger, 1994), there remains relatively little use of the five-factor model with psychiatric patients.

Millon (1999b) raised the question of whether factor analysis is ever an appropriate way to investigate personality. In looking for orthogonal solutions, which would be graphically represented by lines intercepting at right angles, factor analysis assumes that the traits being studied are monothetic and independent. In other words, the method assumes that each factor is made up of characteristics that are unique and different from the characteristics that make up the next factor. He argued that personality has a predominant polythetic structure of overlapping traits (e.g., there is more than one personality style that may be emotive or independent). He argued that as a result, the use of factor analysis should be avoided in the study of personality and psychopathology.

Finally, there is a visualization problem that is inherent in the factorial approach. Even if such factors are the building blocks of any personality system, and even if they can be systematically integrated into a personality style, they do not have the same meaning to the clinician. It may be more scientific to describe a person as being high in extraversion and low in conscientiousness, but somchow the characterization becomes clinically meaningful only when one is told that the patient is histrionic. It would seem that in breaking personality into components, the factorial models make the description less recognizable and practical. The same criticism can be raised about the Edwards Personal Preference Schedule (Edwards, 1959), a measure of needs and motives.

Contrasting with the factorial approach are the theoretical approaches to personality classification. Following Sullivan's (e.g., 1953) writings, Leary proposed the first comprehensive theoretical model of personality (Leary, 1957; Leary & Coffey, 1955). Leary's model defined interpersonal personality styles on the basis of a circle, called the *circumplex.* The two axes of the original circumplex represented the continua of control (domination versus submission arranged on the vertical axis) and affiliation (love versus hate arranged horizontally). The circle was then divided to yield eight basic personality styles: managerial–autocratic, responsible–hypernormal, cooperative–conventional, docile–independent, self-effacing –masochistic, rebellious–distrustful, aggressive–sadistic, and competitive–narcissistic.

Benjamin (1974, 1984, 1993, 1995) expanded the Leary circumplex into three dimensions—focus, affiliation, and interdependence—to allow consideration of intrapsychic phenomena. Kiesler (1983) conducted a great deal of research on his adaptation of the circumplex model, a version he called the *interpersonal circle.* Other psychologists have also developed their own adaptations of the circumplex (e.g., Lorr & McNair, 1963; Wiggins, 1979). For a review of circumplex models, see Pincus (1994).

Leary's (1957) circumplex continues to have a following and has been shown to have commonalities with the third edition of the *Diagnostic and Statistical Manual of Mental Disorders* (*DSM–III;* American Psychiatric Association, 1980) and the Millon system (DeJong, van den Brink, Jansen, & Schippers, 1989; Morey, 1985; Widiger & Kelso, 1983; Wiggins, 1982). Nevertheless, such modes have not been widely accepted.

The lack of support may be partly due to the intricacy of the circumplex models, an intricacy that makes them difficult to learn. The lack of acceptance is undoubtedly also related to the fact that psychiatric nosology is based on distinct prototypes rather than on the kind of continua that circumplex models propose (Schwartz et al., 1989). In other words, the *DSM* does not allow for an individual to be a *little* schizoid and does not readily recognize that psychological traits are a matter of degree. Because clinicians are accustomed to thinking that an individual is either schizoid or not schizoid, in an all-or-none fashion, a system that calls for continua seems foreign and unduly complex. Finally, and perhaps most important, circumplex models generally do not lead to labels such as *schizoid* or *dependent* that are easily recognized by the majority of the professionals in the field.

Millon's Theory

In 1969, in a book entitled *Modern Psychopathology,* Millon proposed a system for organizing many of the existing personality disorders into a coherent whole. Basically, Millon's original model first examines whether the person is inclined to form strong relationships with others (see Figure 2.2). For those who do not form strong relationships, the model then distinguishes between individuals who are loners by design, having little interest in interpersonal relationships (schizoids), and individuals who isolate themselves as a defensive maneuver against the possibility of rejection (avoidants). If the person ordinarily forms strong interpersonal relationships, the model then examines the type of relationship formed in terms of the assumptions the individual makes about the self and the other people in the environment.

Some of the people who form strong relationships with others recognize that they need others to feel safe and comfortable. Of these, the dependent style characterizes a person who believes that others know best. Such people typically establish submissive relationships in which the other person takes responsibility for any decision that is made. By contrast, the histrionic style is not as clearly submissive but frequently needs the attention of others.

Some individuals form relationships with others in which they play the stronger or more dominant role. The first of these two styles is the inverse of the dependent, in that it typifies a person who believes himself or herself to be more capable, gifted, or appealing than other people. Instead of behaving submissively, the narcissistic individual is inclined to tell other people what to do. The second independent personality style defines a person who sees the world as a competitive situation in which those who do well achieve their goals by being dominant and strong, even if at the cost of being unkind or hurtful toward others (antisocial).

Figure 2.2

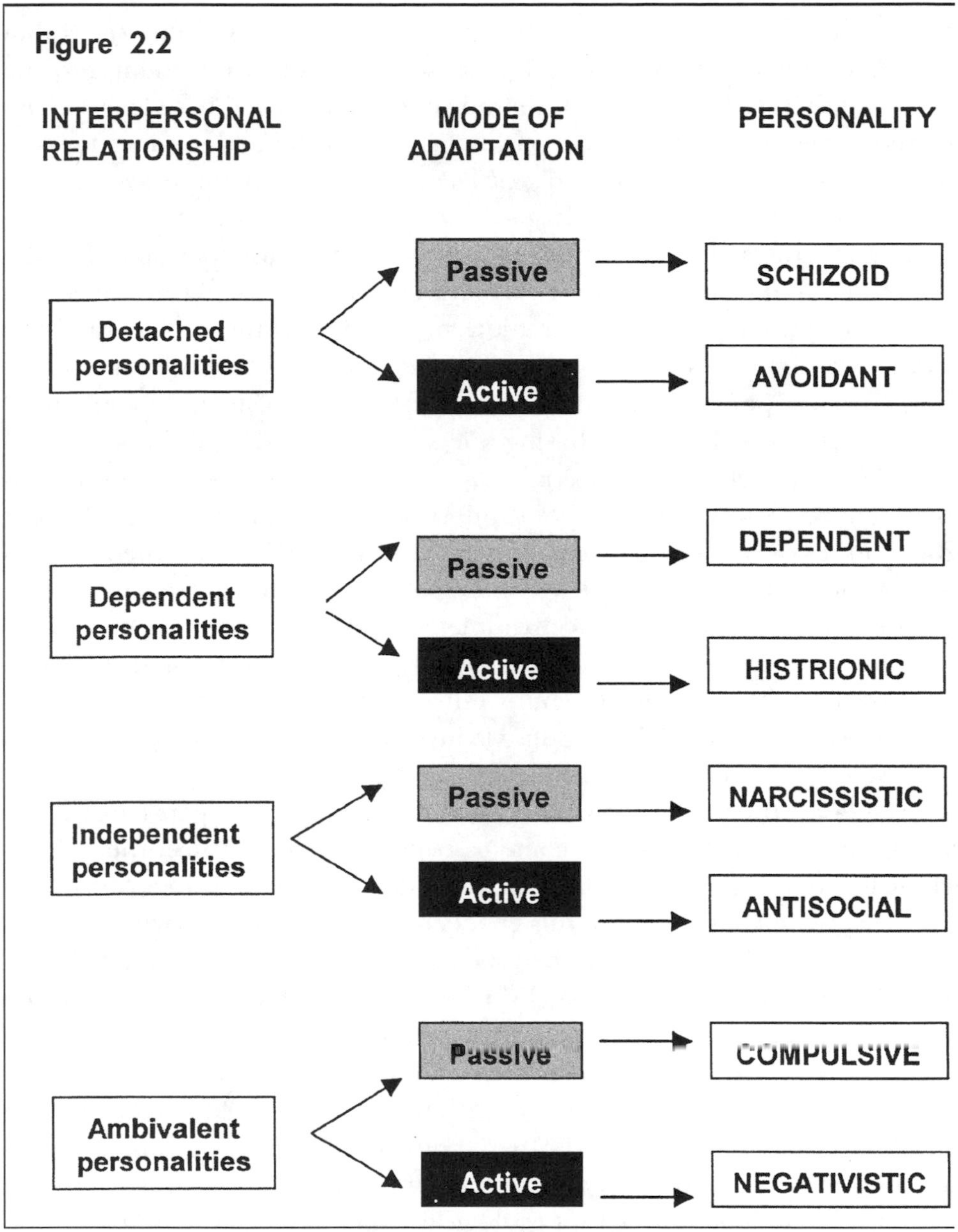

Organizational scheme for the personality prototypes proposed in 1969. The Schizoid personality was labeled Asocial in the original work; this label was changed to the current label of Schizoid to avoid confusion.

Millon acknowledged that there are two other personality styles that have been recognized widely and proposed a way of fitting them into the general scheme. In the model, these two other personality styles are conceived as people who relate in a way that is neither dependent nor independent, a way that Millon labeled *ambivalent*. The first of these two styles is not ambivalent in the usual sense of the word, but it does relate to other people in a way that is not consistently dependent or independent. For the compulsive individual, the world is a hierarchical structure in which a person has either a higher or a lower rank than another. Using this hierarchical view, compulsive individuals relate in a dependent or compliant manner toward those perceived to have higher status and in an independent or authoritative way with those having a lesser rank.

The last style is characterized by individuals who see themselves as being inadequate and in need of support but who are highly cynical about the abilities of others and are not inclined to put others on a pedestal. As a result, they behave in a fairly conflictual way toward others in terms of the dependence–independence parameter. A prevalent substyle of relating for these negativistic individuals is the passive–aggressive substyle, in which the person is able to be overtly compliant while venting his or her conflictual feelings covertly. An explosive substyle involving a cycle of hostile eruptions followed by periods of contrition also can be found.

Millon's theory has evolved considerably through the years (see Choca, 1999, for details). Millon has come to believe that to mature, the field of clinical psychology has to integrate the available knowledge in a process he calls *psychosynergy*. To achieve this goal clinicians must synthesize the truths in the field with those of more established sciences. Psychologists' goal should be to "refashion the patchwork quilt of our facet of science into a well-tailored and aesthetic tapestry that interweaves the many and diverse forms in which nature expresses itself" (Millon, 1999b, p. 441).

Borrowing from the theory of evolution, Millon (1990, 1996; see also R. D. Davis, 1999; Millon & Davis, 1996) pointed to four ecological principles: aims of existence, modes of adaptation, strategies of replication, and processes of abstraction. These four ecological principles lead to four polarities. Of the four polarities, three are used to derive the MCMI–III personalities.

The *aims of existence* principle allows us to distinguish between *life enhancement* and *life preservation*. The dichotomy between these two aims makes up the first of the three polarities upon which the Millon personality types are based, the *pleasure–pain* polarity (see Figure 2.3). The theory proposes that some personality styles seek pleasure as a way of enhancing life (e.g., the narcissistic, histrionic, and antisocial styles), in some cases at the risk

Figure 2.3

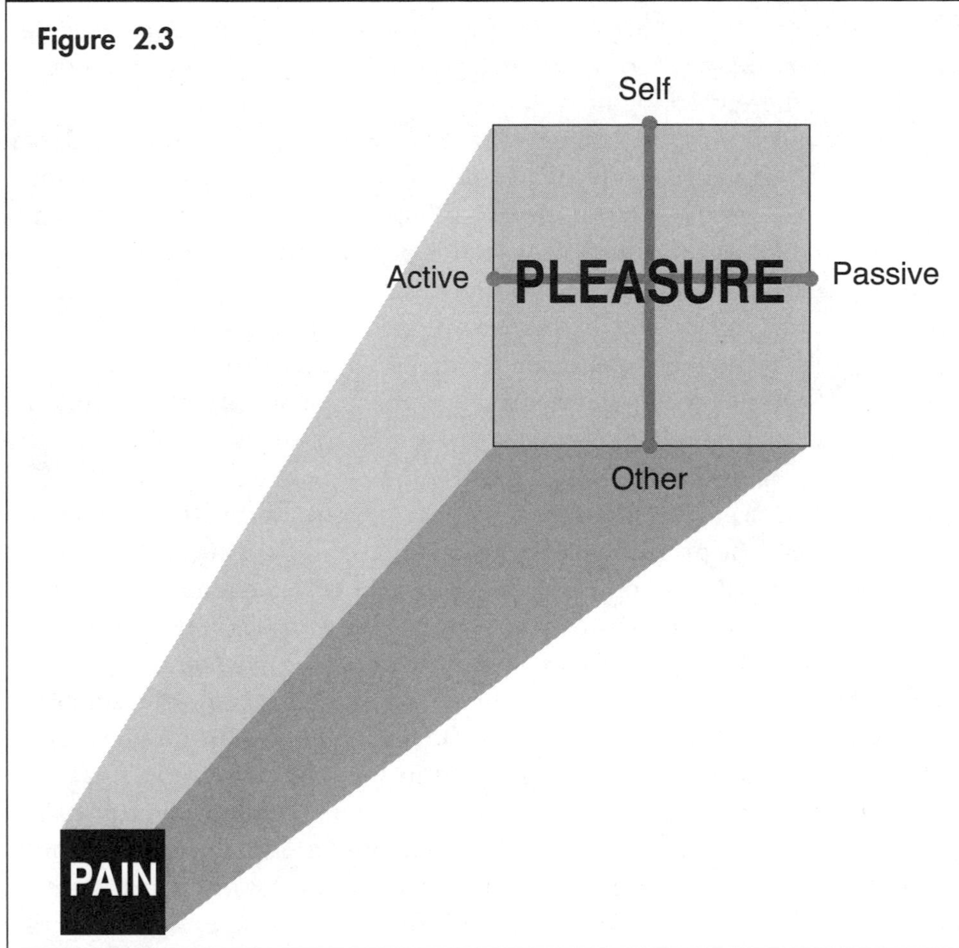

Millon personality polarities.

of placing life in jeopardy. In contrast, other personalities (e.g., the avoidant, the compulsive) emphasize the avoidance of pain and risk at the expense of constricting their existence.

Moving on to the second principle, Millon noted two different *modes of adaptation.* Biological species evolve through a process that calls for both *modification* of the environment and *accommodation* to the environment. These concepts make up the second polarity, the polarity of *active* versus *passive.* In other words, adaptation involves changing unfavorable aspects of the environment (the active mode) and accepting aspects that cannot be changed (the passive mode). Millon proposed that individuals have a natural tendency toward one or the other of these two modes of adaptation.

The proclivity of personalities with the active mode is to attempt a change of the environment, whereas the inclination of the passive personalities is to adjust to the environment.

The reasons why different personalities use a particular mode of adaptation vary. The passive mode of the dependent personality, for instance, results from the belief that the person is inferior and would not be personally able to make any significant changes in his or her environment. The passive mode of the narcissistic personality comes from the opposite belief, the conviction that the person is so special that he or she does not need to make the effort it takes to alter the environment. The active mode of the histrionic personality is generated by the need for attention from others, whereas the active mode of the antisocial is tied to the assumption that the world is a competitive setting where no one is totally trustworthy.

The third principle, *strategies of replication,* speaks to whether the species is best served by the promotion of the individual or the nurturance of others. This self–other polarity contrasts the drive toward self-actualization against the need to have regard for others. Personalities emphasizing the self (the narcissistic and the antisocial) are confident and assertive and seem to have their own ideas on how to conduct their lives. In contrast, the personalities emphasizing others (the dependent and the histrionic) rely on other people for meeting their needs and are invested in the welfare of others.

A personality prototype may be strong, weak, or neutral in any of the polarities. Being strong on a particular element of a polarity does not imply a good attribute, but simply indicates a tendency toward some style of behavior. Using the three sets of polarities, Millon was able to characterize each of the personality prototypes. As Table 2.1 illustrates, the schizoid personality, for instance, is strong in the passive polarity and weak in the pleasure polarity, the pain polarity, and the other polarity. Millon saw the schizotypal personality as involving a reversal of polarities and the borderline personality as involving a conflict between polarities, whereas the paranoid personality was seen as inserting blocks between the poles. Table 2.2 simplifies the mapping by noting only the main source of imbalance for the personality prototypes.

The last of the ecological principles, the *process of abstraction,* addresses the person's capacity to symbolize the world. Here Millon contrasted *thinking* with *feeling* as different modes of understanding. Although this polarity has not played a role in the personality prototypes used for the MCMI, it was used in the development of the Millon test for the nonpsychiatric population, the Millon Index of Personality Styles (MIPS; Millon, Weiss, Millon, & Davis, 1994).

Table 2.1

Characterization of the Millon Personality Prototypes in Terms of the Millon Polarities

	Polarities					
	Survival aims		Adaptive modes		Replication strategy	
MCMI Scale	Pleasure	Pain	Passive	Active	Self	Other
1. Schizoid	–	–	+	–		–
2A. Avoidant	–	+	–	+		
2B. Depressive	–	+	+			
3. Dependent			+	–	–	+
4. Histrionic			–	+	–	+
5. Narcissistic			+	–	+	–
6A. Antisocial		–	–	+		–
6B. Sadistic		–	–	+		–
7. Compulsive	–		+	–	–	
8A. Negativistic	–			+		–
8B. Self-Defeating	–	+	+		–	

Note. A minus sign indicates the relative weakness of a polarity, and a plus sign indicates the relative strength of a polarity. Blank cells indicate neutrality.

As has been noted, personality styles are fairly stable entities that remain mostly unchanged throughout the person's life. What factors can be posited to explain this immutability? Part of the answer can be found in biological factors that Millon saw as significant contributors to the personality makeup. Mostly, however, Millon explained the stability of the personality through the concept of self-perpetuating processes that are embedded in each of the personality prototypes. Millon proposed that there are traits in each of the personalities that feed into a cycle that serves to maintain the permanence of the personality style.

Let us examine, for instance, the histrionic personality. Histrionics are focused on the external world, defining their self-image on the basis of the attention, support, and reaffirmation they obtain from others. They repress their inner feelings and maintain mostly superficial relationships with no real intimacy. These tendencies leave the histrionic with an "empty shell," without an inner definition of who they are (Millon, 1999a, p. 407). This empty shell, or lack of sense of an inner self, in turn pushes the individual

Table 2.2

Simplified Grouping of Millon Personality Prototypes

Prototype	Personality Prototypes
Pleasure deficient	Schizoid
	Avoidant
	Depressive
Interpersonally imbalanced	Dependent
	Histrionic
	Narcissistic
	Antisocial
Intrapsychically conflicted	Sadistic
	Compulsive
	Negativistic
	Masochistic
Structurally defective	Schizotypal
	Borderline
	Paranoid
	Decompensated

to seek the attention, support, and reaffirmation of others, closing the circle of the self-perpetuating process.

Also integrated into Millon's theory are the human developmental stages. Millon recognized four early developmental stages: sensory attachment (from birth to 18 months), sensorimotor autonomy (extending through the 6th year), pubertal gender identity (between the ages of 11 and 15), and intracortical initiative (evolving from the 4th year through adolescence). Millon proposed that the person's development dealing with the four sets of polarities is associated with the experiences the individual had during these four stages. Thus, it is during the sensory attachment period that the individual's orientation toward the aims of existence (pleasure versus pain) is developed. Preferences for the mode of adaptation (active versus passive) are associated to the sensorimotor autonomy period. The pubertal stage is related to the strategy of replication (individuation versus nurturance), and the intracortical initiative development will have an effect on the preference of thinking in contrast to feeling.

Millon considered intensity of the traits, or severity, to be another variable that must be considered. He described mild versions of his personality prototypes that characterize individuals who function well, partly as a result of their personality. Maladjustment results, however, when personality traits become more extreme or rigid. Millon believed that as the severity of the symptomatology increases, the distinctive flavor of the different personality styles is attenuated. As a result of this process, the distinction between the active and the passive mode becomes blurred, and the clinical picture of individuals with different personalities becomes less unique. Borrowing concepts from Kernberg's work on personality dysfunction (e.g., Kernberg, 1984a), Millon proposed that some individuals have a *defective* personality. Progressively higher levels of dysfunction are represented by a *decompensated* and a *terminal* personality. Figure 2.4 maps the Millon personalities at the four levels of dysfunction.

Millon's personality prototypes have both a categorical and a dimensional nature. The dimensional aspect allows one to conceptualize an individual as being stronger or weaker in any of the categorical dimensions. Thus, even when two persons are seen as being in the same personality category, say histrionic, they may be differentiated if one is *more* histrionic than the other. Additionally, in real life people often demonstrate more than one of the personality categories. The person who is mostly compulsive but also has avoidant elements will appear noticeably different from the person who combines the compulsive and the negativistic prototypes.

As will be shown in chapter 6, descriptions of personality profiles that take into account more than one personality are used to interpret the self-report inventories based on Millon's theory. Using that kind of information, Millon recently expanded his descriptions to characterize subtypes of the different prototypes. Among schizoid individuals, for instance, Millon discussed an *affectless* schizoid who—in addition to being schizoid—is compulsive, or a *remote* schizoid, who is both schizoid and avoidant. Whether the person is an *amorous, unprincipled,* or *compensatory* narcissist depends on whether histrionic, antisocial, or negativistic elements accompany the narcissistic traits. The latest edition of Millon's book on personality disorders (1996) recognized 61 such subtypes.

In characterizing the personality prototypes, Millon examined two clinical domains that contain four aspects each (see Table 2.3). The *functional* domain pertains to the dynamic processes that manage our feelings and actions. The four aspects of this domain are expressive behavior, interpersonal conduct, cognitive style, and regulatory mechanisms (defenses). The *structural* domain is an enduring template of imprinted memories and attitudes that guides people's experiences. The aspects of the structural domain are self-image, object relations, morphological organization (the interior congruity and efficiency of the personality), and mood–temperament. Each

Figure 2.4

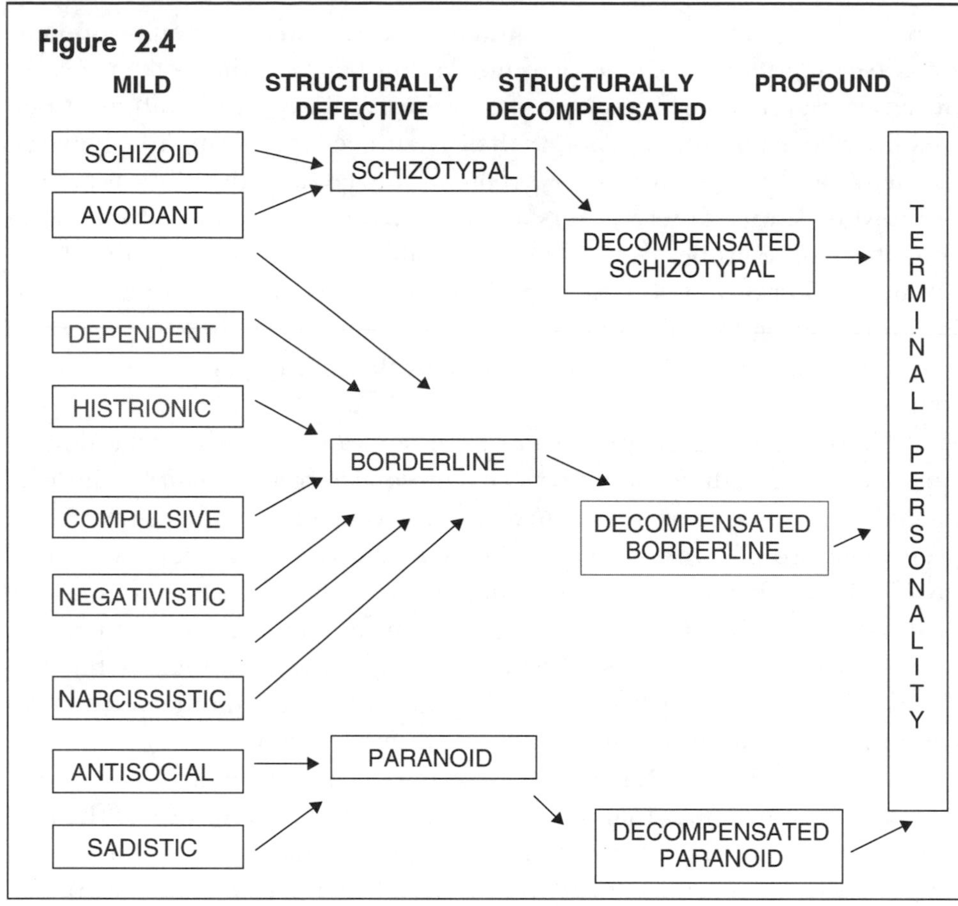

Decompensation of personality prototypes into the severe personality disorders.

Table 2.3

Aspects of the Two Domains Used to Describe Millon Personality Prototypes

Functional Domain	Structural Domain
Expressive behavior	Self-image
Interpersonal conduct	Object relations
Cognitive style	Morphological organization
Regulatory mechanisms	Mood–temperament

of the personality prototypes can be described using the two domains and four levels (R. D. Davis, 1999; Millon & Davis, 1996). The clinical domains are designed to integrate all of the major legacies in the field of psychology. From Millon's point of view, the characterization of personality prototypes should draw on the interest in expressive behaviors of individuals such as Thorndike and Skinner, the interpersonal views of Sullivan or Benjamin, the cognitive styles proposed by Beck and Ellis, and the regulatory mechanisms and object representations of the psychodynamic school (see Millon, 2002).

Borrowing from Jung (1936/1971), Millon recognized four cognitive dimensions: extroversing versus introversing, sensing versus intuiting, thinking versus feeling, and systematizing versus innovating. Like the clinical domains noted above, these cognitive dimensions can be used to further characterize the personality styles (Millon, 1994b; Strack, 1999).

In addition to the personality disorders, Millon proposed three other groups of disorders in his classification system. The *symptom disorders* included anxiety, psychophysiologic, sociopathic, and psychotic disorders. Under *pathological behavior reactions,* Millon recognized transient situational reactions and circumscribed learned reactions. Finally, Millon used the label of *biophysical defects* to cluster disorders that are a direct result of brain dysfunction.

Millon's theory has a substantial following in both North America and Europe. Through his participation on task forces for the different editions of the *DSM,* his ideas have had an impact on the classification system of emotional disorders. His ideas have been expanded into the sphere of industrial organizational psychology (Millon, 1994b). Finally, in what perhaps is the most impressive testimony to the influence a theory may have, Millon's ideas have prompted others to develop their own systems of evaluation and measurement (e.g., Immelman, 1993, 1998; Strack, 1987, 1990).

Critical Views of Millon's Theory

Next to the floor plan of the university building showing the escape route to be followed in case of fire, a friend of the author has pinned a map of the universe. Mirroring the university floor plan, the picture of the universe has a white arrow highlighting one tiny speck; the arrow indicates "You are here." Millon's psychosynergy offers us an ingenious global perspective that we miss when we focus on our microcosm. Like the map of the universe, however, Millon's grand perspective may not be of much practical use to the clinician.

In the sphere of personality theory, clinicians have repeatedly searched for a framework into which the different personality prototypes can be fitted. The ideal framework would be one that is relatively simple, places all of the recognized prototypes without adding unfamiliar ones, enriches clinicians' appreciation of how the prototypes relate to each other and to other forms of psychopathology, and have empirical support. From the present author's point of view, the original formulation of Millon's theory was closer to meeting these goals than his present formulation. In the pursuit of synergy with other bodies of knowledge, and in the many adornments that have been added, Millon's theory lost the simplicity and the clear logic that characterized the original formulation. The additional complexity would have been acceptable if it had expanded the depth of clinicians' understanding of the prototypes or offered empirical support of the theory. It is very questionable, however, if the current formulation has contributed anything further to either of these goals.

Viewing the developments of Millon's theory from the perspective of the *DSM*, some areas have gained consonance, whereas other areas seem more divergent. An example of the former has been the partial abandonment of the idea that affective disorders (what he called the *cycloid personality* and *cyclophrenia*) represent dysfunctional aspects of the personality. On the other hand, Millon's model has acquired three personality prototypes that are not recognized by the official nosology (the depressive, the aggressive, and the self-defeating). Unless his ideas develop more of a following and shape the direction of the future *DSMs*, being at odds with the official nosology is probably not useful.

Going beyond those issues, critics have pointed out that Millon's personality patterns are not always directly derived from a crossing of the three polarities (O'Connor & Dyce, 1998; Widiger, 1999). As illustrated in Figure 2.5, when the self–other polarity is crossed with the active–passive polarity, four personalities result in a straightforward manner (the antisocial, narcissistic, histrionic, and dependent prototypes, respectively). The depressive personality results from the crossing of the pain polarity with the passive mode, but the crossing of the pain polarity with the active mode is not used. No personalities are derived from the pleasure end of the pleasure–pain polarity. Moreover, to derive the rest of the personality prototypes, Millon resorted to concepts that are not related to the polarities (detachment, discordancy, and the ambivalence of some personalities with regard to the

Figure 2.5

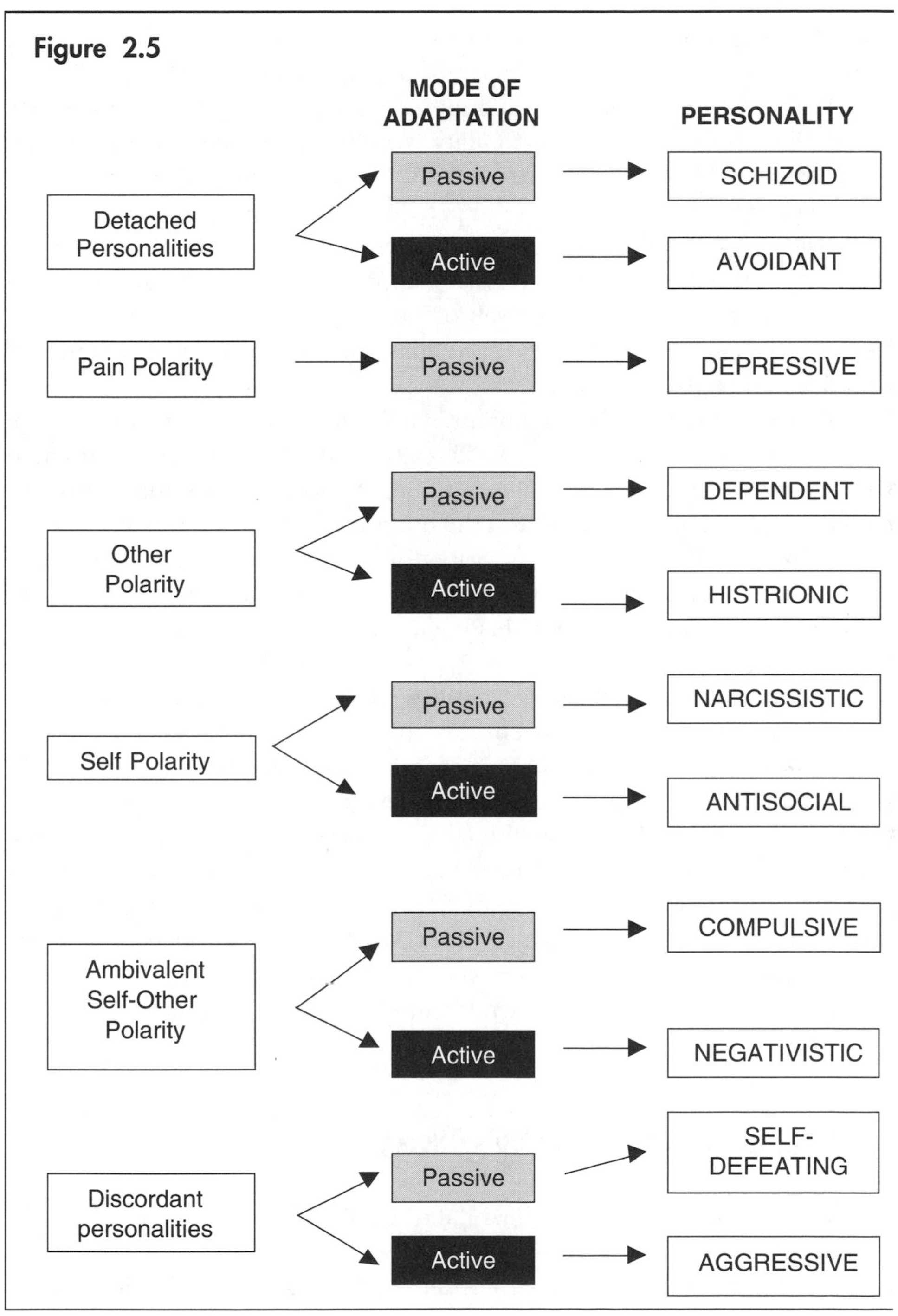

Organizational scheme for the Millon personality prototypes.

self-other polarity). Thus, in some cases the polarities serve to describe personality prototypes that are derived in some other manner.

Widiger (1999) pointed out another incongruence in the model. He noted that the borderline personality is neither high nor low in any of the polarities. He then questioned the value of a theory where "the most dysfunctional personality disorder" (p. 376) is balanced in the most relevant dimensions proposed by the theory. Widiger also pointed out that the scales of the MCMI–III are set to measure complex personality prototypes and not the simpler polarities (e.g., self or other). As a result, the test cannot be used to examine the theoretical model without another instrument that would measure the polarities.

Piersma and his colleagues pointed to Millon's peculiar use of the term *polarity* (Piersma, Ohnishi, Lee, & Metcalfe, 2002). These authors pointed out that the term typically implies a unidimensional continuum, with one element being at one extreme and the other element at the other. If it were taken this way, the self–other polarity, for instance, would imply that the prototype that was high on *self* would be low on *other*, or vise versa. In contrast, Millon proposed that personality entities can be low on both (e.g., the schizotypal personality is expected to be low on both self and other; in fact, this personality and the paranoid personality are hypothesized to be low in all polarities). Thus, Piersma and his group argued that what Millon has proposed are not three, but six separate dimensions.

Millon's recent efforts have been devoted to the development of a treatment system to follow his theory (see chap. 9 for a review). Like the theory, Millon's synergic treatment planning and therapy may be faulted for being too complex and unwieldy. Moreover, in order to use the diverse variety of psychotherapies and modalities that the system endorses, therapists would have to become much more versatile than they are today, or a system of well-coordinated therapy referrals would have to be established.

Empirical Studies on Millon's Theory

Millon's contention that his personality prototypes can be found in the nonpsychiatric population was supported by data gathered on undergraduates by Wiggins and Pincus (1989). After examining personality dimensions from different inventories, these investigators concluded that Millon's conceptions of personality disorders were strongly and clearly related to dimensions of normal personality traits.

In spite of Millon's (1998, 1999a) assertion that personality prototypes do not have the kind of orthogonal structure that could be revealed by factor analysis, the method has been repeatedly used as a way of validating the theory with the MCMI. Partial support for the theory was offered by a factor analysis that Strack, Lorr, Campbell, and Lamnin (1992) performed on the personality scales of the MCMI–III. These investigators found a factor, labeled Introversion–Extraversion, that reflected well Millon's idea of the self–other polarity. The other two factors that were extracted, Aggressive–Assertive and Dependent–Acquiescent, could be seen as mapping into the active–passive polarity. That left only one of the factors extracted as not supporting Millon's theoretical foundation. The factor that was found, labeled Restrained–Emotional, did not appear to resemble the remaining pleasure–pain polarity.

Piersma and his colleagues (2002) took advantage of the polarity scales that Millon created for another test, the Millon Index of Personality Styles (MIPS). When both the MIPS and the MCMI–III were administered to university counseling center students, the findings were unfortunately mostly inconsistent with the underlying theoretical model. Of the 82 predicted correlations, only 32 coefficients were consistent with the theory, and 9 correlations were statistically significant in the opposite direction as would have been predicted by Millon. The greatest discrepancies were found for the expected relationships between the polarity scores and the Narcissistic and Compulsive scales of the MCMI–III, and—to a lesser extent—with Schizoid, Avoidant, Schizotypal, and Negativistic scales (Piersma et al., 2002).

Factorial studies have shown that the Millon personality prototypes emerge nicely from the items included in the second and third editions of the MCMI (Choca, 1997; Choca, Retzlaff, Strack, Mouton, & Van Denburg, 1996). Other such studies have also shown great similarity between the structure of the MCMI and the Personality Adjective Check List in psychiatric and nonpsychiatric samples. The latter findings support the contention that well-adjusted personalities can be found at the mild end of severity in at least eight of the Millon personality prototypes (Dyce, O'Connor, Parkins, & Janzen, 1997; Strack et al., 1989).

In addition to the polarities, Millon (1987) proposed a graphic model that fits all the personality styles in a circle or circumplex. The vertical axis of Millon's circumplex represents affiliation, with the poles of autonomy versus enmeshment; the horizontal axis, which deals with the level of emotionality, has poles representing expressiveness and impassiveness. This circular representation of the personality disorders, which obviously resembles the Leary circumplex, has been shown to have an empirical basis for both the MCMI–II (Sim & Romney, 1990; Soldz, Budman, Demby, & Merry, 1993b; Strack et al., 1990) and the MCMI–III (Strack, Choca, & Gurtman, 2001). As might have been expected, the Millon prototypes that can be clearly defined by the two axes of the circumplex (avoidant, schizoid, dependent, histrionic, and narcissistic) are placed consistently in the same quadrant by different investigations. The dependent, for instance, is on the side of affiliation, whereas the histrionic prototype exemplifies expressiveness. On the other hand, prototypes not clearly defined by affiliation and expressiveness (e.g., compulsive, negativistic) have not been placed in the circumplex in a reliable manner (Matano & Locke, 1995). Moreover, the vertical axis obtained with the MCMI–III scales appeared to represent an impulsivity–compulsivity dimension, rather than the autonomous–enmeshed continuum envisioned by Millon (Strack et al., 2001).

Using a different methodology, Locke (2000) examined the MCMI–III mapping onto the Leary circumplex, with the dimension of agency or dominance on the vertical axis and communion or friendliness on the horizontal axis. The placement of the MCMI–III scales was determined through the scale correlations with three questionnaires designed to measure the circumplex variables. The circumplex location of most of the MCMI–III personality prototypes supported theoretical expectations. For instance, the location of the Avoidant scale (low agency) showed the importance such individuals place on concealing their feelings and avoiding ridicule and rejection. The graphic projection of the Antisocial scale (high agency, low communion) suggested that individuals with high scores on this scale are inclined to use forceful action to obtain or maintain power. The only two MCMI–III prototypes that were not clearly defined in a theoretically consistent manner were the borderline and the schizotypal. The finding indicates that neither of these two prototypes can be reasonably defined by Leary's circumplex.

Another study showed that in the continuum of positive self-regard, the Narcissistic and Histrionic scales of the MCMI–III tend to be positively correlated with a self-serving bias, whereas the Dependent and Avoidant scales are negatively correlated (McAllister et al., 2002). That kind of relationship, of course, is entirely consistent with Millon's theory.

Attempts to fit the Millon personality styles into the five-factor model also have been made (Costa & McCrae, 1990; Dyer, 1994). The five factors that can be used to explain all important personality aspects according to this model are Extraversion, Agreeableness, Neuroticism, Openness to Experience, and Conscientiousness. The contention that the MCMI may be reflecting these five factors can be supported partly by the factor analyses of the MCMI–III items. All the available factor analyses of single items have produced factors that reflect some of the personality aspects included in the five-factor model (Choca et al., 1996; Retzlaff, Lorr, Hyer, & Ofman, 1991; Stewart, Hyer, Retzlaff, & Ofman, 1995). Nevertheless, Millon's model obviously includes attributes that go beyond the five-factor model (Dyer, 1994).

Personality Styles and Personality Disorders

Personality traits or styles are distributed in a continuum that has well-adjusted and maladjusted variants, as was emphasized by Millon's original theory (Millon, 1969; see also Strack, 1999). The adaptive–maladaptive continuum has been well supported in the literature. For instance, after examining personality dimensions from different inventories, Wiggins and Pincus (1989) concluded that "conceptions of personality disorders were strongly and clearly related to dimensions of normal personality traits" (p. 305).

Personality disorders are defined by the *DSM–IV* as an "enduring pattern of inner experience and behavior that deviates markedly from the expectations of the individual's culture" (American Psychiatric Association, 1994, p. 629). The *DSM–IV* adds that the pattern has to be "pervasive and inflexible" and "stable over time" and has to lead to "distress or impairment" (American Psychiatric Association, 1994, p. 629). In other words, the clinician has to contend with both the kind of personality that the client may have and the level of functionality of that personality pattern.

For example, after looking at Charlie Brown, one could decide that he typifies the dependent personality style. The character from Charles Schultz's famous cartoon tends to feel less capable than others and blames the frequent loss of baseball games on his own shortcomings. A cooperative person, he never gets angry and is inclined to follow the advice or recommendations of others.

The fact that this fictitious figure fits nicely the dependent prototype, however, does not mean that Charlie Brown suffers from a personality disorder. Even though he has dependent traits, Charlie Brown does not meet criteria for the dependent personality disorder of the *DSM–IV* because he is able to function well in spite of his dependency. In fact, the success of the Charlie Brown portrayal may be due to his being a typical "normal" neighborhood kid with whom everyone can identify.

By contrast, the figure of Oblomov, characterized by 19-century Russian writer Ivan Goncharov in the novel by the same name, is one of an individual who is constantly comparing himself unfavorably with others. Oblomov feels so inadequate that his life is restricted to the mere essentials. His ability to function leaves much to be desired. Whereas Charlie Brown can be seen as having a dependent personality style, Oblomov suffers from a dependent personality disorder.

What makes a personality style dysfunctional? The differentiation between normal and abnormal personalities is a complex problem (see reviews by Strack & Lorr, 1994, 1997). At a concrete level, the issue can be answered for a particular individual by determining whether the person meets the *DSM–IV* criteria for any of the specific personality disorders. Even this simplistic approach overlooks the complexity of the problem in that individuals may meet several criteria for one disorder and still miss the label using the *DSM–IV* rules. Moreover, there is the issue of individuals from a nonpsychiatric sample—people who are considered "normal"—who nevertheless meet *DSM–IV* criteria for a personality disorder. (For a review of such issues, see Widiger & Corbitt, 1994). Most important, however, this approach evades the real question by relying on what the *DSM–IV* experts could agree on as signs of pathology.

In addition to the above definition, Offer and Sabshin (1991) recognized four other ways of distinguishing between normal and pathological personalities. Using a statistical notion of normality, it could be argued that the extremity of the traits that make up the personality structure could lead to maladjustment (Kiesler, 1983; Leary, 1957; Sim & Romney, 1990). From this viewpoint, the difference between Charlie Brown and Oblomov is that the feelings of inadequacy that Charlie Brown harbors are mild, whereas Oblomov feels so inadequate that he cannot get himself to do any of the things that "others" can do.

More typically, the concept clinicians use to differentiate between functional and dysfunctional personalities is that of adaptive flexibility (Kiesler, 1986; Leary, 1957; Sim & Romney, 1990). Niccolo Machiavelli already had very definite ideas about this issue in the 16th century. In his book *The Prince* (1532/1931), this early political scientist proposed that the person who adapts to the environment tends to prosper, whereas those who "clash with the times" do not (p. 205).

In other words, histrionic individuals who are by nature spontaneous and disorganized could make good pilots only if they learned to check the aircraft compulsively before flying. Individuals with antisocial tendencies will need to drop their guarded competitiveness to some degree if they are to establish intimate relationships. Philosopher Jan Patocka claimed that the real test in life is not how well people can play the role they invented for themselves, but how well they play the role that destiny brings them (cited in Terry, 1990). If individuals are able to be flexible and use personality traits that are not part of their nature in response to specific situations, the results are likely to be more positive than in the case of people who can behave only in the manner that is most egosyntonic.

Inflexibility can also be expected to lead to the vicious cycles that Millon (1981) blamed for much of psychopathology. When compulsive individuals inappropriately persist in using compulsive defenses to deal with the difficulties they are facing, the maladaptive persistence is likely to intensify their problems, which, in turn, could lead to using the compulsive mechanisms even more.

Finally, in addition to the elements of extremeness and inflexibility, Leary (1957) postulated that maladjustment results from a discrepancy between the person's self-perception and the way he or she is perceived by others. Sim and Romney (1990) supported that contention by showing that such discrepancies were significantly larger for a group with personality disorders than they were for a nonpsychiatric control group.

Personality Styles in a Social Context

More than 400 years ago, Machiavelli explained that a person "may be seen happy today and ruined tomorrow," without having changed his or her disposition or behavior (1532/1931, pp. 204–205). This is because personality styles do not exist in a vacuum. People partly define themselves through their social relationships. For instance, we are more inclined to feel adequate or even grandiose when we are relating to people who feel inadequate: An old Spanish proverb holds that "in the land of the blind, the one-eyed is king."

Ibsen's (1879) play *A Doll's House* illustrates the depth of understanding that the concept of personality styles can bring into the assessment of interpersonal relationships. At the beginning of the play, Ibsen portrays an overadequate–underadequate marital relationship. Torvald Helmer is a compulsive–narcissist who carries himself with an air of self-importance and who sets all of the rules for the family. By contrast, the histrionic Nora is a submissive social butterfly. They are seemingly happy until someone attempts to blackmail them. We then learn that at a time when Torvald was seriously ill (in other words, at a time when Nora did not have the kind of support she needed to cope well with her environment), she forged her father's signature on a document. On hearing about the forgery, Torvald is not willing to shelter his wife and does not assume the protecting role that Nora expects him to take.

The decision not to take any blame for the forgery is consistent with Torvald's own personality. The obsessive–compulsive and narcissistic elements of his personality makeup lead to a perfectionistic attitude and an emphasis on avoiding any blemish, and they make it particularly difficult for him to be generous at the time of need. For Nora, however, her husband's decision means that he is undependable and that when the chips are down, she may be left to fend for herself. This realization makes her so uncomfortable that even after the threat to her security miraculously disappears, she is not able to regain her composure or return to the kind of marital relationship she once had. The play ends with Nora leaving the home to "find herself." It is clear at that point that the trauma catalyzed changes in Nora so that she was bound to be a less trusting and more self-sufficient woman in the future.

One could fantasize about the kind of relationship Torvald and Nora would have if a more assertive Nora were to return to the marriage. Faced with the changes that had taken place in Nora's personality, Torvald also could become a higher functioning individual by giving up some of his obsessive controls and his narcissistic need to place others at a level lower than himself. The marriage then might eventually become less of an overadequate–underadequate relationship and more of one in which the partners have more parity. Realistically, before such a development is finalized, one would have to expect a period of unrest. The marriage could turn, at least for a period of time, into a conflictual relationship in which Torvald attempts to reestablish the kind of dominance he once had while dismissing the fact that the changes in Nora would not permit the relationship to return to its origin.

Ibsen's play illustrates how personality styles complement or clash with each other and how the changes in one person affect the entire relationship. This kind of analysis can be helpful in looking not only at the kinds of relationships patients establish in their lives but also at the kind of relationship they will establish with a clinician in the therapeutic setting.

The above interpretation of Ibsen's play was based entirely on his descriptions of the protagonists and on the way they behaved as the drama unfolded. Possibly someone else could read the same work and conceptualize the main characters in a completely different way. Moreover, in our clinical work, we encounter many individuals who would have difficulty describing themselves with the clarity and insight that Ibsen offered in his work. As a result, it is extremely helpful to have an instrument that allows individuals to reveal themselves in a way that permits a formulation of their particular personality style. In the chapters that follow, this book will describe how the MCMI is organized and how well it performs that function.

Psychometric Characteristics

This chapter will cover the psychometric attributes of the Millon Clinical Multiaxial Inventory (MCMI). After a brief introduction of the topic, the discussion will move into the procedures that were used in the development of the test items and the standardization data offered in the test manuals (Millon, 1977, 1987, 1994a). After discussion of the issues associated with the creation of the test, the focus will change to examine how well the test performs. Specifically, the sections that follow will look at the reliability, internal consistency, validity, and factorial structure of the test. The chapter will end with a review of the automated report offered by the test producer, Pearson Assessments. Studies dealing with the concurrent validity of the MCMI (i.e., the relationship of the MCMI to other tests) are not covered in this chapter but are discussed in chapter 8.

Millon saw the change of the MCMI into the second and third versions as a refinement of the instrument rather than the birth of an entirely new test (Millon, 1994a; Millon & Davis, 1997). Considering the criticisms and shortcomings of one version, the developments in psychiatric nosology, and the evolution of his own theory, Millon set out to build one version on the foundations of the preceding version. Because the second and third editions were, from Millon's point of view, refinements of the first, many of the original developmental exercises and studies were not repeated. In consideration of this view, the development and functioning of previous versions are summarized, so that the reader can fully appreciate the current version.

In spite of the changes that have been made for the two revisions, the MCMI has maintained the same basic view of psychopathology and scale organization. To those who were accustomed to one version, the next version seemed like an old friend because it had the same clinical feel. However, clinicians must fight the tendency to assume that because one version looks similar to another, the two versions must have the same psychometric properties. As Rogers and his associates pointed out, the number of items that the MCMI–III has in common with the original MCMI is minimal, the number of scales varies from version to version, and the amount of item overlap and scale length differ as well (Rogers, Salekin, & Sewell, 1999). Given the differences, the three versions must be considered different tests, and the findings obtained with one version cannot be assumed to hold with the next.

Item Development

The initial construction of the MCMI–I involved 3,500 items written on a theoretical basis to comply with the ideas Millon proposed in his 1969 book. Items were grouped into a set of 20 scales and edited to reduce redundancy and increase relevance and simplicity (Millon, 1982b, 1983). Two provisional research forms each containing 556 items were then administered to a diverse clinical sample of 200 patients. Repeated item analyses using item–scale intercorrelations and item endorsement frequencies were used to reduce the item pool to the 175 items that were eventually used in the commercial version of the test.

One problem seen with the MCMI–I was the very high correlation that was found between the different scales (Choca, Bresolin, Okonek, & Ostrow, 1988; Choca, Peterson, & Shanley, 1986a; Wiggins, 1982). Millon (1982b) argued that the intercorrelations mirrored his theoretical position and the clinical realities of the syndromes he was assessing. His point was that scales measuring related constructs would be expected to go up or down together when people took the test. People who are avoidant would be expected to have elevated scores on the Schizoid scale, because both of these personality prototypes describe a socially detached person. However, as Wiggins (1982) noted, "when 20 scales averaging 37 items per scale are scored from a common pool of only 171 items, the psychometric consequences of such a high degree of scale redundancy will almost certainly be unfavorable" (p. 211). The high interscale correlation was one of the problems addressed by the revisions of the test. Although a high interscale correlation continued to plague the MCMI–II, Millon was eventually able to minimize this problem by reducing the number of items that count for more than one scale on the MCMI–III.

Another area of controversy with the early versions of the MCMI was to what degree the test measured, as the automated report implied, the entities of the psychiatric classification system. After Widiger and his collaborators (Widiger, Williams, Spitzer, & Frances, 1985) noted the differences between Millon's theory and the descriptions of the *DSM*, the issue of how well the MCMI reflected *DSM* prototypes became the basis of a public debate. This debate attracted articulate critics and defenders of the MCMI (Flynn, McCann, & Fairbank, 1995; Millon, 1985, 1986; J. Reich, 1985; Torgersen & Alnaes, 1990; Widiger & Frances, 1987; Widiger & Sanderson, 1987; Widiger, Williams, Spitzer, & Frances, 1985, 1986) and highlighted the need to bring the inventory into closer alliance with the changing psychiatric nosology. The emergence of the third edition of the *Diagnostic and Statistical Manual of Mental Disorders* (*DSM–III;* American Psychiatric Association, 1980) and its later successors, the revised *DSM–III* (*DSM–III–R;* American Psychiatric Association, 1987) and the *DSM–IV* (American Psychiatric Association, 1994), provided much of the impetus for revising the MCMI into its second and third editions.

Finally, as noted in chapter 2, Millon's theory evolved considerably through the years. At the time when the MCMI–II was created, Millon wanted to introduce two new personality prototypes and modify the characterization of some of the personality prototypes or clinical scales that were already in existence. The MCMI–III includes an additional personality prototype and an additional clinical syndrome.

To accomplish the three goals noted above, 193 new items were added to the pool of items of MCMI–I after this pool was reduced by 50 "expendable" items. A sample of 108 patients was given the MCMI–II Provisional Form, and through the same procedures used in the external validation studies of the MCMI–I, 175 items were retained to make up the final version of the MCMI–II (Millon, 1987).

For the MCMI–III, a pool of 1,132 additional items were generated. Millon (1997) examined these items to "adequately capture the official criteria" of the *DSM–IV* (p. 26). This method for developing the item pool appeared to be much less involved than that used for the MCMI–I and has been criticized for not meeting the "minimal scientific rigor for establishing content validity" (Rogers, Salekin, & Sewell, 2000). From this pool, 150 new items were eventually derived, selected to measure one additional personality prototype and one additional clinical syndrome. The resulting 325-item form was administered to a sample of 1,000 individuals before the items were again reduced to 175.

In an apparent effort to reduce the high interscale correlation of previous versions, the MCMI–III uses fewer items loading on nearly all of its scales. The MCMI–III Drug Dependence scale, for instance, has 76% fewer items than its MCMI–II counterpart (58 items were used for the MCMI–II, whereas the MCMI–III has only 14 items). The Borderline scale was reduced by 74% (the 62 items of the MCMI–II became 16 items on the MCMI–III). Relatively small proportions of the MCMI–III items are the same or substantially similar to items on the MCMI–II. The MCMI–III Histrionic scale, for instance, retained only 7 items from the MCMI–II (Marlowe, Festinger, Kirby, Rubenstein, & Platt, 1998).

Item Structure

The MCMI follows the classical theory of test development. As opposed to tests developed under the item response theory, classical tests offer no information about the performance of single items (for a review on the contrast between the two theories, see Embretson, 1996). Generally, the test assumes that a single item is unreliable; reliability and validity are achieved through the accumulation of a reasonable number of items. In spite of this fact, a few of the test items are of such a nature that it may be important to review the answers obtained on those items. The few items of the Validity scale, for example, would not be seen by a classical theorist as numerous enough to constitute a scale and are useful only because the content of each of these items makes an endorsement as true very revealing and possibly interpretable. The chapter on psychopathology (chap. 7) will note the items that imply a psychotic state or a suicidal risk. Clinicians should take into consideration any endorsement of these items in the direction that implies psychopathology.

Most of the items of the MCMI are keyed so as to elevate the raw score when the item is endorsed as true. The reason for that way of keying the items is that it is easier to make the items valid and meaningful when they are constructed in that manner. As an illustration, consider the item "I often think about ending my life." A response of true to this item speaks very clearly about the person's suicide potential. The item "I do not often think about ending my life" creates a double negative when it is answered as false and confuses many examinees. A readable version of this item that would reverse the keying may be "I never think about ending my life." A negative response to this item, however, leaves us with the question of whether the person is denying the frequency ("never") or the thought of ending his or her life. The fact that most items are keyed as true, however, makes the test susceptible to inaccuracy with patients who are inclined to answer true to any item, the so-called acquiescent response set (Craig, 1999a).

Standardization

The MCMI–I norms were based on numerous clinical groups and nonclinical samples drawn from industrial plants, colleges, and personnel offices. From these samples, 1,591 clinical respondents provided the basis for MCMI–I norms from the construction phases of the test development (for more information about the samples, see Millon, 1982b). The MCMI–II was standardized with a sample of 1,292 patients (for more information about the sample, see Millon, 1987). The MCMI–III was standardized with 1,079 patients (see Millon, 1994a).

When the population the test is used with is very different from the standardizing population, the test may not perform well (see chap. 1). One problem with the standardization sample used for the norms of the MCMI–III is that it was overwhelmingly White. The developmental sample of 600 individuals, for instance, was 86% White, 9% African American, 3% Hispanic, and 1% of other races or ethnic groups. Although there were more African American men in the cross-validation sample of 398 individuals, the women in this sample were 92% White (Millon, 1997). Whether the constitution of the standardization sample will affect the accuracy of the test with members of a minority group remains to be investigated.

In a population where the prevalence of the different disorders differs considerably from the prevalence found in the standardizing sample, the user would have to adjust the weighted scores. When enough data for an instrument are available in the particular population, a method called *bootstrapping* can be used to adjust the cutoff score (e.g., the Base Rate [BR] score of 75 or 85 in the MCMI) in accordance with the estimated local BR score of the attribute (Rorer & Dawes, 1982).

Reliability

At this point the issues concerning the development of the test have been examined, and the focus will shift to the actual performance of the instrument. The first of the performance indicators is reliability. A scale is reliable if it is likely to yield a similar score on a consistent basis when taken again by the same person. Reliability is the most basic of the performance markers, because the other performance indicators become meaningless if the test is unreliable. Let us consider the analogy of a measuring tape that is so elastic that different readings are obtained on repeated measurements of the same object. The lack of consistency will make it impossible to determine if an object is the same size as another, because the tape cannot lead us to a "true" measurement of the objects in question. In the same manner, a psychological test cannot possibly measure what it is supposed to measure if its readings are inconsistent.

Test–retest studies for the MCMI–I yielded reliability coefficients ranging from the low .60s to the low .90s. Most of the basic personality scales were in the .80s, the pathological personality scales were in the high .70s, and the clinical syndrome scales were in the mid-.60s (Millon, 1982b). Millon's findings were supported by other investigations (Flynn & McMahon, 1983b, 1984b; Libb, Stankovic, Freeman, et al., 1990; McMahon, Flynn, & Davidson, 1985b; T. J. Murphy, Greenblatt, Mozdzierz, & Trimakas, 1990; Overholser, 1989; Piersma, 1986d; J. Reich, 1989; Wheeler & Schwarz, 1989).

Stability coefficients for the MCMI–II scales for a variety of populations are reported in the manual (Millon, 1987). With psychiatric inpatients the stability coefficients ranged from .43 to .75 (Millon, 1987). Piersma (1989b) supported these findings, except that his coefficients were somewhat lower than those of Millon.

Finally, the test–retest correlations obtained as part of the standardization of the MCMI–III showed good stability, ranging from .82 for the Debasement scale to .90 for the Somatoform scale (Millon, 1994a). Craig and Olson (1998) obtained similar scores on an inpatient sample of substance abusers. Correlations tend to be higher for the personality scales than for the clinical syndromes. Because the MCMI is designed to differentiate between enduring personality characteristics and the more transient clinical symptoms, the scales would be expected to perform differently in test–retest studies. Thus, the finding that the personality scales tend to be more stable than the clinical syndrome scales is consistent with the theory. The correlations Craig and Olson reported, however, were consistently lower than the correlations Millon reported.

Internal Consistency

Internal consistency is sometimes seen as a measure of test validity and labeled *internal validity*. It is considered advantageous for items of a particular scale to form a cohesive unit, to go up or down together as the score of the scale increases or decreases. In other words, if one were to examine as an example a scale designed to measure depression, it would be ideal for all of the items to be related to the construct of depression and to have the same tendency to contribute toward the elevation of the total score of that scale. The measure of internal consistency is typically reported for each scale rather than for the entire test. The reason is that because different scales are designed to measure different attributes of the individual, they would not be expected to form a cohesive unit and to rise or fall together. To measure internal consistency, the items keyed on a particular scale are correlated with the total score of that scale, ordinarily using the alpha coefficient.

The internal consistency of the MCMI scales has generally been good. For the MCMI–III the alpha coefficients reported in the test manual (Millon, 1994a) range from .66 for the Compulsive scale to .90 for the Major Depression scale. The alpha coefficients exceed .80 in 20 of the 26 scales, showing that the great majority of the scales are very internally consistent. For at least one case, however, such excellent figures have not been found outside of the standardization data. In their evaluation of the Posttraumatic Stress scale, Hyer and his coworkers reported a low alpha coefficient of .54 (Hyer, Boyd, Stanger, Davis, & Walters, 1997).

Validity

By far the most important measure of test performance is the validity of the instrument. Validity involves the examination of indicators that show the instrument to be measuring what it is designed to measure. This section will discuss the issues involved with the validity of tests in general and with that of the MCMI in particular.

There are three types of validity. The first type, *face validity*, deals with whether test items appear to be the right items to measure the constructs they are intended to measure. An item such as "I feel sad all of the time" may be seen as having more face validity for a depression scale than the item "I do not care if I win or lose." The face validity of the MCMI was partly discussed above in the descriptions of how the test items were developed.

Concurrent validity refers to correlations of one test with another when both instruments are completed by one person at approximately the same time. A study showing that a scale is correlated to another scale measuring a similar construct documents *convergent* concurrent validity. Examples of convergent concurrent validity would be the significant positive correlation found between two depression scales or a significant negative correlation between a depression scale and a mania scale. To show *divergent* concurrent validity, on the other hand, one needs to demonstrate that two scales designed to measure different constructs do not correlate with one another. The near-zero correlation between a scale measuring dependent traits and a scale measuring suicide potential may be an example of divergent concurrent validity. In this book the concurrent validity studies are discussed in chapter 5.

Concurrent validity studies authenticate both of the scales in question. When a low correlation is found between two scales that were supposed to be similar, it is impossible to determine, with this kind of study, which of the two scales may be at fault. In such cases we have learned only that the two scales do not measure the same construct, at least with the kind of population used for the study.

The third type of validity is the *external criterion validity*. Typically the nontest criterion used for questionnaires measuring emotional maladjustment is the diagnosis of the individual as determined by experienced clinicians on the basis of information obtained through interviews. Knowledge of the diagnosis allows the clinician to look at the hit rates of a particular scale, or the times when the scale score agrees with the target diagnosis. There is an established system for organizing these hit rates, referred to as the operating characteristics of a test, and these will be described in the next section.

Operating Characteristics of a Test

When a diagnostic scale—for instance, a scale designed to measure depression—is administered to a heterogeneous group of individuals, the possible hit rates are as shown in Table 3.1. Hit rates involve the agreement of two variables, the test score and the criterion variable. The *criterion variable* is the presence or absence of the attribute (typically the diagnosis) determined in some other way. The agreement of these two variables can then be considered from the point of view of the criterion variable, or from the point of view of the test score, or from both points of view, to produce six different markers.

From the point of view of the criterion variable *presence or absence of the disorder,* the first marker to be considered is the prevalence or base rate. The prevalence of the disorder is the total number of occurrences of the

Table 3.1

Possible Hit Rates When a Diagnostic Scale Is Administered to a Heterogeneous Group

	Patient diagnosis	
Test result	**Positive (e.g., patient is depressed)**	**Negative (e.g., patient is not depressed)**
Positive (score elevated)	Cell A True positives	Cell B False positives
Negative (score not elevated)	Cell C False negatives	Cell D True negatives

disorder (a + c) divided by the total number of individuals (a + b + c + d). *Sensitivity*, the proportion of true positives, is the probability that the test score will be elevated given that the disorder is actually present (a/[a + c]). *Specificity*, the proportion of true negatives, is the probability that the test score will not be elevated given that the disorder is actually absent (d/[b + d]).

If, instead of holding the presence or absence of the disorder as the given, we look at the elevation or lack of elevation of the scale, we come up with two markers that are the other side of the coin from sensitivity and specificity. The first of these markers is the positive predictive power (PPP). The PPP is probably the most clinically relevant marker because it represents the likelihood that the disorder is present given that the test score is elevated. The PPP is calculated as the proportion of true-positive cases across all cases in which the test was positive (a/[a + b]). Negative predictive power (NPP) is the probability that the disorder is absent when the test is negative (d/[c + d]).

The PPP and the NPP are influenced by the magnitude of the sensitivity and specificity of the test and the prevalence of the disorder in the population. When the sensitivity and specificity of the test are high (e.g., 90%), the PPP and the NPP indexes are optimal. As prevalence decreases, so does PPP. In populations that have few cases with a particular diagnosis, even tests with high specificity and sensitivity can have a low PPP for that diagnosis (Baldessarini, Finklestein, & Arana, 1983). This problem will be discussed again below.

Combining both the test score and diagnostic perspectives is the overall diagnostic power (ODP). The ODP represents the proportion of all correct classifications, ([a + d]/[a + b + c + d]). As was true of the PPP and the NPP, the usefulness of the ODP also varies in response to the prevalence rate (Baldessarini et al., 1983).

A good scale should have operating characteristic markers that exceed .70. A sensitivity value of .70, for instance, means that the scale correctly identified 70% of the people as having the particular attribute being measured. A scale would be judged to be fair if the markers are between .50 and .69 and poor if the markers are below .50 (Gibertini, Brandenburg, & Retzlaff, 1986).

The importance of each of the operating characteristics varies according to the kind of use that is made of the test results. In most clinical settings the test user would like to avoid both Type I and Type II errors (i.e., diagnosing individuals with a disorder when they do not have the disorder and failing to diagnose individuals who do have the disorder). In such settings the focus should be on the overall proportion of correct classifications or overall diagnostic power. For forensic work, however, McCann and Dyer (1996) emphasized the PPP because it allows the expert witness to state affirmatively that the examinee has a disorder, because such an affirmative opinion is what is likely to be attacked during the cross-examination.

The external nontest criterion typically used to validate a test is clinician ratings. The gold standard is the rating of experienced clinicians using a structured interview. When several such clinicians offer a rating on the same individual, agreement can be established by calculating the kappa value. Unfortunately, clinicians are not very likely to agree, even after proper training and the use of a *DSM*-based structured interview: *DSM* field trials found kappa values as low as .26 for the personality disorders. The unreliability of the external criterion creates a ceiling for the validity of any scale using that criterion. Retzlaff (1995) noted, for instance, that if the kappa value for the compulsive personality disorder is .26 and the disorder has a prevalence of .05, a scale attempting to measure this construct could not have a PPP of more than .30, and therefore it would accurately identify only 30% of those who scored above the cutoff. The impressive part of this calculation is that it has considered only the reliability of the external criterion and the prevalence of the disorder. Any limitation of the scale, of course, would lower its PPP and usefulness even further.

Another limitation of the PPP is that it is very susceptible to the prevalence of the disorder. For this reason some investigators have advocated the use of an incremental PPP, or IPPP, arrived at by subtracting the prevalence of the disorder from the PPP. The same can be done with the NPP to produce the INPP (Hsu, 2002).

The final problem to be addressed is that all of these values, including the IPPP and the INPP, are affected by the location of the diagnostic cut. On the MCMI, the use of a BR score of 75 as the cutoff will produce a higher sensitivity but a lower specificity than if a BR score of 85 is used. This problem can be resolved with the use of Cohen's effect size. This measure, referred to as Cohen's *d,* is not affected by the location of the cutoff or the prevalence of the disorders, and can show the relative ability of tests to discriminate between groups.

Operating Characteristics of the MCMI

As is typically the case, a mixed picture emerged from the studies assessing the validity of the MCMI–I. Many of the scales of this test were found to be valid and useful with a variety of samples (Bryer, Martines, & Dignan, 1990; Chatham, Tibbals, & Harrington, 1993; Choca et al., 1988; Gibertini et al., 1986; J. O. Goldberg, Shaw, & Segal, 1987; Greenblatt, Mozdzierz, Murphy, & Trimakas, 1992; Jaffe & Archer, 1987; H. R. Miller, Streiner, & Parkinson, 1992; Millon, 1983; O'Callaghan, Bates, Jackson, Rudd, & Edwards, 1990; Sexton, McIlwraith, Barnes, & Dunn, 1987; Streiner & Miller, 1990; Tamkin, Carson, Nixon, & Hyer, 1987; Wetzler, Kahn, Strauman, & Dubro, 1989). Nevertheless, some of the scales were not portrayed well by other studies, pointing to possible diagnostic deficiencies with some populations (Bryer et al., 1990; Calsyn, Saxon, & Daisy, 1990; Chick, Sheaffer, Goggin, & Sison, 1993; Choca et al., 1988; del Rosario, McCann, & Navarra, 1994; Flynn & McMahon, 1983a; Gibertini & Retzlaff, 1988b; J. O. Goldberg et al., 1987; Greenblatt & Davis, 1993; Helmes & Barilko, 1988; Hogg, Jackson, Rudd, & Edwards, 1990; H. J. Jackson, Gazis, Rudd, & Edwards, 1991; J. J. Jackson, Greenblatt, Davis, Murphy, & Trimakas, 1991; Lewis & Harder, 1991; Marsh, Stile, Stoughton, & Trout-Landen, 1988; Nazikian, Rudd, Edwards, & Jackson, 1990; O'Callaghan et al., 1990; Patrick, 1988, 1993; Piersma, 1986a, 1987a; Wetzler & Dubro, 1990; Wetzler et al., 1989). The test generally compared well to the effectiveness of other inventories, such as the Minnesota Multiphasic Personality Inventory (MMPI; Dubro, Wetzler, & Kahn, 1988; Morey, 1986; Uomoto, Turner, & Herron, 1988) but proved to be somewhat inferior in the prediction of recovery from a back surgery (Herron, Turner, & Weiner, 1986).

The MCMI–II performed very well with the standardizing sample (McCann, 1990a; Millon, 1987). With other samples, several of the scales of the inventory were shown to have good operating characteristics, as well as limitations (del Rosario et al., 1994; Fals-Stewart, 1995; Flynn et al., 1997; Ganellen, 1996; Hart, Forth, & Hare, 1991; Messina, Wish, Hoffman, & Nemes, 2001; Piersma, 1991; Retzlaff & Cicerello, 1995; Wetzler & Marlowe, 1993). The MCMI–II was shown to be superior to the MMPI in the diagnosis of affective disorders, schizophrenia, and substance abuse (Libb, Murray, Thurstin, & Alarcon, 1992). The MCMI–II has had some difficulty demonstrating diagnostic efficiency when the personality scales were pitted against semistructured interviews (Hart, Dutton, & Newlove, 1993; Marlowe, Husband, Bonieskie, Kirby, & Platt, 1997; McCann, 1990b; Renneberg, Chambless, Dowdall, Fauerbach, & Gracely, 1992; Soldz, Budman, Demby, & Merry, 1993a; Turley, Bates, Edwards, & Jackson, 1992; Wise, 1996).

As for the MCMI–III, the validity of this instrument has been the source of great controversy. The original version of the test manual provided the prevalence and sensitivity and specificity values obtained with the standardization data (Millon, 1994a). Using these figures, Retzlaff (1996) calculated the PPP figures, which were uniformly poor, ranging from 0 to .32 for the personality scales and from .15 to .58 for the clinical syndrome scales. Millon (personal communication, September 24, 1994) believed that the low PPP values were attributable to the poor quality of the external validity study. The information was taken out of a second edition of the manual (Millon, 1997) and substituted with data collected by R. D. Davis, Wenger, and Guzman (1997). This substitution unfortunately only added fuel to the fire. Because R. D. Davis and colleagues collected data from clinicians who had seen the scores of the MCMI–III, there was concern that the diagnostic formulation was contaminated, possibly inflating the operating characteristics (Rogers et al., 2000). The fact that the values were so dramatically improved in comparison to the values of the first study was seen as a further indictment of the data (Rogers et al., 2000).

The argument came to a head with a meta-analysis, by Rogers and coworkers (1999), of the three validity studies that were available at the time (Millon's, 1994a, standardization data; data from S. E. Davis & Hays, 1997; and data from Dyce, O'Connor, Parkins, & Janzen, 1997). The authors pointed out that the divergence of the 11 personality scales of the MCMI–III with similar scales from other instruments was larger than the level of convergence, so that these instruments disagreed more often than they agreed. They used those findings to argue that the Daubert standard for court, a standard that requires testimony to have a scientific basis and reflect more than the subjective opinions of the expert, could not be met by the MCMI.

Responding to Rogers and his coworkers (1999), Dyer and McCann (2000) noted that the studies Rogers et al. cited "employ a raft of other personality disorders measures" and assume that those instruments are the "adequate benchmarks by which to assess the validity of the MCMI" (p. 488). Dyer and McCann pointed out that the MCMI has actually been used as the benchmark against which other instruments, such as the Structured Clinical Interview for the *DSM–III–R*, were validated (e.g., Renneberg et al., 1992). In other words, when a scale of the MCMI does not correlate well with another scale supposedly measuring the same construct, it is just as likely that the other scale is the one that is not measuring the construct in a valid manner. (For this reason, the present author discusses those concurrent validity studies in chapter 8 and does not take such data as necessarily speaking to the validity of the MCMI). Dyer and McCann (2000) argued that the correct way to validate a test is through the computation of its operating characteristics and not through "a series of Pearson product–moment correlation coefficients, which do not provide any information as to the percentage of cases in which scores on the test correctly diagnose the condition" (p. 494).

In a reply to Dyer and McCann's (2000) article, Rogers and coworkers (2000) further objected that the R. D. Davis et al. (1997) study used the highest elevation in the profile to calculate the hit rate without demanding that the scale be clinically elevated. Their contention continued to be that the MCMI–III did not have enough empirical support to warrant its being used in court (Rogers et al., 2000).

Discussing the issue in what appeared to be a more evenhanded manner, Hsu (2002) expanded the markers from both the Millon (1994a) and the R. D. Davis et al. (1997) studies by calculating values such as the IPPP, the INPP, and Cohen's *d*. Using the new markers, Hsu (2002) noted that the average values for the R. D. Davis et al. study were "3 times larger" (p. 416) and that Cohen's kappa was "nearly 5 times that of the 1994 study" (p. 417). Hsu (2002) concluded that the better values of the R. D. Davis et al. study resulted both from the better familiarity that the participating clinicians had with their patients and from the "extent of criterion contamination" and other problems he found with the study (p. 421).

The idea of submitting a test to the rigor of examining the operating characteristics started with the MCMI (Gibertini et al., 1986) and has been fully supported by Millon, who has reported such statistics with the test revisions (Millon, 1987, 1994a). At the time of this publication, no study approaching such rigor had ever been done with the MCMI's main competitor, the MMPI; as a result, the validity of that test against clinical diagnoses is largely unknown (Schutte, 2001).

It should also be noted that even more than the Axis I clinical syndromes, personality disorders lack clinical consensus (Tyrer, 1988). As a result, instruments that attempt to measure personality style are attempting to hit an ambiguous and unreliable target, a problem that is sure to affect their own validity. H. R. Miller et al. (1992) used maximum-likelihood estimates in a study of personality measures. This procedure statistically computes what combinations of data from different instruments best define the construct to be evaluated (e.g., the dependent personality). After the construct has been defined through this concordance of multiple measures, that definition then becomes the criterion against which the individual measures are compared. Their data showed that none of the instruments (i.e., the MMPI personality scales, the MCMI, and the Structured Interview for the DSM–III Personality Disorders [SIDP; Pfohl, Stangl, & Zimmerman, 1983]) were in consistent agreement either with each other or with the maximum-likelihood estimate definition of the disorder. Similarly, Hunt and Andrews (1992) obtained disappointing results with the revision of the Personality Diagnostic Questionnaire (PDQ–R; Hyler et al., 1988). Problems also have been reported with the Wisconsin Personality Disorders Inventory (Klein, Benjamin, et al., 1993). Greater convergence in the personality area has been reached between the MCMI–II and the MMPI–2 than between either one of these instruments alone when pitted against the results of a structured interview (Butler, Gaulier, & Haller, 1991; Hills, 1995). It is logically impossible to determine whether the difficulties lie with the tests (MCMIs included), with the semistructured interview used, or with the *DSM* itself, which is likely to have its own validity and stability difficulties. In other words, even when clinicians use the best possible methodology and criteria for determining a person's diagnosis, they may still have to accept results that leave something to be desired.

Going beyond the personality scales, we examined the concordance of MCMI–III scores and the clinical syndrome (Axis I) diagnoses given to 371 patients taken into the Chicago Veterans Administration health care system. The diagnoses were formulated by an experienced professional or a trainee working under the direct supervision of the experienced professional. The diagnostic assignments were completed after a thorough interview, in a multidisciplinary team setting, with typically more than one professional having had contact with the patient. In other words, the study did not use the gold standard of multiple raters after a structured interview, but it surpassed the requirements of good contemporary practice. The diagnoses were entered in the chart prior to scoring the MCMI–III. As can be seen from Table 3.2, the overall diagnostic power ranged from a low of .39 to a high of .85 (Choca, Gibeau, Craig, & Van Denburg, 2000). With the exception of the Anxiety scale, all other scales had ODP values of .65 or better. The excellent NPP values indicate that the MCMI–III clinical syndrome scales are very seldom elevated when the disorder is absent. However, several of the scales cannot be trusted to be elevated when the disorder is present (low PPP values).

Looking at MCMI–III results of more than 10,000 inmates of the Colorado department of corrections, Retzlaff et al. (2002) reported significant correlations with the interview-based intake professional assessment of the need for mental health interventions and anger management. Similar results were obtained when the MCMI–III scores were compared with the inmates' eventual need for treatment and medications. Although several scales (e.g., Narcissistic, Paranoid, Negativistic, and Schizoid) were correlated with the eventual incidence of fighting or assaults, those results showed more modest test performance.

Other researchers have looked at specific MCMI–III scales. Craig and Olson (1997) published operating characteristics for the Posttraumatic

Table 3.2

Operating Characteristics for the MCMI–III, Axis I Scales (Base Rate Score > 75)

Scale	Prevalence	Sensitivity	Specificity	PPP	NPP	ODP
Dysthymia	.42	.73	.58	.56	.75	.65
Anxiety	.11	.73	.35	.13	.91	.39
Somatoform	.03	.50	.81	.08	.98	.80
Mania	.10	.19	.92	.22	.91	.85
Alcohol or Drug Abuse	.48	.64	.90	.85	.72	.77
Posttraumatic Stress Disorder	.11	.83	.79	.34	.97	.80
Thought Disorder	.05	.09	.86	.05	.94	.82
Delusional Disorder	.12	.23	.93	.31	.89	.85
Major Depression	.42	.45	.79	.60	.67	.65

Note. MCMI–III = Millon Clinical Multiaxial Inventory, 3rd ed.; NPP = negative predictive power; ODP = overall diagnostic power; PPP = positive predictive power.

Stress scale. The prevalence of posttraumatic stress disorder (PTSD) in the sample of substance abusers they used for the study was .16. The scale (Scale R) proved to have a sensitivity of .68, a specificity of .83, a PPP of .43, an NPP of .93, and an ODP of .80. Although the sensitivity was not optimal, the scale was still able to detect more than two thirds of the PTSD group and was able to accurately exclude 83% of patients who did not have PTSD. The average BR score for the PTSD substance-abusing patients was 22 points higher than the average for the non-PTSD substance-abusing patients. Hyer and his coworkers (1997) were able to show that the scale significantly differentiated between a PTSD group and a non-PTSD group.

Craig (1997) used a sample of African American drug-abusing men to check the effectiveness of the substance abuse scales. He reported a very impressive sensitivity of .82 for the Drug Abuse scale. The sensitivity of the Alcohol Abuse scale in detecting coexisting alcohol misuse was .80. The latter scale, however, did not perform as well in terms of the specificity with which it detected alcohol misuse as opposed to other drugs (value of .59). Based on these values, the substance abuse scales of the MCMI–III can be seen as an improvement over previous versions of the test, but they continue to have the problem of being a bit redundant in relation to one another.

Daubert and Metzler (2000) examined the effectiveness of the Modifying Indices in the detection of fake-good and fake-bad responses. The overall rates of successful classification showed moderate effectiveness in detecting dissimulated responding, with the PPP varying from .67 to .94 depending on the score used. It was noted, however, that at low base rates of faking, the MCMI–III cutoff points yielded a high number of false positives.

Psychometric Structure

Factor analytic techniques have been used with the Millon instruments, even though the application of such techniques is fraught with difficulties and limitations. Perhaps the most basic problem is that the Millon instruments are, by design, essentially nonfactorial: The underlying structural model calls for built-in scale overlaps and considerable item redundancy (Millon, 1982b). Hess (1985) observed that all but four of the items for the Anxiety scale on the MCMI–I appeared on at least one of the other five scales. The impact of item overlap and the resultant high interscale correlation on an overdetermined factor structure has been cited repeatedly in the literature (Choca et al., 1986a; Gibertini & Retzlaff, 1988a; Hess, 1985; Montag & Comrey, 1987; Widiger, 1985).

As Guilford (1952) noted, factor analyzing a group of scales that share items may be inappropriate. Gibertini and Retzlaff (1988a) explained the reason for this in the following manner:

> When two or more scales share items they become linearly dependent to an extent proportional to the percentile of the item-overlap. This essentially guarantees that the correlation matrix to be factored has some degree of structure not provided by the subject response patterns. Some part of the resulting factor pattern, in other words, will be artificial. This artificial structure will be constant across populations. If this effect is large relative to that of the subject response patterns, then the artificial structure will "drive" the factor analysis and create very stable factors which have little to do with subject responses. (p. 66)

Note that the same problem has been cited with regard to the MMPI (Shure & Rogers, 1965).

Beyond the essentially nonfactorial structure of the Millon tests, there are important additional conceptual and methodological difficulties. For instance, selecting a factor method and choosing a solution to summarize the covariation matrix involve complex methodological questions. There also are the issues of weighing, for various sample populations, the influence of differences in demographic features and clinical homogeneity (Millon, 1982b).

Nevertheless, the structure of a test offers much useful information, and many factor analytic studies have been reported for the Millon instruments. Researchers have examined populations of general psychiatric patients (Choca et al., 1986a; Choca, Greenblatt, Tobin, Shanley, & Van Denburg, 1989; Choca, Shanley, Peterson, & Van Denburg, 1990; Greenblatt, Mozdzierz, Murphy, & Trimakas, 1986; Lorr, Retzlaff, & Tarr, 1989; Millon, 1982b, 1987; Piersma, 1986b; Retzlaff, Lorr et al., 1991; Strack et al., 1992; Strauman & Wetzler, 1992), women with eating disorders (Head & Williamson, 1990), alcohol abusers (Gibertini & Retzlaff, 1988a; Lorr et al., 1989; McMahon, Applegate, Kouzekanani, & Davidson, 1990; McMahon & Davidson, 1988; McMahon, Gersh, & Davidson, 1989), drug abusers (Flynn & McMahon, 1984a; McMahon, Kouzekanani, & Bustillo, 1991), substance abusers (Millon, 1982b), and U.S. Air Force trainees (Gibertini & Retzlaff, 1988a; Retzlaff & Gibertini, 1987). Nonpsychiatric samples of college students are available (Dyce et al., 1997; Retzlaff, Lorr, et al., 1991), as are combined factor analyses of the MCMI and other tests (Ownby, Wallbrown, Carmin, & Barnett, 1990).

Some investigators have attempted to deal with the overlap problem by using correlations of shared and unshared scale items (Dyce et al., 1997;

Lumsden, 1986, 1988). Others have performed a factor analysis on the matrix of the item-overlap coefficients (Gibertini & Retzlaff, 1988a). Attempts have been made to use the Bashaw and Anderson statistical correction to change the correlation matrix (Helmes, 1989). Studies factor analyzing the items rather than the scales (Choca et al., 1989; Lorr, Strack, Campbell, & Lamnin, 1990; Retzlaff, Lorr, et al., 1991) obviously bypass the entire issue but lead to factors that resemble the test scales rather than the more global structure typically expected out of factor analysis.

The MCMI–III has considerably reduced the technical difficulties by reducing the amount of item overlap between scales. Using nonoverlapping items, Dyce and associates (1997) reported a 4-factor structure for the MCMI–III. The structure was seen as consistent with 4 of the 5 factors of the five-factor model of personality (for a review of the model, see Costa & Widiger, 1994). The first factor, labeled Neuroticism, had positive loadings on the Avoidance, Depressive, and Self-Defeating scales. The second factor, seen as reflecting Low Agreeableness, was defined by positive loadings on the Narcissistic, Aggressive, Antisocial, and Paranoid scales. A bipolar third factor, with the Schizoid and Avoidant scales at one end and the Histrionic scale at the other, was thought to resemble Low Urgency–Extraversion. Another bipolar factor emerged fourth, with a strong positive loading for the Compulsive scale and a moderate negative loading for the Antisocial scale. This factor was interpreted as reflecting Conscientiousness. The MCMI–III did not appear to have any measure of the Openness to Experience factor from the five-factor model, but the authors pointed out that the latter factor has typically not been associated with the personality disorder prototypes.

The *DSM–IV* proposes that the 11 personality disorders can be grouped into three clusters. Cluster A is associated with odd, eccentric, or asocial inclinations; Cluster B is characterized as flamboyant and dramatic; and Cluster C describes anxious or fearful tendencies (American Psychiatric Association, 1994). That system of grouping was partially supported with MCMI–II data (Bagby, Joffe, Parker, & Schuller, 1993) but has not emerged with the MCMI–III (Dyce et al., 1997).

Validity of the Pearson Assessment Automated Report

The diagnostic accuracy of the computer-generated MCMI diagnoses was found to be deficient in the case of the MCMI–I (Bonato, Cyr, Kalpin, Prendergast, & Sanhueza, 1988; DeWolfe, Larson, & Ryan, 1985; Piersma,

1987b) but has not been studied with later versions. The validity of previous versions of the Pearson Assessment report as a whole has been supported by some studies (C. J. Green, 1982; Moreland & Onstad, 1987), but not without a certain amount of controversy (Cash, Mikulka, & Brown, 1989; Lanyon, 1984; Siddall & Keogh, 1993).

Effect of Individual Variables

This chapter reviews studies in which demographic variables, such as gender, race, age, socioeconomic status, birth order, and education, have been shown to influence the results obtained on the MCMI. Traditionally, this effect has been called *test bias* and has been seen as an unwanted error of the measurement, an element that lowers the validity of an instrument.

Regarding the effect of the examinee's race, the outcome of litigation has demanded that evaluations not lead to a disproportionate number of individuals being chosen from one race over another, even if the difference in test performance could be explained in terms of the characteristics of the minority groups involved (e.g., *Larry P. v. Wilson Riles* [Lambert, 1981]; the "Golden Rule" settlement [Anrig, 1987]; *Watson v. Fort Worth Bank & Trust* [Bersoff, 1988]). This particular interpretation has been controversial (Denton, 1988) because it is just as logical to argue that the test is measuring what it is supposed to measure and that different groups have different qualities or attributes.

Regardless of our viewpoint on the cause of group differences, it seems imperative for clinicians to be aware of the effect that particular examinee variables may have on the test results. For example, if women were much more prone than men to score higher on the Self-Defeating scale of the MCMI–III, then an elevation on this scale by female respondents would be seen as less pathological than the same elevation by male respondents. Such knowledge then could be used to modulate our interpretations. A marginally elevated score may be dismissed in some cases, whereas more significant elevations may be seen as partly constituting a socioculturally determined defense. In the review that follows, the literature is examined from that perspective, seeing any differences found between groups not necessarily as a flaw of the test, but rather as data with which clinicians must be familiar.

Gender

Wierzbicki and Goldade (1993) asked college students to rate the items of the MCMI–I on whether they were more likely to be endorsed by men or women. Their data showed that items on 10 of the 11 personality scales of this inventory were perceived to be more associated with one gender than the other. The standardizing data for all versions of the MCMI have shown that men and women do respond differently on this test. As a result, Millon (1982b, 1987, 1994a) thought it necessary to use different tables for the conversion of raw scores to the Base Rate (BR) score for men and women. It is important to examine how effectively the use of different conversion tables equalizes the test results if one is going to offer the same interpretation to similar elevations regardless of the person's gender.

Studies with previous editions of the MCMI led to the concern that the test tended to pathologize stereotypically feminine traits (Bornstein, 1995; Cantrell & Dana, 1987; Lindsay & Widiger, 1995; Piersma, 1986c). However, this has not been the case with the MCMI–III. Examining the Histrionic, Dependent, Antisocial, and Narcissistic scales, Lindsay and her coworkers (Lindsay, Sankis, & Widiger, 2000) found no significant differences between the average scale scores of the two biological sexes. Only three items, all of them in the Histrionic scale, were judged to be biased against the biological sex of the respondent. As an example, the authors cited Item 80, "It is very easy for me to make friends," as one that is more likely to be endorsed by women than by men.

To distinguish between the biological sex and gender characteristics, the authors used their own self-report measure of masculinity and femininity to characterize study participants. Using that measure, 17 MCMI–III items were considered potentially gender biased. Four of these items were in the Histrionic scale, one was in both the Antisocial and the Narcissistic scales, and the remaining 12 items were from the Narcissistic scale. The items of the Narcissistic scale mostly concerned a sense of confidence and efficacy and were more likely to be endorsed by the masculine participants (Lindsay et al., 2000).

The above findings would be an issue only if the diagnostician used these personality scales as a measure of a personality disorder, a use that is not advocated in this book. Even then, the fact that there were no differences in average scores between the two biological sexes indicates that the error would be subtle and, most likely, not clinically relevant.

Race

Public and scientific debate over the adequacy of psychological instruments in evaluating members of minority groups has been around for decades (assertion taken from Cronbach, 1975). Although the original conversion tables for the MCMI did not distinguish between individuals of different races, a 1984 manual supplement included separate conversion tables for Black, White, and Hispanic examinees for the MCMI–I. In spite of these efforts, racial differences were repeatedly noted on both the MCMI–I and the MCMI–II (Calsyn, Saxon, & Daisy, 1991; Choca, Peterson, & Shanley, 1986b; Choca et al., 1990; W. E. Davis, Greenblatt, & Choca, 1990; W. E. Davis, Greenblatt, & Pochyly, 1990; Hamberger & Hastings, 1992; J. J. Jackson et al. 1991, Pochyly, Greenblatt, & Davis, 1989; Weekes, Morison, Millson, & Fettig, 1995). Some data were also available to show that the tests tended to measure accurately the same characteristic on both races (Greenblatt & Davis, 1992).

No information regarding the performance of the MCMI–III with different races appeared to be available at the time of this writing. Unfortunately, however, the lack of adequate representation of minority groups in the standardization sample (see chap. 3) should make MCMI–III users uncomfortable with minority examinees. Especially in those cases, it is imperative that the clinician support test findings with other sources of information.

So as not to mislead readers, it is noteworthy that the kind of racial differences that have been found with the MCMI are typically found with psychological tests in general. As the reviews by Reynolds (1982, 1983) and Jensen (1980) have indicated, this problem plagues most of the measures of intellectual ability. Although the MMPI–2 is presently thought to perform better than its predecessor (Ben-Porath, Shondrick, & Strafford, 1995; Butcher, 1999), this version contains basically the same items as the original version, and the original version was well known for the differences it showed between minority group members and White Americans (Butcher, Braswell, & Raney, 1983; Costello, Fine, & Blau, 1973; Costello, Tiffany, & Gier, 1972; W. E. Davis, Beck, & Ryan, 1973; Genther & Graham, 1976; S. B. Green & Kelley, 1988; Gynther, 1972, 1981, 1989; Gynther & Green, 1980; Hibbs, Kobos, & Gonzalez, 1979; Holcomb & Adams, 1982; Marsella, Sanaborn,

Kameoka, Shizuru, & Brennan, 1975; McCreary & Padilla, 1977; McGill, 1980; C. Miller, Knapp, & Daniels, 1968; C. Miller, Wertz, & Counts, 1961; Page & Bozlee, 1982; Plemons, 1977; Pollack & Shore, 1980).

Age

Studies on aging follow either a cross-sectional or a longitudinal design. In the cross-sectional design, a group of younger cohorts is compared with a group of older cohorts at one point in time. The advantage of this design is that it avoids confounding variables such as test–retest unreliability and the cultural and environmental changes that may have taken place between measures. The drawback to the cross-sectional study is that it measures two different groups, contaminating the aging changes with differences that may have existed between the two groups. In contrast, a longitudinal design studies the same individuals over a period of years. The problems of the longitudinal design include the difficulty with participant retention, test–retest unreliability, and extraneous variables (e.g., social, political, economic events) that may have played a role in the change from one test session to another. D. T. Campbell and Stanley (1963) recommended a combination of the cross-sectional and longitudinal approach as the ideal design.

After collecting MCMIs from patients at the Chicago Veterans Administration for several decades, the author and his colleagues (Dean & Choca, 2001) examined the data using both a cross-sectional and a longitudinal design. The cross-sectional study included MCMIs from 2,093 psychiatric male patients, divided into younger (18–40 years) and older (60 years and older) age groups. The longitudinal study included patients who had taken another MCMI as part of an intake at least 10 years later and patients who had been seen more than 10 years ago and who could be recruited to take the test a second time. In those cases, the version of the MCMI that the patient had taken before was administered the second time.

As can be seen in Figure 4.1, the younger group obtained lower scores in only four of the scales (Histrionic, Narcissistic, Compulsive, and Desirability), with the older group obtaining significantly lower scores on all of the rest. It should be noted that the four scales on which the younger group had lower scores could be considered indicators of psychological health (see chap. 2 for more details). Thus, the cross-sectional data show the younger individuals as substantially more pathological and symptomatic than the older group.

Figure 4.1

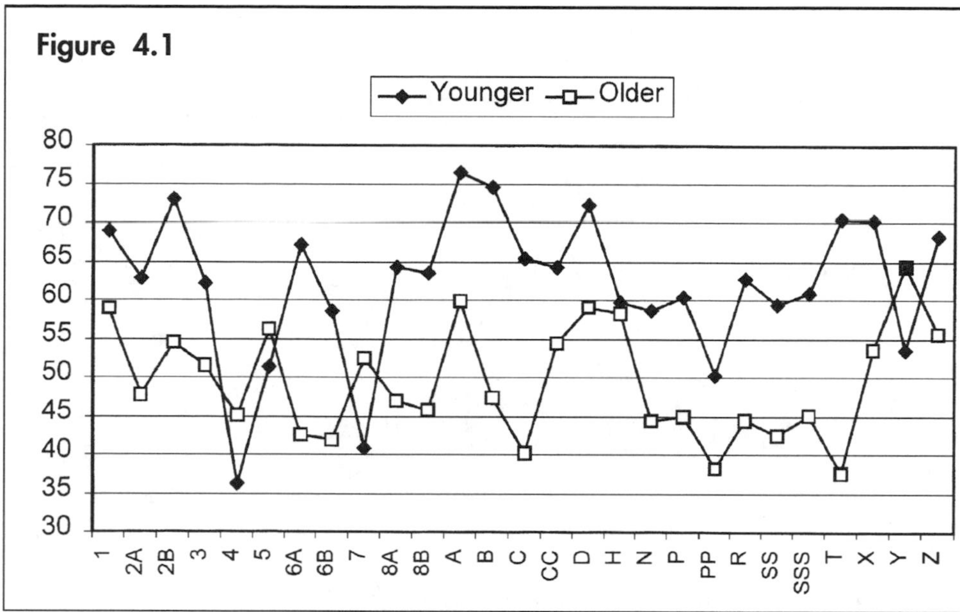

Cross-sectional comparison of younger (n = 610) versus older (n = 435) psychiatric male patients on the MCMI–III. The difference between the two groups was significant ($p < .001$) for all scales except Bipolar Manic (Scale H).

Figure 4.2 shows the longitudinal findings. For this figure we subtracted the first score from the second score obtained when the individual was at least 10 years older. A score at the 0 line indicates that there was no change from the first testing to the second. The negative scores below that line show that the score obtained on the second testing, when the individual was older, was lower than the score obtained the first time the person was seen. The solid circles on the graph indicate significant differences. Of the 24 scales examined, 11 scales showed significant differences, and all of the significant differences were in the direction of the second score being lower than the first. As McCrae and Costa (1990) would have led us to expect, the personality scales were less prone to change, with only 3 of the 13 scales showing reduced scores with age. Judging from our data, however, men become less antisocial, negativistic, and borderline as they become older. On the other hand, 7 of the 9 clinical syndrome scales showed a significant drop in scores when the person was at least 10 years older. The trend toward lower scores in the older population was consistent with the cross-sectional data.

The mellowing trend in the aging of psychiatric male patients had been previously shown by W. E. Davis and Greenblatt (1990) with the MCMI–I. The

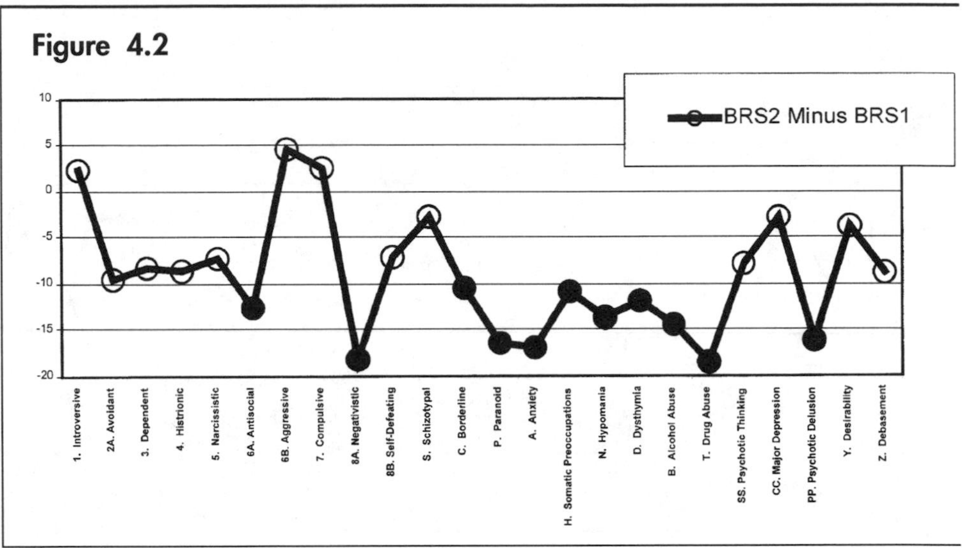

Difference between the Base Rate scores obtained on the second and the first administration of the MCMI, at least 10 years apart.

"mellowing" of pathology in emotionally disturbed individuals means that the older folks report their symptoms as being less severe. The finding speaks for being a bit more tolerant of higher scores in the young and being more concerned with milder elevations with individuals of mature ages.

Birth Order

Curtis and Cowell (1993) investigated correlations of birth order and scores on the Narcissism scale. They found that firstborn and only children tended to score higher than middle-born and last-born children on both the MCMI–I and the Narcissistic Personality Inventory.

Culture

Glass, Bieber, and Tkachuk (1996) contrasted the MCMI–II scores of 46 Alaska Native incarcerated men with scores of 21 non-Native incarcerated men. Natives obtained a higher Debasement index than the non-Native group and scored significantly higher on the Compulsive, Avoidant, and Schizoid personality scales, as well as on the Alcohol and Thought Disorder scales. These findings were used to characterize the Alaska Native inmates as more deprecating, self-restrained, and detached than non-Natives and more inclined to abuse alcohol.

Gunsalus and Kelly (2001) compared a group of Korean college students with American college students on the personality scales of the MCMI–III. The Korean group spoke English as a second language, and the test was administered in English to both groups. The Koreans obtained higher scores on 6 of the 11 personality scales investigated (Schizoid, Avoidant, Depressive, Dependent, Aggressive, and Self-Defeating). The American group showed a higher average score on the Histrionic scale. The authors cautioned against interpreting elevations of MCMI–III personality scales as indications of a personality disorder with Korean Americans without corroboration from another data source.

Invalidity and Defensiveness

This chapter discusses the use of Millon's Validity scale and Modifying Indices in assessing the usefulness of the scores obtained with a particular individual and in the adjustment of the Base Rate (BR) scores. The chapter will start with an introduction to the topic, review the work that has been done with the different scales of the MCMI, and discuss the response sets that can make an MCMI protocol untrustworthy.

Introduction

The MCMI–I had only one scale for evaluating the response set of the examinee (Millon, 1977). This scale, the Validity scale, consists of items that are blatantly implausible and mostly measures how well the examinee is paying attention and understanding what he or she is doing. The assessment of the examinee's response set became more involved with the second and third versions of the MCMI. The latter versions used the Validity scale of the MCMI–I and formalized the computation of an index from the raw scores of the personality scales under the name of the Disclosure Index. Two additional scales were introduced with the MCMI–II to assess whether the examinee is trying to create a positive or a negative image. These scales are the Desirability and Debasement scales. The Disclosure, Desirability, and Debasement scales, as well as other internal calculations, then are used to adjust the BR scores of certain scales.

In spite of the fact that the adjustments to the BR scores have been criticized as being excessive (see chap. 3), these adjustments are not strong enough to correct for response sets in many cases (McNiel & Meyer, 1990). It would seem that when the primary intent of the examinee is to draw a biased picture of himself or herself, no amount of score adjustment will correct the profile so that it can be interpreted without taking the response set into consideration.

Validity Scale

The first score one looks at when interpreting the MCMI is the score obtained on the Validity scale (see chap. 10). A Validity score of 1 or more may mean that the other MCMI–III scores are untrustworthy. Such a score indicates that the examinee was not reading and understanding the inventory for some reason and that the answers could even represent random choices.

Using the MCMI–II, Bishop (1993) showed that a high proportion of substance abusers (16%) obtained an invalid protocol, possibly because of subtle intellectual impairment present during the withdrawal phase. The Validity score was correlated negatively with the Vocabulary score of the Shipley Institute of Living Scale (SILS; Shipley, 1986). This finding seems to indicate that examinees who are unable to understand the meaning of words or unwilling to give the time and effort necessary to read and comprehend each item will not respond to the MCMI adequately.

Although Millon has accepted protocols containing a Validity score of 1 as valid, much caution should be used with such protocols. After all, a score of 1 on the Validity scale means that the examinee claimed that one blatantly absurd item was true about himself or herself. (For example, the examinee may claim never to have had any hair on any part of his or her body.) The reason a Validity score of 1 is acceptable is that, unfortunately, many examinees used in the standardization studies scored some points on this scale; as a result, a score of 1 was not statistically out of the acceptable range. Even if statistically acceptable, clinicians have to consider whether the same person who would make some outlandish claim on the MCMI can evaluate accurately, for example, the connotations of believing that the world would be a better place if people's morals were improved.

Thus, users should look carefully at protocols that have a Validity score of 1. If it is possible to explain such a score in a way that still allows one to think that the rest of the items were answered accurately, the rest of the scores may be examined. If no such explanation is obvious, the examiner is encouraged to disregard all the other findings. In clinical practice, the author typically tells the examinee that the test was invalid and suggests that he or she may not have been paying close attention to all the items. In most cases, one can have the examinee fill out the inventory again, asking the examinee this time to make certain to read the items carefully.

In cases in which the bad Validity scale item is explainable in some way, the rest of the scores may be examined to see whether they make clinical sense. If the rest of the scores are in any way surprising for the particular patient, the protocol should be seen as invalid and the findings should be disregarded. For research work, the best practice is to include only protocols with a Validity score of 0.

Disclosure Index

The Disclosure index is a composite score derived from the raw scores obtained on the personality scales. For the MCMI–I, this index is a simple addition of the applicable raw scores (Millon, 1982b). The MCMI–II and the MCMI–III use an equation to weigh the raw scores of the different personality scales in a way that makes theoretical sense (Millon, 1987, 1994a). The Disclosure index was found to accurately identify more than 90% of the simulated fake-bad protocols with the MCMI–II (Retzlaff, Sheehan, & Fiel, 1991).

If the Disclosure index obtained is outside of the acceptable range, the acceptability of the profile is in question. An unacceptably low Disclosure index score is obtained by individuals who mark most of the items false. One possibility is that the individual did not read or understand the inventory. If all items are answered false, the Validity scale score would be 0, because the items were written in a way that indicates an invalid protocol only if they are answered true. If this possibility seems to have been the case, refer to the comments in the previous section on invalid protocols.

Another possibility that may lead to an unacceptably low Disclosure index score would be that the examinee is highly defensive. In that case, the individual might have read and understood all of the items but claimed that few of the traits or psychological attributes included in the inventory applied to him or her. Unfortunately, this index tended to remain in the acceptable range when examinees were asked to fake good in the inventory (Retzlaff, Sheehan, & Fiel, 1991; Van Gorp & Meyer, 1986). In cases in which the unacceptably low Disclosure index score is attributable to defensiveness, the thinking would be that the defensiveness is so profound that little can be learned from looking at any other score and that the protocol should be seen as invalid. In such cases it may be possible to coach the individual into completing the inventory again, this time in a less defensive manner.

When accompanied by a Validity scale score of 1 or above, an unacceptably high Disclosure index score usually is associated with an invalid protocol. For such cases, refer to the discussion in the first part of this chapter. Otherwise, an unacceptably elevated Disclosure index score is an indication of faking bad on the examinee's part. Such an individual usually claims to have so many symptoms and psychological traits that it does not seem possible, even when the person is compared with the most incapacitated of psychiatric patients. The validity of the Disclosure index in the case of fake bad conditions was supported by both of the studies available (Retzlaff, Sheehan, & Fiel, 1991; Van Gorp & Meyer, 1986).

Disclosure index scores within the acceptable range may be outside the average range. In such cases, the protocol is seen as valid, but the index betrays a particular response set that the individual is using. In that case, Millon would use the score to adjust the weighted scores of the clinical scales so that they may better represent the actual clinical picture. In addition, however, the fact that the Disclosure index is outside the normal range is interpretable. When the index score is elevated, the indication would be that the individual has a tendency to think that he or she has more traits or symptoms than the average patient in the standardizing population. Elevations of this scale have been shown to indicate a tendency to exaggerate one's psychopathology (Grossman & Craig, 1994). In the case of a low (but acceptable) Disclosure index score, the implication would be one of defensiveness (see the section on defensive personality styles).

Millon (1994a) recommended using a Disclosure index of more than 178 as the cutoff for invalidity. Schoenberg and his coworkers, however, found that particular cutoff ineffective, because it did not identify any of the students taking the inventory while trying to fake bad (Schoenberg, Dorr, & Morgan, 2003). The best classification rates in their study were obtained with a cutoff of more than 89.

Desirability and Debasement Scales

The Desirability and Debasement scales were first introduced with the MCMI–II and were kept for the MCMI–III. Desirability measures the tendency to portray oneself in a good light. Items included make the examinee look confident, gregarious, cooperative, efficient, and well organized and allege a regard for authority and a respect for the rules of society. Elevations indicate a tendency to minimize psychological problems (Grossman & Craig, 1994).

The Debasement scale, on the other hand, was designed to tap an attempt to look bad in the inventory. Prominent items deal with feeling physically and emotionally empty, having low self-esteem, becoming angry or tearful at the slightest provocation, feeling unwanted or disliked, feeling tense, being uncomfortable in the presence of others, or feeling guilty and depressed. Erratic moods, a desire to hurt people, a suspicious attitude, and mental confusion also may be present. This scale typically becomes elevated when the examinee responds to the instrument in a way that exaggerates psychopathology (Grossman & Craig, 1994). The Debasement scale was found to identify accurately more than 90% of the simulated fake-bad protocols (Retzlaff, Sheehan, & Fiel, 1991).

Millon (1987) used the difference between the scores obtained on these two scales to modify some of the clinical scales so that they better reflect the picture that others may see looking at the individual. Elevations of these two scales, however, are obviously interpretable using the descriptions provided previously.

The effectiveness of the Desirability and Debasement scales in detecting dissimulation or malingering has been the subject of several studies. Retzlaff, Sheehan, and Fiel (1991) found these two scales to have only modest effectiveness in detecting malingering. In their study, only 52% of their fake-good groups were screened by the scales; the scales detected 48% of the examinees in one of their fake-bad groups and 92% in the other. Bagby, Gillis, and Dickens (1990) used a discriminant function to discover which participants had been asked to fake good or fake bad; they were able to classify correctly only 67% of their sample during the cross-validation phase of the study.

Wetzler and Marlowe (1990), on the other hand, reported that 17% of their psychiatric inpatients scored higher than a BR score of 84 on the Debasement scale. Their finding suggested that this index may reflect a "cry for help" and be an expression of distress rather than intentional dissimulation in the case of severely disturbed examinees. Schoenberg et al. (2003) recommended using a cutoff of less than 21 as indicating an attempt to fake bad on the MCMI–III.

Defensive Personality Styles and Fake-Good Response Sets

As will be discussed in chapter 6, it is the author's contention that an elevation of any of the eight basic personality scales is indicative only of the presence of a personality style and is not necessarily suggestive of psychopathology. Nevertheless, an MCMI protocol containing no elevations is theoretically indicative of a healthy personality. It is possible to obtain such a personality profile, referred to as *Profile 000,* in a nondefensive manner, a manner that leads to acceptable Disclosure index levels and average scores on the other Modifying Indices. Respondents fitting such a profile typically admit having some dependent traits, narcissistic traits, competitive traits, and so on, but they do not have enough of a tendency in any one of these areas to cause an elevation on the particular personality scale score.

Such people may be described as not having a characteristic style, a ready-made routine, or a typical way in which they react to environmental events. Being this way may have the advantage of allowing individuals to readily vary their response according to the situation. It may have the disadvantage of preventing individuals from having an automatic response, or a pattern of behavior that comes out naturally and predictably regardless of the situation at hand.

Clinicians must remember, however, that most individuals taking the MCMI will have an elevation in at least one of the personality scales. In Repko and Cooper's (1985) sample of nonpsychiatric workers' compensation examinees, for instance, only 4% did not have any elevated scores. Thus, when no elevations are obtained, one possibility to be considered is that of defensiveness on the examinee's part. Two defensive no-elevation profiles can be readily recognized.

In the first such profile, the Compulsive scale is the highest elevation of the protocol and is significantly more elevated than the rest of the personality scales. This style is referred to as *Profile 070* and is indicative of individuals who have an air of perfectionism and a tendency to deny faults or limitations. Typically, this profile describes individuals who are guarded, private, and uncommunicative. Interpersonally, they seem distant and unavailable and have difficulty expressing emotions. In spite of appearing somewhat uncomfortable, they may speak of themselves in an overly superficial manner and try to project the image of someone who is doing well after having solved most of his or her problems. Behind this facade one may find an individual who is feeling vulnerable and insecure, at least about the outcome of the psychological testing.

The other defensive profile is similar to the first, but instead of having only the Compulsive scale score elevated above the rest, the Compulsive and the Narcissistic scale scores both are prominent. This profile is referred to as *Profile 075* and is described as follows: The compulsive aspects shown by the MCMI suggest that such individuals place an emphasis on perfectionism and maintaining good control of their environment. Similar individuals are somewhat defensive and unlikely to admit failures or mistakes. At times, they may be seen as being too inflexible, formal, or proper and may relate to others somewhat distantly. Together with these compulsive elements, these individuals may have a tendency to feel that they are special and have few faults. Similar individuals believe that they are more capable or worth more than almost everyone else. People with this profile attempt to tell others what to do and are most comfortable when placed in a position of leadership, but they usually share little of their own private affairs with those around them.

In support of the aforementioned contentions, it has been shown that fake-good groups tend to yield a narcissistic–compulsive profile (Craig, Kuncel, & Olson, 1994; Retzlaff et al., 1991). Lampel (1999) used the MCMI–III to evaluate custody litigants. Because these parents were seeking the custody of their children, they wished to present themselves in a good light. Lampel found that the majority of her examinees had elevated scores on the Compulsive, Histrionic, or Narcissistic scales, as well as on the Desirability scale. Looking at such data, Halon (2001) raised the issue of whether the profile represents a pattern that many healthy individuals give in a custody battle type of situation.

The fake-good pattern also includes a tendency to reduce scores in all the scales (Fals-Stewart, 1995). The fact that it is difficult to distinguish between fake-good malingering and a valid profile also has been demonstrated repeatedly (Craig et al., 1994; Retzlaff et al., 1991; Van Gorp & Meyer, 1986). This would be especially true in the case of people who have mild emotional problems because, for them, the lack of significant elevations among the symptom scales cannot be used as further evidence that the inventory was not completed meaningfully. Additionally, investigators have shown that the fake good condition tends to elevate the Desirability index and may depress both the Debasement and the Disclosure scale scores of the MCMI–II or the MCMI–III (Bagby, Gillis, Toner, & Goldberg, 1991; Fals-Stewart, 1995; Grossman & Craig, 1994; Lampel, 1999).

One group of patients especially prone to minimize their pathology is substance abusers. Because recreational use of alcohol and drugs is widely accepted in American society, the boundary between pathological and non-pathological use is blurred and easily permits a denial of problem abuse. Results of several studies have shown that the majority of substance abusers are able to avoid detection of their substance abuse problem on the MCMI–II

(Craig et al., 1994; Fals-Stewart, 1995). It seems that patients whose substance abuse is milder in severity are more able to avoid detection than those who have a more chronic and severe problem (Craig et al., 1994). Clinicians should examine the prototypical items for the substance abuse scales, because many of the patients avoiding detection still endorsed one or more of the prototypical items in the scorable direction. Additionally, diagnosticians may want to investigate further an MCMI showing the modal substance abuse denial profile. This profile is characterized by elevations on the Narcissistic, Antisocial, and Aggressive scales; no elevations on the clinical syndrome scales; and low Disclosure and Debasement scores (Craig et al., 1994).

Fake-Bad Response Sets

Fake-bad profiles are easily discernible on the MCMI. Typically, such profiles have many scales with a BR score of 85, the Disclosure and Debasement scale scores are moderately high, and the Desirability scale score is moderately low (Bagby, Gillis, Toner, & Goldberg, 1991; Grossman & Craig, 1994). The clinical scales that tend to be elevated include the Schizoid, Avoidant, and Negativistic personality scales; the severe personality scales; and the Anxiety and Dysthymia scales (McNiel & Meyer, 1990; Retzlaff et al., 1991; Van Gorp & Meyer, 1986).

Lees-Haley (1992) studied MCMI–II scores of personal injury claimants who fraudulently claimed to have posttraumatic stress disorder after a relatively minor incident at work. Using a BR cutoff score of 60, Lees-Haley classified correctly 73% of the fraudulent claims using the Disclosure scale, 87% using the Debasement scale, and 97% of the real-injury control group using either scale. These findings should be viewed with caution, however, because in my experience the nonfraudulent clinical population routinely scores above a BR of 60 on those scales.

In a study with the MCMI–III, the test unfortunately did not show any promise in its ability to detect the individuals exaggerating their symptomatology (Schoenberg et al., 2003). In a sample in which dissimulation had a 37% prevalence rate, the MCMI–III performed only slightly better than chance. In a real clinical sample, the fake-bad prevalence is probably much lower than 37%, a fact that would worsen the MCMI–III's performance. When the authors computed the operating characteristics using a 10% prevalence rate of malingering, the test performed worse than chance. (In a real clinical scenario, where malingering is expected to be less than 10%, if the clinician assumes that no one is malingering, this clinician would be right 90% of the time.)

Random-Response Set

Some individuals who are not willing or able to take the test properly will enter answers at random. Because the items of the Validity scale are keyed so that they should all be false, the scale should be sensitive to random responding as long as the response set was not that of answering all of the items as false (Retzlaff et al., 1991). Simulation studies in fact showed this scale to effectively identify more than 90% of the randomly answered protocols (Bagby, Gillis, & Rogers, 1991; Retzlaff et al., 1991).

In actual practice, however, the MCMI–III has not done so well. Charter and Lopez (2002) discovered that when a Validity score of 1 is accepted, half of the random responders will escape detection. They found, furthermore, that neither the Disclosure scale nor the clinical personality scale pattern was useful in detecting random responding. This study clearly raises the concern that protocols completed through random answering of the items may not be detectable on the MCMI–III.

Untrustworthy-Response Sets and Personality Characteristics

As has been noted, interpreting the MCMI often requires distinguishing possibly untrustworthy-response sets from personality characteristics. This distinction is problematic at best. In a recent study, Wise (2002) found significant correlations between the validity scales of the second edition of the Minnesota Multiphasic Personality Inventory (MMPI–2) and 11 of the 13 personality scales of the MCMI–II.

Subtle and Obvious Subscales

Peterson, Clark, and Bennet (1989) found little difference between MCMI–I profiles under instructions to fake good and those obtained when examinees were asked to answer the items honestly. That finding led them to suggest that the subtle–obvious distinction that has been used so often with the MMPI is not important for the MCMI.

Studies done with the MCMI–I led to the establishment of Subtle and Obvious subscales for that version of the test (Wierzbicki, 1993a, 1993b; Wierzbicki & Daleiden, 1993; Wierzbicki & Howard, 1992). Unfortunately, no such scales are available for the current version of the test.

Part II

Interpreting the MCMI

Assessment of Personality Styles

From the author's perspective, the original eight personality scales of the Millon Clinical Multiaxial Inventory (MCMI)—Schizoid, Avoidant, Dependent, Histrionic, Narcissistic, Antisocial, Compulsive, and Negativistic—are best conceptualized as representing personality *styles,* rather than necessarily personality *disorders* (Choca, Shanley, et al., 1992). The author agrees with Birtchnell's (1991) warning against interpreting high scores on these personality scales as indicators of psychopathology. Instead, he views the scales as measuring basic assumptions, predominant attitudes, and typical ways of interacting, which may or may not be pathological.

Much evidence can be cited in support of the contention that the original eight scales measure personality styles. The original prototypes from which these scales were derived described personalities of mild severity and were not designed to be very pathological. Craig (1999a) reached the same conclusion for the Histrionic, Compulsive, and Narcissistic scales by looking at the results of factor analyses and noting that these scales tend to load negatively on the psychological maladjustment factor.

Additionally, there is the finding that when these scales are interpreted as measuring personality disorders, they have been shown to "overpathologize" respondents. Investigations typically show that almost everyone who takes the MCMI will have an elevation on at least one of these personality scales. This was true of the MCMI–I (Brown, 1992; Calsyn & Saxon, 1990; Cantrell & Dana, 1987; Chambless, Renneberg, Goldstein, & Gracely, 1992; Chick, Sheaffer, Goggin, & Sison, 1993; Craig, 1988; Hart, Forth, & Hare, 1991; Holliman & Guthrie, 1989; Inch & Crossley, 1993; R. E. King, 1994; Piersma, 1987c; Repko & Cooper, 1985; Wetzler, Kahn, Cahn, van Praag, & Asnis, 1990) and the MCMI–II (Chambless et al., 1992; Hart, Dutton, &

Newlove, 1993; Inch & Crossley, 1993; Renneberg, Chambless, Dowdall, Fauerbach, & Gracely, 1992; Sinha & Watson, 2001; Turley, Bates, Edwards, & Jackson, 1992).

From the author's point of view, a serious, unfortunate mistake that is commonly made with the MCMI is to interpret elevations on the eight basic personality scales as evidence of a personality disorder. This caveat is not meant to include the other personality scales (Depressive, Aggressive, Self-Defeating, Schizotypal, Borderline, and Paranoid) because those scales appear to have many items that seem obviously pathological and yield higher scores in a psychiatric sample (Strack et al., 1989). Because this is the area in which the author differs the most from the automated interpretations generated by the Pearson Assessments program for the MCMI, the methodology and narratives that are used to describe the personality *styles* are offered in this book.

Interpreting the Basic Eight Personality Scales

The least sophisticated way of interpreting the results of psychological inventories such as the MCMI is to take one elevated scale score at a time and describe what that particular elevation indicates about the examinee. Such a simplistic method forfeits the more finely detailed information that would be derived from an integrative view of the elevated scales. Consider, for instance, two individuals for whom the Negativistic scale (Scale 8A) constitutes the highest elevation. One such individual may have as a second elevation the Dependent scale (Scale 3); in that case, one may talk about a person who feels inadequate but does not typically behave cooperatively because he or she does not feel that other people are going to adequately meet his or her dependency needs. By contrast, if the second elevation is found on the Antisocial scale (Scale 6A), the negativistic tendencies may be discussed more accurately in terms of the juxtaposition of feelings of inadequacy and the view of life as a tournament in which every person has to fend for himself or herself. Therefore, the ideal would be a system that allows any one finding to be adjusted and expanded by any other finding.

Although this is a goal worth striving for, those who work with the MCMI typically operate in a way that represents a compromise between the simplistic interpretations based on "1-point" elevations and the ideal report that takes into account every scale elevation at the same time. For one thing, at times one may not have a clear idea of how the cluster of traits that are described by one elevation are altered by the presence of another elevation.

Moreover, those who routinely administer this test have ready-made interpretations, and the number of narratives needed would be prohibitive if every scale were to be considered in combination with every other scale.

Once the idea of considering more than one of the personality scales is accepted, the issue to be raised is how many of the personality prototypes may be clinically relevant when several scales are elevated. To answer that question, the clinician needs to look at how elevated the scores are and at how wide the gap is between the score of one scale and the next highest score. An interpretation that includes the highest two prototypes (a "2-point" interpretation) is most appropriate when only two scales are elevated, when there is a sizable gap between the scores obtained on the second highest scale and the third, and when the score of the third highest scale is closer to the cluster of scores to follow than to the cluster made up by the two highest scales.

Clinicians using the MCMI typically take into consideration the highest three personality scores (a "3-point" interpretation). Some elements of the fourth or the fifth elevations are occasionally added, in cases where those scores also cluster with the other high scores and especially in cases where such additions offer some information that appears to be of particular clinical relevance for the examinee.

A Base Rate (BR) score of 75 is typically used as the cutoff determining whether or not a scale is elevated. A knowledgeable clinician does not have to adhere strictly to that guideline. Although cutoff scores constitute a practical way of determining if an attribute is present or absent, they impose an artificial dichotomy on an essentially continuous distribution. As Dwyer (1996) pointed out, there is no statistical difference between a score just below the cutoff (e.g., a BR score of 74) and one just above it (e.g., a BR score of 76); nevertheless, the use of the cutoff makes it so that one would not be seen as elevated and the other would be. Consideration of such issues would lead to advocating a more flexible and clinically informed approach.

In cases where the entire score profile is elevated, the clinician may decide to disregard or deemphasize some of the scales that did not yield the predominant elevations, even if the BR score was actually above 75. Conversely, with a low score profile, a clinician may use data from scales with scores that did not quite reach the cutoff, especially in cases where such a decision can be supported with other sources of information about the individual. In other words, the emphasis when the clinician is personally interpreting an MCMI protocol should be on the cluster of scores that has primacy, rather than on adopting a mechanistic rule about what scores are to be interpreted. Of course, the license to interpret scores below the cutoff has to be exercised with caution: We must remember that the BR score of 50 represents the average for the nonpatient population, so that as the scores get into the 60s, they become more indistinguishable from the mass of scores that, being in the average range, do not indicate a salient characteristic.

The author recommends looking at the personality style by separating the original eight personality style scales from the rest. Thus, the first interpretive step would include the Schizoid (1), Avoidant (2A), Dependent (3), Histrionic (4), Narcissistic (5), Antisocial (6A), Compulsive (7), and Negativistic (8A) scales. In taking this step, we temporarily disregard the new personality scales that were added to the MCMI–II and MCMI–III to measure depressive (2B), aggressive (6B), and self-defeating (8B) personalities, as well as the three severe personality scales. These latter six scales, which inherently denote the presence of psychopathology, would be considered for interpretation later on. The author recommends interpreting only the three highest elevations among the original eight scales. Taking all possible permutations of the eight different scales results in 336 interpretive narratives, an unwieldy number.

Although all 336 of these permutations would theoretically constitute discrete personality profiles, this book will narrow the range of narratives to approximately 80, because empirical data indicate that many of these possible permutations are seldom encountered. A study using a larger number of participants found 20 common 2-point profiles that accounted for 82% of the examinees (Retzlaff, Ofman, Hyer, & Matheson, 1994). For a review of all the profiles found in the literature from 1980 to 1993, the reader is referred to Craig (1995).

The system advocated here involves giving an individual a narrative that approximates his or her particular profile, even if it does not exactly fit the elevations that the respondent obtained. Table 6.1 shows a mapping of all possible profiles among the personality styles onto the available narratives. The coding of the profiles is performed in the following manner: The first number represents the highest elevation above the cutoff (BR) score of 75, the second number represents the second such elevation, and the third number represents the third such elevation. A 0 denotes that no scale is elevated above the cutoff, so that 12A0 means that the Schizoid and Avoidant scales were the only two scales having significant elevations. When fewer than three numbers are given, it does not matter which other scale is elevated; in other words, 51 means that the Narcissistic scale is the most elevated, followed by an elevation on the Schizoid scale, which may be followed by an elevation of any other scale or no other elevations. Having decided which narrative may constitute the best fit using the table, the reader then can go on to find the narrative later in the chapter.

Three different methods have been used to develop narratives for instruments such as the MCMI. The *theoretical* approach generates such descriptions based on theoretical notions of what an individual with a particular score profile should look like. In contrast, the *item* approach relies on a review of the items actually endorsed by individuals obtaining a particular profile or on the findings of factor analytical studies of the items of the scales involved. Finally, the *actuarial* approach examines empirical data, typically demographic data or data derived from sources outside of the inventory, to characterize individuals obtaining a particular profile. The narratives offered in this chapter were created by using, as much as possible, all three of these approaches.

Note that some liberties have been taken in the inclusion of actuarial data into the narratives. For instance, a study by Hamberger and Hastings (1986), who investigated the 6A54 profile, is cited in the 6A50 narrative because that is the narrative that this book recommends for that particular personality style. A second caveat: No effort was made to distinguish between the different versions of the MCMI in this section. In the majority of the citations, the MCMI–I was used. It is hoped that the findings also apply to the MCMI–II and the MCMI–III, but that expectation remained largely untested at the time this book was written. Finally, many of these citations note the prevalence of a personality style among individuals with other characteristics, such as alcoholism or posttraumatic stress disorder. Such data, however, cannot be used in isolation to infer the presence of the other characteristic. In other words, even though profile 12A0 has been shown to be prevalent among schizophrenics (Josiassen, Shagass, & Roemer, 1988), it has also been found with other clinical syndromes (Fals-Stewart, 1992; McNiel & Meyer, 1990; Retzlaff & Bromley, 1991), and the mere presence of the profile does not imply the diagnosis of schizophrenia.

The narratives provided were generated from actual clinical work. Each of these narratives was originally written for one examinee. Repeated use of the narratives led to further refining of the descriptions, often involving the omission of statements that did not apply to subsequent examinees obtaining the same test profile. Nevertheless, the narratives have not been validated systematically and experimentally; they are offered as an aid to clinicians, who would decide what part of the narrative, if any, applies to the individual being evaluated.

In spite of the attempt to make the narratives as benign as possible, negative terms are often used. There are two reasons for this. First, negative

Table 6.1

Mapping of Personality Profiles Into Narrative Clusters

Cluster	Profile	Cluster	Profile	Cluster	Profile	Cluster	Profile	Cluster	Profile	Cluster	Profile	Cluster	Profile	Cluster	Profile
0	000	2A0	2A00	30	300	40	400	50	500	6A0	6A00	70	700	8A0	8A00
070	070	2A10	12A0	310	32A0	41	400	51	500	6A10	6A12A	71	72A0	8A10	8A12A
075	075	2A13	32A1	312A	32A1	42A	400	52A	52A0	6A12A	6A12A	72A	72A0	8A12A	8A12A
10	100	2A14	2A00	314	32A0	430	430	53	530	6A13	6A12A	730	730	8A13	8A00
12A0	12A0	2A15	2A00	315	32A0	431	430	540	540	6A14	6A00	731	730	8A14	8A00
12A3	2A31	2A16A	2A00	316A	32A0	432A	430	541	540	6A15	6A00	732A	730	8A15	8A00
12A4	12A0	2A17	2A00	317	32A0	435	430	542A	540	6A17	6A12A	734	730	8A16A	8A00
12A5	12A0	2A18A	18A2A	318A	32A0	436A	430	543	540	6A18A	6A12A	735	730	8A17	8A70
12A6A	12A0	2A30	2A30	32A0	32A0	437	430	546A	546A	6A2A	2A6A0	736A	736A	8A2A0	8A2A0
12A7	12A0	2A31	2A31	32A1	32A1	438A	438A	547	540	6A3	6A34	738A	738A	8A2A1	8A2A0
12A8A	12A8A	2A37	32A7	32A4	32A0	450	450	548A	548A	6A40	6A40	74	740	8A2A3	8A2A3
130	132A	2A34	2A38A	32A5	32A0	451	450	56A	56A4	6A41	6A40	75	750	8A2A4	8A2A3
132A	132A	2A35	2A38A	32A6A	32A0	452A	450	57	750	6A42A	6A40	76A	6A70	8A2A5	8A2A0
134	138A	2A36A	2A38A	32A7	32A7	453	450	58A	58A0	6A43	6A40	78A	8A70	8A2A6A	8A2A6A
135	138A	2A38A	2A38A	32A8A	32A8A	456A	456A			6A45	456A			8A2A7	8A2A0
136A	138A	2A4	2A38A	340	340	457	450			6A47	6A40			8A30	38A0
137	137	2A5	2A50	341	340	458A	458A			6A48A	46A8A			8A31	38A0
138A	138A	2A6A0	2A6A0	342A	340	46A	46A8A			6A50	6A50			8A32A	38A2A
14	100	2A6A1	2A6A0	345	354	470	470			6A51	6A50			8A34	38A0
15	150	2A6A3	2A6A0	346A	340	471	470			6A52A	6A50			8A35	38A0
16A	100	2A6A4	2A6A0	347	340	472A	470			6A53	6A53			8A36A	38A0
17	170	2A6A5	2A6A0	348A	348A	473	470			6A54	6A50			8A37	8A37
18A0	18A2A	2A6A7	2A6A7	350	530	475	470			6A57	6A50			8A4	8A40

18A2A	18A2A	2A6A8A	2A6A0	351	530	476A	470			6A58A	6A58A			8A50	58A0
18A3	138A	2A7	2A70	352A	530	478A	48A0			6A7	6A70			8A51	58A0
18A4	138A	2A8A0	2A8A0	354	354	48A0	48A0			6A8A0	6A8A0			8A52A	58A0
18A5	138A	2A8A1	2A8A0	356A	356A	48A1	48A0			6A8A1	6A8A0			8A53	58A0
18A6A	138A	2A8A3	2A38A	357	357	48A2A	48A0			6A8A2A	6A8A0			8A54	548A
18A7	138A	2A8A4	2A8A0	358A	356A	48A3	48A0			6A8A3	6A8A0			8A56A	8A56A
		2A8A5	2A8A	36A	36A0	48A5	458A			6A8A4	6A8A0			8A57	8A57
		2A8A6A	8A2A6A	370	370	48A6A	46A8A			6A8A5	6A58A			8A6A0	8A6A0
		2A8A7	2A8A0	371	370	48A7	48A0			6A8A7	6A8A0			8A6A1	8A6A0
				372A	32A7									8A6A2A	8A2A6A
				374	370									8A6A3	8A6A0
				375	370									8A6A4	8A6A4
				376A	370									8A6A5	8A56A
				378A	38A0									8A6A7	8A6A0
				38A0	38A0									8A70	8A70
				38A1	38A0									8A71	8A70
				38A2A	38A2A									8A72A	8A70
				38A4	38A0									8A73	8A37
				38A5	38A0									8A74	8A70
				38A6A	38A0									8A75	8A70
				38A7	38A0									8A76A	8A70

Note. Profile clusters (first number) and the narrative prototype that may be appropriate are shown. A zero among the profile clusters means that no other scale is elevated above the Base Rate score of 75. When only two numbers are given, the third elevation is unimportant (e.g., 14 means that the Schizoid scale [Scale 1] is the highest elevation, the Histrionic scale [Scale 4] is the second elevation, and it does not matter what else is elevated).

terms unfortunately tend to be more meaningfully descriptive: Most individuals would claim to be cooperative, but only a few would admit being submissive or compliant, even though all three of those terms have a very similar meaning to the clinician. Second, because the MCMI was designed for a psychiatric population, clinicians are often in the position of having to highlight problem areas without giving equal emphasis to psychological strengths.

If read in sequence, these narratives are highly repetitive because they often describe traits that already were described in a previous narrative. The intention is for the reader to use these narratives in a cookbook fashion, examining only the one that applies for the particular respondent in question.

Schizoid Profile Clusters

Profile 100: Schizoid

The Schizoid scale of the MCMI contains items that deal with a lack of close relationships with others and a lack of interest or ability in expressing feelings or emotions. Individuals who obtain elevated scores on this scale are probably private and prefer to be alone rather than with others.

Similarly scoring individuals, labeled "affectless schizoids" by Millon (1996), tend to be uninsightful and are not interested in exploring their personal feelings. Their detachment may result from relating better to inanimate objects and not caring about interpersonal rewards. They lead unemotional lives and are not inclined to get too disturbed when things do not go their way, but they also do not experience much excitement when good things happen. This tendency to remain on an even keel can be a real asset, because emotions will seldom interfere with the decision-making process. These individuals may be seen, however, as being emotionally bland and lacking an effective rapport with the people around them. In terms of coping strategies, higher scores on this scale are associated with lower levels of seeking social support, higher levels of acceptance of the status quo, and a greater tendency to use alcohol or drugs (Vollrath, Alnaes, & Torgersen, 1995).

Given this personality style, these individuals may be reluctant to engage in therapy. Because they are not likely to value the explorations and insights that are often seen as being an important part of therapy, establishing a therapeutic alliance is likely to be problematic. Modes of treatment that deemphasize emotional rapport or the understanding of psychodynamics may be more in tune with the individuals' approaches to life. In addition, the therapist must be comfortable with a distant relationship and must accept that, although cooperative, these clients may never be active collaborators in the therapeutic process.

Profile 12A0: Schizoid–Avoidant

High scores on the Schizoid and Avoidant scales of the MCMI characterize people who keep a significant emotional distance from others. Such individuals are most comfortable when they are alone and are referred to as the "remote schizoids" (Millon, 1996). They tend to like jobs or hobbies that involve objects and that have minimal human contact. In extreme cases, these individuals may be single, and their history may show signs of an inability or unwillingness to establish a meaningful relationship outside of the nuclear family. Otherwise, these individuals restrict the number of relationships that they form and tend to have superficial friendships when they do exist.

For these individuals, the inclination to be loners seems to be the result of two different dynamics. First, they appear to be uninterested in interpersonal relations. They are not too adept at understanding and enjoying the subtleties and nuances of interpersonal emotions and communications, a situation that might then have led to their being apathetic about relationships. They typically do not have strong emotions and live fairly bland affective lives.

A second dynamic in their lives is that they seem to be sensitive and afraid of being rejected by others. As a result, social situations are a source of significant tension; they feel nervous about and do not look forward to this type of activity. They would like to be accepted and appreciated and realize that they have to take part in social events to obtain that kind of satisfaction. Relating to others, however, is so uncomfortable that they avoid social situations in spite of the positive effects that they could have.

On the positive side, schizoid–avoidant individuals are self-sufficient individuals who do not depend on others for the fulfillment of their own needs. They often lead lives that are fairly free of overemotionality and in which psychological issues tend not to interfere with their behavior. On the other hand, others may perceive them as isolated loners who lead somewhat empty and unproductive lives.

Research indicates that this profile prevails among schizophrenics (Josiassen et al., 1988); this profile also has been found among forensic inpatients (McNiel & Meyer, 1990), alcoholics (Retzlaff & Bromley, 1991), and drug addicts treated in a therapeutic community (Fals-Stewart, 1992). In the latter study, schizoid–avoidant addicts were found to be likely to become self-critical and discouraged and to drop out of treatment; they also had worse outcomes, were less able to maintain abstinence, and relapsed faster than the rest of the group. Concomitant Minnesota Multiphasic Personality Inventory (MMPI) codes have been reported as either 28/82 (Antoni, Tischer, Levine, Green, & Millon, 1985a) or 78/87 (Antoni, Levine, Tischer, Green, & Millon, 1987).

Individuals with this personality style may have difficulty establishing therapeutic alliances. The discomfort that they experience in interpersonal relationships will probably make the sessions unenjoyable. In addition, a therapist also would have to be concerned about such clients feeling rejected any time he or she makes an uncomplimentary interpretation. When the treatment plan involves giving negative feedback or is intended to confront objectionable aspects of the personality or behavior, the client will experience the therapeutic context as threatening or stressful. To maintain the alliance but still contribute to the client's growth, the therapist must achieve a careful balance between uncritical support and threatening therapeutic work. The therapist also must be ready to allow the emotional distance that such clients may need and to tolerate their inability to talk about their lives and feelings nondefensively. These individuals will feel most enhanced with a therapist who treats them with admiration and respect.

Profile 12A8A: Schizoid–Avoidant–Negativistic

The schizoid–avoidant–negativistic profile characterizes individuals with introversive, avoidant, and negativistic elements in their personality styles. Such individuals have little interest in experiencing the subtle aspects of interpersonal relationships. Because of their lack of interest in interpersonal matters, these clients are likely to have turned their attention to areas that do not involve direct contact with people, such as reading or art. At worst, such individuals may be perceived as being emotionally insensitive in a distant and apathetic way. Such individuals probably have few friends and little real interpersonal involvement.

High scores on these three scales also suggest a general unresponsiveness to stimuli. Similar individuals are not particularly energetic or enthusiastic, and their thinking is usually vague, unclear, and somewhat impoverished. They are not prone to understanding or interpreting past events or to planning for the future. At times, they may appear evasive and overly defended, but most typically they just seem somewhat apathetic, dull, and uninteresting.

The detachment from others is accompanied by conflicts these clients experience when they are in social situations. They typically feel somewhat inadequate and often wish that someone would provide nurturance, shelter, and guidance. They fear rejection, however, and often seem nervous, moody, and resentful. At times, they may be friendly and cooperative, but anger and dissatisfaction soon color most of their relationships. Results of one study showed this profile to be the modal code for depressed clients who responded to tricyclic antidepressants (Joffe & Regan, 1989a).

Given their personality styles, these clients may have some difficulty establishing therapeutic alliances. The discomfort experienced in interpersonal relationships probably will make the sessions unenjoyable. In addition, a therapist would have to be concerned about clients feeling rejected any time he or she makes an uncomplimentary interpretation. Finally, the clients' dependency conflicts will mean that they are likely to respond negatively to the therapist's leadership. Thus, it may be difficult to get them to be motivated collaborators in the treatment process. The therapist must be ready to allow the emotional distance that these clients may need and to tolerate their inability to talk about their own lives and feelings nondefensively. If the therapist takes care not to issue many directives or much advice, he or she can minimize the resentment that such clients usually develop when they feel dependent on a relationship.

Profile 132A: Schizoid–Dependent–Avoidant

Labeled "ineffectual dependent" by Millon (1996), the schizoid–dependent–avoidant personality style emphasizes introversive aspects accompanied by dependent and avoidant traits. These individuals lack interest in other people. They do not seem happy when things come out well, nor are they too upset by unfortunate events. They are not interested in interpersonal situations. They are quiet and often stay by themselves, typically taking the role of passive observer, seldom taking sides or verbalizing a strong opinion. Rarely the center of attention, these individuals typically fade into the background. They have few friends; when relationships do exist, they tend to be superficial. They are socially indifferent and have little apparent need to communicate or to obtain support from others.

With the emotional indifference, such clients tend to feel less important or capable than other people. Similar individuals are easily led by others and are submissive and dependent. They are uncomfortable with highly competitive situations, are humble, and try to be as congenial as possible to the people around them. They often are afraid of being rejected by others and, as a result, feel some discomfort when relating to others.

These individuals are probably detached and uninvolved. Cooperative and agreeable individuals, they may be perceived as easygoing and emotionally stable. However, they may be criticized as being somewhat dull, quiet, indifferent, dependent, or apathetic.

Research suggests that this profile is common among psychiatric inpatients (McCann & Suess, 1988). Tango and Dziuban (1984) found that this profile, at a subclinical level, is correlated with the Strong–Campbell Interest Inventory's vocational interests of music and office practice among college students seeking career counseling. Indecisiveness about career choices was thought to be associated with discomfort with interpersonal contact.

A therapist attempting to work with these clients may have difficulty establishing the therapeutic alliance. The therapist will have to be tolerant of these clients' distant way of relating. A somewhat unexciting course of treatment also can be expected. A supportive relationship will be one in which the therapist takes a protective and parental attitude, reassuring clients that problems can be worked out and that help will be available.

Profile 137: Schizoid–Dependent–Compulsive

The schizoid–dependent–compulsive personality profile emphasizes introversive aspects seen with dependent and disciplined traits. These individuals are characterized by a lack of interest in and awareness of feelings and interpersonal situations. They usually lead relatively unemotional lives: They do not seem particularly happy when things turn out well, nor are they saddened by unfortunate events. They tend to be quiet loners and passive observers who remain uninvolved and seldom take sides or express a strong opinion. Rarely the center of attention, they often fade into the social background. They have few friends, and when relationships do exist, they tend to be superficial. It is not that such individuals fear or actively avoid others, but that they are somewhat indifferent and apparently have little need to communicate or to obtain support from others.

These clients also think of themselves as unimportant and incapable. Individuals with the same pattern of scores tend to be led by others and to be submissive and dependent. They also tend to shy away from highly competitive situations. They are humble and try to be as congenial as possible to the people around them.

These individuals typically assume that if they do not make mistakes, they can depend on other people to provide for their needs. This perfectionism both serves their dependency needs and fuels their tendency to be distant from others, with an emphasis on controlled and hidden thoughts and feelings. Such individuals often seem rigid, unexpressive, detached, dull, apathetic, and excessively formal. From a more positive perspective, they also appear objective, orderly, dependable, well organized, and responsible.

Profile 138A: Schizoid–Dependent–Negativistic

Individuals with the schizoid–dependent–negativistic profile have an introversive personality style with dependent traits that make them uncomfortable. They tend to be unemotional: When things turn out well for them, they do not seem particularly happy, nor are they saddened by unfortunate events. They tend to be quiet, private individuals—loners and passive observers who seldom take sides or have a strong position. Rarely the center of attention, these individuals tend to fade into the background. They have few friends, and relationships are usually superficial. It is not that they fear or actively avoid people, but that they are somewhat indifferent and apparently have little need to communicate with or to obtain support from others.

Perhaps related to this lack of interpersonal interest and know-how are the low self-esteem and submissive attitude that typically plague these clients. They avoid competitive situations and try to be congenial and conciliatory. Toward this end, they may cover up aggressive or objectionable feelings.

Some submissive individuals feel comfortable when they are able to establish a dependent relationship with another person who seems to be competent and trustworthy. The lack of emotional interest and awareness exhibited by these clients, however, makes it hard for them to establish a strong relationship of any kind, even a dependent one. These clients often come across as moody or negativistic—their only means of expressing their discomfort with personal relationships.

Profile 150: Schizoid–Narcissistic

The scores that schizoid–narcissistic individuals obtain on the test describe a personality with schizoid and narcissistic elements. Similar individuals typically have little interest or ability in experiencing the subtle aspects of interpersonal relationships. Because of this, they turn their attention toward matters that do not involve social relationships, like reading or art. Such individuals may be seen as emotionally insensitive to others in a distant and apathetic way. The end result of this particular trait is that the person probably has few friends and little real interpersonal involvement.

Similar individuals also tend to feel that they are a "special" kind of person. They see themselves as superior to others and tend to exaggerate their abilities and positive attributes, constructing rationalizations to inflate their own worth and depreciating those who refuse to accept or enhance their self-image. They typically view themselves as intelligent, outgoing, charming, or sophisticated. They have a need to be conspicuous and to evoke affection and attention from others. They often make good first impressions because they are able to express their feelings, may have strong opinions, and have a natural ability to draw attention to themselves. These are proud individuals who carry themselves with dignity, and they may have a good sense of humor.

Given this type of personality, such individuals may have little interest in psychotherapy and may find it difficult to establish a strong therapeutic alliance. Similar individuals would be most comfortable in situations where they feel looked up to and admired, or at least respected. If confrontation is used in therapy, much tact has to be exercised so as not to injure their narcissism more than they can tolerate. On the other hand, the danger also exists that a therapist would be so supportive of the patient's narcissism that he or she gives no negative feedback and does not facilitate growth. Thus, it is important to find ways of helping these individuals accept their fallibilities and work on their problems without feeling unrecognized or humiliated.

Profile 157: Schizoid–Narcissistic–Compulsive

The scores that schizoid–narcissistic–compulsive individuals obtain on the test describe a personality with schizoid, narcissistic, and compulsive elements. Individuals with similar personalities typically have little interest or ability in experiencing the subtle aspects of interpersonal relationships. Because of this, they turn their attention toward matters that do not involve people, like reading or art. Such individuals may be seen as emotionally insensitive to others in a distant and apathetic way. The end result of this particular trait is that the person probably has few friends and little real interpersonal involvement. Additionally, the indications are that these individuals tend to feel that they are a "special" kind of individual. Individuals who obtain similar test scores see themselves as superior to others and tend to exaggerate their abilities and positive attributes, construct rationalizations to inflate their own worth, and depreciate those who refuse to accept or enhance their own self-image. They typically view themselves as intelligent, outgoing, charming, or sophisticated. They have a need to be conspicuous and to evoke affection and attention from others. They often make good first impressions because they are able to express their feelings, may have strong opinions, and have a natural ability to draw attention to themselves. These are proud individuals who carry themselves with dignity, and they may have a good sense of humor. However, these individuals may have trouble if they feel that they are not properly recognized or when they have to accept the opinions of others and compromise.

Given these personality traits, such individuals may have little interest in psychotherapy and would find it difficult to establish a strong therapeutic alliance. Similar individuals would be most comfortable in situations where they felt looked up to and admired, or at least respected. If confrontation is used in therapy, much tact has to be exercised so as not to injure their narcissism more than they can tolerate. On the other hand, the danger also exists that a therapist would be so supportive of the patient's narcissism that he or she gives no negative feedback and does not facilitate growth. Thus, it is important to find ways of helping these individuals accept their fallibilities and work on their problems without feeling unrecognized or humiliated.

Profile 170: Schizoid–Compulsive

The schizoid–compulsive personality profile characterizes individuals who are fairly distant and controlled. Similar individuals have little interest in or ability to experience the subtleties of interpersonal relationships. Because of this, they usually concentrate on matters that do not involve people, such as reading or art. They may be perceived as emotionally insensitive to others or apathetic. As a result, they are likely to have few friends and little real interpersonal involvement.

Additionally, such clients tend to be overly controlled, disciplined, and proper. It is as if the emotions that they feel are so confusing or threatening that they must be hidden. Individuals with similar personality profiles try hard to avoid making mistakes. They are orderly, conscientious, well prepared, and controlled. They try to be efficient, dependable, industrious, and persistent. These individuals usually relate in an overly respectful, ingratiating manner to those in authority. With subordinates, however, they are more likely to be perfectionistic, even disdainful. These individuals often believe in discipline and practice self-restraint. This overcontrol causes them to appear overly formal and proper, and they may be perceived as rigid or indecisive when they have not had a chance to study all possible alternatives. On the positive side, they tend to be well organized and usually do well in situations in which it is important to be accurate and meticulous.

Profile 18A2A: Schizoid–Negativistic–Avoidant

Individuals with elevated scores on the Schizoid, Negativistic, and Avoidant scales typically are resentful and socially detached. This was the most common profile found among schizophrenics in a Veterans Administration hospital (J. J. Jackson et al., 1991). Antoni, Tischer, Levine, Green, and Millon (1985b) found this personality style to represent a subgroup of the clients obtaining the 24/42 MMPI code.

Similar individuals have little interest in experiencing the subtle aspects of interpersonal relationships. They may turn their attention instead to areas that do not require social contact, such as reading or art. At worst, these individuals may be seen as emotionally insensitive, distant, and apathetic. Such individuals probably have few friends and minimal interpersonal involvement.

The MCMI scores also suggest that these individuals generally are unresponsive to stimuli. This may be true regardless of whether the stimulus comes from their own processes or from the outside. Similar individuals are not particularly energetic or enthusiastic, and their thinking is usually vague, unclear, and somewhat impoverished. They typically are not interested in understanding or interpreting past events or in planning for the future. Although they sometimes appear evasive and overly defended, they are more likely to seem apathetic, dull, and uninteresting.

Underlying the detachment from others are conflicts related to feelings of inadequacy and the wish that someone would provide nurturance, shelter, and guidance. These individuals fear, however, that when others get to know them, they will be rejected. At times they may be friendly and cooperative, but they are more typically moody and resentful: Anger and dissatisfaction eventually color most of their relationships.

Given their personality style, establishing a therapeutic alliance will be difficult. The discomfort that they experience in interpersonal relationships will probably make the sessions unenjoyable. In addition, the therapist will need to be sensitive to their feelings of rejection when he or she makes an uncomplimentary interpretation. Finally, their dependency conflict will mean that they are likely to respond resentfully to the therapist's leadership, so that it may be difficult to motivate them to collaborate in their own treatment. The therapist must allow the emotional distance that these clients may need and tolerate their inability to talk about their own life and feelings. If care is taken not to issue directives or advice, the resentments that the clients usually develop when feeling dependent on a relationship may be avoided.

Avoidant Profile Clusters

Profile 2A00: Avoidant

Avoidant individuals are hypersensitive to the possibility of rejection. They assume that people will not value their friendship and fear interpersonal humiliation. Because these "hypersensitive avoidants" (Millon, 1996) feel they have to put their best foot forward and to constantly be on guard, they often are ill at ease in social situations. Even though they often are understanding and compassionate, their perfectionism and anxiety cause them to shy away from social contact and to forfeit the support and acceptance they want from others. As a result, similar individuals tend to be isolated and to function best in situations in which they do not have to interact with many people. Their coping style is characterized by passivity, social withdrawal, a lack of an active interventional approach, and cognitive negativism (Vollrath, Alnaes, & Torgersen, 1994). The use of alcohol and drugs as a coping mechanism also has been reported (Vollrath et al., 1995).

Profile 2A30: Avoidant–Dependent

Individuals with the avoidant–dependent profile, referred to as "phobic avoidants" by Millon (1996), usually do not have any close friends, so they tend to remain detached and isolated. They view themselves as weak, inadequate, unresourceful, and unattractive. Strongly wishing to be liked and accepted by others, they nevertheless have a great fear of rejection. They often are guarded and experience social situations negatively. They seem apprehensive, shy, or nervous in social situations. These clients usually avoid relating to others, which forces them to give up the support and affection that the relationship might have brought. Thus, life is experienced as a conflict between taking a risk and accepting the discomfort of forming a relationship or retreating to the unfulfilling safety of their isolation. Although these individuals usually are sensitive, compassionate, and emotionally responsive, they also are nervous, awkward, mistrustful, and isolated.

This profile has been shown to be common among forensic inpatients (McNiel & Meyer, 1990), patients with an obsessive–compulsive disorder (Joffe, Swinson, & Regan, 1988), and women with a history of sexual abuse (Bryer, Nelson, Miller, & Krol, 1987). Many clients with this personality style have a 28/82 MMPI code type (Antoni et al., 1985a) or a 78/87 MMPI code type (Antoni et al., 1987).

Profile 2A31: Avoidant–Dependent–Schizoid

The avoidant–dependent–schizoid profile characterizes individuals with interpersonal apprehensiveness, feelings of inadequacy, and introversiveness. Individuals with similar scores are preoccupied with being liked and appreciated and consequently constantly anticipate rejection. This creates a bind: By avoiding interactions with others, they feel comfortable and at ease on the one hand and concerned about their lack of social support on the other. Should they actually risk a relationship, the fear of rejection makes them tense, nervous, and uncomfortable and overrides whatever pleasure the relationship brings.

Such individuals tend to devalue themselves and to think that other people are more capable and more worthy. As a result, they are typically cooperative to the point of submissiveness. This dependency fits well with the discomfort in interpersonal relationships because it supports the client's assumption that if others got to know him or her, they would see how worthless the client really was and would lose interest in the friendship.

Individuals obtaining similar profiles often are unaware of their own emotions and tend to remain aloof and detached. They are distantly complacent, appear somewhat apathetic, and do not experience strong emotional ties with others. They are private individuals, often loners, who may have some acquaintances but typically lack intimate friendships.

Bartsch and Hoffman (1985) found this profile to be prominent in their sample of alcoholics. They believed that drinking may serve to alleviate social anxiety, diminish insecurity, and allow these individuals to establish some social contact. Because of their typical avoidance of social relationships, therapy and involvement in Alcoholics Anonymous would be difficult. Bartsch and Hoffman reported MMPI code type 24/78 for this group.

Profile 2A38A: Avoidant–Dependent–Negativistic

Found to be common among women with a history of physical and sexual abuse (Bryer et al., 1987) and alcoholics (Mayer & Scott, 1988), the avoidant–dependent–negativistic profile indicates a fear of rejection, feelings of inadequacy, and a tendency to have mood changes. These individuals want to be liked by others but anticipate that their social approaches likely will be rejected.

Individuals with this personality profile usually underestimate themselves: They feel less capable, less attractive, or worth less as human beings than others. They tend to be unassertive and seldom make demands on others, although they can be controlling in a dependent and submissive manner. They are more comfortable when they can rely on others to make the important decisions in their lives. These individuals assume that people will eventually develop uncomplimentary opinions about them and will reject them.

As a result of this basic personality structure, such individuals tend to be apprehensive, shy, and nervous in social situations. They are likely to feel caught in a bind: On one hand, they would like to interact with others and to be liked and appreciated. On the other hand, they feel compelled to avoid social situations to avoid the anxiety that the situations evoke.

The psychic conflict manifests itself behaviorally in vacillation and ambivalence. At times open and friendly, they also may be aloof, distant, abrasive, moody, and disinterested in others. Occasionally, similar individuals project the feelings created by this basic conflict, becoming even more distrusting, hostile, and prone to blame others for their failures. This pattern will be short-lived, and these individuals eventually come back to feeling inadequate and blaming themselves for everything that happens to them.

In the light of this personality style, these individuals can be expected to have difficulty establishing a therapeutic alliance. They must overcome discomfort in the relationship and mistrustfulness that mitigates against confiding in the therapist. Even after the relationship has been established, the therapist will need to be careful not to offer interpretations that can be experienced as rejections. The therapist also will need to be able to tolerate moodiness and overt or covert expressions of resentment. These clients may derive much benefit from experiencing the closeness of the therapeutic relationship, once established, because they may not have many other opportunities for emotional closeness.

Profile 2A5O: Avoidant–Narcissistic

Individuals obtaining elevated scores on the Avoidant and Narcissistic scales are hypersensitive to the possibility of rejection. They typically assume that people will not value their friendship and often are concerned with the risk of humiliation. This fear causes them to feel ill at ease in social situations. They constantly are on guard, preoccupied with putting their best foot forward. Even though they often are sensitive individuals who can show understanding and compassion for others, they also tend to be nervous about and uncomfortable with interpersonal contact and will shy away from social situations. They probably would like to have friends and to be well accepted, but their discomfort leads them to forfeit the support that they could have derived from others rather than risk mistreatment. As a result, they tend to be isolated and may function best in situations in which they do not have to interact with many other people.

The fear of rejection has roots in the tendency to overestimate their own value. Individuals obtaining this personality profile typically feel that they are special and superior to others in some way. Such individuals may tend to exaggerate their abilities and positive attributes and to construct rationalizations to inflate their own worth. Such individuals are likely to view themselves as intelligent, outgoing, charming, or sophisticated. They have a need to evoke affection and attention from others. Whenever they feel slighted, rejected, or mistreated by others, they tend to use projection as a defense and depreciate those who refuse to accept or enhance their self-image. Thus, these individuals may be a bit grandiose, ego centered, and unappreciative of others.

In the light of this personality style, these individuals can be expected to have difficulty establishing a therapeutic alliance. They must overcome a certain amount of discomfort in the relationship and an inability to develop enough trust to truly confide in a therapist. Even after an alliance has been established, the therapist must be careful not to offer interpretations that can be experienced as rejections and must be able to tolerate expressions of resentment. These clients will feel most enhanced when a therapist treats them with admiration and respect and allows them to be as much in control as possible during the therapy session. Clients will experience a relationship in which they treat the therapist more like a colleague than a superior as egosyntonic and supportive. To the extent that treatment involves giving negative feedback or confronting objectionable behavior or aspects of the personality, such clients will experience the therapeutic context as threatening or stressful. To maintain the therapeutic alliance but contribute to a client's growth, the therapist must achieve a careful balance between uncritical support and threatening therapeutic work.

Profile 2A6A0: Avoidant–Antisocial

According to the MCMI, avoidant–antisocial individuals are hypersensitive to the possibility of rejection and look at the environment as a competitive place. Similar individuals feel that to function in this world, they have to fend for themselves. Somewhat distrusting and suspicious, they also see themselves as assertive, energetic, self-reliant, strong, and realistic. They imagine that they have to be tough to make it in the rat race. Justifying their assertiveness by pointing to others' hostile and exploitative behaviors, they may be contemptuous of the weak and may not care whether they are liked, claiming that "good guys come in last."

Individuals with this type of personality are concerned that others will take advantage of their friendship if they are not careful. This fear causes them to be uncomfortable in social situations because they feel that they constantly have to be on guard. As a result, they tend to be nervous and uncomfortable.

To avoid the discomfort that is commonly attached to interpersonal contact, they shy away from social situations. These individuals typically like to have friends, but the discomfort associated with the social risk often leads them to forfeit the support that could have been derived from others rather than to take the chance of being mistreated. Such individuals typically are isolated and may function best in situations in which they do not have to interact with many other people.

Individuals obtaining similar MCMI scores usually are impulsive. They typically are perceived as being somewhat aggressive and intimidating and perhaps as cold, callous, or insensitive to the feelings of others. They may be argumentative and contentious, even abusive, cruel, or malicious. When matters go their way, they may act in a gracious, cheerful, and friendly manner. More characteristically, however, their behavior is guarded, reserved, and resentful. Greenblatt and Davis (1992) found this avoidant–antisocial personality to be prevalent among angry Black men in their psychiatric sample.

In the light of this personality style, such clients can be expected to have some difficulties in establishing a therapeutic alliance. They must overcome a certain amount of discomfort in the relationship and an inability to develop enough trust to truly confide in the therapist. Even after the relationship has been established, the therapist will need to be careful not to offer interpretations that can be experienced as a rejection. To the extent that treatment involves giving negative feedback or confronting objectionable aspects of their personalities or behaviors, these clients will experience the therapeutic context as threatening or conflictual. To maintain the therapeutic alliance while contributing to the client's growth, the therapist must strike a balance between uncritical support and threatening therapeutic work.

Profile 2A6A7: Avoidant–Antisocial–Compulsive

According to the scores that avoidant–antisocial–compulsive individuals obtain on the MCMI, they have a personality style characterized by avoidant, antisocial, and compulsive traits. Typically, similar individuals are hypersensitive to the possibility of rejection. They look at their environment as a competitive situation and feel that to function in it, they have to fend for themselves. Most individuals with this view are, as a result, somewhat distrusting and suspicious. They see themselves as assertive, energetic, self-reliant, strong, and realistic. They imagine that they have to be tough in order to make it in the rat race. Justifying their assertiveness by pointing to the hostile and exploiting behaviors of others, they may be contemptuous of the weak and may not care if they are disliked, claiming that "good guys come in last."

Individuals with this type of personality are concerned that people will take advantage of their friendship if they are not careful. This fear has the effect of making them ill at ease in social situations, because they feel that they have to be constantly on guard. As a result, they tend to be nervous and uncomfortable. To avoid the discomfort that is commonly attached to interpersonal contact, similar individuals shy away from social situations. These persons probably would like to have friends, but the discomfort associated with the social risk often makes it easier to forfeit the support that could have been derived from others rather than take the risk of being mistreated. Similar individuals are typically isolated and may function best in situations where they do not have to interact with many other people.

Individuals obtaining similar scores hold the assumption that people should work hard to avoid making a mistake. Such individuals are usually orderly and plan for the future. They are conscientious; they typically prepare well and do their work on schedule. They tend to be efficient, dependable, industrious, and persistent. To those in authority, these individuals relate in an overly respectful and ingratiating manner. This style of relating often changes when the relationship is with a subordinate. In that case such individuals may become somewhat perfectionistic and demanding. Often similar individuals believe in discipline and practice self-restraint, especially concerning their own emotions, which they usually keep under control. The overcontrol of emotions tends to give this type of individual a characteristic flavor: They are formal and proper and unlikely to open up and act spontaneously in front of others. They are sometimes seen as perfectionistic, distant, occasionally inflexible, and perhaps indecisive before they have a chance to study all possible alternatives. However, they are often careful, deliberate, righteous, honest, dependable, and hardworking individuals.

This type of personality style may make it hard for this individual to work with some aspects of the environment. For instance, situations that can change abruptly from one moment to the next in an unpredictable manner, or situations in which following the rules does not lead to the desired outcome, can be expected to be particularly stressful. However, disciplined individuals are well suited for situations in which it is important to be accurate and meticulous.

In the light of this personality style, these individuals can be expected to have some difficulties in establishing a therapeutic alliance. They will have to overcome a certain amount of discomfort in the relationship and an inability to develop enough trust to truly confide in the therapist. Even after the relationship has been established, the therapist will need to be careful not to offer interpretations that can be experienced as rejections. Inasmuch as the treatment plan involves giving such clients negative feedback or guiding them to confront objectionable aspects of their personality or behavior, they will experience the therapeutic context as threatening or conflictual. To maintain the therapeutic alliance while contributing to the patient's growth, the therapist must strike a very careful balance between uncritical support and threatening therapeutic work. Such individuals may find it easier to establish a therapeutic alliance with a professional who is formal, proper, punctual, and predictable. Explanations of the diagnosis, the nature of the "illness," the expected course of treatment, and the like hold a very special appeal for similar persons.

Profile 2A70: Avoidant–Compulsive

Judging from their MCMI scores, avoidant–compulsive individuals have an avoidant personality with compulsive traits. Individuals with this type of personality are concerned that people will humiliate them if they are not careful. This fear has the effect of making them ill at ease in social situations, because they feel that they have to be constantly on guard. As a result, they tend to be nervous and uncomfortable. To avoid the discomfort that is commonly attached to interpersonal contact, similar individuals shy away from social situations. Such persons probably would like to have friends, but the discomfort associated with the social risk often makes it easier to forfeit the support that could have been derived from others rather than take the risk of being mistreated. Similar individuals are typically isolated and may function best in situations where they do not have to interact with many other people.

Individuals obtaining similar scores hold the assumption that people should work hard to avoid making a mistake. Such individuals are usually orderly and plan for the future. They are conscientious; they typically prepare well and do their work on schedule. They tend to be efficient, dependable, industrious, and persistent. To those in authority, these individuals relate in an overly respectful and ingratiating manner. This style of relating often changes when the relationship is with a subordinate. In that case these individuals may become somewhat perfectionistic and demanding. Often, similar individuals believe in discipline and practice self-restraint, especially concerning their own emotions, which they usually keep under control. The overcontrol of the emotions tends to give this type of individual a characteristic flavor: They are formal and proper and unlikely to open up and act spontaneously in front of others. They are sometimes seen as perfectionistic, distant, occasionally inflexible, and perhaps indecisive before they have a chance to study all possible alternatives. However, they are often careful, deliberate, righteous, honest, dependable, and hardworking individuals.

This type of personality style may make it hard for such individuals to work with some aspects of the environment. For instance, situations that can change abruptly from one moment to the next in an unpredictable manner, or situations in which following the rules does not lead to the desired outcome, can be expected to be particularly stressful. However, disciplined individuals are well suited for situations in which it is important to be accurate and meticulous.

In the light of this personality style, these individuals can be expected to have some difficulties in establishing a therapeutic alliance. They must overcome a certain amount of discomfort in the relationship and an inability to develop enough trust to truly confide in the therapist. Even after the relationship has been established, the therapist will need to be careful not to offer interpretations that can be experienced as rejections. Inasmuch as the treatment plan involves giving such clients negative feedback or guiding them to confront objectionable aspects of their personality or behavior, they will experience the therapeutic context as threatening or conflictual. To maintain the therapeutic alliance while contributing to growth on the part of the patient, the therapist must strike a very careful balance between uncritical support and threatening therapeutic work. These individuals may find it easier to establish a therapeutic alliance with a professional who is formal, proper, punctual, and predictable. Explanations of the diagnosis, the nature of the "illness," the expected course of treatment, and the like hold a very special appeal for similar persons.

Profile 2A8A0: Avoidant–Negativistic

Elevated scores on the Avoidant and Negativistic MCMI scales indicate a fear of rejection and a tendency to be resentful. Millon (1996) labeled this cluster the "conflicted–avoidant" cluster. Individuals with this personality profile perceive interpersonal situations as risky and likely to lead to humiliation or rejection. Similar individuals would like to be appreciated, but their fear of rejection makes them apprehensive; they would like to meet people and establish strong emotional ties, but they are so uncomfortable in social situations that they tend to avoid interpersonal contacts altogether. These individuals typically are loners to some degree. They retreat into their own worlds and are interpersonally nervous and uncomfortable. They tend to be sensitive, however, to their own feelings and the emotional reactions that they evoke in others.

Individuals with similar MCMI profiles tend to question their own abilities and to see themselves as not being interesting or worthwhile. However, they do not see others as being much better and, in fact, tend to perceive humanity as cold and rejecting. So, in spite of their poor self-image, they do not look up to others and generally are aware of the limitations that other individuals may have.

When these clients are able to establish significant relationships, the interactions tend to be conflictual. They tend to be moody and resentful. They may be friendly and cooperative at times, but they may become negativistic or hostile, only to feel guilty later and behave contritely. In some cases, these mood fluctuations are less noticeable, with the clients handling the conflict through a more stable form of covert obstructionism.

This profile represents the modal personality makeup for alcoholics (Donat, 1988; Donat, Walters, & Hume, 1991), psychotic Black men in a psychiatric sample (Greenblatt & Davis, 1992), psychiatric patients with mixed diagnoses (T. J. Murphy et al., 1990), psychiatric inpatients who attempted suicide (McCann & Gergelis, 1990), and patients with a dissociative identity personality disorder (Ellason, Ross, & Fuchs, 1995; Fink & Golinkoff, 1990).

In the light of this personality style, these individuals can be expected to have some difficulties in establishing a therapeutic alliance. They must overcome a certain amount of discomfort in the relationship and an inability to develop enough trust to truly confide in the therapist. Even after the relationship has been established, the therapist will need to be careful not to offer interpretations that can be experienced as rejection. A tolerance for moodiness and overt or covert expressions of resentment also will be needed. Therapists can minimize projected hostility by trying not to give advice to such clients and allowing them to control any aspect of the therapy sessions that the therapist does not need to control. Interpretations dealing with both the fear of rejection and the tendency to blame others also can be helpful. If successful, the clients may derive much benefit from experiencing the closeness of the therapeutic relationship because they may not have many other opportunities for emotional closeness.

Dependent Profile Clusters

Profile 300: Dependent

Individuals obtaining elevations on the Dependent scale have a cooperative personality style. These "immature dependent" (Millon, 1996) individuals feel that they are not very able to take care of themselves and must find someone dependable who will protect them and support them, at least emotionally. They tend to feel inadequate or insecure and to see themselves as being less effective or capable than everyone else. They also tend to form strong attachments to people who will be the decision makers. They are followers rather than leaders and are often submissive in social interactions, shying away from competitive situations.

Concerned with the possibility of losing friends, similar individuals may cover up their true emotions when they are aggressive or otherwise objectionable. These are humble individuals who try to be as congenial as possible to those around them. They probably are well liked but occasionally may be considered wishy-washy because they never take a strong position on controversial issues. They also may be criticized for their submissive dependency, their lack of self-esteem, and their tendency to always look outside of themselves for help. They show a lack of active intervention as their coping style when under stress (Vollrath et al., 1994), as well as a tendency to turn to religion (Vollrath et al., 1995). Similar individuals characterize their family of origin as noncohesive social systems that were controlling, allowed little independence and expressiveness, and were not intellectually or culturally oriented (Baker, Capron, & Azorlosa, 1996; Head, Baker, & Williamson, 1991).

This MCMI profile was found to be the most prevalent profile among psychiatric patients (Donat, Geczy, Helmrich, & LeMay, 1992). Additionally, the profile was commonly found in a group of individuals with head injuries being evaluated for workers' compensation claims (Snibbe, Peterson, & Sosner, 1980), among women who elected mastectomy as opposed to another treatment approach for breast cancer (Wolberg, Tanner, Romsaas, Trump, & Malec, 1987), and among people with bulimia (Tisdale, Pendleton, & Marler, 1990).

In the light of this personality style, such individuals can be expected to form a quick alliance with any therapist willing to play a benevolent parental role. Such clients will experience as supportive an approach in which they are given guidance in an affectionate and understanding manner. It may be difficult if part of the treatment plan is to move clients toward more independence or increase their ability to compete assertively or effectively. If that is the case, these clients may feel vulnerable and threatened and may respond with maladaptive behaviors.

Profile 32A0: Dependent–Avoidant

Dependent–avoidant, or "disquieted dependent," individuals (Millon, 1996) tend to have low self-esteem and to see others as being more capable or worthwhile. They likely are followers rather than leaders, often taking passive roles. They would like to seek emotional support and the protection of others, but together with these wishes they experience discomfort.

The discomfort comes from the assumption that if others got to know the clients, they would develop the same uncomplimentary views that these clients have of themselves. As a result, these individuals tend to be guarded and apprehensive when relating to others. Similar individuals try to put their best foot forward and hide their true feelings, especially when the feelings are aggressive or otherwise objectionable. They may seem tense, nervous, and distant. Because they feel ill at ease in social situations, they often avoid them, which results in loneliness and isolation.

Research indicates that this personality style prevails among women with eating disorders (Kennedy, McVey, & Katz, 1990; Pendleton, Tisdale, & Marler, 1991) and among nonangry psychotic White men in a psychiatric sample (Greenblatt & Davis, 1992). Similar individuals characterize their family of origin as noncohesive social systems that were controlling, allowed little independence and expressiveness, and were not intellectually or culturally oriented (Baker et al., 1996; Head et al., 1991).

On the positive side, dependent–avoidant individuals try to be cooperative and conciliatory. They can be sensitive and unassuming and can maintain any relationship they have been able to establish.

Given the personality style just described, these clients will experience as supportive a relationship in which the therapist has a benevolent and protective attitude toward them.

These clients will be reassured by the feeling that the therapist is a powerful expert and will give good advice and guidance. Because of their fear of rejection, they may require frequent reaffirmation and the promise of support.

Profile 32A1: Dependent–Avoidant–Schizoid

Common among psychiatric inpatients (Donat, Geczy, et al., 1992) and among individuals in marital therapy (Craig & Olson, 1995), the dependent–avoidant–schizoid personality profile characterizes socially detached individuals with low self-esteem, who tend to perceive others as being more capable and worthy. Similar individuals characterize their family of origin as noncohesive social systems that were controlling, allowed little independence and expressiveness, and were not intellectually or culturally oriented (Baker et al., 1996; Head et al., 1991). This profile has been found to be the modal profile among unipolar depressed clients (Wetzler, Khadivi, & Oppenheim, 1995). Levine, Tischer, Antoni, Green, and Millon (1985) found this personality style to represent a subgroup of clients with the 27/72 MMPI code.

Similar individuals are likely to be followers rather than leaders, often taking a passive role in social affairs. Although they would like to seek the emotional support and protection of others, they are uncomfortable in social relationships. They also often have trouble understanding the feelings and motivations of others and appear somewhat bland and apathetic.

They tend to assume that if others got to know the clients, they would develop the same uncomplimentary views that these clients have of themselves. As a result, they are guarded and apprehensive when relating to others. They try to put their best foot forward and to hide their true feelings, especially when the feelings are aggressive or otherwise objectionable. They may seem tense, nervous, and distant. Because they feel ill at ease in social situations and lack interest and understanding in the interpersonal area, they often do not have any strong relationships. Thus, they frequently are lonely and isolated from others. However, these clients may be fairly cooperative and gentle, seldom experiencing intense feelings and feeling fairly pleasant and controlled.

Given the personality style just described, these clients will experience a therapeutic relationship as supportive if the therapist has a benevolent and protective attitude toward them. These clients will be reassured by the feeling that the therapist is a powerful expert who will offer helpful advice and guidance. Because of their fear of rejection, they may require frequent reaffirmation and the promise of support; the therapist must tolerate clients' discomfort during the sessions.

Profile 32A7: Dependent–Avoidant–Compulsive

The dependent–avoidant–compulsive profile characterizes individuals with a cooperative, avoidant, and disciplined nature. Similar individuals characterize their family of origin as noncohesive social systems that were controlling, allowed little independence and expressiveness, and were not intellectually or culturally oriented (Baker et al., 1996; Head et al., 1991).

Individuals with similar scores tend to have low self-esteem and to see others as being more capable and worthy. They are followers rather than leaders, often assuming passive roles. They would like to seek the emotional support and protection of others, but together with these wishes they experience a certain amount of discomfort.

The discomfort comes from the assumption that if others got to know the clients, they would develop the same uncomplimentary views that these clients have of themselves. As a result, such individuals typically are guarded and apprehensive when relating to others. They try to put their best foot forward and have a tendency to hide their true feelings, especially when the feelings are aggressive or otherwise objectionable. They may seem tense, nervous, and distant. Because they feel uncomfortable in social situations, they often avoid them and are frequently lonely and isolated.

Thus, one way in which these individuals defend against the insecurity engendered by their low self-esteem is by counting on the guidance and protection of others. Another defense mechanism that they use is thinking that if they manage to avoid making mistakes, the outcome always will be positive. Individuals with a similar perfectionistic bent are orderly and plan for the future. They are conscientious and do their work on schedule. Other characteristics of these individuals include efficiency, dependability, industriousness, persistence, extreme respectfulness and ingratiating behavior, perfectionism, and self-discipline. They tend to be indecisive and have significant problems making decisions by themselves. Their perfectionism also may magnify the underlying feelings of inadequacy in that, whenever bad things happen, they will be inclined to look for what mistakes they made that might have led to the undesirable outcome.

In the light of this personality style, these clients will experience as supportive a therapeutic relationship in which the therapist has a benevolent and protective attitude. They will be reassured by the feeling that the therapist is a powerful expert who will advise and guide them. Their fear of rejection may require frequent reaffirmation and the promise of support.

Profile 32A8A: Dependent–Avoidant–Negativistic

High scores on the Dependent, Avoidant, and Negativistic scales characterize individuals who have cooperative, avoidant, and negativistic personality traits. Individuals with similar scores tend to have low self-esteem. Furthermore, they are likely to assume that if others got to know these clients, they would develop the same uncomplimentary views that these clients have of themselves. They would like to seek the emotional support and protection of others, but at the same time they fear rejection. As a result, they may experience much interpersonal discomfort and tend to be guarded and apprehensive. They may seem tense, nervous, and distant when they are with others. Because they feel ill at ease in social situations, they often avoid them and become loners.

Such individuals are somewhat resentful of others and are inclined to blame negative events on external factors. The anger may be expressed overtly or covertly. In either case, they occasionally may become uncooperative and hard to handle. The projective defense mechanism fits well with the social avoidance because the hostility tends to alienate others. Projections also give them a rationale for rejecting others before they have a chance to be rejected. At the same time that they resent the control of others, however, they are probably uncomfortable in competitive situations in which they have to act independently and make their own decisions. This discomfort creates a vicious cycle of needing to depend on others but feeling resentful of that need.

Research shows that this personality style prevails among depressed individuals (Piersma, 1986c), especially those with no family history of depression (Joffe & Regan, 1991), and among alcoholics (Craig, Verinis, & Wexler, 1985).

Clients with this dependent, avoidant, and resentful personality style will have difficulty establishing a therapeutic alliance. They may be most at ease in situations in which they feel protected, supported, and safe (i.e., not likely to be rejected or humiliated). This same relationship, however, also is likely to precipitate conflict over dependency, heighten their fear of rejection, and activate their discomfort with intimacy. These clients then may become critical of the therapist, and it may be even more difficult to keep them in treatment.

Appropriate interpretations that help them understand how the defensive resentment is generated may increase the clients' understanding, and they may be able to become less dependent, defensive, and conflicted.

Profile 340: Dependent–Histrionic

Elevated scores on the Dependent and Histrionic scales describe an "accommodating dependent" or "appeasing histrionic" individual (Millon, 1996) with a cooperative personality style and dramatic overtones. The most prominent trait these individuals display is low self-esteem. They think of themselves as being less gifted and worthy than others. Their poor self-image usually leads to feelings of insecurity and anxiety, especially when they are in competitive situations.

Such individuals need a lot of attention from others and actively seek affirmation, approval, and affection. They often develop a sensitivity to the moods of others and use this knowledge to evoke the reactions that they desire. They can be charming and outgoing, dramatic, or seductive, usually with the result of having their need for approval met.

These individuals usually are cooperative and congenial, colorful, and in touch with their emotions. However, they may have a difficult time in situations in which they feel alone or have to depend on themselves. The loss of meaningful others often is strongly felt.

With regard to psychotherapy, clients with a dependent–histrionic personality style feel the most comfortable when the therapist recreates a parental role and offers a good deal of attention, support, nurturance, and protection. In spite of the dependency, similar clients tend to be occasionally contrary and conflictual in the therapeutic relationship as a result of the histrionic overtones. The therapist should be tolerant on these occasions. Therapeutic change may come from processing the perceived lack of support, from encouraging clients to be more independent, and from helping them understand the source of low self-esteem and its relationship to their strong need for attention and support.

Profile 348A: Dependent–Histrionic–Negativistic

Individuals with the dependent–histrionic–negativistic profile have a combination of cooperative, dramatic, and negativistic elements in their personality. Their MCMI scores suggest that they are caught in the bind of having low self-esteem but feeling that they mask it with a confident and self-assured presentation.

Similar individuals think they are less gifted or valuable than others. Their poor self-image leads to feelings of insecurity and results in anxiety when they are in competitive situations. They are followers rather than leaders, usually trying to be cooperative and to get along well with others. They are "people who need people": They tend to relate to others in an easy and meaningful manner but often depend on those relationships to function. Because they trust others to protect and guide them, these individuals may not be well prepared to take independent responsibility for attaining goals or life accomplishments.

An elevated Histrionic scale score indicates the need for attention from others. Similar individuals often are conspicuous in their seeking of frequent reaffirmations of approval and affection. Their ability to appreciate the feelings of others may be used to evoke the reactions they desire. They can be charming and outgoing, colorful, dramatic, or seductive. Depending on how functional they are, they may use these traits to cope effectively with the environment or to manipulate or exploit others.

When such individuals feel inadequate, they are friendly and cooperative. However, they may shift rapidly to a more arrogant and demanding posture to project an image of greater adequacy. They may become bored with stable relationships and displace some of their inner conflicts into interpersonal resentments. Thus, they may seem moody and easily irritated, unpredictable, or negativistic.

Given their personality style, these individuals will benefit from a therapeutic relationship in which the therapist takes a parental role and offers guidance and protection. An emphasis on formalities such as being on time for the session or keeping an interpersonal distance during the session is likely to be perceived as unfriendly and dissatisfying. More egosyntonic to the clients would be a relationship in which they are the center of attention, with demonstrations of affection and support flowing readily from the therapist. The limits to the support that the therapist can offer, however, eventually may become an issue if clients become clingy, demanding, and dissatisfied. Such developments may threaten the therapeutic alliance, but the therapist can manage this by making clients aware of inappropriate expectations and helping them work through the dependency conflict.

Profile 354: Dependent–Narcissistic–Histrionic

Elevated scores on the Dependent, Narcissistic, and Histrionic scales characterize individuals who appear to be cooperative, confident, and dramatic but for whom the most prominent personality trait is low self-esteem. Individuals with similar scores tend to feel less gifted or worthy than others. This poor self-image usually leads to insecurity and anxiety in competitive situations.

Such individuals also tend to publicly overrate their own self-worth. This inclination may come from disparate assumptions that they hold about themselves, so that even though they do not value themselves in some areas, they seem to be highly confident in others. Often, however, this ego inflation is a defensive reaction to the low self-esteem. In either case, there is an obvious conflict between the two images that they try to project. This conflict may play out in vacillations between congeniality and obstructionistic arrogance.

These individuals also need a lot of attention, approval, and affection. Individuals with similar profiles actively pursue the attention they need. They often become sensitive to other people's moods and use this knowledge to evoke the reactions they want. They may seem charming and outgoing, dramatic, or seductive in their relationships with others.

On the positive side, these individuals usually are cooperative and congenial, colorful, and in touch with their emotions, qualities that provide a good foundation for developing effective coping strategies (Leaf, Alington, Ellis, DiGiuseppe, & Mass, 1992; Leaf, Alington, Mass, DiGiuseppe, & Ellis, 1991; Leaf, DiGiuseppe, et al., 1990; Leaf, Ellis, DiGiuseppe, Mass, & Alington, 1991; Nakao et al., 1992; Retzlaff & Deatherage, 1993; Strack et al., 1989). Tango and Dziuban (1984) correlated this profile with the Strong–Campbell Interest Inventory's interests in adventure, music, writing, religion, public speaking, and office management and with somewhat exhibitionistic roles (e.g., writer, orator, executive, merchant, adventurer, musician). However, these individuals may have a difficult time in situations in which they feel alone or have to depend on themselves. The loss of meaningful others often is strongly felt.

Profile 356A: Dependent–Narcissistic–Antisocial

Individuals with the dependent–narcissistic–antisocial profile have a personality that is driven partly by a sense of personal inadequacy. Similar individuals often are cooperative and ingratiating. They want to be liked by others and often try to be generous and congenial. In spite of viewing themselves as being less capable than others, however, they feel that they have some quality or innate worth that makes them special and superior to others.

Such individuals adapt to these conflictual self-assumptions by developing a posture that allows both of the assumptions to remain in place. Individuals obtaining similar scores emphasize the competitive aspects of the world and see themselves as needing to be tough to come out ahead. They experience the world as a place where everyone is in competition for the same limited assets, and they focus on the advantages of having personal strength. They often try to hide their own inadequacies because they assume that if others learn about them, the knowledge will become a liability that will work against them. Although they do feel emotionally dependent on others, they try to appear as if they do not need other people and can make it on their own. They try to control others and may be somewhat mistrusting. When confronted by people who question their control, they may have an abrasive or hostile reaction that represents their attempt to bolster their own self-confidence.

On the positive side, this MCMI profile characterizes proud individuals who portray themselves in a positive light, tend to behave in a congenial and cooperative manner, and may be resourceful in meeting their own emotional needs. These qualities can provide a basis for effective coping strategies (Leaf et al., 1992; Leaf, Alington, et al., 1991; Leaf, DiGiuseppe, et al., 1990; Leaf, Ellis, et al., 1991; Nakao et al., 1992; Retzlaff & Deatherage, 1993).

Profile 357: Dependent–Narcissistic–Compulsive

The dependent–narcissistic–compulsive profile characterizes individuals who are cooperative, confident, and disciplined but whose most prominent personality trait is low self-esteem. Individuals with similar scores tend to feel less gifted or worthy than others. Their poor self-image usually leads to feelings of insecurity and anxiety when they are in competitive situations. They try to be cooperative and feel most comfortable when they are under the guidance and protection of a powerful mentor.

Even though they do not value themselves in some areas, they seem to be highly confident in others and sometimes may publicly overrate their self-worth. This ego inflation—their propensity to rationalize away their failures and paint themselves in a good light—may be seen as a defensive reaction to the low self-esteem, a way of quieting their insecurities and comforting themselves.

Such individuals also may use compulsive ways of enhancing their self-image. Similar individuals likely are proper and respectful in their relationships with others and adopt a somewhat perfectionistic and moralistic outlook. They usually are hardworking individuals who see the world in terms of right and wrong (black and white) and who may be somewhat meticulous and picayunish. This proper and disciplined facade frequently is used to emphasize their intrinsic value and to combat the fear that they may not be worthwhile. On the positive side, both the narcissistic and the compulsive elements have been shown to contain effective coping strategies (Leaf et al., 1992; Leaf, Alington, et al., 1991; Leaf, DiGiuseppe, et al., 1990; Leaf, Ellis, et al., 1991; Nakao et al., 1992; Retzlaff & Deatherage, 1993; Strack et al., 1989).

Profile 36A0: Dependent–Antisocial

The dependent–antisocial profile defines a cooperative personality style with competitive overtones. The life assumption of individuals with this profile is that they are not capable of taking care of themselves and must find someone dependable who will support and protect them. They tend to feel inadequate or insecure and see themselves as being less effective or able than everyone else. They tend to form strong attachments to people who will be the decision makers and take responsibility for their welfare. Concerned with the possibility of losing friends, they may hide their true emotions when the feelings are aggressive or objectionable. These are humble, congenial individuals.

Such individuals perceive the environment as a competitive place. As a result, they are somewhat mistrustful and suspicious of others. Typically, their behavior is guarded and reserved, but they hope that with the help of the people they have risked depending on, they can be strong, realistic, and determined in the rat race of life. Although they do not feel tough or secure by themselves, they look to others to provide protection from a cruel and insensitive world in which people are interested only in personal gain.

In the light of the personality style just described, such clients are likely to be guarded and distant at first, but they nonetheless will be able to form an alliance with any therapist willing to play a benevolent parental role. If guidance is given in an affectionate and understanding manner, the client will experience it as supportive. If part of the treatment plan is to move clients toward more independence or increase their ability to compete in an effective or aggressive manner, clients may feel vulnerable and threatened and may respond with maladaptive behaviors.

Profile 370: Dependent–Compulsive

Dependent–compulsive individuals tend to have low self-esteem and an orderly and disciplined nature. Similar individuals believe that other people are more capable, interesting, or valuable than they are. They are humble and personable and often are capable of forming strong interpersonal relationships. They aim to be as congenial as possible to obtain the support they need. As a result, they tend to be fairly submissive, or at least compliant. They shy away from competitive situations in which they feel unsupported and vulnerable. When they feel protected, however, they tend to be at ease and conflict free.

Thus, one way in which these individuals defend against their insecurity is by counting on the guidance and protection of others. They also are likely to retreat to a perfectionistic defense that is organized around avoiding mistakes to ensure positive outcomes. Toward that end, they are compulsive and orderly. They prepare in a conscientious manner and complete work on schedule. They try to be efficient, dependable, industrious, and persistent. These individuals relate in an overly respectful and ingratiating manner, and they can be somewhat demanding. In their quest for perfection, they may be indecisive and have significant problems making decisions by themselves. The compulsive tendency also may serve to strengthen the feelings of inadequacy that are beneath it in that whenever bad events happen, they blame themselves for the outcome.

This personality profile has been found to be prominent among people seeking marital therapy (Craig & Olson, 1995), perhaps because it also is common among men with a history of domestic violence (Hamberger & Hastings, 1986). The profile also is common among individuals suffering from chronic headaches (Jay, Grove, & Grove, 1987) and among clients with affective disorders in remission who have no family history of depression (Joffe & Regan, 1991). The profile also is prevalent among psychiatric inpatients (Donat, Geczy, et al., 1992) and alcoholics (Mayer & Scott, 1988). Such individuals characterize their family of origin as noncohesive social systems that were controlling, allowed little independence and expressiveness, and were not intellectually or culturally oriented (Baker et al., 1996; Head et al., 1991). They are likely to have a 27/72 MMPI profile (Levine et al., 1985).

Clients with this personality style will benefit from a therapeutic relationship in which the therapist has a benevolent and protective attitude. These clients will feel reassured by the feeling that the therapist is a powerful expert who will give appropriate advice and guidance. Such clients can be expected to establish a strong therapeutic alliance without much difficulty and to find such a relationship helpful.

Profile 38A0: Dependent–Negativistic

Individuals with the dependent–negativistic personality profile tend to feel insecure, to have low self-esteem, and to feel uncomfortable in competitive situations. Many individuals with low self-esteem look to others for protection and support. However, individuals with this profile seem to have a conflict in this area. Although they are unsure of their own abilities and need to depend on others, they also tend not to trust others to be reliable or dependable. They resent being in the vulnerable position of needing others and lack confidence that their needs will be met.

Some individuals faced with this conflict externalize it by appearing to be cooperative and compliant but actually resist the leader in some way. Others tend to vacillate between friendly cooperation and resentful distrust, only to feel guilty and contrite and begin the cycle again.

Research has shown this style to be common among alcoholics (Retzlaff & Bromley, 1991), drug abusers (Stark & Campbell, 1988), and spouse-abusing men (Hamberger & Hastings, 1986). Clients with this personality profile commonly obtain the MMPI profile codes of 89/98 (Antoni, Levine, Tischer, Green, & Millon, 1986), 27/72 (Levine et al., 1985), or 24/42 (Antoni et al., 1985b).

These clients may need a therapeutic relationship in which the therapist assumes the dominant role and offers parental guidance and protection. The limits to the support that the therapist can offer, however, eventually may become an issue, at which time the clients can become clingy, demanding, and dissatisfied. If not handled properly, such developments may threaten the therapeutic alliance. One way to handle such issues is to make clients aware of their inappropriate expectations and help them work through the dependency conflict.

Profile 38A2A: Dependent–Negativistic–Avoidant

Individuals with the dependent–negativistic–avoidant profile tend to feel that they are not capable or gifted and that if they are left to their own devices, they would not be able to make ends meet. They would like to have someone else take care of them and provide for their needs, but they tend to be distrustful and resent the abilities of others, a fact that eliminates the option of becoming dependent on some benefactor.

These individuals tend to be moody and to experience sudden, seemingly inexplicable mood shifts. At times they may be friendly and engaging, but they typically have periods when they are angry and resentful. Later yet, they may feel guilty and behave contritely. The cycle is completed when they again become friendly and cooperative. In other words, they defend against their insecurities by projecting blame, sometimes onto themselves and sometimes onto others. A variation of the same basic personality makeup involves the use of a negativistic defense; these individuals may try to control resentment through obstructionistic maneuvers that allow the venting of anger in covert ways without blatantly jeopardizing the dependent relationship.

Most individuals with similar MCMI scale scores have considerable feelings of insecurity. They tend to perceive others as being more gifted, more capable, and more worthy. In addition, they fear that others may recognize their lack of value and reject them; they also tend to be nervous and uncomfortable in social situations because they fear that other people do not really like them and that they are imposing. They avoid some of the discomfort by avoiding social relationships altogether. As a result, similar individuals tend to isolate themselves and may establish fairly distant relationships with people they experience as untrustworthy and judgmental.

On the positive side, individuals with this personality style are sensitive individuals who would like to be appreciated by others and to be able to relate better than they do. They feel conflicted, however, over wanting to depend on others but believing that if they trust others, they will be hurt in the end.

This personality profile was found to be common among depressed clients (Wetzler et al., 1989) and appears to be associated with a poor response to tricyclic antidepressants (Joffe & Regan, 1989a). Similarly, this profile is common among alcoholics (Retzlaff & Bromley, 1991), especially alcoholic women experiencing major depression (McMahon & Tyson, 1990). The personality profile also can be found with some frequency among spouse-abusing men (Hamberger & Hastings, 1986; Lohr, Hamberger, & Bonge, 1988). In the case of workers' compensation claimants with low back pain, this personality style is thought to indicate that psychosocial stress factors may be aggravating the pain complaints (Snibbe et al., 1980).

These clients will probably demand much attention and reassurance in the therapeutic context. In spite of being somewhat distant and mistrustful, similar individuals react negatively to the unavailability of the therapist or to the therapist's perceived attempts to control their behaviors. It may be useful to set clear limits in the therapeutic relationship and to give these clients as much independence as possible, getting them to make their own decisions rather than offering suggestions or recommendations, because any advice given is likely to trigger their dependence–independence conflict.

Histrionic Profile Clusters

Profile 400: Histrionic

Referred to as "theatrical histrionics" by Millon (1996), individuals with an elevation in the Histrionic scale score show a predominance of dramatic traits in the basic personality structure. They are colorful and emotional and are likely to seek stimulation, excitement, and attention. They tend to react easily to situations around them and often become very absorbed, but typically the involvement does not last. This pattern of getting involved and ending up bored is repetitive.

Histrionic individuals are good at making positive first impressions. Their ability to react to unexpected situations, their alertness, and their search for attention make them colorful and charming socialites at parties or other social gatherings. Individuals with this style have been found to have good coping strategies (Leaf et al., 1992; Leaf, Alington, et al., 1991; Leaf, DiGiuseppe, et al., 1990; Leaf, Ellis, et al., 1991; Nakao et al., 1992; Retzlaff & Deatherage, 1993; Retzlaff & Gibertini, 1988; Strack et al., 1989). Such individuals characterize their family of origin as controlling and intellectually or culturally oriented (Baker et al., 1996). The predominant use of repression as a defense was suggested by one study of Italian examinees (Rubino, Saya, & Pezzarossa, 1992).

However, histrionic individuals can be too loud, exhibitionistic, and dramatic. They can be demanding and uncontrollable, especially when they are highly involved. They typically have intense emotional moments in friendships, but these friendships may be short-lived and replaced when boredom sets in. Their dependency has a much different flavor from the dependency of inadequate individuals in that they need the attention of others rather than protection and guidance. As a result, they may be much less submissive than other types of dependent individuals. They cope with stress by seeking emotional support, reinterpreting events in a positive light, and attempting to find humor in their life situations, but they are too inclined to focus on emotional distress and the discharge of emotions (Vollrath et al., 1994).

Given the histrionic personality style, an emphasis on formalities, such as being on time for the session or keeping an interpersonal distance during the session, is likely to feel unfriendly and dissatisfying. The therapist may need to be tolerant of the clients' emotionality and even a certain amount of conflict. These clients view as egosyntonic therapeutic relationships where they are the center of attention and where demonstrations of affection and support flow readily, especially from the therapist to the client.

Profile 430: Histrionic–Dependent

Judging from their MCMI scores, histrionic–dependent individuals have a histrionic personality style with dependent overtones. Histrionic individuals are colorful and emotional. They seek stimulation, excitement, and attention. They react very readily to situations around them and often become very involved with events, but typically the involvement does not last. The pattern of becoming involved and ending up bored is repeated time and again. Histrionic individuals are very good at making positive first impressions. Their ability to react to unexpected situations, their alertness, and their search for attention make them colorful and charming socialites at parties or other social gatherings. Often, however, they can be too loud, exhibitionistic, and overly dramatic. They can be demanding and uncontrollable, especially on occasions when they are highly involved.

Individuals with similar MCMI scores also tend to have low self-esteem and to feel less gifted or worth less as human beings when they compare themselves with others. The low self-image usually leads to feelings of insecurity and some anxiety when the individual is in a competitive situation.

The histrionic–dependent individual may always seek to be conspicuous and may want constant affirmations of approval and affection. Individuals with similar profiles take an active role in obtaining the attention they need. They often develop sensitivity to the moods of others and use this knowledge to evoke the reactions that they desire. They may seem charming and outgoing, dramatic, or seductive.

This type of person is usually cooperative and congenial, colorful, and in touch with their emotions. However, they may have a difficult time in situations where they feel alone or have to depend on themselves. The loss of meaningful others is often strongly felt.

With regard to psychotherapy, such persons would feel most comfortable when the therapist re-creates a parental role and offers them a good deal of attention, support, nurturance, and protection. An emphasis on formalities such as being on time for the session or keeping an interpersonal distance during the session is likely to feel unfriendly and dissatisfying to them. The therapist may need to be tolerant of emotionality on the part of such clients and even a certain amount of conflict. These individuals feel comfortable in therapeutic relationships in which they are very much the center of attention and where demonstrations of affection and support flow readily, especially from the therapist to the individual. Therapeutic change may come from their processing instances of perceived withdrawal of support, as well as from the encouragement of more independent functioning and an enhanced understanding of their primitive needs for attention.

Profile 438A: Histrionic–Dependent–Negativistic

The MCMI profile of the histrionic–dependent–negativistic individual shows a combination of dramatic, dependent, and negativistic traits as components of the basic personality structure. Individuals with this type of personality are colorful and emotional and seek stimulation, excitement, and attention. They react easily to situations around them and often become emotionally involved, but typically this involvement does not last. The pattern of getting involved and ending up bored is repetitive.

The scores suggest that these individuals are caught in the bind of having low self-esteem but having to conceal their self-appraisal and appear confident and self-assured. They tend to feel less gifted or valuable compared with others. Nevertheless, they are aware that dependency on others projects an undesirable image and are uncomfortable with that particular coping strategy. Faced with this conflict, some individuals externalize it by appearing to be cooperative and compliant but actually resisting the leader in some covert way; others may vacillate. At times, they may be friendly and cooperative, but they start to feel resentful and may become angry and aggressive, only to feel guilty and contrite and begin the cycle again. Such a solution allows them to reconcile the wish to be protected and the wish to appear independent and self-sufficient at the expense of being in frequent conflict with others.

These individuals may be criticized for being somewhat loud, exhibitionistic, or overly dramatic. They need support from others and may be moody or temperamental. However, they often are colorful and expressive individuals who are able to engage others effectively in a reasonably short period of time. The predominant use of repression as a defense was suggested by one study of Italian examinees (Rubino et al., 1992).

Given this type of personality style, an emphasis on formalities, such as being on time for the session or keeping an interpersonal distance during the session, is likely to feel unfriendly and dissatisfying. The therapist may need to be tolerant of these clients' emotionality and conflict. Such clients see as egosyntonic therapeutic relationships where they are the center of attention and where demonstrations of affection and support flow readily, especially from the therapist to the client. The lack of exciting issues during the sessions, or the limits to the support that the therapist can offer, eventually may become an issue, with clients becoming clingy, demanding, or dissatisfied. If not handled properly, such developments may threaten the therapeutic alliance. One way to handle such issues is to make clients aware of their inappropriate expectations and help them work through their attentional needs and dependency conflict.

Profile 450: Histrionic–Narcissistic

The histrionic–narcissistic profile highlights a need for attention and conspicuousness. These "vivacious histrionic" individuals (Millon, 1996) tend to feel that they are special and may view themselves as being intelligent, outgoing, charming, or sophisticated. They often exaggerate their own abilities, constructing rationalizations to inflate their own worth and belittling others who refuse to enhance the image they try to project. They make good first impressions because they are able to express their feelings, have a flair for the dramatic, and have a natural ability to draw attention to themselves. They also are colorful and may have a good sense of humor.

These individuals are probably perceived as friendly and helpful; they may actively seek praise and may be entertaining and somewhat seductive. Individuals with histrionic and narcissistic elements have been found to have good coping strategies (Leaf et al., 1992; Leaf, Alington, et al., 1991; Leaf, DiGiuseppe, et al., 1990; Leaf, Ellis, et al., 1991; Nakao et al., 1992; Retzlaff & Deatherage, 1993; Retzlaff & Gibertini, 1988; Strack et al., 1989). However, they are bored easily and lack self-definition when they are alone. The predominant use of repression as a defense was suggested by one study of Italian examinees (Rubino et al., 1992).

Studies finding this profile in their samples include an investigation of nonpsychiatric individuals with high electroencephalographic alpha waves (Wall, Schuckit, Mungas, & Ehlers, 1990) and drug addicts (Fals-Stewart, 1992). At a subclinical range, this personality was well represented in a group of U.S. Air Force pilot trainees (Retzlaff & Gibertini, 1987, 1988).

Given this personality style, clients may find it easier to establish a relationship with a therapist who is attentive and inclined to appreciate their charms and successes. Allowing clients to take a leading role in the therapeutic context and to control as much as possible what goes on in the sessions also would contribute to making the treatment palatable. Once the therapeutic relationship is well established, the therapist will undoubtedly need to offer occasional interpretations that will sound negative if psychological growth is to occur. The therapist should take care to choose both the timing and manner of such interpretations to avoid injuring these clients' narcissism beyond a point that they can tolerate.

Profile 456A: Histrionic–Narcissistic–Antisocial

Elevations on the Histrionic, Narcissistic, and Antisocial scales define a dramatic personality style with confident and competitive overtones. Individuals obtaining similar scores have a great need for attention and affection. They constantly seek stimulation and conspicuousness with a dramatic flair. Typically, they are adept at manipulating social situations so that others give them the attention they need. They do this partly by becoming sensitive to others so that they can decide what reactions will evoke the responses they want.

These individuals often easily express their feelings and have fairly intense, short-lived emotions. They may appear outgoing, charming, and sophisticated. Individuals with this profile have been found to have good coping strategies (Leaf et al., 1992; Leaf, Alington, et al., 1991; Leaf, DiGiuseppe, et al., 1990; Leaf, Ellis, et al., 1991; Nakao et al., 1992; Retzlaff & Deatherage, 1993; Strack et al., 1989). However, their other-directedness makes them vulnerable to the lack of acceptance from others. They may be somewhat capricious and intolerant of frustration. At times, their dramatic presentations may appear shallow, phony, or overly seductive rather than expressions of real feelings. They also may have some difficulties in developing a self-identity.

For these individuals, the histrionic style has narcissistic and antisocial components. This finding suggests that in striving for attention, they may feel that they are special and that they will be successful in most enterprises. They tend to feel that they are better than everyone else, a feeling that is apparent in their interactions with others. They also view the world as being competitive: Everyone is competing for attention, and only those who are better at getting attention will actually have their needs fulfilled. As a result of these attitudes, they may be somewhat abrasive or conflictual at times.

The histrionic–narcissistic–antisocial personality has been found to be common among alcoholics (Bartsch & Hoffman, 1985; Craig & Olson, 1990; Donat, 1988; Donat et al., 1991) and among adult children of alcoholics (Hibbard, 1989). A subclinical version of this profile often was seen in a group of U.S. Air Force pilot trainees (Retzlaff & Gibertini, 1987).

Given this personality style, these clients may find it easier to establish a relationship with a therapist who is attentive and inclined to appreciate their charms and successes. Allowing the clients to take a leading role in the therapeutic context and control as much as possible what goes on in the sessions also would help to make the treatment palatable. Accepting the clients' matter-of-fact, tough, and antisocial view of the world should help to establish rapport.

Once the therapeutic relationship is well established, the therapist will undoubtedly need to offer occasional interpretations that will sound negative but have to be made if the clients are to grow psychologically. The therapist should take care, however, in choosing the timing and manner of such interpretations to avoid injuring these clients' narcissism beyond the point that they can tolerate.

Profile 458A: Histrionic–Narcissistic–Negativistic

Elevated scores on the Histrionic, Narcissistic, and Negativistic scales indicate a personality composed of dramatic, confident, and oppositionistic traits. These scores characterize individuals with prominent needs for attention who live fast-paced lives and enjoy stimulation and excitement; they may be thrill seekers, easily interested in the prospects of some new adventure. Perceived as charming socialites, these individuals are typically colorful, dramatic, and emotional; they can be flippant, capricious, and demanding but also skilled at attracting others and appearing in a good light. They are easily infatuated, but their enthusiasm is often short-lived. They tend to be immature and unable to delay gratification, are undependable, and often lack discipline. However, they are lively extraverts who present themselves with a certain color and flair.

Their MCMI scores also show that these individuals have a fairly high self-regard. They tend to feel that they are better or more capable than most people. As a result, they are prone to behave in a confident and self-assured manner and to be comfortable taking a strong position on important issues, even when other people disagree. This trait, however, also may present a problem in that they may treat others in a disdainful and insensitive manner or be threatened when someone questions their superiority.

When these individuals encounter some sort of opposition, the negativistic elements are likely to emerge. They may become angry and provocative and show their feelings in aggressive or even hostile ways. This highly emotional state is probably short lived, followed by a return to prominence of the other aspects of their personalities.

Given the personality style just described, these clients may find it easier to establish a relationship with a therapist who is attentive and inclined to appreciate their charms and successes. Allowing such clients to take a leading role in the therapeutic context and control as much as possible what goes on in the sessions also would help the treatment. It may also be useful to refrain from giving these clients directives or setting up unnecessary rules, because they tend to resent controls. Part of the therapist's task is to maintain their clients' perception that the therapist is on their side; otherwise, the relationship becomes competitive and conflictual, and the clients' goal is no longer solving their problems but winning the fight with the therapist.

Once the therapeutic relationship is well established, the therapist undoubtedly will need to offer occasional interpretations that will sound negative to the clients. The therapist should carefully choose the timing and manner of such interpretations to avoid injuring these clients' narcissism beyond the point they can tolerate.

Profile 46A8A: Histrionic–Antisocial–Negativistic

Elevated scores on the Histrionic, Antisocial, and Negativistic scales characterize the dramatic, competitive, and oppositionistic tendencies of the "disingenuous histrionic" (Millon, 1996) personality style. Individuals with similar scores enjoy being the center of attention. In addition to being somewhat emotional and dramatic and enjoying social situations, they are colorful and lively, but they can be seen as somewhat superficial and not serious enough in their approach to the world. Because they have a tendency to get bored easily, they may not always finish one task before moving on to another.

Another important aspect of the personality pattern characterizing these individuals is a competitive worldview: Such individuals feel that there is a limited supply of the things for which everyone is striving. As a result, life is a rat race, and the world is a somewhat cruel and unfriendly place in which no one can really be trusted and in which individuals have to fend for themselves. Most of these individuals see themselves as tough realists and are always trying to avoid getting into situations in which they may be taken advantage of.

These two tendencies usually cause conflict for similar individuals. The attention-getting tendency is people loving and tends to make the individuals somewhat dependent on others. The antisocial outlook, on the other hand, makes them somewhat distrusting. Therefore, they typically are caught in this conflict and may resolve it in one of two ways. Some individuals handle the conflict through mood fluctuations. At first they are friendly and cooperative; they then become afraid that they will be taken advantage of and suddenly seem resistant, distant, and mistrustful or even angry and aggressive. In more pronounced cases, they may even become explosive and hard to handle. Other individuals may handle the conflict with a passive–aggressive maneuver by superficially complying but actually being obstructionistic and thus acting out their aggressive impulses.

Given this personality style, these clients may find it easier to establish a relationship with a therapist who is attentive and inclined to appreciate their charms and successes. Allowing such clients to dominate and control as much as possible what goes on in the sessions also would help the therapy. It is also useful to avoid giving directives or setting up unnecessary rules, because these clients are prone to eventually resent any control. Part of the therapist's task is to maintain their perception that the therapist is on their side; otherwise, the relationship becomes competitive and conflictual and the clients' goal is no longer solving their problems but winning the fight with the therapist. On the other hand, it is just as important to stand firm when a rule has been established, making sure that infractions have an appropriate consequence. Clarity, firmness, and certainty about what areas are controlled by whom can eventually lessen some of the conflicts that would otherwise occur.

Once the therapeutic relationship is well established, the therapist undoubtedly will need to offer occasional interpretations that will sound negative to the clients. The therapist should choose carefully the timing and manner of such interpretations to avoid getting involved in a competitive struggle and evoking a defensive and unproductive reaction.

Profile 470: Histrionic–Compulsive

High scores on the Histrionic and Compulsive scales characterize colorful and emotional individuals who usually seek stimulation, excitement, and attention. They tend to be conspicuous and search actively for affirmation or approval and affection. They often become sensitive to other people's moods and use this knowledge to evoke the reactions they want. They respond readily to situations around them and often become emotionally involved, but typically the involvement does not last. These individuals make good first impressions. Their ability to react to unexpected situations, their alertness and interest, and their search for attention make them colorful socialites at parties and similar gatherings.

Similar individuals value an image hinging on propriety and dependability. They also want to appear conscientious, efficient, dependable, industrious, and persistent, and they may place an emphasis, for instance, on dressing right, having a clean and orderly house, and so on.

In some ways, the histrionic and compulsive tendencies conflict with one another. The histrionic inclination makes individuals seem emotional, intense in their relationships, and impulsive. Compulsive individuals, on the other hand, overcontrol their emotions, are somewhat distant when relating to others, and carefully plan their behaviors. Individuals who have these two tendencies together are often unable to integrate them well and are conflicted as a result. They may then seem moody or emotionally labile. At times, they may be more emotional and intense, but then they may fear where this behavior would lead and become more rigid and controlled.

Both the histrionic and the compulsive elements, however, have been shown to contain good coping strategies (Leaf et al., 1992; Leaf, Alington, et al., 1991; Leaf, DiGiuseppe, et al., 1990; Leaf, Ellis, et al., 1991; Nakao et al., 1992; Retzlaff & Deatherage, 1993; Strack et al., 1989). The predominant use of repression as a defense was suggested by a study of Italian examinees (Rubino et al., 1992).

Profile 48A0: Histrionic–Negativistic

High scores on the Histrionic and Negativistic scales characterize individuals with dramatic and oppositionistic traits. Elevations on the Histrionic scale suggest that such individuals often seek to be the center of attention. They are dramatic, emotional, sensitive, and perceptive about other people's moods, using that knowledge to fulfill their needs for attention and support. They often are colorful socialites who can charm and entertain others and thrive in the superficial relationships of parties and social gatherings. However, they usually need a certain amount of stimulation and become bored easily. When this happens, they are prone to move on to something different without much forethought.

These individuals are often highly aware of the images that people project. For them, the building of their own image is based partly on a negative attitude toward others. These individuals are prone to putting others down or showing disdain. This aspect adds a particular flavor to their basic personality makeup by introducing an aggressive or hostile element.

Some individuals handle this aggressiveness by being consistently obstructionistic, a behavioral pattern that allows them to vent the aggressive element without jeopardizing their ability to gain emotional support and be the center of attention. Otherwise, these individuals may try to control or repress their angry feelings. In that case, the aggressive element will eventually surface through some kind of hostile explosion. After such an incident, however, the individuals are likely to feel guilty and apologize, an action that they hope will appease the offended party and place them back in their original position. Such a mode of operation may make these individuals seem moody, overemotional, and unpredictable.

Given this basic personality style, such clients need a therapeutic relationship in which they are the center of attention. The therapist may need to tolerate displays of emotion and accept a certain amount of conflict. The therapist must also take care not to foster undue enthusiasm and positive responses in these clients and should prepare them for the times ahead when the treatment will become more mundane and they will want to terminate. To avoid future resentment, it also may be important to keep some distance and not to intrude in decisions that clients can make on their own.

Narcissistic Profile Clusters

Profile 500: Narcissistic

High scores on the Narcissistic scale of the MCMI characterize "elitist narcissists" (Millon, 1996), whose basic assumption in life is that they are special. These individuals feel superior to others and have a tendency to exaggerate their abilities and positive attributes, construct rationalizations to inflate their own worth, and depreciate others who refuse to accept or enhance their own self-image.

Such individuals typically view themselves as being intelligent, outgoing, charming, and sophisticated and have a need to be conspicuous and to evoke affection and attention from others. They often make good first impressions because they are likely to have their own opinions and have a natural ability to draw attention to themselves. They are proud individuals, carry themselves with dignity, and may have a good sense of humor. However, they may have trouble if they do not feel properly recognized or are forced to accept the opinions of others or to compromise.

This personality profile has been found to be predominant among claimants for workers' compensation (Repko & Cooper, 1985) and among women who chose a conservative treatment for breast cancer as opposed to a mastectomy (Wolberg et al., 1987) and among substance abusers (Craig & Olson, 1990; Craig et al., 1985). Clients with MMPI 42/24 or 89/98 profile codes tend to have this personality profile on the MCMI (Antoni et al., 1985b, 1986). The Narcissistic scale has been shown to represent a healthy aspect of personality for many individuals (Leaf et al., 1992; Leaf, Alington, et al., 1991; Leaf, DiGiuseppe, et al., 1990; Leaf, Ellis, et al., 1991; Nakao et al., 1992; Retzlaff & Deatherage, 1993; Strack et al., 1989).

Given this personality style, such individuals can be expected to be most comfortable in situations in which they feel admired or at least respected. If confrontation is used in therapy, the therapist must exercise much tact so as not to injure these clients' narcissism more than they can tolerate. On the other hand, there also is a danger that a therapist would be so supportive of clients' narcissism that he or she gives no negative feedback and does not facilitate growth. Thus, it is important to find ways of helping clients accept their fallibilities and work on their problems without feeling unrecognized or humiliated.

Profile 52A0: Narcissistic–Avoidant

Individuals obtaining elevated scores on the Narcissistic and Avoidant scales assume that they are special and feel superior to most other people. They tend to exaggerate their abilities and positive attributes, construct rationalizations to inflate their own worth, and depreciate others who refuse to accept or enhance their own self-image. Viewing themselves only in positive terms, they tend to think of themselves as intelligent, outgoing, charming, and sophisticated. Any negative attributes that they do accept usually are minimized.

For these individuals, however, there also is a certain amount of apprehension regarding relationships with others. They tend to feel that other people are not going to appreciate how capable and outstanding they really are. Such individuals are extremely sensitive to any sign of rejection, because they interpret a rejection as a negation of the kind of image that they feel they must have. As a result, when they interact with others, they always feel they have to put their best foot forward. They tend to be tense, nervous, and self-conscious with most of the people with whom they interact. Therefore, their social outlook is conflicted: In some ways they would like to relate to people well so that they would be appreciated, but they are so socially uncomfortable that they find themselves avoiding people altogether much of the time.

Profile 530: Narcissistic–Dependent

The narcissistic–dependent profile shows predominant confident and cooperative traits in the personality makeup. The juxtaposition of these two styles is a bit unusual and possibly problematic. An elevation on the Narcissistic scale usually indicates that they value themselves highly. Such individuals are prone to assume that they are more capable than others; they think of themselves as being special in some way. As a result, they tend to exaggerate their own positive attributes and to minimize their liabilities. They like to be conspicuous and relate to others with an air of self-assurance. They wish to be leaders and to hold positions of status and power, and they are not particularly interested in following somebody else's directions.

The problem with this personality profile is that the second elevation occurs on a scale that is almost the direct opposite of the first. The Dependent scale characterizes individuals who are followers rather than leaders. This score tends to indicate that they are not sure about their own abilities. Given those two divergent assumptions about their role in life, the test scores suggest that these individuals may experience conflict. At times they may relate in a submissive and overly congenial manner; at other times they may be assertive and try to be dominant.

The task in establishing a therapeutic relationship with clients having this personality style may involve catering to both of the basic emotional needs. The therapist may need to provide the parentlike guidance and support that they seem to need while allowing them to control enough of the situation that they do not feel humiliated. In some ways such individuals will need to be treated like children, but they will still have to be afforded the respect given a peer. The conflict between the two opposing tendencies may lead to some anger and interpersonal discomfort that the therapist will have to handle well for the treatment to be successful.

Profile 540: Narcissistic–Histrionic

The main assumption that narcissistic–histrionic individuals have about themselves is that they are special and probably superior to most other people. Tendencies to exaggerate their abilities and positive attributes, emphasize their past achievements, and depreciate those who refuse to accept their inflated self-image may be present. This narcissism probably is manifested in an air of conviction and self-assurance. When extreme, these individuals are perceived to be conceited and arrogant.

Something that these individuals pay attention to when feeling superior to others is their personal image. They seem to value appearances: A good person is one who looks intelligent, outgoing, competent, sophisticated, and so on. Beneath this surface, however, there is a need for approval and a striving to be conspicuous, to evoke affection, and to attract attention from others. These individuals may be impressive at first glance because they are able to express their thoughts easily, have a flair for the dramatic, and enjoy a natural capacity to draw attention to themselves. However, they may be capricious and intolerant of frustration. They often are emotional, but the emotions may be short-lived. There also is an inclination to be easily bored, at which times they may go do something else. Millon (1996) called this style the "amorous narcissistic" style because of the seductive flavor that these individuals tend to have.

This personality style has been found to be common among drug addicts (Craig & Olson, 1990; Yeager, DiGiuseppe, Resweber, & Leaf, 1992). Generally, however, individuals with this personality style have been found to have good coping strategies (Leaf et al., 1992; Leaf, Alington, et al., 1991; Leaf, DiGiuseppe, et al., 1990; Leaf, Ellis, et al., 1991; Nakao et al., 1992; Retzlaff & Deatherage, 1993; Strack et al., 1989). In a study of U.S. Air Force pilots in training, at a subclinical level the individuals were described as sociable, level-headed, and well adjusted (Retzlaff & Gibertini, 1987).

Clients having this personality style can be expected to be most comfortable in situations in which they feel admired, or at least respected, and the center of attention. If confrontation is used in therapy, the therapist must exercise tact so as not to injure these clients' narcissism more than they can tolerate. On the other hand, there also is a danger that a therapist would be so supportive of the clients' narcissism that he or she gives no negative feedback and does not facilitate growth. Thus, it is important to find ways of helping the clients accept their fallibilities and work on their problems without feeling unrecognized or humiliated.

Profile 546A: Narcissistic–Histrionic–Antisocial

High scores on the Narcissistic, Histrionic, and Antisocial scales suggest a personality style characterized by confident, dramatic, and competitive elements. The main assumption these individuals hold about themselves is that they are special and superior to most other people. Such individuals may tend to exaggerate their abilities and positive attributes, emphasize their past achievements, and depreciate those who refuse to accept their inflated self-image. This narcissism typically is manifested in an air of conviction and self-assurance. When extreme, some individuals are perceived as being conceited and arrogant.

There is evidence that individuals with this profile pay attention to their personal image when they are feeling superior to other people. They seem to value appearances: A good person is someone who appears intelligent, outgoing, competent, sophisticated, and so on. Beneath this surface, however, there is a need for approval and a striving to be conspicuous, to evoke affection, and to attract attention from others. These individuals may be impressive at first because they easily express their thoughts, have a flair for the dramatic, and enjoy a natural capacity to draw attention to themselves. They may be capricious, however, and intolerant of frustration. They often are emotional, but the emotions may be short-lived; they become bored easily and may move from one enterprise to another.

Another factor in the feelings of superiority may be related to the individuals' tendency to view the environment as a competitive place. They feel that they have to fend for themselves to function. As a result, they are somewhat mistrustful and suspicious. *Assertive, energetic, self-reliant, strong,* and *realistic* are adjectives they use to describe themselves. They feel that they have to be tough to survive in a tough world. For them, compassion and warmth are weak emotions that will place them in an inferior position. The competitive outlook fits well with the feelings of superiority as long as they are in situations in which they have a good chance of "winning."

This profile often has been found among substance abusers (Donat, 1988; Donat et al., 1991; Fals-Stewart, 1992; Retzlaff & Bromley, 1991). It also is indicative of an absence of depression among alcoholics (McMahon & Davidson, 1986b).

Clients with this personality style may require a therapeutic context in which they feel admired or at least respected. They need to be the center of attention. If confrontation is used in therapy, the therapist must use tact to avoid injuring these clients' narcissism more than they can tolerate. Another problem could arise if clients interpret the confrontation as being part of a competitive relationship and fight it rather than accepting it as useful feedback. On the other hand, there also is a danger that a therapist would be so supportive of the clients' narcissism that he or she gives no negative feedback and does not facilitate growth. Therefore, it is important to find ways to help clients accept their fallibilities and work on their problems without feeling unrecognized or humiliated.

Profile 548A: Narcissistic–Histrionic–Negativistic

Individuals who obtain high scores on the Narcissistic, Histrionic, and Negativistic scales assume that they are special and superior to other people. They tend to exaggerate their abilities and positive attributes, construct rationalizations to inflate their own worth, and depreciate others who refuse to accept or enhance their own self-image.

In addition, similar individuals want to appear intelligent, outgoing, charming, and sophisticated and have a need to be conspicuous and evoke affection and attention from others. They typically make good first impressions because they are able to express their feelings, have a flair for the dramatic, and have a natural ability to draw attention to themselves. They are colorful, usually have a good sense of humor, and can be perceived as being friendly and helpful in interpersonal relationships. Actively solicitous of praise, they may be entertaining and somewhat seductive. Their preoccupation with external rewards and approval may leave them feeling empty when they are alone.

These individuals also tend to be conflicted. On one hand, they see themselves as colorful, very capable, and generally superior to others. On the other hand, they depend on a flow of attention and approval from others. With some, this conflict surfaces in a hypersensitive or oppositionistic way of reacting: They may be compliant but resentful. Others handle this conflict by showing mood changes: They may be submissive and compliant at times; resentful and angry in other instances; and contrite, apologetic, and overly cooperative in other instances. In terms of research, a variant of this personality style (code 854) was found to be the most common among clients with major depression (Wetzler et al., 1990).

Profile 56A4: Narcissistic–Antisocial–Histrionic

Elevated scores on the Narcissistic, Antisocial, and Histrionic scales characterize "unprincipled narcissistic" (Millon, 1996) individuals, who are confident, competitive, and dramatic. A major assumption they have is that they are special: Such individuals typically feel superior to most other people. Such individuals may tend to exaggerate their abilities and positive attributes, construct arguments to emphasize their own worth, and depreciate those who refuse to accept their self-image. This tendency probably is externalized through an air of conviction, security, and self-assurance. When extreme, these individuals can be perceived as conceited and arrogant.

Some of the feelings of superiority come from a tendency to view the world in competitive terms. Similar individuals feel they have to fend for themselves to function. As a result, they are somewhat mistrustful and suspicious. They see themselves as being assertive, energetic, self-reliant, strong, and realistic and feel that they have to be tough to make it in a tough world. These individuals usually justify their aggressiveness by pointing to the hostile and exploitative behavior of others. In their view, compassionate or warm people are weak and will be taken advantage of. This antisocial outlook fits particularly well with their feelings of superiority if they are in a situation in which they have a chance of winning.

These individuals tend to pay attention to their image when they are feeling superior to others. They seem to value appearances: A good person is someone who appears intelligent, outgoing, charming, sophisticated, and so on. Beneath this surface, there typically is a need for approval and a striving to be conspicuous and to evoke affection and receive attention from others. These individuals usually make good first impressions because they easily express their thoughts and feelings, have a flair for the dramatic, and naturally draw attention to themselves. However, they may be capricious and intolerant of frustration.

This personality style has been found to be common among male inpatients in both an alcoholic population (Mayer & Scott, 1988) and a more general psychiatric ward (Donat, Geczy, et al., 1992). It also is well represented among drug abusers (Marsh, Stile, Stoughton, & Trout-Landen, 1988).

Therapy may be more effective for clients with this personality if they feel admired, or at least respected, by the therapist. Similar individuals frequently also need to be the center of attention. If confrontation is necessary, the therapist must use tact so as not to injure these clients' narcissism more than they can tolerate. Moreover, there is the risk that clients could interpret confrontation as part of a competitive relationship and fight it rather than accepting it as useful feedback. On the other hand, it also is possible that a therapist could be so supportive of the clients' narcissism that he or she gives no negative feedback and does not facilitate growth. Therefore, it is important to find ways to help clients accept their fallibilities and work on their problems without feeling unrecognized or humiliated.

Profile 58A0: Narcissistic–Negativistic

This personality profile defines individuals who have a confident and explosive personality. Similar individuals assume that they are special and superior to most people. They tend to exaggerate their abilities and positive attributes, construct rationalizations to inflate their own worth, and depreciate others who refuse to accept or enhance their own self-image.

Such individuals typically want to appear intelligent, outgoing, charming, and sophisticated and have a need to be conspicuous, evoking affection and attention from others. They often make good first impressions because they can be friendly and helpful in interpersonal relationships. However, they are unlikely to accept criticism and tend to project whatever feelings of inadequacy they have, attempting to dismiss their failures as resulting from the irresponsibility or incompetence of others.

Individuals with similar MCMI scores tend to be conflicted. On one hand, they want to see themselves as being superior to others. On the other hand, they are insecure and painfully aware of their own limitations. This conflict may surface through mood changes: They may be compliant at times, only to become resentful and angry in other instances and to be contrite, apologetic, and overly cooperative on still other occasions.

Given this personality style, these clients may benefit most from a therapeutic relationship in which they feel admired or at least respected. If therapists confront these clients, they should use tact to avoid injuring their narcissism more than they can handle. On the other hand, the therapist should not be so supportive of the clients' narcissism that he or she gives no negative feedback and does not facilitate growth. Thus, it is important to find ways of helping such individuals accept their fallibilities and work on their problems without feeling unrecognized or humiliated.

In addition, it may be important not to try to control these clients in ways that are not necessary for the therapy to function. Because these individuals are bound to resent any control placed on them, this tactic can prevent the therapeutic relationship from becoming overly conflictual. Such individuals also may benefit from learning how they normally operate and project negative feelings onto others.

Antisocial Profile Clusters

Profile 6A00: Antisocial

Antisocial individuals see their environment as if it were a tournament, and they feel they have to fend for themselves to function. As a result, most individuals with this personality profile are competitive and somewhat mistrustful and suspicious of others. They see themselves as being assertive, energetic, self-reliant, strong, and realistic. To make it in the rat race, they have to be tough. These individuals justify their assertiveness by pointing to the hostile and exploitative behavior of others. They may be contemptuous of the weak and may not care whether they are liked because "good guys come in last."

Such individuals are impulsive. They typically are perceived as somewhat aggressive and intimidating. At times, they may appear cold, callous, and insensitive. They may be argumentative and contentious. They may even be abusive, cruel, or malicious. When matters go their way, they may be gracious, cheerful, and friendly. More characteristically, however, their behavior is guarded, reserved, and competitive. When crossed, pushed on personal matters, or faced with embarrassment, they may respond impulsively and become angry, vengeful, and vindictive. This type of personality has been found in a therapeutic community for drug addicts and was associated with difficulty obeying rules, staying in treatment, and maintaining abstinence (Fals-Stewart, 1992).

In the light of this personality style, the establishment of a therapeutic alliance may be somewhat difficult. Clients are not inclined to see psychotherapy as valuable unless it offers a tangible material benefit, such as a way out of a jam. One approach to establishing an alliance in spite of this difficulty may be to accept, at least temporarily, the same competitive outlook that the clients favor. The therapist then may be in the position to help them explore the behaviors and attitudes that get in the way of their being a "winner."

Profile 6A12A: Antisocial–Schizoid–Avoidant

Competitive, introversive, and avoidant traits characterize this "nomadic antisocial" (Millon, 1996) personality profile of the MCMI. Such individuals see their environment as if it were a tournament, with one person pitted against the other. To be able to function in such a situation, they feel that they have to fend for themselves. Such individuals are self-sufficient and do not depend on others to fulfill their needs. They may be somewhat mistrustful and suspicious. They see themselves as being assertive, energetic, self-reliant, strong, and realistic. To make it in the rat race, they believe they must adopt a tough stance. Their assertiveness is justified by pointing to the hostile and exploitative behavior of others.

Individuals with this type of personality may be contemptuous of the weak; they may appear cold, callous, or insensitive to the feelings of others and may tend to be argumentative and contentious. When matters go their way, they may be gracious, cheerful, and friendly. More characteristically, however, their behavior is guarded, reserved, and aggressive. When crossed, pushed, or embarrassed, they may respond impulsively and become angry, vengeful, and vindictive.

In addition, these individuals keep an emotional distance from others. They are uninterested in interpersonal relations and may not be adept at understanding and enjoying the subtleties of emotions, which could result in apathy about relationships. Moreover, they typically are afraid of being rejected by others who also are looking out for themselves in the competitive world. As a result, social situations are avoided because they are uncomfortable and tension provoking. These individuals restrict the number of relationships they form and tend to have superficial friendships when they exist and alliances that are more like acquaintanceships than strong friendships.

In the light of this personality style, the establishment of a therapeutic alliance may be somewhat difficult. Clients are not inclined to see psychotherapy as valuable unless it offers a tangible material benefit, such as a way out of a jam. The fact that they are likely to be threatened by or uninterested in emotional closeness also may impede the forming of a relationship. One approach to establishing an alliance in spite of this difficulty may be to accept, at least temporarily, the same competitive outlook that the clients favor. The therapist then may be in the position to help them explore the behaviors and attitudes that get in the way of their being a "winner."

Profile 6A34: Antisocial–Dependent–Histrionic

The MCMI scores antisocial–dependent–histrionic individuals obtain describe an antisocial personality with dependent and histrionic elements. Similar individuals experience an internal conflict between their competitive and aggressive nature on the one hand and their insecurity and need for people's attention on the other.

One part of such individuals' nature is characterized by a view of the environment as a competitive, tournament-like situation. To be able to function, similar individuals feel they have to operate on their own. They see themselves as assertive, energetic, self-reliant, strong, and realistic. They feel that they have to be tough in order to make it in the rat race. They may be somewhat distrusting of others. These individuals justify their assertiveness by pointing to the hostile and exploitative behaviors of others. They may be contemptuous of the weak and may not care if they are disliked, claiming that "good guys come in last." They are typically impulsive and insensitive to the feelings of others.

Conflicting with their competitive nature is a part of these individuals that is insecure and that strives for attention. Individuals with similar scores feel less gifted or worthwhile than others around them. The low self-image usually leads to feelings of insecurity and anxiety when such individuals are expected to be on their own. They may seek to be conspicuous and may want frequent affirmations of approval and affection.

The fact that aspects of this personality style do not blend well creates an inner tension that may lead to anxiety, moodiness, or other uncomfortable subjective experiences. This conflict, however, has a positive element in that it may moderate the two influences. For instance, having low self-esteem does not fit well with the competitive outlook on life and may cause these individuals some problems, but it also reigns in the aggressiveness of the competitive style.

It should also be stated that each of these styles has advantages to go with the disadvantages already noted. The competitive tendencies prepare these individuals well for many activities that intrinsically involve competition against others. The dependent inclination creates a side of these individuals that is cooperative and wanting to please, whereas the histrionic element makes them colorful and interesting individuals.

One issue such individuals may present in therapy is a tendency to become competitive with the therapist, which can create trouble in forging a real alliance. Such individuals would feel most comfortable when the therapist recreates a parental role and offers them a good deal of attention, support, nurturance, and protection. However, in spite of the dependency, similar clients tend to be oppositional and conflictive in their therapeutic relationships as a result of their competitive nature and histrionic personality overtones. The therapist may need to be tolerant on these occasions. Therapeutic change may come from processing perceived withholding of support, as well as from an enhanced understanding of these clients' primitive needs for attention and the results of their behaviors.

Profile 6A40: Antisocial–Histrionic

Elevations on the Antisocial and Histrionic scales reveal an antisocial personality style with histrionic elements. Those with similar scores look at their environment as a competitive situation. To be able to function, they feel that they have to fend for themselves. Most individuals with this view are, as a result, somewhat distrusting and suspicious of others. They see themselves as assertive, energetic, self-reliant, strong, and realistic. They feel that they have to be tough in order to make it in the rat race. These individuals usually justify their assertiveness by pointing to the hostile and exploitative behaviors of others. They may be contemptuous of the weak and may not care if they are disliked, claiming that "good guys come in last." They are often seen as somewhat aggressive or intimidating. At times they may be cold, callous, or insensitive to the feelings of others. They may be argumentative and contentious. Some such individuals may even be abusive, cruel, or malicious.

Individuals with this type of personality are typically impulsive. They are colorful and emotional. They seek stimulation, excitement, and attention. They react very readily to situations around them and often become involved, but typically the involvement does not last. This pattern of becoming involved and ending up bored is repeated time after time. Similar individuals are good at making positive first impressions. Their ability to react to unexpected situations, their alertness, and their search for attention make them colorful and charming socialites at parties or other social gatherings. Often, however, they can be too loud, exhibitionistic, and overly dramatic. They can be demanding and uncontrollable, especially on occasions when they are highly involved.

Individuals with an antisocial–histrionic personality style tend not to value therapy for its own sake. One approach to establishing a therapeutic alliance may be to accept, at least temporarily, the same competitive outlook they favor. The therapist may be in the position to help such individuals explore the behaviors and attitudes they hold that get in the way of their being a "winner." An emphasis on formalities such as being on time for the session or keeping an interpersonal distance during the session is likely to feel unfriendly and dissatisfying to them. The therapist may need to be tolerant of emotionality on the part of the patient and a certain amount of conflict. These individuals feel comfortable in therapeutic relationships where they are very much the center of attention and where demonstrations of affection and support flow readily, especially from the therapist to the client.

Profile 6A50: Antisocial–Narcissistic

The antisocial–narcissistic personality profile is characterized by competitive and confident traits. Because the environment is perceived to be competitive by nature, individuals with this profile feel they have to fend for themselves to function. As a result, most individuals with this view are somewhat distant, mistrustful, and suspicious of others. They see themselves as being assertive, energetic, self-reliant, strong, and realistic. For them, one must be tough to make it in this "dog-eat-dog" world. These individuals usually justify their assertiveness by pointing to the hostile and exploitative behavior of others. They may not object if they are not liked; after all, "good guys come in last."

Another aspect of this personality style is an inflated self-image. These individuals typically see themselves as being more capable, more interesting, and more worthwhile than other people. This tendency often is externalized through an air of conviction, independent security, and self-assurance. When extreme, this tendency may make the bearer appear conceited or arrogant.

Other people may perceive these individuals as being somewhat aggressive and intimidating. Their assertiveness may be sensed as a cold insensitivity to the feelings of others. Such individuals tend to be argumentative and contentious and may even be abusive, cruel, or malicious at times. When things go their way, they may be gracious, cheerful, and friendly. More characteristically, however, they are guarded, reserved, and resentful. When crossed, pushed on personal matters, or faced with embarrassment, they may respond quickly and become angry, vengeful, and vindictive.

This type of personality has been found to be common among men in a domestic violence abatement program (Hamberger & Hastings, 1986; Lohr et al., 1988). The men were described as self-centered, likely to insist that their values and rules be accepted, and inclined to use others to meet their own needs. They felt entitled to be treated differently from others. This personality style also has been found to be prevalent in correctional inmates (Hart et al., 1991; McNiel & Meyer, 1990) and can be found among alcoholics (Corbisiero & Reznikoff, 1991; Craig et al., 1985). Antoni et al. (1986) found this personality style to represent a subgroup of the clients obtaining the 89/98 MMPI code.

In the light of this personality style, establishing a therapeutic alliance may be somewhat difficult. These clients will not see the benefit of psychotherapy unless it offers a tangible material benefit, such as a way out of trouble. They also resent the kind of superior position that the therapist has in the therapeutic context, perhaps because the therapist is the "expert" whose opinions are solicited during the therapy session. One approach to establishing an alliance in spite of these difficulties may be to accept, at least temporarily, the same competitive outlook that the clients favor. The therapist then may be in the position to help them explore the behaviors and attitudes that prevent them from being "winners." Treating them with as much respect and deference as possible also may contribute to the formation of the therapeutic alliance.

Profile 6A53: Antisocial–Narcissistic–Dependent

The antisocial–narcissistic–dependent personality profile indicates the predominance of competitive, confident, and cooperative traits in the personality makeup. The juxtaposition of these three styles is unusual and possibly problematic. An elevation on the Antisocial scale typically is associated with viewing the environment as a contest in which people are pitted against each other. To be able to function, these individuals feel that they have to fend for themselves. As a result, they are somewhat distant, mistrustful, and suspicious of others. They see themselves as assertive, energetic, self-reliant, strong, and realistic; they feel that they have to be tough to make it in the world.

Another aspect of this personality style is an inflated self-image. Such individuals may tend to think that they are more capable, interesting, or worthwhile than other people. These individuals like to be conspicuous and admired. Their wish to be leaders and hold positions of status and power, and their lack of interest in following someone else's directions, may become externalized through an air of conviction, independent security, and self-assurance. When extreme, this tendency may make such individuals look somewhat conceited and arrogant.

Similar individuals may be perceived as aggressive or intimidating; their assertiveness often is sensed as a cold insensitivity to other people's feelings. When events go their way, they may be gracious, cheerful, and friendly. At other times, however, they may be guarded, reserved, and resentful. When crossed, pushed on personal matters, or faced with humiliation, they may become angry and vindictive.

The inflated self-image fits well with the competitive outlook in that it provides the security that these individuals need to engage in the rivalry they are likely to experience when they are with others. One problem with this personality profile is that the third elevation occurs on a scale that is almost the direct opposite of the first two. The Dependent scale typically characterizes individuals who are followers rather than leaders. High scores on this scale describe individuals who are unsure of their abilities and would feel more comfortable if they had someone whom they trust to take care of them. One way of integrating all the findings would be to think of these individuals as actually feeling fairly inadequate but compensating against these feelings by putting up an overconfident facade.

In the light of this personality style, establishing a therapeutic alliance may be difficult. These individuals are not likely to see psychotherapy as valuable unless they will benefit from it in a tangible way. They are inclined to resent the kind of superior position the therapist assumes during the sessions. One approach to establishing an alliance may be to accept, at least temporarily, the same competitive outlook that the clients favor. The therapist then may be able to help them examine the behaviors and attitudes that keep them from being successful. It also will help to treat the clients with special respect and deference.

Profile 6A58A: Antisocial–Narcissistic–Negativistic

Individuals obtaining elevations on the Antisocial, Narcissistic, and Negativistic scales likely will have a competitive personality style with confident and negativistic overtones. In terms of empirical data, this personality profile has been found to be common among alcoholics (Corbisiero & Reznikoff, 1991).

Individuals with this personality style view their environment as primarily competitive, and to be able to function they feel they must fend for themselves. As a result, they are somewhat distant, mistrustful, and suspicious of others, but they see themselves as being assertive, energetic, self-reliant, strong, and realistic. They feel that they have to be tough to survive in such a competitive environment, and they justify their assertiveness by pointing to the hostile and exploitative behavior of others. They probably will not care whether other people like them, because one does what one must do to get ahead.

An unfortunate effect of adversarial relationships is that the loser suffers as a result of the other person winning. Although this may not be the goal of behaving in a particular way, individuals with this personality style try not to be bothered by humanistic sentiments or guilt. In fact, they may feel that worrying about such issues implies a weakness or liability instead of something admirable. These individuals strive to be tough, thick-skinned, street-wise, and capable of taking care of themselves.

Another aspect of the antisocial–narcissistic–negativistic personality style is an inflated self-image. They tend to think they are more able, more interesting, and more worthwhile than others. They have an air of conviction, independent security, and self-assurance. When extreme, these individuals may appear to be conceited and arrogant.

This personality style also may make the bearer appear aggressive, intimidating, cold, or insensitive. Such individuals tend to be argumentative and contentious and may even be abusive, cruel, or malicious at times. When events go their way, they may be gracious, cheerful, and friendly. More characteristically, however, they are guarded, reserved, and resentful. When crossed, pushed on personal matters, or embarrassed, they may respond quickly and become angry, vengeful, and vindictive.

In fact, high scores on these scales suggest the presence of interpersonal conflicts. At times these individuals may want to have closer and warmer relationships and may regret having mistreated others in their antisocial struggle. The unresolved conflict is projected in the form of a negativistic resentment or anger. Instead of overtly venting the resentment, some of these individuals are more inclined to be obstructionistic.

The predominance of the antisocial personality style probably makes these individuals function particularly well in situations that are inherently competitive, such as some businesses, sales, or competitive sports (e.g., boxing, football). Their superficiality in interpersonal relationships and their aggressive attitude, on the other hand, may have a negative effect in situations in which loyalty and team coordination are needed.

In the light of the personality style just described, the establishment of a therapeutic alliance may be difficult. These clients may not see value in psychotherapy. Moreover, the therapist's superior position as an expert will be resented. One way of fostering the relationship may be to accept, at least temporarily, the competitive outlook that the clients favor. The therapist then may be better able to help them figure out what behaviors and attitudes hinder their becoming a "winner." The therapist also may have to remain unintrusive, being careful not to take a stance if it is not necessary. Not taking a strong position will encourage clients to make their own decisions and will decrease the amount of conflict present in the therapeutic relationship. Giving interpretations at times when clients are using dysfunctional projective mechanisms may be necessary. However, any confrontation has to be carried out with care, because these individuals will be inclined to approach such feedback in a competitive manner and fight the insights that are offered. The therapeutic alliance has to be protected by doing whatever is necessary to keep them feeling that the therapist is on their side.

Profile 6A70: Antisocial–Compulsive

Elevated scores on the Antisocial and Compulsive MCMI scales indicate predominant competitive and disciplined personality traits. Individuals with this profile view life as a sort of tournament. Everyone, in their view, is competing for the same rewards, and these valuables are in limited supply. To be able to function well, they feel they have to fend for themselves. As a result, most such individuals are somewhat mistrustful or even suspicious of others. They see themselves as assertive, energetic, self-reliant, strong, and realistic and feel that they have to be tough to make it in the world. These individuals may be somewhat contemptuous of the weak and may not care whether they are liked, claiming that "good guys come in last." Characteristically, their behavior is guarded and reserved.

Additionally, these individuals assume that the way to become a "winner" is to avoid making a mistake. They usually are orderly and conscientious, plan for the future, prepare well, and do their work on schedule. They tend to be efficient, dependable, industrious, and persistent. These individuals often believe in discipline and practice self-restraint, especially when it concerns their own emotions, which are usually kept under control. The overcontrol of the emotions gives them their typical flavor: They are formal and proper and somewhat unlikely to open up and act spontaneously in front of others. They sometimes are perceived as perfectionistic, distant, and inflexible; they tend to be indecisive at times when they have had no chance to study all the possible options. In other words, their strategy to win the rat race is to be careful, deliberate, dependable, and hardworking.

About 15% of the alcoholic population has been found to have this personality style. The group is associated with the MMPI 42 code. Alcohol for these clients is thought to dampen an overly exuberant conscience and to permit escape from responsibility and the expression of anger (Bartsch & Hoffman, 1985). Retzlaff and Gibertini (1987) found this personality to be common among U.S. Air Force pilot trainees.

Profile 6A8A0: Antisocial–Negativistic

The antisocial–negativistic personality profile indicates a predominance of competitive traits with negativistic elements. Clients tend to experience life as if it were a tournament. Assuming that everyone is struggling for things that exist in limited supply, they probably are somewhat mistrustful and superficial in the way they relate to others. They need to be strong and self-sufficient. They feel that asking others for help is counterproductive because it lessens their own chances of ending up ahead of those on whom they depend. These individuals are proud of their "realistic" views, which emphasize tangible achievements and material gains.

An unfortunate effect of adversarial relationships is that the loser suffers as a result of the other person winning. Although this may not be the goal of behaving in a particular way, individuals with this profile probably try not to be bothered by humanistic sentiments or guilt. In fact, they may feel that worrying about those issues implies some weakness or liability instead of something to be admired. They want other people to perceive them as tough, thick-skinned, streetwise, and capable of protecting their own interests.

However, these individuals may have some conflicts in the way that they relate to others. At times they may want closer and warmer relationships and may regret having mistreated others in their competitive struggle. The unresolved conflict typically is projected in the form of a negativistic resentment or anger. Instead of overtly venting their resentment, some individuals may use an obstructionistic or passive–aggressive strategy.

The predominance of the antisocial personality style probably makes such individuals function particularly well in situations that are inherently competitive, such as business, sales, or sports. Their superficiality in interpersonal relationships and their aggressive attitude, on the other hand, may have a negative effect in situations in which loyalty and teamwork are needed.

In the light of this personality style, such clients may have difficulty establishing a therapeutic alliance. They are not likely to see psychotherapy as valuable unless it offers a tangible material benefit. They also resent the therapist's superior position in the therapeutic context, perhaps because the therapist is the "expert" whose opinions are solicited during the therapy session. One approach to establishing an alliance is to accept, at least temporarily, the same competitive outlook that the clients favor. The therapist then may be able to help the clients identify the behaviors and attitudes that hinder the chance of their becoming "winners."

The therapist also may have to remain unintrusive and to be careful not to take a stance. Not taking a stance will encourage the clients to make their own decisions and will decrease the amount of conflict present in the therapeutic relationship. Giving interpretations when the clients are using maladaptive projective mechanisms may be necessary. However, any confrontation has to be done carefully because these clients will be inclined to react to such feedback in an antisocial manner and to fight the insights that are offered. The therapeutic alliance must be protected, and the therapist has to do whatever is necessary to keep the clients feeling that the therapist is on their side.

Compulsive Profile Clusters

Profile 700: Compulsive

Elevated scores on the Compulsive scale indicate the predominance of disciplined traits in the basic personality structure. Individuals with this "conscientious compulsive" (Millon, 1996) type of personality profile place a premium on avoiding mistakes. They usually are orderly and plan for the future. Moreover, they are conscientious, prepare well, and do their work on schedule. They tend to be efficient, dependable, industrious, and persistent. To people in authority, these individuals typically act in a respectful and ingratiating manner. This style of relating often changes when the relationship is with a subordinate. When this is the case, these individuals may become somewhat perfectionistic and demanding.

Individuals with this profile believe in discipline and practice self-restraint, especially when it concerns their own emotions, which are usually kept well under control. The overcontrol of emotions tends to give them a characteristic flavor: They are formal and proper and unlikely to open up and act spontaneously in front of others. Sometimes seen as perfectionistic, distant, or inflexible, these individuals tend to be indecisive before they have had a chance to study all possible alternatives. However, they are careful, deliberate, righteous, honest, dependable, and hardworking individuals.

This type of personality style may make it difficult for such individuals to work with some aspects of their environment. For instance, situations that unpredictably change abruptly from one moment to the next or in which following the rules does not lead to the desired outcome can be particularly stressful. However, disciplined individuals are well suited for situations in which it is important to be accurate and meticulous.

Individuals with a compulsive personality style have been found to have good coping strategies, and this has been seen as a possible source of psychological strength (Leaf et al., 1992; Leaf, Alington, et al., 1991; Leaf, DiGiuseppe, et al., 1990; Leaf, Ellis, et al., 1991; Nakao et al., 1992; Retzlaff & Deatherage, 1993). The style has been found to be common among seminarians (Piersma, 1987c) and missionaries (Adams & Clopton, 1990). However, compulsive individuals also constitute a large portion of the alcoholic population (Craig et al., 1985; Donat, 1988; Donat et al., 1991).

Unfortunately, an elevation on the Compulsive scale also can be obtained by individuals who are not all that proper or orderly but who are interested in "looking good" in the testing or are defensive psychologically (Craig et al., 1994; Retzlaff, Sheehan, & Fiel, 1991). This is because these individuals do not endorse personality "flaws" and answer the testing in a perfectionistic manner. If this turns out to be the case, the description has to be changed to emphasize the defensive outlook rather than the meticulousness, orderliness, or interest in careful planning.

If these clients do have a compulsive personality style, however, they would find it easier to establish a therapeutic alliance with a professional who is formal, proper, punctual, and predictable. Keeping some distance and allowing the clients to control significant parts of the session also would make them feel more at ease. Explanations of the diagnosis, the nature of the "illness," and the expected course of treatment will probably be appreciated. It may, however, be difficult to move such individuals from a superficial therapeutic alliance to a more meaningful dependency on the relationship. Helping them explore the defenses that they use or enhancing their tolerance for allowing others to hold the controls also can be difficult to accomplish.

Profile 72A0: Compulsive–Avoidant

Individuals with high scores on the Compulsive and Avoidant scales have disciplined and avoidant tendencies in their personality structure. An important motivational force behind this basic personality structure is the avoidance of mistakes. Such individuals tend to be orderly and plan for the future. To those in authority, they are inclined to be respectful, ingratiating, and dependent. This approach probably changes when they relate to a subordinate. In that case, they may become somewhat arrogant, perfectionistic, or disdainful. They often believe in discipline and practice self-restraint, especially when it concerns their own emotions, which are always kept under control.

There are indications that these individuals would like to relate to others and enjoy the affection and appreciation of others. People in general, however, present a problem to those with this personality style, because they can be emotional and unpredictable. This unpredictability and emphasis on the emotional aspects of relationships can make these individuals uncomfortable. Thus, relating to others represents a risk that makes them feel particularly vulnerable. They may be inclined to avoid relationships or to relate in a cold and distant manner to minimize the risks taken. Individuals with similar MCMI personality scores tend to be proper and formal. They usually are conscientious, well prepared, efficient, dependable, industrious, and persistent. However, they also may be perceived as perfectionistic, rigid, picayunish, and indecisive.

Given this type of personality style, such clients may find it easier to establish a therapeutic alliance with a professional who is formal, proper, punctual, and predictable. Keeping some distance and allowing the clients to control significant parts of the session also will make them feel at ease. Explanations of the diagnosis, the nature of the "illness," and the expected course of treatment can be important. However, it may be difficult to move from a superficial therapeutic alliance to a more meaningful dependency on the relationship. Helping such clients explore defenses or enhance their tolerance for allowing others to be in control also can be difficult to accomplish.

Profile 730: Compulsive–Dependent

Elevated scores on the Compulsive and Dependent scales describe a personality style with both compulsive and dependent elements. Individuals with similar personalities hold the life assumption that one must work hard to avoid making a mistake. Such individuals are usually orderly and plan for the future. They are conscientious; they typically prepare well and do their work on schedule. They tend to be efficient, dependable, industrious, and persistent. To those in authority, these individuals relate in an overly respectful and ingratiating manner. They believe in discipline and practice self-restraint, especially concerning their own emotions, which are usually kept under control. The overcontrol of the emotions tends to give this type of individual a characteristic flavor: They are formal and proper and unlikely to open up and act spontaneously in front of others. They are sometimes seen as perfectionistic, distant, occasionally inflexible, and perhaps indecisive before they have had a chance to study all possible alternatives. However, they are careful, deliberate, righteous, honest, dependable, and hardworking individuals.

These individuals tend to feel that other people are more capable than they are. Similar individuals are unconceited and personable and are inclined to form strong interpersonal relationships with others. They aim to be as congenial as possible to those around them to secure the support they need. As a result, similar individuals tend to be fairly submissive, or at least compliant. They shy away from competitive situations because such situations make them feel unsupported and vulnerable. When they feel protected, however, they tend to be quite at ease and conflict free.

The compulsive–dependent personality style may make it hard for these individuals to work with some aspects of the environment. For instance, situations that can change abruptly from one moment to the next in an unpredictable manner, or situations in which following the rules does not lead to the desired outcome, can be expected to be particularly stressful. However, disciplined individuals are very well suited for situations in which it is important to be accurate and meticulous.

Unfortunately, the compulsive–dependent MCMI profile is also obtained by individuals who are not all that proper or orderly, but who are interested in "looking good" in the testing and are fairly defensive psychologically. The reason is that such persons do not endorse items containing personality "flaws" and answer the test in a perfectionistic manner. If this is thought to be the case with an examinee, the description given above has to be changed to emphasize the defensive outlook rather than the meticulousness, orderliness, or interest in careful planning of the future.

Given the type of personality style described, this individual may find it easier to establish a therapeutic alliance with a professional who is formal, proper, punctual, and predictable. Keeping a bit of a distance from these clients and allowing them to control significant parts of the session would also make them feel at ease. Explanations of the diagnosis, the nature of the "illness," the expected course of treatment, and the like can hold a very special appeal for this individual.

Profile 736A: Compulsive–Dependent–Antisocial

Individuals with this personality profile are disciplined, cooperative, and competitive. This profile has been described in the literature as representing individuals who attempt to avoid expected criticism by presenting themselves in a superficially friendly and compliant manner but who also are fairly guarded and defensive (Donat, Geczy, et al., 1992; Lorr & Strack, 1990). These individuals tend to feel inadequate and have low self-esteem. Superficially, they may appear to be cooperative and congenial and to be searching for support from others. However, they tend to have their own ideas, and although they may sometimes comply with the wishes of others, they are not likely to enthusiastically support someone else's plan.

These individuals see the world as a competitive place. Because they believe that people are out to satisfy their own needs, they are somewhat mistrustful in their interpersonal relationships; they probably will not share all of their feelings and will harbor suspicions that other people may be trying to use them in some way. Combined with their feelings of inadequacy, the competitive view of the world reinforces the compulsive traits because such individuals feel that they have to avoid making mistakes, which can be used to gain advantage over them.

Individuals with this profile may seem somewhat rigid, unsure, distant, and mistrustful. On the other hand, well-adjusted individuals with this personality cluster may be able to use some of these traits to their benefit. Their disciplined nature may contribute to their being conscientious, hardworking individuals with an ability to pay attention to detail and follow rules. Their dependent inclinations may translate into a certain congeniality and motivation to be liked and appreciated. Finally, their competitiveness may make them realistic individuals who are mature enough to appreciate that people do not usually get something for nothing and that one has to look at the risks and alternatives before making a decision.

Profile 738A: Compulsive–Dependent–Negativistic

Elevated scores on the Compulsive, Dependent, and Negativistic scales indicate a personality style with disciplined, dependent, and negativistic traits. This MCMI profile has been described in the literature as representing individuals who attempt to avoid expected criticism by presenting themselves in a superficially friendly and compliant manner but who are fairly guarded and defensive (Donat, Geczy, et al., 1992; Lorr & Strack, 1990). Individuals with high scores on these scales emphasize the need to avoid making mistakes. Such individuals usually are orderly and plan for the future. They are highly conscientious and well prepared and like to do their work on schedule; they try to be efficient, dependable, industrious, and persistent.

In spite of their perfectionistic inclinations, these individuals fear that they are not capable enough, so that if left completely to their own devices, they would not be able to make ends meet. They would like to have someone else take care of them and provide for their needs, but they tend to resent any control that others may exert as the price for the emotional support. This resentment eliminates the option of becoming dependent on some benefactor.

The conflict of wanting support but fighting control and dependency also makes these individuals likely to change their overall feelings without an obvious reason. At times, they may be friendly and engaging; they then may become angry and resentful. After that, they may feel guilty and contrite. The cycle is completed when they again become friendly and cooperative. In other words, they defend against their insecurities by projecting blame, sometimes on themselves and sometimes on others. A different style brought about by the same basic conflict involves the use of a passive–aggressive defense. In such cases, they try to control their resentment through obstructionistic maneuvers that allow them to vent their anger in covert ways without blatantly jeopardizing the dependent relationship.

The compulsive element in this personality style may make it difficult for such individuals to deal with some aspects of their environment. For instance, situations that can change abruptly from one moment to the next, or situations in which following the rules does not lead to the desired outcome, can be more stressful for these individuals than for other people. However, such individuals are well suited for situations in which it is important to be accurate and meticulous.

Given the type of personality style just described, these clients may find it easier to establish a therapeutic alliance with a professional who is formal, proper, punctual, and predictable. Keeping some distance and allowing clients to control significant parts of the session also would make them feel better. Explanations of the diagnosis, the nature of the "illness," and the expected course of treatment also can be helpful. Moving these individuals from a superficial therapeutic alliance to a more meaningful dependency on the relationship may be difficult. Helping them explore defenses or enhance their tolerance for not being in control also can be difficult to accomplish. These clients will probably demand some support and reassurance in the therapeutic context. It may be useful to set clear limits and to give them as much independence as possible, encouraging them to make their own decisions rather than offering suggestions or recommendations.

Profile 740: Compulsive–Histrionic

Individuals obtaining the compulsive–histrionic personality profile have predominant disciplined and dramatic traits. In some ways, the dramatic and disciplined tendencies conflict with one another. Dramatic individuals, for instance, tend to be emotional, intense in their relationships, and impulsive. Disciplined individuals, on the other hand, overcontrol their emotions, are somewhat distant when relating to others, and carefully plan their behaviors. Individuals who have these two tendencies together often are unable to integrate them well and tend to be conflicted. As a result, they may seem moody or emotionally labile. At times they may be more invested and intense, but they then may fear where this behavior would lead and become more rigid and controlled.

These individuals may tend to emphasize appearances, placing a premium on propriety and dependability and living their lives trying to avoid the appearance of making a mistake. A high value may be placed, for instance, on dressing right, having a clean and orderly house, and so on. They probably try to be conscientious, efficient, dependable, industrious, and persistent.

Nevertheless, there is a side to these individuals that is not all that conscientious or dependable and that often breaks through the controls they try to exert. This is the side that seeks stimulation, excitement, and attention and is colorful and emotional. Thus, at times, these individuals are conspicuous and actively search for affirmation or approval and affection. They often become sensitive to the moods of others and use this knowledge to evoke the reactions they desire. They are highly reactive to their environments and often become deeply involved, but typically this involvement does not last.

Similar individuals are good at making positive first impressions. The ability to react to unexpected situations, the alertness and interest, and the search for attention help make them colorful at parties and similar gatherings. Individuals with this personality style have been found to have good coping strategies (Leaf et al., 1992; Leaf, Alington, et al., 1991; Leaf, DiGiuseppe, et al., 1990; Leaf, Ellis, et al., 1991; Nakao et al., 1992; Retzlaff & Deatherage, 1993) and to be well represented—with scores at a subclinical range—in well-functioning groups (e.g., Lemkau, Purdy, Rafferty, & Rudisill, 1988). However, similar individuals typically have difficulty balancing the disciplined control of their emotions and their need to get attention, stimulation, and affection.

Given this personality style, forming a therapeutic alliance may be easier if the therapist conducts formal and orderly sessions. Even more important may be making sure that clients are the center of attention and receive a great deal of reassurance, affection, and support.

Profile 750: Compulsive–Narcissistic

Elevated scores obtained on the Compulsive and Narcissistic scales indicate the prominence of disciplined and confident personality traits, what Millon (1996) called the "bureaucratic compulsive." Individuals with these traits have been found to have good coping strategies (Leaf et al., 1992; Leaf, Alington, et al., 1991; Leaf, DiGiuseppe, et al., 1990; Leaf, Ellis, et al., 1991; Nakao et al., 1992; Retzlaff & Deatherage, 1993; Strack et al., 1989) and, in some cases, to have an enhanced ability to function. However, this type of personality has been found among spouse-abusing men (Lohr et al., 1988).

The disciplined aspects indicate an emphasis on perfectionism and maintaining good control of the environment. Individuals obtaining elevations on these scales are somewhat defensive and unlikely to admit to failures or mistakes. At times they may be seen as too inflexible, formal, or proper and may relate to others somewhat distantly.

Together with the disciplined elements, these individuals have a tendency to feel that they are more special or capable than others. They are field-independent individuals who rely more on their own feelings or judgments than they do on the opinions of others.

A confident air of self-assurance may be present. They may have trouble accepting someone else's ideas and doing what they are told. Such situations may cause conflict between them and the other people involved.

Given the type of personality style just described, these clients may find it easier to establish a therapeutic alliance with a professional who is formal, proper, punctual, and predictable and able to admire them in some manner. Keeping some distance and allowing them to control significant parts of the session also would make them feel at ease. Other helpful ideas include explaining the diagnosis, the nature of the "illness," and the expected course of treatment. It could be difficult to move such individuals from a superficial therapeutic alliance to a more meaningful dependency on the relationship. Helping them explore psychological defenses or enhance their tolerance for not being in control also could be difficult.

Negativistic Profile Clusters

Profile 8A00: Negativistic

The Negativistic scale describes resentful individuals. This personality style results from holding two assumptions about the world that are difficult to integrate. Such individuals first assume that they need to rely on others because they are not able to do well without their support; they are "people who need people." The second premise is that they cannot afford to depend on others. They may feel that others are not interested enough to be dependable, that the dependence on others is not socially acceptable and will make them look bad, and that others would take advantage of them if they were not constantly on guard.

These two assumptions about life typically bring about one of two different behavior patterns. In the passive–aggressive substyle, the individuals handle conflict by being compliant on the surface but not fully supporting the efforts of others along the way. By contrast, the explosive variant involves a vacillation between feeling lucky and able to get more out of life than expected and feeling cheated or mistreated.

The behavior of negativistic individuals changes accordingly. At times, these individuals treat others in an agreeable and friendly manner, and on other occasions they may be irritable, aggressive, or hostile. At still other times, they may experience guilt and appear eagerly cooperative and remorseful. They frequently may be optimistic and see the future as bright, but this changes, seemingly without reason, into the opposite view. An energetic and productive mood, together with high goals, may characterize them on some occasions, but in other instances these individuals are inclined to lower their goals and become less productive.

Similar individuals can be flexible and changeable, sensitive, and responsive to their environments, but they also may seem moody and unpredictable. Projection is an important defense, but the direction of the projection tends to change from self to other or vice versa. Mostly, these individuals tend to be angry, conflicted, and resentful. They typically are difficult to handle and present some problems wherever they go. A high level of emotional venting as a coping mechanism under stress has been reported (Vollrath et al., 1995). Elevations on the Negativistic scale are accompanied by more elevations on other scales than would be expected for any of the other seven basic personality scales (Chick et al., 1994). The style has been reported to be prominent among alcoholics (Craig et al., 1985), drug addicts (Craig & Olson, 1990), chronic pain clients (Jay et al., 1987), and clients with panic disorders who prematurely terminate treatment (J. Reich, 1990).

Given this personality style, the therapist may find it useful to try not to control these clients in ways that are not necessary. Because clients are bound to resent any control that is placed on them, this tactic can prevent the therapeutic relationship from becoming overly conflictual. These clients also may benefit from learning how they normally operate and tend to project negative feelings onto others.

Profile 8A12A: Negativistic–Schizoid–Avoidant

The negativistic–schizoid–avoidant personality profile is indicative of a negativistic personality style with introversive and avoidant elements. This profile was found to be the most common profile in a group of angry, nonpsychotic White men with psychiatric disorders (Greenblatt & Davis, 1992). Elevations on the Negativistic scale are accompanied by more elevations on other scales than would be expected for any of the other seven basic personality scales (Chick et al., 1994).

This personality style results from holding two assumptions about the world that are difficult to integrate. Such individuals first assume that they need to rely on others because they are not able to do well without their support; they are "people who need people." The second premise is that they cannot afford to depend on others. They typically feel that others are not interested enough to be dependable.

These two assumptions about life typically cause one of two different behavior patterns. In the passive–aggressive substyle, these individuals deal with conflict by being compliant on the surface but not fully supporting the efforts of others along the way. The other variant involves an explosive pattern in which individuals vacillate between feeling that they are lucky and get more out of life than they have a right to expect and feeling cheated or mistreated. Their behavior changes accordingly. At times these individuals are agreeable and friendly; at other times they may be irritable, aggressive, or hostile; at still other times, they may experience guilt and appear overly cooperative and remorseful. These individuals frequently may be optimistic and see the future as bright, but this changes, seemingly without reason, into the opposite view. An energetic and productive mood, together with high goals, may characterize some occasions, but in other instances similar individuals are inclined to lower their goals and become less productive.

These individuals can be flexible and changeable, sensitive, and responsive to their environment, but they also can seem moody and unpredictable. Projection is an important defense that can be aimed at themselves or others. For the most part, though, these individuals tend to be angry, conflicted, and resentful; they often are difficult to handle and may present problems wherever they go.

These individuals also keep an emotional distance from others. To some degree, they are uninterested in interpersonal relations and may not be too adept at understanding and enjoying the subtleties and nuances of emotions. This attribute may lead to their being apathetic about relationships. Moreover, they typically are afraid of rejection. As a result, social situations are uncomfortable and are avoided. Such individuals restrict the number of relationships that they form and tend to have superficial friendships when they exist and alliances that are more like acquaintanceships than friendships.

In trying to establish a therapeutic relationship, it might be useful for the therapist to avoid trying to control these clients in ways that are not necessary. Because the clients probably will resent any control placed on them, the use of minimal controls and directives can prevent the therapeutic relationship from becoming overly conflictual. Clients also may benefit from learning how they normally operate and from exploring their tendency to project negative feelings onto others.

Profile 8A2A0: Negativistic–Avoidant

The negativistic–avoidant profile defines a personality style characterized by resentment and a fear of rejection. Elevations on the Negativistic scale are accompanied by more elevations on other scales than would be expected for any of the other seven basic personality scales (Chick et al., 1994). This profile, with the additional elevation of the Aggressive scale, was part of the most typical profile for individuals diagnosed with a borderline personality disorder (McCann, Flynn, & Gersh, 1992); it was shown to represent 18% of the psychiatric inpatient population, and it is likely that such individuals will have high levels of psychiatric symptoms (Donat, Geczy, et al., 1992). According to Greenblatt and Davis (1992), the negativistic–avoidant style is the most common profile for the angry and psychotic men in their psychiatric sample. This personality style, with the two variants described next, is so prevalent among men with posttraumatic stress disorder that the presence of this personality style has significant diagnostic value for it (Hyer & Boudewyns, 1987; Hyer, Davis, Woods, Albrecht, & Boudewyns, 1992; Hyer, Woods, & Boudewyns, 1991; Hyer, Woods, Boudewyns, Bruno, & O'Leary, 1988; Hyer, Woods, Boudewyns, Harrison, & Tamkin, 1990; McDermott, 1987; Munley, Bains, Frazee, & Schwartz, 1994; Sherwood, Funari, & Piekarski, 1990). This style also has been found among alcoholics (Corbisiero & Reznikoff, 1991; Mayer & Scott, 1988; McMahon & Davidson, 1986b; McMahon, Davidson, & Flynn, 1986; Retzlaff & Bromley, 1991), especially those who are depressed (McMahon & Davidson, 1986b); opiate addicts (Craig et al., 1985); and bulimics (Garner et al., 1990). Unfortunately, this personality style also has been associated with a poor response to treatment (Garner et al., 1990; Hyer, Woods, Bruno, & Boudewyns, 1989; McMahon & Tyson, 1990). Antoni et al. (1985a) found that this personality style represents a subgroup of the clients obtaining the 28/82 MMPI code type.

Individuals with high scores on these scales usually have low self-esteem and see themselves as inadequate or unworthy. Projection is an important part of their psychological defense; the tendency to search for someone to blame is common. In their pessimistic view of the world, other people are typically portrayed as cold and rejecting. Therefore, in spite of their poor self-image, these individuals do not put others up on a pedestal and tend to be aware of the limitations that others may have.

Individuals with this profile have conflicts in their interpersonal relationships. Because they are afraid that they may not be seen in a good light, interpersonal situations are associated with having to take considerable emotional risks. Some individuals are loners who retreat into their own world of fantasy and are nervous and uncomfortable when they are with others. However, they tend to be sensitive individuals who are aware of their own feelings and the emotional reactions they evoke in others.

Together with the conflict over whether they should relate to others, these individuals tend to be moody and resentful. Thus, they may be friendly and cooperative at times, but then they may become obstructionistic, negativistic, or hostile, only to feel guilty later and behave contritely. In some cases, these mood fluctuations are less noticeable, and the conflict is handled through covert obstructionism. This pattern works well because it allows these individuals to cope with the conflict over dependency and their fear of relating to others through the same projective defenses. Thus, the negativistic response allows cooperation without submission and contributes to the formation of relationships that keep others at a distance. The negativism occasionally may have a positive side, because there are some individuals who are able to excel while being a rebel.

Clients such as these are likely to be ambivalent about the prospect of therapy and will probably be uncomfortable during the session. The therapist may be able to make establishing the therapeutic alliance easier by finding ways of minimizing the controls and demands that are made on such clients to make the relationship more conflict free. Although reassurance of acceptance may be necessary, the therapist should not be too warm and embracing, because such an approach may be too threatening to individuals who have to keep some interpersonal distance. In addition, the therapist may have to be tolerant of clients who may be irritable, or even hostile, during the sessions.

Once the therapeutic alliance has been established, the therapist might want to use the relationship to help the clients explore their emotional reactions and develop more productive ways of dealing with their feelings. The therapist has to be careful not to be perceived as being on the other side of the fence and joining the mass of individuals who are, in these clients' view, callous and rejecting.

Profile 8A2A3: Negativistic–Avoidant–Dependent

The negativistic–avoidant–dependent profile combines resentment, fear of rejection, and feelings of inadequacy into a personality style. Elevations on the Negativistic scale are accompanied by more elevations on other scales than would be expected for any of the other seven basic personality scales (Chick et al., 1994). Moreover, the negativistic–avoidant–dependent profile commonly is associated with a borderline personality disorder (Lewis & Harder, 1991). As a variant of the negativistic–avoidant style, this profile commonly has been found with men suffering from posttraumatic stress disorder (Hyer & Boudewyns, 1987; Hyer et al., 1988, 1991, 1992; Hyer, Woods, Boudewyns, et al., 1990; McDermott, 1987; Munley et al., 1994; Piekarski, Sherwood, & Funari, 1993; Sherwood et al., 1990). The style is common in alcoholics (Bartsch & Hoffman, 1985; McMahon et al., 1986, 1989) and has been associated with higher characterological disturbances and a more continuous alcohol abuse use pattern (McMahon, Davidson, Gersh, & Flynn, 1991). The appearance of this profile also is likely in clients with major depression (Stankovic, Libb, Freeman, & Roseman, 1992) and has been associated with a history of suicide attempts (Joffe & Regan, 1989b). Depressed clients with this personality profile, however, are likely to respond to antidepressants (Joffe & Regan, 1989a), and there is evidence that the MCMI profile will change significantly when the depression improves (Joffe & Regan, 1988; Libb, Stankovic, Sokol, et al., 1990).

Individuals with this personality style tend to be moody and to change their overall feelings without any obvious reason. At times, they may be friendly and engaging and then may become angry and resentful; later yet, they may feel guilty and contrite. The cycle is completed when they again become friendly and cooperative. A different substyle of the same basic personality makeup is found in individuals who vent their resentment through obstructionistic maneuvers that allow them to dissipate their anger without threatening their interpersonal support.

Most of these individuals have considerable feelings of insecurity. They tend to feel that others are more gifted, capable, and worthy than they are. However, they may feel that if others got to know them, they would recognize these individuals' lack of value and reject them. They tend to be nervous and uncomfortable when relating to others, because they often feel that other people do not actually like them. By avoiding social relationships altogether, they can avoid some of their discomfort. As a result, these individuals tend to lead lonely lives, fairly distant from the people they see as untrustworthy and judgmental. Similar individuals would like to be appreciated and wish they could relate better than they do.

As clients, these individuals are likely to be highly ambivalent about the prospect of therapy and will probably be uncomfortable during the sessions. However, their dependency may allow the therapist to have some influence and injects a measure of "likeability" (Hyer et al., 1991, p. 179). Establishing a therapeutic alliance may be made easier by finding ways to minimize the controls and demands that are made on such clients. The therapist may need to provide frequent reassurance of acceptance; he or she needs to take care, however, not to make the relationship so warm and embracing that it becomes threatening to the kind of individual who has to be able to keep a certain interpersonal distance. The therapist may have to be tolerant of clients who are irritable or even somewhat hostile.

Once the therapeutic alliance has been established, the therapist should try to use the relationship to help clients explore their emotional reactions and develop more productive ways of dealing with feelings. This plan has to be executed tactfully so that the therapist does not come to be perceived as the enemy and join the mass of individuals who are, in these clients' view, callous and rejecting.

Profile 8A2A6A: Negativistic–Avoidant–Antisocial

The negativistic–avoidant–antisocial personality profile characterizes individuals with conflictual, avoidant, and competitive traits. Elevations on the Negativistic scale are accompanied by more elevations on other scales than would be expected for any of the other seven basic personality scales (Chick et al., 1994). As a variant of the negativistic–avoidant style, this profile has been found commonly in men suffering from posttraumatic stress disorder (Hyer & Boudewyns 1987; Hyer et al., 1988, 1991, 1992; Hyer, Woods, Boudewyns, et al., 1990; McDermott, 1987; Munley et al., 1994; Piekarski et al., 1993; Sherwood et al., 1990). This personality style represented about 10% of a sample of men undergoing treatment for spousal abuse (Hamberger & Hastings, 1986).

Probably the most predominant feature of this personality style is an ambivalence in relating to others. Similar individuals have low self-esteem and feel that they are not particularly able or gifted. They tend to generalize this assessment to also include other people. Thus, even though they do not feel good about themselves, they are inclined to put others down and to judge others as being just as unworthy.

Such individuals usually feel that they need the help of others to make ends meet. However, they have difficulties accepting the help of others, because they see the world as a competitive place where everyone is struggling to obtain the same limited benefits. For them, relying on others risks the possibility that people will take advantage of their trust and use the relationship for their own purposes.

These individuals tend to be extremely sensitive about negative feedback. They fear that others may form poor opinions of them and would not value their friendship. The end result is a constant vigilance for signs of rejection when they are in social situations. They experience interpersonal relationships as anxiety producing and uncomfortable. Because they tend to be nervous when they are relating to others, they often choose to avoid this stress by keeping to themselves. When they do relate, they are distant, superficial, and apprehensive.

These individuals typically experience a great deal of anger. Some handle their anger through obstructionistic maneuvers. More typically, however, these are explosive individuals who demonstrate hostile affectivity, fearlessness, and vindictiveness. Hyer et al. (1991) spoke of this personality style as working on the stance that "I'm-gonna-get-you-before-you-get-me" (p. 179). The hostile feelings eventually may subside and leave them in a contrite mood, so that they will try to be friendly and cooperative once more, only to be overcome by resentment later on.

When treating clients with this personality style, the therapist should consider that such clients are likely to be ambivalent about therapy and will be uncomfortable during the sessions. The therapist may be able to facilitate establishing a therapeutic alliance by minimizing the controls and demands made on these clients. However, the therapist should not be too warm and embracing, because this may be threatening to individuals who have to be able to keep some interpersonal distance. In addition, the therapist may have to be tolerant of clients who may be irritable or even somewhat hostile.

Once the therapeutic alliance has been established, the relationship could be used to help the clients explore their emotional reactions and develop more productive ways of dealing with their feelings. The therapist should be careful not to be perceived as being on the other side of the fence and joining the mass of people who are, in these clients' view, callous and rejecting.

Profile 8A37: Negativistic–Dependent–Compulsive

A combination of resentment, feelings of inadequacy, and a perfectionistic attitude represent the hallmarks of the negativistic–dependent–compulsive personality style. Individuals who have this kind of personality do not have a high regard for their abilities or accomplishments and feel that they need the help of others to make ends meet. Their low self-image is partly the result of their high expectations. These individuals strive to lead a flawless life. They have set ideas about how things should be done, and seldom will anyone be able to meet those expectations. Their world is highly idealistic and devoid of heroes, because neither they nor their cohorts can measure up. This kind of situation leaves them in a bind. On one hand, they feel inadequate to meet their own needs and would like to have another person on whom they could depend. However, they have reservations about the abilities of others and often object to the kind of help that they might receive.

As with many individuals bearing this personality style, the psychological adaptation to these forces is evident in the clinical picture. At times these individuals may seem cooperative and in search of help, attention, and reassurance. However, they also come across as proper, formal, and controlling. Although occasionally they may seem obstructionistic and angry, this anger will be kept well under control and will tend to be vented in covert ways. Elevations on the Negativistic scale are accompanied by more elevations on other scales than would be expected for any of the other seven basic personality scales (Chick et al., 1994).

Profile 8A40: Negativistic–Histrionic

The negativistic–histrionic, or "tempestuous histrionic" (Millon, 1996), personality style describes an individual who is both resentful and dramatic. [These individuals do not have a high opinion of themselves or others. Some individuals who are insecure about their own abilities can obtain peace of mind by finding someone on whom they can depend. The interpersonal attitude that the negativistic–histrionic person has, however, tends to eliminate the option of obtaining help as a viable alternative. Similar individuals feel that dependency on others is not acceptable, that the dependency would make them look bad, and that eventually people would criticize them for needing this type of relationship. As a result, they probably face an unsolvable approach–avoidance conflict: If they do not depend on others, they feel uncomfortable because they fear that they will not be able to provide for their needs. If they do form a dependent relationship, they do not have to worry about making ends meet, but they will become uncomfortable about the type of position in which they will be placed.

The behavior of individuals with the negativistic–histrionic personality style usually fluctuates. At times they may be friendly and congenial. Soon, however, they resent others and may become inappropriately aggressive or even hostile; this also may change and turn into guilt and repentance. The friendly and congenial behavior that may follow completes the behavioral cycle. By contrast, other individuals with a similar personality work out their conflicts with a more stable pattern of behavior. This pattern involves appearing to be friendly and congenial on the surface while covertly playing a negativistic and obstructionistic role.

Individuals obtaining similar scores have a great need for attention and affection. They constantly seek stimulation and conspicuousness with a dramatic flair. These individuals often easily express their feelings and have fairly intense, short-lived emotions. When they are at their best, they may appear outgoing, charming, and sophisticated.

Elevations on the Negativistic scale are accompanied by more elevations on other scales than would be expected for any of the other seven basic personality scales (Chick et al., 1994). Furthermore, research has shown that about one third of the alcoholics in treatment have a negativistic–histrionic personality style (Donat, 1988; Donat et al., 1991). This personality was the predominant style among clients with a panic disorder (J. Reich, 1990). The style was found with many individuals who obtained the 78/87 profile code in the MMPI (Antoni et al., 1987).

Given this personality style, it may be best to avoid placing any controls on these clients beyond the minimum. Because these clients are likely to resent any control, this tactic can prevent the therapeutic relationship from becoming overly conflictual. A supportive relationship would be one in which the client is the center of attention. The therapist should have tolerance for displays of emotion and be able to accept a certain amount of conflict. The therapist must also take care to prepare these clients for the times ahead when they become angry with the therapist, the treatment has become mundane, and they are ready to terminate. Such clients also may benefit from learning how they normally operate and about their tendency to project negative feelings onto others.

Profile 8A56A: Negativistic–Narcissistic–Antisocial

The negativistic–narcissistic–antisocial personality profile defines a conflictual personality style with confident and competitive traits. The combination often leads to resentments and difficulty in handling anger. Many individuals who have the same pattern of scores appear conflicted and moody and change their feelings and behaviors from one moment to the next. They seem irritable, unstable, or erratic and typically have a low tolerance for frustration. Similar individuals may vacillate between being enthusiastic and cheerful or resentful and ornery. At times they may feel guilty and try to be friendly and cooperative, but they soon start resenting others and become critical, angry, or spiteful. Instead of being moody or explosive, individuals with this pattern of MCMI scores vent their resentment by adopting an oppositional pattern of behavior. Their anger then may be less obvious, but in their negativism, irresponsibility, and passivity, they "get even" by making others angry.

Part of the resentment these individuals experience comes from the perception that they are better than the people around them. They see the world as a competitive place where every person has to fight for the same limited rewards. However, they are unable to integrate these two assumptions about the world, because if they were truly superior, they should have their needs fulfilled without having to compete with "lesser" human beings. It is this conflict and lack of integration that often lead to whatever problems they present in psychological functioning.

This personality style has been found to be common among drug abusers (Craig & Olson, 1990). Elevations on the Negativistic scale are accompanied by more elevations on other scales than would be expected for any of the other seven basic personality scales (Chick et al., 1994). On the positive side, individuals with this personality style are independent people who do not cling to others. They tend to be proud and to avoid situations in which they may be humiliated, an issue that may be important for them.

In the light of this personality style, the therapist should pay attention to these clients' narcissistic needs if a strong therapeutic alliance is to be established. Such clients may tend, for instance, to reject any interpretation that sounds critical. Feeling threatened, they may become angry and blame the therapist for real or imagined faults or mistakes. Keeping clients feeling that the therapist is on their side and avoiding competitive or conflictual dealings will require tact and effort. The therapist must strike a balance between being unconditionally supportive and dealing with these clients' issues in an aggressive manner. Often, such a balance will require the therapist to allow clients much control over the relationship and to limit the areas of exploration in which negative feedback is given.

Profile 8A6A0: Negativistic–Antisocial

The negativistic–antisocial personality style is characterized by resentful and competitive traits, a combination that leads to conflicted and moody individuals who are inclined to change their feelings and behaviors from one moment to the next. Similarly scoring individuals are upset easily and have a low tolerance for frustration. At times they may feel guilty and try to be friendly and cooperative, but they soon start resenting others and become more critical, which may even have an angry or spiteful element.

This kind of vacillation theoretically results from conflictual views about the self and the environment. On one hand, such individuals tend to be aware of their own limitations and may feel that they need to depend on others to provide for some of their needs. On the other hand, they seem to view the world as a competitive place, a rat race in which one has to be strong, dominant, adequate, and willful to survive. These individuals typically suppress the softer emotions of kindness, generosity, and gentility because of the belief that these emotions will make them weak and vulnerable to the exploitation of others. In their minds, the way to survive is to be assertive, energetic, self-reliant, and on guard. They feel that they must be aware of the possible manipulations of others and try to gain the upper hand whenever possible. Elevations on the Negativistic scale are accompanied by more elevations on other scales than would be expected for any of the other seven basic personality scales (Chick et al., 1994).

In the light of the negativistic–antisocial personality style, the therapist may want to remain unintrusive, being careful not to take a position among the options available unless necessary. This stance will encourage clients to make their own decisions and will decrease conflict in the therapeutic relationship. The therapist may need to provide interpretations when clients use maladaptive projective mechanisms. However, any confrontation has to be done carefully, because these clients will be inclined to perceive the feedback in a competitive manner and fight the insights that are offered. The therapist must protect the therapeutic alliance and do whatever is necessary to keep these clients feeling that the therapist is on their side.

Profile 8A6A4: Negativistic–Antisocial–Histrionic

Resentful, competitive, and dramatic elements characterize individuals with the negativistic–antisocial–histrionic personality profile. Such individuals tend to be angry and moody and are inclined to change their feelings and behaviors from one moment to the next. They typically are perceived as obstructionistic, are inclined to approach life by turning everything around, and seldom accept views in the manner in which they were presented.

There often is a conflictual aspect to these individuals' oppositionism; they typically are aggressive, if not hostile, in their interactions with others. Similarly scoring individuals tend to emphasize their ability to remain independent and are not inclined to do what others tell them to do. They are competitive by nature and may be seen as behaving in a callous manner in the struggle to get ahead of everyone else. They are likely to be mistrustful, to question the motives of others, and to assume that they have to be vigilant and on guard if they are to protect themselves. These individuals tend to blame others for anything that goes wrong. They are "touchy" individuals: Excitable and easily upset, they are inclined to treat others in a rough or mean manner and to become angry whenever they are confronted or opposed.

The anger and emotional lability that such clients seem to have theoretically results from conflictual views regarding the self and the environment. On one hand, they tend to be aware of their own limitations and may feel that they need to depend on others to provide for some of their needs. On the other hand, they seem to view the world as a competitive place in which one has to be strong, dominant, adequate, and willful to survive. They may be inclined to suppress the softer emotions of kindness, generosity, and gentility, feeling that these emotions will make them weak and vulnerable to the exploitation of others. These individuals typically are vigilant of the possible manipulations of others and try to gain the upper hand whenever possible.

These individuals' negativism may be fueled partly by their histrionic tendencies. They seem to need to be the center of attention and may become easily bored with any situation that becomes routine. Their contrariness probably serves to fulfill their need for attention—albeit in an abrasive and unproductive manner—because uncooperative behaviors are likely to be noticed. In fact, the oppositionism and the search for attention may create a vicious cycle that may be hard to break, because their oppositionism tends to meet several of their psychological needs. Elevations on the Negativistic scale are accompanied by more elevations on other scales than would be expected for any of the other seven basic personality scales (Chick et al., 1994).

Profile 8A70: Negativistic–Compulsive

The negativistic–compulsive personality style may be described as resentful and disciplined. A variant of this personality style (code 871, with the Schizoid scale also elevated) was found to be the modal profile for the angry and psychotic Black psychiatric clients (Greenblatt & Davis, 1992). Elevations on the Negativistic scale are accompanied by more elevations on other scales than would be expected for any of the other seven basic personality scales (Chick et al., 1994).

The negativistic–compulsive style results from holding two assumptions about the world that are difficult to integrate. These individuals first assume that they need to rely on others because they are not able to do well without their support. The second premise is that they should strive toward perfection on their own. These two assumptions about life typically bring about one of two different behavior patterns.

In the passive–aggressive substyle, the person handles conflict by being compliant on the surface but not fully supporting the efforts of others along the way. By contrast, the moody variant involves a vacillation between feeling lucky and being able to get more out of life than expected and feeling cheated or mistreated. The behavior changes accordingly. At times these individuals treat others in an agreeable and friendly manner, but they also may be irritable or hostile. Still at other times, these individuals may experience guilt and appear eagerly cooperative and remorseful. An energetic and productive mood, together with high goals, may characterize them on some occasions, but in other instances these individuals are inclined to lower their goals and become less productive.

Such individuals place a premium on avoiding mistakes. They tend to be orderly and plan for the future. They prepare in a conscientious manner and try to do the work on schedule. They strive to be efficient, dependable, industrious, and persistent. They often relate in an overly respectful and ingratiating manner, but they may be somewhat rigid, perfectionistic, and demanding. They have significant problems making decisions by themselves.

Negativistic–compulsive individuals can be moody and irritable. Projection is an important defense, but the direction of the blame tends to change from the self to others. Mostly, these individuals tend to be resentful and conflicted. They typically are difficult to handle and present some problems wherever they go.

Given this personality style, it may be useful to try not to control these clients in ways that are not necessary. Because these clients are bound to resent any control that is placed on them, this tactic can prevent the therapeutic relationship from becoming overly conflictual. They also may benefit from learning how they normally operate and tend to project negative feelings onto others.

Assessment of Psychopathology

This chapter will focus on the use of the Millon Clinical Multiaxial Inventory (MCMI) in assessing the different psychopathological patterns. The diagnostic entities from the fourth edition of the *Diagnostic and Statistical Manual of Mental Disorders (DSM–IV)* will be used to organize the information, as will the *DSM–IV* distinction between clinical syndromes (Axis I) and personality disorders (Axis II).

As opposed to other chapters, this chapter includes many studies done with previous versions of the MCMI. There are several reasons for this policy. First, the findings obtained with previous versions typically revealed information that transcends the instrument being used. In a recent article, for instance, the MCMI–I was used to characterize elderly benzodiazepine abusers (Petrovic et al., 2002). The study mostly revealed the other problems these individuals had, in addition to the benzodiazepine addiction. The results were so logical (see later discussion of this study for more details) that, if the study were to be repeated with any other instrument, the author would expect all of the findings to be replicated. If these studies were discarded, a great deal of useful information would be lost.

Second, the MCMI–III is so highly correlated with previous versions of the test (see chap. 8) that similar findings would be expected on the basis of that relationship. This argument would not be so valid if the studies were examining the instrument itself, such as the psychometric studies covered in chapter 3. However, the work included in this chapter deals with different aspects of psychopathology; these are aspects that—if the instrument is valid—would be expected to endure.

Finally, probably for the reasons already noted, journals have continued to publish articles on studies using previous editions of the MCMI. If the policy was made to use only MCMI–III articles, this book would be disregarding a good amount of the MCMI literature that is emerging.

Clinical Syndromes and Personality Disorders

As useful as the distinction between the two axes may be, it is a distinction that is often difficult to make (Hirschfeld, 1993). Part of the problem is that many of the Axis II prototypes have elements in common with the Axis I disorders. The borderline personality disorder, for instance, includes affective instability, which also is part of the Axis I affective disorders (Widiger, 1989). Presumably as a result of this commonality, patients with affective disorders are likely to obtain an elevation on the Borderline scale of the MCMI (H. J. Jackson, Rudd, Gazis, & Edwards, 1991). To consider another example, the dependent personality disorder is characterized partly by the kind of helplessness and feelings of inadequacy that also constitute an important aspect of many types of depression (Overholser, 1991). It should not be surprising, then, that depressed patients generally have elevated scores on the Dependent scale on the MCMI–I (G. E. Alexander, Choca, Bresolin, et al., 1987; G. E. Alexander, Choca, DeWolfe, et al., 1987).

Also blurring the distinction between the two axes is the way some disorders affect the individual so as to increase his or her chances to meet criteria for other disorders: There is a reasonable amount of literature showing that the emotional *state* of the individual alters the personality *traits* that are demonstrated (e.g., Hirschfeld et al., 1983). Personality traits are often thought to predispose the individual to developing certain clinical syndromes (e.g., schizoid or avoidant personality styles may increase a person's tendency toward schizophrenia; Millon, 1981). Whenever there are more specific data about the interaction between the two axes of the *DSM–IV*, the information is included in the discussion of the disorder in this chapter.

The MCMI profile of people suffering from a *DSM–IV* syndrome typically has several elevations, more than would be expected if the profile were to reflect only the primary diagnosis. B. K. Campbell and Stark (1991), for instance, gave the MCMI–I to 100 consecutive clients admitted to a community outpatient drug program. The substance abusers obtained significantly higher means for 8 of the 20 scales compared with those of the normative sample. In some cases, the multiple elevations may be indicative of comorbidities, additional psychiatric problems that merit professional attention. In other cases, however, the multiple elevations may be attributable to a lack of selectivity of MCMI scales or to the natural clustering of particular pathological traits. Thus, an elevation on the Alcohol Abuse scale is almost expected in the case of a cocaine addict, because this scale shares items with the Drug Abuse scale and because the majority of cocaine addicts also have abused alcohol. Diagnosticians have to develop the skill of deciding what part of the profile should be seen as part and parcel of a particular diagnosis and what findings are indicative of other problems. In addition to the history and other diagnostic data, clinicians can use the knowledge of what MCMI scales tend to be elevated for particular disorders. This information is offered in Tables 7.1 and 7.2. The interpretive logic would be that if the profile in question looks similar to the modal profile for a particular disorder, the findings should not be seen as pointing to additional problems.

This chapter discusses personality disorders first because many of them are related to the personality styles discussed in the previous chapter. Along with the *DSM–IV* clinical syndromes, articles that have dealt with pathologies

Table 7.1

Expected Primary and Secondary Elevations on the Millon Clinical Multiaxial Inventory for the Different Personality Disorders

Disorder	Highest scale	Other elevated scales
Schizoid	Schizoid	Avoidant, Schizotypal
Avoidant	Avoidant	Schizoid, Negativistic, Self-Defeating, Dysthymia
Dependent	Dependent	Avoidant, Self-Defeating
Histrionic	Histrionic	Narcissistic
Narcissistic	Narcissistic	Histrionic, Aggressive
Antisocial	Antisocial	Narcissistic, Negativistic, Aggressive, Borderline, Paranoid, Drug Abuse
Compulsive	Compulsive	
Negativistic	Negativistic	Aggressive
Schizotypal	Avoidant	Schizoid, Negativistic, Self-Defeating, Schizotypal, Borderline, Anxiety, Dysthymia, Thought Disorder, Major Depression
Borderline	Borderline	Avoidant, Negativistic, Self-Defeating, Anxiety, Dysthymia
Paranoid	Aggressive	Narcissistic, Antisocial, Compulsive, Paranoid, Anxiety, Dysthymia

Table 7.2

Expected Primary and Secondary Elevations on the Millon Clinical Multiaxial Inventory for the Different Clinical Syndromes

Problem area	Highest scale	Other elevated scales
Anxiety	Anxiety	Avoidant, Negativistic, Self-Defeating
Somatoform	Somatoform	Anxiety, Histrionic, Compulsive
Eating Disorder	Borderline	Schizoid, Avoidant, Dependent, Schizotypal
Mania	Hypomania	Histrionic, Narcissistic, Antisocial, Paranoid, Drug Abuse, Psychotic Delusion
Dysthymia	Dysthymia	Avoidant, Negativistic
Alcohol Abuse	Alcohol Abuse	Negativistic, Antisocial, Dependent, Anxiety, Dysthymia, Drug Abuse
Drug Abuse	Drug Abuse	Alcohol Abuse, Antisocial, Negativistic, Narcissistic, Histrionic
Schizophrenia	Avoidant	Schizotypal, Schizoid, Dependent, Narcissistic, Negativistic, Self-Defeating
Major Depression	Dysthymia	Major Depression, Anxiety, Avoidant, Dependent, Self-Defeating, Negativistic
Delusion	Psychotic Delusion	Psychotic Thinking, Paranoid, Narcissistic, Aggressive

that are not specifically recognized *DSM–IV* diagnoses, such as partner abuse and thought disorders, also are reviewed.

Personality Disorders

Table 7.1 shows a modification of the data that Millon (1987) presented for the typical patient suffering from the different personality disorders, adjusted with any relevant literature found (e.g., Lewis & Harder, 1991; Retzlaff et al., 1994; Swirsky-Sacchetti et al., 1993). Knowledge of such typical profiles may be helpful in making decisions about patients' diagnoses. The reader should remember that there is much variance within any diagnostic group. When a protocol is obtained that does not fit typical patients within a diagnostic category, the finding can often be used to further understand the patient and does not necessarily mean that the person does not suffer from the particular clinical syndrome.

A person can have a personality disorder in one of two ways. Seven of the 10 *DSM–IV* personality disorders constitute syndromes that can be seen as exaggerations of basic personality styles. In other words, the clusters of personality traits that have been discussed in this book sometimes occur in a pathologically exaggerated or rigid fashion. Such a pattern can then be classified as a personality disorder.

In addition, there are three *DSM–IV* personality disorders that are not represented among the personality styles: the borderline, the schizotypal, and the paranoid. There are also MCMI scales for personality disorders that are part of Millon's theory but are not included in the *DSM–IV*. The MCMI–II contains two such scales (the Aggressive and the Self-Defeating scales), and the MCMI–III additionally includes the Depressive personality scale. All six of these lifelong dysfunctional characterological tendencies, in the author's opinion, do not have a "normal" or nonpathological equivalent; in other words, the pattern is intrinsically pathological, even in cases in which the disorder is not severe.

Most research in which the MCMI personality scales were used has dealt with the validity of the scales or the characterological issues related to particular clinical syndromes. (These studies were discussed in chap. 3.) The investigations included in this chapter are those that have examined personality styles or personality disorders in their own right. Thus, the rest of this section will review studies in which the MCMI was used to investigate a personality disorder.

To start with, Overholser, Kabakoff, and Norman (1989) compared individuals with a significant elevation on the Dependency scale with other psychiatric inpatients. They reported that this group was unlikely to be married and was more likely to have been hospitalized repeatedly for psychiatric problems. Overholser (1991) also found that patients displaying elevated levels of dependency over a 6-week period tended to report a mild but persistently elevated level of depression. The findings were said to agree with previous evidence relating depression to dependency (see the section on affective disorders).

Looking at whether particular professions attract different kinds of characterological pathology, Patrick (1990) evaluated the incidence of pathological narcissism in the clergy. The scores she obtained with the MCMI–I Narcissistic scale generally failed to reveal the presence of narcissistic personalities. On the other hand, judging from the MCMI–I, such narcissism is more likely to occur among adults who are firstborn or only children (Curtis & Cowell, 1993).

DiGiuseppe, Robin, Szeszko, and Primavera (1995) reported a cluster analysis of individuals presumed to have a narcissistic personality disorder on the basis of an elevation of the MCMI–II Narcissistic scale scores. As has been noted, the present author does not see the mere elevation of an MCMI scale as showing the presence of a personality disorder. To this author, the fact that many of the participants had higher scores on personality scales other than the Narcissistic scale made the findings even more uninterpretable.

Hart et al., (1991) examined men with an antisocial personality disorder and found support for Millon's picture of the scores these individuals would obtain on the MCMI–II. The convicts they tested obtained their highest elevation on the Antisocial scale, but psychopathy also was associated with elevations on the Narcissistic, Aggressive, and Drug Abuse scales.

Data gathered from a group of borderline patients suggest that difficulties with interpersonal attachments are related to the severe personality scales of the MCMI–I. Specifically, avoidant attachment difficulties may be related to elevated scores on the Borderline scale, whereas difficulties consisting of resistant or hostile attachments are correlated modestly with the Schizotypal and Borderline scales (Sperling, Sharp, & Fishler, 1991).

Studies examining the MCMI–I elevations of obsessive–compulsive patients suggested a personality constellation of avoidant, dependent, and passive–aggressive features (Joffe et al., 1988; J. S. Silverman & Loychik, 1990). Fals-Stewart and Lucente (1993) cluster analyzed the MCMI–I results of 137 obsessive–compulsive patients and found four cluster types that were reasonably well defined and differentiated. The authors found that patients with little character pathology and those with dependent and compulsive features did best in behavioral treatment.

Finally, members of the Belgian military found to have longstanding authority problems were shown to have a higher rate of personality scale elevations on the MCMI–I (62%) than a control group with acute authority problems (11%). The Negativistic scale was the most prevalent elevation (42%) with the longstanding authority problem sample (Vereycken, Vertommen, & Corveleyn, 2002).

Clinical Syndromes

Table 7.2 shows the author's rendition of the data Millon presented for typical patients suffering from the different clinical syndromes, adjusted with any other data found (e.g., Craig, 1993a; Craig, Kuncel, & Olson, 1994;

Craig & Weinberg, 1992a, 1992b; Hogg et al., 1990; Hyer, Carson, Nixon, Tamkin, & Saucer, 1987; Kennedy et al., 1990; Retzlaff et al., 1994; Simonsen, Haslund, Larsen, & Borup, 1992; Wetzler, Khadivi, & Oppenheim, 1995; Yeager, DiGiuseppe, Resweber, & Leaf, 1992). As before, knowledge of such typical profiles may be helpful, but considerable variance exists within any diagnostic group.

In the remainder of this chapter, I review the literature on the MCMI for the different Axis I disorders. Clinicians typically have hypothesized about underlying or predisposing personalities behind most clinical syndromes, and the MCMI has proved to be a good instrument for testing some of the hypotheses. When such data are available, the findings are presented first, followed by a discussion of any other information on that disorder.

Attention-Deficit-Hyperactivity Disorder (ADHD)

May and Bos (2000) gave the MCMI–II to 104 adults with ADHD. Participants with uncomplicated ADHD were characterized by an elevation on the Histrionic scale. Those who, in addition to ADHD, met criteria for an oppositional defiant disorder tended to also have elevations on the Narcissistic, Aggressive, and Negativistic scales. Patients with a comorbid clinical syndrome (e.g., mood disorder, anxiety disorder) were found to have elevations on other scales as well.

Schizophrenic Disorders

Hogg et al. (1990) investigated the comorbidity of personality disorders in a sample of 40 patients with recent-onset schizophrenia. Using the personality scales of the MCMI–I, they found elevations on the Dependent, Narcissistic, and Avoidant scales. Also using the MCMI–I, Greenblatt and Davis (1992) found the Avoidant scale to be effective in predicting psychosis.

Anxiety Disorders

Alnaes and Torgersen (1990) compared a group of 84 patients with anxiety disorders with other outpatients using the MCMI–I. They reported that the individuals with "pure" anxiety disorders tended to be more schizotypal than depressed patients. The individuals with "pure" anxiety disorders were more schizoid and avoidant and less histrionic than patients with other mental disorders.

Wetzler, Kahn, Cahn, van Praag, & Asnis (1990) compared patients with panic disorders with depressed and normal individuals. The findings showed that the patients with panic disorders scored higher than normal individuals on the Schizoid, Avoidant, Negativistic, Schizotypal, Borderline, Anxiety, Somatic Preoccupation, Dysthymic, Psychotic Thinking, and Psychotic Depression scales of the MCMI–I. The patients scored significantly lower than the normal respondents on the Narcissistic and Compulsive scales (Wetzler et al., 1990). Finally, there seems to be a high level of dependency on the MCMI–I among individuals suffering from phobias (J. Reich, Noyes, & Troughton, 1987).

Dissociative Disorders

College students scoring high on the Dissociative Experience scale (Bernstein & Putnam, 1986) were found to have a significantly higher score on the Borderline scale of the MCMI–I compared with students scoring low on the Dissociative Experience scale (Ross, Ryan, Voigt, & Eide, 1991). A group of 96 patients with a dissociative identity (multiple personality) disorder were found to have elevations on the Avoidant, Self-Defeating, Borderline, and Negativistic scales of the MCMI–II. Elevated Axis I scales have included Dysthymia and Major Depression (Ellason et al., 1995; Fink & Golinkoff, 1990). The MCMI–II was able to differentiate between the dissociative identity disorder and schizophrenia but did poorly when the differentiation was between the dissociative identity disorder and a borderline personality (Fink & Golinkoff, 1990).

Affective Disorders

In this section, I examine the relationship between personality traits and affective disorders. This relationship has been used to develop notions about the causes of the disorder, and a completely different approach uses the information about personality traits to classify and understand different types of affective disorders.

The association between personality traits and affective symptomatology has been well established in the literature (see Bronisch & Klerman, 1991, for a review). A state of depression or a manic state is likely to elevate some personality scales. For this reason, there is a need to characterize the typical test results during the acute episode as well as during remission.

Work with previous versions of the MCMI showed depressed patients appearing more schizoid, avoidant, dependent, and negativistic and less narcissistic than their nondepressed cohorts (G. E. Alexander, Choca, Bresolin, et al., 1987; G. E. Alexander, Choca, DeWolfe, et al., 1987; Hyer, Harrison, & Jacobsen, 1987; Libb, Stankovic, Freeman, et al., 1990; J. Reich & Troughton, 1988; Stankovic, Libb, Freeman, & Roseman, 1992; Wetzler et al., 1990, 1995). Manic bipolar patients have been found to be more histrionic, narcissistic, antisocial, and compulsive than their euthymic cohorts on both of the previous versions of the MCMI (G. E. Alexander, Choca, DeWolfe, et al., 1987; Alnaes & Torgersen, 1991; Turley, Bates, Edwards, & Jackson, 1992; Wall, Schuckit, Mungas, & Ehlers, 1990; Wetzler & Marlowe, 1993). Showing the other side of the coin, Joffe and Regan (1988) reported reductions of scores on six of the personality scales of the MCMI–I (i.e., Schizoid, Avoidant, Dependent, Negativistic, Schizotypal, and Borderline) when complete remission was achieved with depressed patients.

Judging from these findings, individuals suffering from affective disorders may have elevations on the measures of personality traits on the MCMI, both during the episode and after remission. Several theories have been proposed to account for such findings. The *common cause theory* proposes a common element, such as a chemical imbalance, that is responsible for both the personality traits and the mood disorder. A family history of depression, for instance, has been found to be associated with higher scores on the Dependent and Compulsive scales of the MCMI–I among depressed patients (Joffe & Regan, 1991).

According to another explanation, personality traits are presumed to be subclinical signs of the mood disorder (the *spectrum model*), and the personality is seen as predisposing the individual to the affective pathology. It also is possible that personality and mood are independent but capable of affecting each other (the *pathoplasty model*), or that the personality traits are scars that are left over from the affective disorder episodes (for reviews of these models, see Farmer & Nelson-Gray, 1990; Klein, Wonderlich, & Shea, 1993). As is now well recognized, this etiological controversy will not be resolved until a longitudinal study is available that assesses participants premorbidly, during the episode, and after remission (Klein, Wanderlich, & Shea, 1993).

Another way of looking at the relationship between affective disorders and personality styles is to conceptualize the personality elements as defining different depressive styles. J. O. Goldberg, Segal, Vella, and Shaw (1989), for instance, found two such styles after administering the MCMI to depressed patients. The first of these styles was characterized by an elevated Negativistic scale on the MCMI–I and was seen as being similar to Beck's (1983) "autonomous" depressive. Such individuals typically feel misunderstood and unappreciated; they tend to anticipate disappointment and to precipitate failures through obstructive behaviors. By contrast, the other style was marked by elevations on the Dependent and Avoidant scales of the MCMI and was seen as representing Beck's "sociotropic" subtype. These individuals are self-effacing, noncompetitive people who seek relationships in which they can lean on someone for guidance and security.

Overholser (1991; Overholser et al., 1989) examined the difference between dependent and nondependent depressed individuals. Their data indicated that dependent depressed respondents were more likely to be older and female than nondepressed psychiatric control respondents, were more likely to demonstrate reduced activity and energy levels, and were more likely to have more pathological views of success and happiness than nondependent depressed respondents.

In another study, individuals who suffered from seasonal depression were compared with other depressed individuals. The findings showed that the seasonally depressed individuals had less of an elevation on the Schizotypal and Avoidant scales of the MCMI–I and obtained higher scores on the Narcissistic scale. The findings were interpreted as indicating a lower level of psychopathology for the seasonal group (Schuller, Bagby, Levitt, & Joffe, 1993).

In terms of the psychopathology scales of previous MCMIs, depression typically was associated with scales measuring anxious–fearful syndromes, as opposed to the extraverted–projective syndromes that are more typical comorbidities of the manic group. Thus, depressed patients typically scored higher than other respondents on the Schizotypal, Borderline, Anxiety, Dysthymia, and Psychotic Depression scales and lower on the Aggressive, Paranoid, Bipolar, Drug Abuse, and Delusional Disorder scales (Wetzler et al., 1990; Wetzler & Marlowe, 1993). The manic group tended to score higher than other patients on the Paranoid, Hypomania, Drug Abuse, and Psychotic Delusion scales on both the MCMI–I and MCMI–II (Wetzler & Marlowe, 1993). The modal profile for depressed individuals on the MCMI–III shows elevations on the Depressive Personality, Anxiety, Dysthymia, and Major Depression scales (Piersma & Boes, 1997b).

Eating Disorders

Norman, Blais, and Herzog (1993) used MCMI–I data to support their claim that 84% of patients with eating disorders suffered from a personality disorder. The fact that practically every person who takes the MCMI will obtain an elevation on at least one of the personality scales (see the discussion in chap. 6) renders that finding relatively useless.

Tisdale et al. (1990) compared a group of bulimic individuals with psychiatric patients who did not have an eating disorder and with a group of normal control individuals. The data showed that bulimic respondents obtained significantly higher scores on the Dependent, Avoidant, and Schizoid scales; their average score on the Narcissistic scale was significantly lower than the average score of the other two groups. The average Base Rate (BR) score obtained by the bulimic patients on the Dependent scale was 75, indicating that most of them had a dependent personality style. The investigators considered their findings to be consistent with previous descriptions of bulimic women as dependent, unassertive, eager to please, and concerned with social approval. This contention has been supported, at least in part, by other studies with the MCMI–I (Kennedy et al., 1990; Norman et al., 1993; Pendleton et al., 1991; Schmidt, Sanders, Burdick, & Lohr, 1991) and the MCMI–II (Wiederman & Pryor, 1997). Anorexic women, on the other hand, are prone to have elevations on the Compulsive scale of the MCMI–II (Wiederman & Pryor, 1997).

In terms of the pathology scales, elevations on the Borderline, Anxiety, and Dysthymia scales have been found among bulimic individuals before treatment (Garner et al., 1990; Kennedy et al., 1990). Elevations on the Schizoid and Schizotypal scales were found with the larger group, which included participants with both bulimia and anorexia (Kennedy et al., 1990).

Caution should be exercised so as not to overdiagnose personality disorders during an acute phase of the disorder. The MCMI–I scores have been found to change considerably after the acute phase has resolved (Garner et al., 1990; Kennedy et al., 1990).

Lundholm, Pellegreno, Wolins, and Graham (1989) compared a group of women receiving treatment for bulimia with a normal control group. They found that 27 items from the MCMI–I, mostly dealing with social withdrawal and depression, successfully differentiated the two groups.

Substance Abuse

A great deal of work has been done with the MCMI and substance abusers. This review will discuss first the cluster analyses of MCMI scores with alcoholics. The findings of these studies have much clinical utility, because they allow the practitioner to characterize different types of alcoholics using the MCMI and possibly to become more sophisticated regarding the treatment plan of such individuals. MCMI studies examining other aspects of alcoholism are presented after the discussion of the cluster analyses. The same approach will be used to review the studies dealing with drug abuse, with the presentation of the cluster analyses preceding that of other studies. Finally, other studies dealing with substance abuse and the MCMI will be reviewed at the end of this section.

The idea that substance abuse is fueled by characterological tendencies probably dates back to Freud. The Freudian contention that all alcoholic individuals represented an "oral" personality (the precursor of the dependent personality) has not been supported by the literature. Instead, the current thinking is that there are several alcoholic subtypes. In a comprehensive review of the literature, Nerviano and Gross (1983) identified seven such subtypes. Several MCMI–I studies done by different investigators have revealed clusters among alcoholic patients supporting the presence of several of the theoretically derived subtypes (Bartsch & Hoffman, 1985; Craig, Verinis, & Wexler, 1985; Donat, Walters, & Hume, 1991; Gibertini & Retzlaff, 1988b; Matano, Locke, & Schwartz, 1994; Mayer & Scott, 1988; Retzlaff & Bromley, 1991).

In most of the MCMI–I studies, there was a group of alcoholic patients with elevated scores on the Negativistic scale. It appeared that they often had additional elevations on the Borderline or Paranoid scales and were thought to be demonstrating moderate-to-severe-personality dysfunctions. Specifically, the patients were characterized as having "substantial variations in mood, irritability, suspiciousness" and "an ambivalent and indecisive approach" to life (Bartsch & Hoffman, 1985, p. 711). Drinking is typically done with friends (Donat et al., 1991) and often serves a "self-medicating" function for them (Bartsch & Hoffman, 1985). This group tended to be anxious and demonstrated borderline and paranoid tendencies (Craig et al., 1985), being less likely than other alcoholic groups to "inhibit interpersonal anxieties, frustrations and discouragements" (Donat et al., 1991, p. 343). In terms of prevalence, this cluster accounted for 38% of Mayer and Scott's (1988) sample. The presence of a massive pathological factor on the MCMI–II of alcoholics, with heavy loadings on the Negativistic and Borderline scales

(Litman & Cernovsky, 1993), suggested that this test would lead to the diagnosis of a similar type of alcoholic.

Several investigators have found a variant of the negativistic type, characterized by additional elevations on the Avoidant and Schizoid scales of the MCMI–I (Corbisiero & Reznikoff, 1991; Retzlaff & Bromley, 1991). With significant elevations on the Anxiety and Dysthymia scales, individuals in this cluster were seen as having widespread symptomatology. They have a "poor and alienated self-image . . . are mistrustful of others, and have difficulty managing and expressing emotions" (Corbisiero & Reznikoff, 1991, p. 295). Scores on the Alcohol Use Inventory showed a serious drinking problem, even though these individuals were typically concerned about their drinking (Corbisiero & Reznikoff, 1991).

Another cluster of patients was defined by elevated scores on the Narcissistic and Histrionic scales of the MCMI–I. For those patients, the drinking was conceptualized as "recreational in nature" and a "manifestation of a lifestyle of self-indulgence and thrill seeking" (Bartsch & Hoffman, 1985, p. 711). According to Donat et al. (1991), these individuals are interpersonally insensitive and value personal willpower and self-reliance. Ironically, they report obtaining few benefits from drinking and are likely not to recognize the deleterious effects that the drinking has in their lives. Matano et al. (1994) saw these individuals as being especially prone to use "ego-protecting defenses" and thought that the first goal of treatment should be to break through the denial. This cluster may account for 22% to 28% of the alcoholic population (Gibertini & Retzlaff, 1988b; Mayer & Scott, 1988). The emergence of a Histrionic–Narcissistic–Manic factor of alcohol abusers with the MCMI–II (Litman & Cernovsky, 1993) suggested that a similar cluster would be obtained with that version of the inventory.

An antisocial narcissistic alcoholic also has been found with the MCMI–I. Constituting as much as 20% of some alcoholic samples, these individuals have been described as "exploitive, defiant, and often hostile, with an inflated self-image or sense of entitlement, with a lack of sensitivity or indifference to the rights of others" (Corbisiero & Reznikoff, 1991, pp. 295–296). Scores on the Alcohol Use Inventory indicated serious drinking problems and less concern with the drinking than is seen with other alcoholics.

Accounting for about 20% of the samples (Craig et al., 1985; Matano et al., 1994; Mayer & Scott, 1988) were alcoholic patients with elevated scores on the MCMI–I Compulsive scale. Bartsch and Hoffman (1985) talked about this cluster as representing an "overly exuberant conscience," so that the function of the alcohol is to "permit escape from feelings of responsibility, or permit the expression of anger" (p. 711). They typically are unaware of any positive or negative effects that the drinking may have in their lives (Donat et al., 1991). This type of alcoholic also is represented by one of the factors found with the MCMI–II (Litman & Cernovsky, 1993).

In most of the MCMI–I studies, there was a cluster with schizoid, avoidant, and dependent elements that constituted as much as 28% (Craig et al., 1985) or as little as 5% (Gibertini & Retzlaff, 1988b) of the examinees. Besides the MCMI–I personality scales that measure those three traits, some of the investigators found elevations on the Borderline and Schizotypal scales (Bartsch & Hoffman, 1985; Donat et al., 1991; Mayer & Scott, 1988). Craig et al. (1985) described these respondents as being "anxious and depressed" (p. 159). Such individuals were thought to demonstrate "widespread and severe maladjustment" and to be typically "caught between feelings of loneliness and social apprehension"; drinking may serve to "mediate social anxiety to a level that produces self-assurance and permits social contact" (Bartsch & Hoffman, 1985, p. 712). They are inclined to become "self-critical, discouraged, and socially withdrawn and, as a result, are more likely than patients in other clusters to engage in solitary drinking" (Donat et al., 1991, p. 343). It is particularly difficult for this group to recognize the cognitive impairment that results from their drinking (Donat et al., 1991). Participation in treatment programs is especially difficult for this type of alcoholic (Fals-Stewart, 1992). Given the level of pathology that these individuals demonstrate, Matano et al. (1994) advised an emphasis on the reduction of the level of distress experienced by the patient as the first goal of treatment.

Retzlaff and Bromley (1991) found a cluster of dependent and anxious individuals who otherwise did not show much other pathology. There appears to be a small group of alcoholics who do not have characterological or emotional problems besides their drinking behavior (Corbisiero & Reznikoff, 1991; Retzlaff & Bromley, 1991). According to scores on the Alcohol Use Inventory, the drinking of these individuals also is likely to be less problematic than the drinking of other alcoholics (Corbisiero & Reznikoff, 1991). Finally, Retzlaff and Bromley (1991) also found a "denial" group that "rejects all personality and clinical symptoms" (p. 306) in a defensive manner.

Similar work also has been done with drug abusers using previous editions of the MCMI (Bartsch & Hoffman, 1985; Craig & Olson, 1990; Craig et al., 1985; Dougherty & Lesswing, 1989; Fals-Stewart, 1992; Litman & Cernovsky, 1993). In the case of drug abusers, however, there is some concern that the distinguishing features of the MCMI for different kinds of substance abusers may be caused by demographic and other group differences besides the drug of choice (Cannon, Bell, Fowler, Penk, & Finkelstein, 1990; Donat, Walters, & Hume, 1992).

The modal profile of cocaine abusers on the MCMI–II was shown to have elevations on the Antisocial, Aggressive, Narcissistic, Negativistic, Borderline, Drug Dependence, and Alcohol Dependence scales (McMahon & Richards, 1996). The modal MCMI–III personality profile for drug abusers is represented by a single elevation of the Antisocial scale (Craig, 2000; Craig, Bivens, & Olson, 1997). Using a sample of inpatient African American drug-abusing men, Craig et al. (1997) went beyond that single peak to characterize four different cluster groups.

The first cluster group of drug abusers represented 37% of the sample and was seen as the most disturbed. In addition to the spike on the Antisocial scale, this group had elevations on the Schizoid, Negativistic, and Dependent personality scales. Clinical scales showed difficulties with anxiety and depression, and historical data pointed to a higher rate of suicide attempts. These individuals were described as having a tendency toward social withdrawal and detachment, and their interpersonal relationships, when present, were fraught with conflict. Their coping mechanisms were ineffective, their emotions were erratic, and they were likely to demonstrate antisocial behaviors.

The elevation on the Antisocial scale was slightly below the clinical cutoff for the second cluster group, which made up 22% of the sample. Because this group was mostly characterized by the elevation on the Drug Abuse scale, the thinking was that the antisocial behaviors resulted from the drug abuse and would probably diminish if the person recovered from the substance abuse.

The antisocial personality and the substance abuse seemed to be the most predominant for the third group, which represented 31% of the sample. Finally, a fourth group with 10% of the sample appeared the healthiest, showing no MCMI–III elevations in the pathological range. This group, however, exhibited a strong social desirability bias and may have been guarded or defensive. Other researchers have reported a similar breakdown of clusters using the MCMI–II (McMahon, Malow, & Penedo, 1998; Penedo, Malow, McMahon, & Kouzekanani, 1996).

A sizable percentage (43%) of drug abusers were thought to have a personality disorder on the basis of MCMI–II scores (Caudill, Flynn, Hamilton, & Hoffman, 1992). In addition to characterological problems, researchers have noted a prevalence of depression among alcohol abusers. McMahon and Davidson (1986a) found that 66% of male alcoholics undergoing inpatient treatment obtained elevated scores on the Dysthymia scale of the

MCMI. McMahon and colleagues (McMahon & Davidson, 1986b; McMahon & Tyson, 1989, 1990) demonstrated how the MCMI–I can be used to discriminate between patients who will experience only transient depressive episodes and those for whom the depressive feelings may be more enduring and problematic. In their work, the enduring depression was associated with higher scores on the Negativistic and Avoidant scales and was correlated negatively with Compulsive scale scores. In other words, the more enduring depressive feelings tended to include a pattern of interpersonal ambivalence, low self-image, irritable affectivity or explosive anger, hypersensitivity to rejection, and social isolationism. On the other hand, the more transient episodes tended to be associated with excessive emotional control, fear of social disapproval, and psychological restraint (McMahon & Davidson, 1985b; McMahon & Tyson, 1989, 1990).

McMahon, Schram, and Davidson (1993) further examined the interplay among personality type, alcoholism, depression, and other variables. They attempted to study the relationship of depression, personality subtypes, and social supports. The three subtypes included dependent, detached/ambivalent, and independent. They gathered data from 125 participants drawn from inpatient and outpatient substance abuse units in the Miami area. The MCMI–I was used, along with a life experience survey, perceived support network inventory, and depression rating scale. Results indicated that the detached/ambivalent group reported greater levels of depression than the other groups. Both detached/ambivalent and dependent types reported higher levels of depression under high stress than under low stress. Social support was not found to buffer the negative stress effects in any of the groups, contrary to predictions.

Alcoholics also can be differentiated in terms of the level of their social functioning on the basis of the MCMI. McMahon, Davidson, & Flynn (1986) found the low-social-functioning group of alcoholics to have a significantly higher mean score on the Schizotypal scale of the MCMI–I and a significantly lower mean on the Compulsive scale.

Additionally, the MCMI–I can be used to describe the pattern of drinking used by alcoholic patients. McMahon and associates (McMahon & Davidson, 1989; McMahon, Davidson, Gersh, & Flynn, 1991; McMahon, Gersh, & Davidson, 1989) found that continuous drinkers tended to have higher scores on the Psychotic Thinking scale than did episodic drinkers. A group of the alcoholics in the Craig et al. (1985) sample also had such elevations, a finding that was attributed to the possible development of an organic mental disorder that causes "disorganization of thinking, regressive behavior, confusion, and disorientation" (p. 159). McMahon et al. (1989) found associations of lesser magnitude between continuous drinking and higher scores on the Drug Abuse, Paranoid, and Hypomanic scales. Episodic drinking, on the other hand, was associated with higher scores on the Compulsive scale. On the basis of their data, McMahon et al. (1989) characterized continuous drinkers as being more likely to be confused, agitated, and disorganized in their thinking than episodic drinkers; the former also are more likely to feel misunderstood and unappreciated and to be discontented and socially alienated. Although continuous drinkers are likely to be more stable in terms of their social and occupational functioning than episodic drinkers and to have greater prospects for controlled drinking, McMahon and Davidson (1989) cited data indicating that continuous drinkers are more psychologically disturbed and at greater risk for neuropsychological impairment and liver problems.

Some older folks who did not abuse chemicals in their younger days become addicted to prescribed benzodiazepines. Petrovic et al. (2002) studied this population with the MCMI–I. The findings showed a tendency for this group to have elevations on the Borderline scale of this inventory, a scale that was originally called Cyclothymic and mostly measured mood instability. Other scale elevations included the Anxiety, Dysthymic, and Alcohol Dependence scales.

Children of substance abusers also have been studied with the MCMI. Hibbard (1989) examined whether adult children of alcoholics had greater emotional and characterological problems than did a matched control group of adults with nonalcoholic parents. Adult children of alcoholics overall scored higher on the Borderline and Negativistic scales of the MCMI–I and lower on the Compulsive scale than did the control group respondents.

Given the tendency of many substance abusers to deny or minimize their addiction, the issue of whether they can avoid detection becomes particularly poignant. Craig et al. (1994) found that 52% of their substance abusing sample were able to fill out the MCMI–II without elevations on the substance abuse scales when they were asked to try to hide their addiction. Even with those instructions, however, 48% of the study participants were unable to avoid detection. The patients who were able to fake good were more likely to have been classified by the clinicians as "mild" abusers than those who could not avoid detection. The test profile obtained by those who avoided detection was the usual fake-good profile discussed in chapter 5.

Substance Abuse Codependence

Many substance abusers have non-substance-abusing friends or relatives who have enabled or encouraged the person's addiction. The concept of codependence was popularized by self-help books (e.g., Beattie, 1986; Black, 1981) but is now seen by some professionals as a diagnosable problem in its own right (Cermak, 1986). Codependent individuals are thought to have their own personal needs for contributing to the continuation of the substance abuse. Loughead, Spurlock, and Ting (1998) cluster analyzed the MCMI–II results of a group of self-identified codependent individuals. The first of the clusters obtained was characterized by an MCMI–II profile resembling that of the dependent personality disorder. Clinical elevations were obtained on the Self-Defeating and Avoidant scales, followed by subclinical (below a BR score of 75) scores on the Negativistic, Dependent, and Schizoid scales. The other three clusters did not show any significant elevations on the MCMI–II and were thought to be composed of individuals who were not emotionally disturbed.

Posttraumatic Stress Disorder (PTSD)

The exposure to severe or repeated life-threatening situations leaves emotional scars that often cause problems for many years after the event. The great majority of PTSD patients taking the MCMI–III obtain elevations on the Depressive, Self-Defeating, Borderline, and Dependent personality scales (Allen, Coyne, & Huntoon, 1998; Allen, Huntoon, & Evans, 1999; Craig & Olson, 1997). Because it is so prevalent (e.g., 90% of the Menninger sample described by Allen and coworkers), elevations on this group of scales may be seen as constituting the core of the disorder. The elevations describe a pattern of sadness and dissatisfaction, low self-esteem, emotional instability, and a tendency toward behaviors that undermine the individual's welfare. This core pattern was well documented with previous editions of the MCMI (Busby, Glenn, Steggell, & Adamson, 1993; Hyer, Davis, Woods, Albrecht, & Boudewyns, 1992; Hyer, Woods, & Boudewyns, 1991; Hyer, Woods, Boudewyns, Bruno, & O'Leary, 1988; Hyer, Woods, Boudewyns, et al., 1990; McDermott, 1987; T. W. Miller, Martin, & Shapiro, 1991; Munley, Bains, Bloem, Busby, & Pendziszewski, 1995; Robert et al., 1985; Sherwood et al., 1990).

One of the clusters that emerged from the Menninger Clinic sample basically reflected the core PTSD pattern described above, without any other elements. This cluster, labeled the *suffering* cluster by Allen et al. (1999), made up approximately 20% of the sample.

Beyond the core symptoms, the PTSD patients appear to divide into several clusters with different types of pathology. Accounting for 36% of the Menninger Clinic sample was the *aggressive* cluster. Individuals in this cluster showed elevations on the Negativistic, Aggressive, and Antisocial scales (Allen et al., 1999). Although studies with previous MCMI versions did find the Negativistic scale commonly elevated, an elevation of the Avoidant scale was usually part of the profile (Hyer & Boudewyns, 1987; Hyer et al., 1988, 1991, 1992; Hyer, Woods, Boudewyns, et al., 1990; McDermott, 1987; Munley et al., 1994; Piekarski, Sherwood, & Funari, 1993; Sherwood et al., 1990).

The tendency toward social isolation split the Menninger group into two additional clusters. From the perspective of the MCMI–III scales, however, these two clusters seemed strikingly similar and will be discussed together here. The *alienated/withdrawn* group made up 35% of the Menninger sample and was characterized by elevations on the Avoidant and Schizoid scales (Allen et al., 1999). A profile showing both schizoid and antisocial tendencies emerged as the modal profile in Craig and Olson's (1997) work. These individuals would be mostly loners who may never have been able to talk to others about their traumatic experiences and have used isolation as a way of coping with their feelings. No differences were found in the profile obtained by Hispanic PTSD patients in comparison to the non-Hispanic population (Himmelfarb, Strack, & Amanat, 1993).

Adjustment Disorders

MCMI–I studies with recently diagnosed cancer patients have consistently shown elevations on the Anxiety, Dysthymia, and Somatic Preoccupation scales (Baile, Gibertini, Scott, & Endicott, 1993; Malec, Romsaas, Messing, Cummings, & Trump, 1990; Malec, Wolberg, Romsaas, Trump, & Tanner, 1988). A similar MCMI–I pattern was found with individuals experiencing the stress of a recent return from a "cult" living environment (Martin, Langone, Dole, & Wiltrout, 1992).

Suicidal Patients

This section will discuss the use of the MCMI to determine the suicide potential of the examinee and ways to use the test to distinguish between different kinds of suicidal patients. Clinicians often face the task of evaluating the suicidal risk that a particular patient may present. As indicated in chapter 5, the MCMI was not designed to permit interpretation of single responses with scientific certitude. Nevertheless, McCann and Dyer (1996) pointed out the need to follow up any information that reveals a possible suicidal risk. The MCMI–III has two items of this type (items 154 and 171). If either of these items is endorsed as true, the examiner should note the finding and undertake further inquiry to determine the risk involved.

Earlier versions of the MCMI showed the instrument's usefulness in the assessment of suicide potential (Hull, Range, & Goggin, 1992; Joffe & Regan, 1989b; Lall, Bongar, Johnson, Jain, & Mittauer, 1999; McCann & Gergelis, 1990; McCann & Suess, 1988). Typically, the suicide risk was reflected in the elevation of numerous scales in a pattern consistent with a high level of distress, interpersonal alienation, depression, and deficient adaptive coping mechanisms. Craig and Bivens (2000) compared the MCMI–III scores of substance abusers with a history of suicide attempts to the MCMI–III scores of substance abusers without such a history. The individuals with a suicide history scored higher in 7 of the 11 personality scales (Schizoid, Avoidant, Depression, Dependent, Negativistic, Self-Defeating, and Paranoid) and lower on 2 of the remaining 4 personality scales (Histrionic and Compulsive). All of the clinical syndrome scales were higher for the group with a history of suicide attempts except for the Drug Dependence and Delusional Disorder scales. The results point to a higher level of disturbance for the group of substance abusers with a history of suicide attempts when compared with the group of substance abusers without such attempts (the only scales where this former group scored lower than the latter—Histrionic and Compulsive—have been associated with psychological health, as noted in chap. 2). A discriminant function correctly predicted 90% of the patients with a suicide history and 63% of the patients without a suicide history. At least with substance abusers, the findings speak for a higher suicide risk of any individual showing a good deal of pathology on the MCMI–III.

The MCMI has also been used to distinguish among different types of suicidal patients. In their cluster analysis of 299 suicidal psychiatric outpatients in the military, T. E. Ellis, Rudd, Rajab, and Wehrly (1996) uncovered four different types. Approximately half of the group was defined by elevations on the Negativistic, Avoidant, and Schizoid scales of the MCMI–I. These emotionally distant patients were seen as angry, difficult, and unpredictable. Accounting for 18% of the sample was the avoidant–dependent–negativistic type, a group that had been already described by McCann and Suess (1988). Identifiable traits in this group included low self-esteem, fear of rejection, feelings of inadequacy, ruminative guilt, moodiness, and anxiety. This group was seen as representing the greatest suicide risk because of their sense of hopelessness and the impairment they showed in problem-solving skills. Twenty-two percent of the sample had a single elevation on the Antisocial scale. These individuals were seen as competitive, aggressive, impulsive, and somewhat intimidating. Finally, the histrionic–narcissistic group was described as in constant need of attention and general conspicuousness. This group made up 8% of the sample and was seen as the least symptomatic of the sample (T. E. Ellis et al., 1996).

Sleep Disorders

One investigation of six patients with a sleep terror disorder concluded that the patients also suffered from a personality disorder because they had elevated personality scale scores on the MCMI–II (Llorente, Currier, Norman, & Mellman, 1992). Because the overwhelming majority of individuals who take the MCMI will obtain at least one such elevation, however, the authors' argument is not very convincing.

Neuropsychological Dysfunction

The MCMI often has been used as part of neuropsychological evaluations. Like the Minnesota Multiphasic Personality Inventory (MMPI), which is considered part of the Halstead–Reitan Neuropsychological Battery, the MCMI provides a measure of the overall level of psychopathology. The test can be used to assess the possibility that the examinee is experiencing a diagnosable emotional problem such as depression or paranoid delusions. In the author's opinion, the superiority of the MCMI lies in its focus on personality.

Even individuals who do not have a diagnosable emotional disorder may experience difficulty coping with intellectual losses. A determination of the individuals' basic personality can give clinicians some indication of the way the individuals may be reacting to the stress of the neuropsychological dysfunction. Elevations on the Schizoid or Avoidant scales, for instance, suggest the possibility of social withdrawal and isolation; elevations on the Dependent scale warn clinicians of the possibility of clinging dependency. See Table 7.3 for other theoretical expectations of the individual's reactions to neuropsychological problems.

Table 7.3

Theoretical Strengths and Liabilities Presented by the Different Personality Styles in Coping With Disability or Impairment

Personality style	Likely reaction to neuropsychological impairment: Liabilities	Strengths
1. Avoidant	Withdrawal and isolation Difficulty sharing problems or allowing other people to help	These individuals will attempt to handle problems on their own and are unlikely to be bothersome to others.
2. Schizoid	Anxiety and nervousness Defensive distancing from others Heightened discomfort in social situations, now with the fear that the neuropsychological problems have created another area that may lead to rejection by others	These individuals will attempt to handle problems on their own and are unlikely to be bothersome to others.
3. Dependent	Overly dependent and clinging Wants help and support all of the time Will not take responsibility for needs that he or she is capable of meeting May complain that others are not helping enough	These individuals are likely to accept their limitations gracefully and to be cooperative when other people offer help.
4. Histrionic	May exaggerate the problems being experienced as a way to attract attention May appear melodramatic and needy May show superficial and short-lived emotions, including displays of anger	These individuals are likely to accept their limitations gracefully and will have no trouble discussing their problems and processing their losses.

5. Narcissistic	Pride may prevent recognition of the full extent of impairment May have trouble accepting any limitations (e.g., inability to drive a car) or help in a situation in which the other person is in control and dictates what is done Likely to project difficulties as problems created by others (e.g., some demented individuals explain lost objects by contending that they were stolen)	These people are likely to remain independent and functional for as long as possible.
6. Antisocial	May become distrustful of others; may question offers for help as attempts to access the person's possessions or take advantage in some other way May have trouble accepting the control that others exert Likely to project difficulties as problems created by others	Such persons are invested in remaining as independent as possible and may accept limitations or treatment if it is seen as the means toward the goal of remaining independent.
7. Compulsive	May become overly concerned with trivial matters May experience heightened interest in saving or hoarding objects or organizing one's life may be heightened Likely to be very bothered by personal losses and to seek information about the illness in an obsessive manner	Compulsive individuals are likely to follow all instructions and be in good compliance with the treatment prescribed.
8. Negativistic	Easily angered by frustrating situations May both seek and resent the help of others A humble acceptance of personal liabilities may change into angry accusations about the lack of help or limitations of others	These individuals are likely to accept personal limitations and the help of others.

Clinicians using the MCMI with acutely disturbed individuals should heed the usual caveat about assuming that the score profile obtained reflects premorbid clinical realities. In other words, an elevation of the Dependent scale may often, *but not always*, indicate that the examinee was a dependent type before the onset of the neuropsychological dysfunction. In individuals for whom the MCMI personality profile can be shown to represent their premorbid inclinations, the personality profile can be used to speculate about the underlying dynamics of an emotional disturbance. For intelligent narcissistic individuals, for instance, a loss of intellectual abilities could undermine the basic assumption that they are superior to others; for those with a compulsive nature, the occurrence of unforeseeable and unpreventable brain impairment could shake the lifelong belief that unwanted events can be avoided by not making any mistakes.

Clinicians using the MCMI should remember that scale elevations do not imply causality. The neuropsychological literature has demonstrated that damage to particular areas of the brain can lead directly to mood instability, disinhibition, and so on. Elevations on the MCMI suggest, at best, the clinical picture at the time of the testing and do not reveal the causative factors that may have generated the clinical picture. Whether the elevations represent lifelong pathology, an adjustment reaction to the brain damage, or the direct result of a dysfunctional brain has to be argued on the basis of patients' histories, the neurological findings, or the neuropsychological literature.

Unfortunately, empirical information on the use of the MCMI as part of a neuropsychological battery is limited. Swirsky-Sacchetti et al. (1993) investigated the cognitive impairment of 10 patients with a borderline personality disorder. They failed to find any difference in the MCMI–I profiles of borderline patients with or without cognitive impairment.

Problem-Solving Deficits

Gilbride and Hebert (1980) examined the MCMI characteristics of good and poor interpersonal problem solvers. The measure of problem-solving ability used was the Means–Ends Problem Solving Procedure (Platt & Spivack, 1975), which requires the examinee to finish a story that presents some sort of problem. Black individuals who were poor problem solvers showed significant elevations on the Paranoid and Psychotic Delusions scales compared with good problem solvers of the same race. For White individuals, the poor problem solvers had higher means on the Schizoid and Schizotypal scales.

Object Representations and Relatedness

The MCMI–II was used to show that affective dimensions of object representations were related to the severity of psychopathology in an outpatient sample (Porcerelli, Cogan, & Hibbard, 1998). Attachment difficulties have been associated with higher scores on the Histrionic, Narcissistic, Antisocial, Borderline, and Aggressive scales of the MCMI–II (Bender, Farber, & Geller, 2001).

Chronic Pain

Papciak and Feuerstein (1991) administered the MCMI–II to 186 chronic back pain sufferers. The Anxiety and Dysthymia scales were found to be modestly but significantly associated with a computerized measure of trunk strength. The authors concluded that the two scales measure psychological factors that negatively affect the recovery of workers' compensation examinees. Elliott, Jackson, Layfield, and Kendall (1996) found that 35% of a sample of outpatients in a chronic pain treatment program showed a Cluster C personality (Avoidant, Dependent, Compulsive, or Negativistic) on the MCMI–I.

Chronic Fatigue Syndrome

The MCMI–II was given to a small sample of patients diagnosed with chronic fatigue syndrome (CFS; also known as chronic Epstein–Barr virus). The score pattern that emerged included elevations on five of the personality scales (i.e., Histrionic, Schizoid, Avoidant, Narcissistic, and Aggressive) as well as the Anxiety, Dysthymia, and Somatoform scales. The results were interpreted as indicating the presence of "severe personality pathology and affective distress" (C. Millon et al., 1989, p. 131).

Vorce, Jones, Helder, Pettibon, and Reiter (1995), however, would argue that the MCMI–II elevations partly are caused by the intrinsic nature of CFS and may not be indicative of an additional psychiatric problem. Vorce et al. asked five experts to rate the MCMI–II items in terms of their possible association with CFS. They found that the content of 54 of the MCMI–II items were thought to be part of the CFS symptomatology. Eliminating from this pool of items those items that had a low endorsement rate for CFS patients reduced the number of items to 46. The scales that were most affected were the Anxiety, Debasement, Somatoform, Dysthymia, Major Depression, Self-Defeating, Alcohol Dependence, and Negativistic scales. Vorce and coworkers noted that most of the affected scales represented constructs (e.g., depression, somatoform disorders) that have been used to explain CFS symptoms. They discussed several possible corrections that could be used to separate more the diagnosis of CFS from psychiatric disorders.

Sexual Disorders

Several MCMI studies have evaluated men convicted of child molestation or rape. The general MCMI–I profile of sexual offenders portrays such individuals as being more negativistic, dependent, interpersonally isolated, and depressed and less narcissistic than control group examinees (Chantry & Craig, 1993; Langevin et al., 1988). Cluster analyses have led to the characterization of several distinct groups among the sexual offenders. Perhaps one third of these individuals have an avoidant–schizoid–dependent personality on the MCMI–I. A second group, appearing to include many of the rapists, had a narcissistic–antisocial–histrionic personality and elevations on the substance abuse scales. As many as 50% of the sexual offenders, however, obtained no significant MCMI–I elevations (Bard & Knight, 1987; Chantry & Craig, 1994).

Looking at sexual abuse from the victim's viewpoint, P. C. Alexander (1993) showed that MCMI–II findings were not associated with the kind of sexual abuse the person experienced as a child. Rather, her findings pointed to the importance of characteristics in the relationship the person had with the adult abuser. A preoccupied attachment, as measured on the Relationship Questionnaire, was associated with dependent, self-defeating, and borderline personality attributes. Fearful attachment, on the other hand, was linked to higher scores on the Avoidant and Self-Defeating scales of the MCMI–II.

Legal Offenders

Working with a population of emotionally disturbed incarcerated men, Blackburn (1986) characterized four personality types that he labeled *primary psychopath, secondary psychopath, controlled,* and *inhibited.* Distinguished by elevations on the Narcissistic, Antisocial, and Histrionic scales of the MCMI–I (Blackburn, 1996), the primary psychopath profile also has been found to be prominent among Canadian prisoners (Weekes & Morison, 1993). The secondary psychopath is defined by elevations on the Negativistic, Avoidant, Schizoid, and Antisocial scales (Blackburn, 1996) and bears some resemblance to one of the clusters reported by Weekes and Morison (1993). Primary and secondary psychopaths had more convictions for assaultive crimes than the other two types and had spent a significantly longer period of time incarcerated (Blackburn, 1975, 1996). Studies also have found a group of patients with a compulsive personality (Blackburn, 1996; Weekes & Morison, 1993) and a fourth group in which the prominent feature was their social detachment (indicated by elevations on the Schizoid and Avoidant scales; Blackburn, 1996).

Misconduct of Incarcerated Felons

The MCMI–III has proved to be a valuable tool in the prediction of misconduct for incarcerated felons (Kelln, Dozois, & McKenzie, 1998). The incarcerated group receiving more behavioral penalties showed higher scores on the Schizoid, Narcissistic, Antisocial, Aggressive, Negativistic, Borderline, Alcohol Dependence, and Thought Disorder scales and lower scores on the Compulsive scale. The overall classification rate increased substantially when the MCMI–III findings were added to the demographic information; an overall correct classification rate of 79% was obtained when both demographic information and MCMI data were used.

Marital Discord

Craig and Olson (1995) examined 75 women and 70 men seeking marital therapy. A cluster analysis of MCMI–II results led to the characterization of four different types of individuals who seemed inclined to have difficulties in their marriages. The first type is a narcissistic–aggressive–histrionic individual; Craig and Olson (1995) thought that such individuals would form either a conflictual or an overadequate controlling relationship with their spouse depending on the type of person they married. The second type is characterized by generalized maladjustment and elevations on the Negativistic, Aggressive, Self-Defeating, Narcissistic, and Borderline scales. Such individuals also would be expected to form a conflictual or dictatorial relationship with their spouse. Finally, there were two types of dependent individuals: an anxious dependent–avoidant–schizoid type and a dependent–compulsive type. It was assumed that these individuals likely would play the underadequate role in an overadequate–underadequate relationship. The psychotherapeutic goals offered for the different types of relationships are reviewed in chapter 10.

Partner Abuse

In his review of the literature, Craig (2003) noted that studies on domestic violence have generally reported elevations on the Antisocial, Aggressive, Negativistic, or Narcissistic scales for male batterers. Personality disorders appear to be common and may characterize as many as 90% of these individuals (Hamberger & Hastings, 1986, 1988a; Hart, Dutton, & Newlove, 1993).

Much of the information on batterers was gathered by Hastings and Hamberger (1988, 1994). In a 1988 study, for instance, they were able to show marked differences between the MCMI–I personality elevations of batterers when compared to a control group of nonbatterers. These findings have been replicated with the MCMI–II (Beasley & Stoltenberg, 1992; Hart et al., 1993; C. M. Murphy, Meyer, & O'Leary, 1993).[1] Batterers with a poor premorbid history (defined by a lack of a high school education, unemployment, a history of alcohol abuse, or a history of having witnessed or experienced abuse) showed more elevations on the MCMI–I than did batterers with a good premorbid history (Hastings & Hamberger, 1994).

Hamberger and Hastings (1988a, 1991) distinguished wife abusers from a nonabuser control group. The differences in MCMI–I scale elevations suggested that wife abusers may have difficulty regulating affective states and feel uncomfortable in intimate relationships. These individuals were seen as being more alienated, in more need of approval, and more sensitive

[1] Hart et al. (1993) diagnosed numerous abusers with a personality disorder entirely on the basis of the MCMI–II. These authors assumed that mere elevations on the personality scales of the MCMI–II could be used to diagnose personality disorders, an assumption that the author and his colleagues have described as untenable (Choca, Shanley, et al., 1992). The fact that no control group was used further compromised, in our opinion, the power of their conclusions. The problem was corrected, however, by the work of Beasley and Stoltenberg (1992), who did use a control group.

to rejection than the nonbatterers. According to the MCMI–I scores, the batterers were more prone to experience anxiety and depression, have somatic complaints, and abuse drugs or alcohol than the members of the control group. Whenever alcohol abuse was present, as revealed by elevations on the MCMI–I scale, this problem was associated with an even greater tendency toward overall pathology and a propensity toward interpersonal ambivalence and alienation (Hamberger & Hastings, 1987, 1991; Hastings & Hamberger, 1988).

Using the MCMI–II, Dutton (1994) discussed the prevalence of the negativistic–avoidant personality profile when the test results of men in treatment for wife assault were compared with a control sample of blue-collar workers. He interpreted the findings as indicating that wife assaulters are caught in a bind between perceived abandonment and being smothered.

As informative as this characterization may be, it is of limited clinical utility when one must evaluate or treat a particular individual. Perhaps of greater clinical value is the factor analysis that Hamberger and Hastings (1986, 1988a) carried out using the eight personality scales of the MCMI–I. This procedure led to the emergence of three factors associated with wife batterers. The findings allow the classification of such individuals in a way that elucidates the psychodynamics behind the spouse abuse. Using the proposed system, three "pure" types are recognized: borderline–schizoid, narcissistic, and dependent.

The borderline–schizoid abuser typically shows a prominence on those two MCMI–I scales; other scales that may be elevated with this group are the Negativistic and Avoidant scales (Lohr, Hamberger, & Bonge, 1988). These men were described as withdrawn, moody, and hypersensitive to interpersonal slights. Hamberger and Hastings (1986, 1988a) characterized such individuals as "Dr. Jekyll and Mr. Hyde" types who can be very calm and sociable one moment but then turn uncontrollably hostile the next because of the unpredictable lability. These individuals theoretically require a symbiotically supportive relationship that offers external validation of their value and existence. If their partners fail to recognize their worth, these individuals are devastated and physically express their anger. Once the incident is over, however, they tend to express considerable guilt and remorse. The relationship between a borderline personality structure and wife abuse has been supported by Dutton's (1994) work using the MCMI–II and the Borderline Personality Organization Inventory (Oldham et al., 1985). People having this cluster type are considered to hold more irrational beliefs than those in other clusters of relational partner abusers (Lohr et al., 1988).

By contrast, individuals obtaining elevated scores on the Narcissistic scale of the MCMI–I have self-centered approaches to life. These men typically feel that they are important people and demand respect and admiration. A refusal to look at them with awe invites threat and aggression. Hamberger and Hastings (1986, 1988a) felt that for this type of person, the abuse is like a punishment handled in a matter-of-fact manner; their sense of superiority and entitlement leads them to believe it is appropriate for them to show others the error of their ways. The presence of a narcissistic group also has been supported by other studies (Lohr et al., 1988).

Finally, dependent individuals lack self-esteem and feel in dire need of support from others. The failure of other people to meet their dependency needs is eventually translated into rebellious and hostile feelings. In addition to individuals who are "pure" types, Hamberger and Hastings (1986, 1988a) found many who represent a combination of the pure types, as well as some individuals whose scores on the MCMI–I personality scales would not be indicative of any personality tendencies.

Another system for classifying wife abusers was used by Dutton (1994). Dutton used the results of the Psychological Maltreatment of Women Inventory (Tolman, 1989) to classify wife abusers into a dominance/isolation group—for whom the issues are the rigid observance of traditional sex roles, demands for subservience, and isolation from resources—and an emotional/verbal-abuse group—who tend to withdraw emotional resources, take part in verbal attacks, and engage in behaviors that degrade women. The dominance/isolation group was mostly associated with the Negativistic and Self-Defeating scales of the MCMI–II, whereas the emotional/verbal-abuse group was characterized by elevations on the Aggressive–Sadistic and Narcissistic scales.

This kind of information can be applied readily when evaluating a wife batterer who meets one of the described types. Clinicians can use the MCMI to theoretically predict the kind of situation that evokes the aggressive feelings within the context of the family system. The information also can be used in working with patients to make them aware of the personal issues that they are reacting to when they act in a hostile manner toward their wives. The critical issues of treatment completion and recidivism also have received some attention in the literature (see chap. 11). Other than personality problems, the research has tended to show that there is not much incidence of Axis I clinical syndromes among spouse abusers (Gondolf, 1999).

Victims of Abuse

The MCMI–I was given to 30 clients of a university counseling center who had reported experiencing physical, sexual, or emotional abuse as children. This group scored higher on the Borderline scale than did a control group of 54 nonabused clients, even though the group score was not clinically elevated (a BR score of 73). The 19 clients who reported only emotional abuse did not differ from the clients reporting sexual or multiple forms of abuse (Braver, Bumberry, Green, & Rawson, 1992). (Recall that the Borderline scale of the MCMI–I was originally called Cyclothymia and mostly measured mood instability.)

Abortions in Adolescents

N. B. Campbell, Franco, and Jurs (1988) compared young women who had abortions as adolescents or adults on the MCMI–I and Beck Depression Inventory. The authors reported that 25% of their overall sample had significant elevations on the Anxiety, Dysthymia, and Somatoform scales. It is unclear how this would compare with other comparable clinical populations. N. B. Campbell et al. also included some data demonstrating that those who had abortions as adolescents had greater elevations on four scales of the MCMI–I. However, their mean scores were well below BR scores of 75 (range = 58.9–63.4). Thus, their conclusions about the meanings of these differences seem suspect.

Parents of Children With Selective Mutism

Kristensen and Torgersen (2001) administered the MCMI–I to both parents of children exhibiting selective mutism. When compared with a control group, the mothers of selectively mute children were distinguished by a higher Avoidance scale, whereas with the fathers, the Schizoid scale was the predictor variable.

The MCMI and Other Psychological Instruments

This chapter reviews investigations comparing one version of the Millon Clinical Multiphasic Inventory (MCMI) to another version of the test, or one version of the MCMI to another instrument, when both tests were given to the same individuals. In spite of the substantial differences between the three versions of the MCMI, they are very highly correlated, as will be seen in this chapter. As a result, this chapter continues to include studies with previous versions of the MCMI on the presumption that the MCMI–III would relate in a similar manner to other instruments.

This review is intended to serve three purposes. First, some of the studies address the concurrent validity of the MCMI, such as when the test results resemble the results obtained with another instrument designed to measure a similar construct. Second, in comparing different instruments, these studies can make clinicians aware of situations in which the use of the MCMI may be more or less advantageous than the use of the other instrument. Finally, some of the studies offer information that clinicians can use to integrate the findings of the two sources. Although the other source of information typically has been another psychological test, the procedures for integrating MCMI results with clinician ratings using canonical variates are available in the literature (Robbins & Patton, 1986).

In his review of the literature involving the MCMI and the Minnesota Multiphasic Personality Inventory (MMPI), Gallucci (1990) criticized the available studies for not meeting the criteria he proposed as optimal. In particular, Gallucci noted that few of the studies estimated the incremental validity that is gained from using more than one test. That criticism would apply not only to the MMPI studies discussed in this chapter, but to almost all of the studies in this chapter. In theory, having the results from more than one psychological instrument would increase the amount of certainty clinicians would have about the diagnosis of the patient. In practice, however, that potential has been hard to actualize. A study by Marlowe and Wetzler (1994), for instance, showed little improvement in diagnostic efficiency over single scale elevations when the MCMI–I, the MCMI–II, the MMPI, the Symptom Check List (SCL-90-R), and the psychiatrist's diagnosis were used.

In any event, this chapter will first discuss the instruments that are most similar, in structure or scope, to the MCMI–III. Other instruments designed to measure personality traits are discussed next, followed by the instruments that emphasize the clinical syndromes.

The MCMI–I and the MCMI–II

Millon (1987) reported high correlations between the corresponding scales of the first two versions of the MCMI. Hyer, Davis, Woods, Albrecht, and Boudewyns (1992) gave both versions to 100 veterans diagnosed with post-traumatic stress disorder (PTSD). Although their corrclations were not as high as Millon's, the corresponding scales were found to be similar enough that the two versions could be "used interchangeably," at least with a PTSD group (Hyer et al., 1992, p. 878). When the patients were grouped together, both of the MCMI versions resulted in the typical PTSD profile, with elevations on the Avoidant and Negativistic scales. Even the high-point codes showed some stability, as one or both of the highest two elevations on the MCMI–I turned out to be elevated on the MCMI–II the great majority (85%) of the time. However, the data also showed significant differences between the two instruments. The Base Rate (BR) scores on the MCMI–II were significantly higher for most of the scales, and the 2-point code involved the same two scales in only 17.5% of the cases (Hyer et al., 1992).

The MCMI–II and the MCMI–III

The correlation of the MCMI–III BR scores and those of its immediate predecessor ranged from .59 on the Dependent scale to .88 for the Dysthymia scale. The mean was approximately .70 (Millon, 1994a).

Marlowe, Festinger, Kirby, Rubenstein, and Platt (1998) gave both versions of the test to 40 cocaine abusers receiving outpatient treatment. They reported a striking similarity of group profiles in terms of the shape of the profile, with modal elevations on the Antisocial, Narcissistic, Aggressive,

Alcohol Dependence, and Drug Dependence scales. However, the overall MCMI–III group profile was significantly lower than the profile obtained with the MCMI–II. Some of the correlations between respective scales were very low (.13 for the Somatoform Disorder, .23 for Drug Dependence, .27 for Negativistic), and only two of the correlations were at or above .70. Ninety percent of the participants produced discrepant 2-point code-types on the two tests. Based on these data, one may conclude that the two versions of the test retain some basic similarity, but are mostly different instruments.

The MCMI and the Millon Behavioral Health Inventory (MBHI)

Like the MCMI, the MBHI (Millon, 1982a) is rooted in Millon's theory and contains the eight basic personality prototypes that Millon (1969) proposed. In addition to the personality scales, the MBHI contains scales designed to measure attributes thought to be relevant in the treatment of medically ill patients. Wise (1994b) administered both of these inventories to a group of psychiatric patients with medical symptoms. In looking at the personality scales, his data showed that the two tests were not significantly different in the number of scales that were elevated. A significant and positive correlation was found between the complementary scales of the two instruments. However, the actual code-type correspondence was a disappointing 30% for single scales and 21% for 2-point code-types.

The MCMI and the Personality Adjective Check List (PACL)

Strack (1987, 1990) developed the PACL to measure the eight basic Millon personality scales in normal individuals. When both instruments were given to a sample of 140 university students, six of the eight PACL scales obtained their highest correlation with their MCMI–II counterpart (Strack, 1991a). One of the exceptions was the Introversive scale of the PACL, which was not only related to the Schizoid scale of the MCMI–II, but also was negatively related to the Avoidant and the Histrionic scales. The PACL's Forceful scale was more associated with the Dependent (negatively) and the Narcissistic scales than with its MCMI–II counterpart (Antisocial).

Strack's (1991a) factor analysis of the two scales together led to four factors that accounted for 77% of the variance. Three of these factors (labeled Social Dominance Versus Submissiveness, Emotionality Versus Restraint, and Social Introversion Versus Extraversion) showed the theoretically expected loadings on both the MCMI–II and the PACL. The last factor, thought to measure general maladaptiveness, loaded only on five of the eight scales of the MCMI–II.

The correlations obtained by Strack (1991a) between the matching scales of the two instruments ranged from .41 to .72. These values seem to indicate that the scores produced by the two instruments have definite similarities but are far from equivalent. The difference between the two could be explained partly by the difference in format (the PACL is an adjective checklist as opposed to a true–false questionnaire), the presence or absence of items designed to measure pathological traits, and the adjustments made to the Millon typologies to align the descriptions with the revised third edition of the *Diagnostic and Statistical Manual of Mental Disorders* (*DSM–III–R*; American Psychiatric Association, 1987).

The MCMI–III and Craig's Adjectival Descriptions of Personality Disorders

Expanding the idea of the PACL into the pathological range, Craig and Olson (2001) developed a set of adjectives to measure personality disorders. All but one of the personality scales of the MCMI–III were found to correlate significantly with a great number of the corresponding adjectives. The exception was the Narcissistic scale; this scale produced a correlation of .20 or above with only two adjectives. The authors blamed the nonconvergence on a lack of adjectives describing a narcissistic trait that do not pertain to healthy narcissism and good ego functioning (Craig & Olson, 2001).

The MCMI–II and the Coolidge Axis II Inventory (CATI)

The CATI (Coolidge & Merwin, 1992) was designed to assess all 13 of the *DSM–III–R* personality disorders, as well as anxiety, depression, and brain dysfunction. The instrument is a self-report inventory with responses in a 4-point scale format. Modest correlations (median r = .55 to .58, depending on the study) between equivalent scales of the CATI and the MCMI–II have been reported (Coolidge & Merwin, 1992; Sinha & Watson, 2001; Smith Silberman, Roth, Segal, & Burns, 1997).

The MCMI–II and the Revised Version of the Personality Diagnostic Questionnaire—Revised (PDQ–R)

Wierzbicki and Gorman (1995) gave the MCMI–II and the PDQ–R (Hyler et al., 1988) to a group of college students. The two instruments were significantly but modestly correlated (the median correlation was .49).

The MCMI and the Wisconsin Personality Disorders Inventory (WPDI)

The WPDI is a self-report questionnaire designed to measure the 11 personality disorders of the *DSM–III–R* from the interpersonal perspective of Benjamin's (1984) structural analysis of social behavior (SASB; Benjamin, 1974). The SASB is based on Leary's circumplex model (see the historical section in chap. 1 for more information). The instrument consists of 360 items that are rated on a 10-point scale (Klein et al., 1993). All but two of the scales of the WPDI (Narcissistic and Antisocial) were significantly correlated with the corresponding personality scale of the MCMI–I. The reported correlations ranged from –.26 to .68.[1] When corrected for attenuation, the average correlation between the two instruments was .46 (Klein et al., 1993). Except for two scales, these questionnaires measure constructs that have much in common, although they clearly are different tools.

The MCMI and the Inventory of Interpersonal Problems

The Inventory of Interpersonal Problems is a self-report inventory designed to assess maladaptive interpersonal dispositions (Horowitz, Rosenberg, Baer, Ureño, & Villaseñor, 1988). Alden, Wiggins, and Pincus (1990) developed scales for this instrument that allow placement of the individual on the nurturant–cold and domineering–unassertive axes of the circumplex. Using the MCMI–I and the Alden scales, Matano and Locke (1995) found that

[1] The report that the two compulsive scales had a significant negative correlation seemed odd to us. The issue is not addressed in the paper. Klein (personal communication, January 11, 1994) felt that the finding was due to discrepancies between the MCMI compulsive prototype and that of the *DSM–III–R*. We are not convinced that this factor could explain a negative correlation but have no better explanation.

schizoid, avoidant, and negativistic alcoholics were excessively guarded interpersonally, narcissistic patients were too domineering, compulsive individuals were unassertive, antisocial individuals were guarded and domineering, and dependent individuals were both open and unassertive.

The MCMI and the NEO Personality Inventory (NEO–PI)

The NEO–PI (Costa & McCrae, 1985) was designed to measure personality in accordance with their five-factor model (Neuroticism, Extraversion, Openness to Experience, Psychoticism, and Agreeableness). In terms of that model, Costa and McCrae (1985) reported that the Schizoid scale of the MCMI–I was related negatively to the Extraversion scale, specifically showing low warmth, gregariousness, positive emotions, assertiveness, and openness to feelings. In addition to being related negatively to Extraversion scores, avoidants in T. Millon's (1969) typology scored highly on the Neuroticism scale, showing problems with self-consciousness, depression, and vulnerability. Dependent scale scores were related to low Openness to Experience scores and to high Agreeableness scores in terms of the five-factor model. Histrionic individuals obtained positive correlations with the Extraversion scale and negative correlations with the Conscientiousness scale. The high Extraversion scores were thought to be attributable to histrionic individuals' gregariousness, positive emotions, assertiveness, and excitement seeking.

Individuals who had high scores on the Narcissistic scale were found to have high scores on the Extraversion scale and low scores on the Agreeableness scale. These people were high in assertiveness and saw themselves as being low in self-consciousness and vulnerability. The Antisocial scale also was correlated negatively with Agreeableness scores. Compulsive individuals were found to have extremely high scores on the Conscientiousness scale. Finally, scores on the Negativistic scale have been correlated with Neuroticism scores (Costa & McCrae, 1990; McCrae, 1991). Using the MCMI–III, Dyce and O'Connor (1998) tested the predictions that Widiger and his associates had proposed to characterize the relationship between the five-factor model and the *DSM–IV* personality categories (Widiger, Trull, Clarkin, Sanderson, & Costa, 1994). Dyce and O'Connor obtained significance for 63% of the 150 predicted relationships.

The MCMI and the Gordon Personality Profile Inventory (GPPI)

The GPPI (Dyer, 1984) is another measure of the five-factor model of personality. Dyer (1994) administered this inventory and the MCMI–II to 50 participants. His data showed that the MCMI–II Schizoid and Avoidant scales characterize individuals lacking assertiveness, goal-directed behavior, and drive. Dependent participants turned out to be cautious and behaviorally inhibited. Unexpectedly, histrionic people showed a capacity for original thinking on the GPPI. The Antisocial scale of the MCMI–II correlated negatively with both the Cautiousness and Vigor scales of the GPPI. Correlating negatively with GPPI's Responsibility, Personal Relations, and Vigor scales was the MCMI–II's Aggressive scale, but the Self-Defeating scale had a negative correlation with every GPPI scale. Compulsive participants tended to be routine oriented, behaviorally inhibited, emotionally contained, and responsible. The Negativistic and Borderline scales had significant negative correlations with all but one of the GPPI scales. Finally, schizotypal individuals were found to be introverted, socially isolated, irresponsible, and lacking in drive.

The MCMI and the 50-Bipolar Self-Rating Scales (50-BSRS)

A third measure of the five-factor model, the 50-BSRS, is a 50-item self-report questionnaire (L. R. Goldberg, 1992). When both the MCMI–II and the 50-BSRS were given to psychiatric patients, the Schizoid, Schizotypal, and Avoidant scales were found to be related negatively to Extraversion, Emotional Stability, and Openness to Experience; the Avoidant scale also was related to low Agreeableness. Dependent individuals are thought of as introverted and closed to experience, whereas histrionic individuals are agreeable, undependable, and open to experience. Narcissists and antisocials are both extraverted, but the narcissists also are open to experience.

The Compulsive scale was characterized as measuring introversion and conscientiousness. MCMI–II negativists were disagreeable, neurotic, and undependable on the 50-BSRS. The MCMI borderline prototype was shown to be related to disagreeableness and lack of conscientiousness, and paranoid individuals were unstable. Finally, those with high scores on the Self-Defeating scale were introverted, disagreeable, undependable, and neurotic, whereas those with high scores on the Aggressive scale were disagreeable, neurotic, and open to experience (Soldz, Budman, Demby, & Merry, 1993b).

The MCMI and the Eysenck Personality Questionnaire

Similar constructs to those used by the five-factor model are represented by the Psychoticism, Extraversion, and Neuroticism scales of the Eysenck Personality Questionnaire (Eysenck & Eysenck, 1975). Using a psychiatric sample, Gabrys et al. (1988) found an association between low Psychoticism scores and a compulsive personality style, whereas high Psychoticism scores led to elevations of the Schizoid, Avoidant, and Negativistic scales of the MCMI–I. Introversion was related to the Schizoid, Avoidant, Dependent, Negativistic, Schizotypal, Borderline, Anxiety, Somatoform, Dysthymia, Psychotic Thinking, and Major Depression scales. Finally, examinees scoring low on Neuroticism tended to score high on the MCMI–I's Histrionic, Narcissistic, and Compulsive scales.

The MCMI and the Sixteen Personality Factor Questionnaire (16PF)

The 16PF (Cattell, Ever, & Tatsuoka, 1970) has validity scales that appear similar to the Desirability and Debasement scales of second and third editions of the MCMI. Because of this apparent similarity, the 16PF has been used to study the performance of the MCMI Modifying Indices. The Fake-Bad scale of the 16PF has a significant positive correlation with the Disclosure and Debasement scales of the MCMI–II. On the other hand, the Motivation Distortion (Fake-Good) scale of the 16PF is correlated positively with the Desirability scale and correlated negatively with both the Disclosure and Debasement scales (Grossman & Craig, 1994).

On the personality scales, DeLamatre and Schuerger (1992) found support for the convergent validity of 10 of the 11 MCMI–I scales and the 16PF dimensions. General convergence also was reported using five broad factors (i.e., Extraversion, Anxiety, Practicality, Independence, and Self-Control) from a new version of the 16PF and the MCMI–I (Terpylak & Schuerger, 1994).

Hyer, Woods, Boudewyns, Harrison, and Tamkin (1990) gave both the MCMI and the 16PF to a group of veterans diagnosed with posttraumatic stress disorder (PTSD). Their findings were always consistent with Millon's (1977) conceptualizations of the different MCMI scales. For example, the Schizoid and the Avoidant scales were related inversely to the Assertiveness scale and related positively to the Self-Sufficiency scale of the 16PF. The Avoidant scale also was related to the Anxiety scale. The Dependent scale was related positively to the Sensitivity scale but related inversely to the Self-Sufficiency scale.

Patients with high scores on the Histrionic scale also tended to have high scores on the Intelligence, Assertive, Happy-Go-Lucky, Boldness, Extraversion, Tough Poise, and Independence scales of 16PF. Both the Narcissistic and the Antisocial scales appeared to be associated with assertiveness and independence; the Narcissistic scale also was correlated with the Happy-Go-Lucky, Boldness, and Extraversion scales, whereas the Antisocial scale was found to be associated with the Tough Poise scale and related negatively to the Sensitivity scale. Correlating positively with the Conformity and Self-Discipline scales, the Compulsive scale of the MCMI was related negatively to the Tension, Anxiety, and Tough Poise scales.

Finally, judging from these two inventories, respondents with negativistic personality styles tend to be tense and anxious and are not inclined to be warm, emotionally stable, happy-go-lucky, conforming, bold, and self-disciplined. Correlations for the Schizotypal, Borderline, and Paranoid scales of the MCMI also are included, along with the correlations obtained by the symptom formation scales on the traits of the 16PF (Hyer, Woods, Boudewyns, et al., 1990).

Craig and Olson (1992) administered the MCMI–II and the 16PF to 75 women and 70 men involved in outpatient marital therapy. They found 75 significant correlations between the Millon personality scales and the 16PF and 40 significant correlations between the latter test and Millon clinical syndrome scales. All the obtained correlations were thought to reflect a "meaningful and logical" relationship between the two tests (Craig & Olson, 1992, p. 703).

The MCMI and Other Measures of Narcissism

The MCMI has received some attention for its ability to measure narcissism. Prifitera and Ryan (1984) administered both the MCMI and the Narcissistic Personality Inventory (NPI), which was developed by Raskin and Hall (1979) using a counterbalanced design and psychiatric patients. Prifitera and Ryan reported a correlation of .66 between the Narcissistic scale of the MCMI and the NPI. They also found significant correlations between the NPI and the Histrionic and Negativistic scales of the MCMI. They explained the latter correlations on the basis of the similarities between the narcissistic personality prototype and the prototypes for the histrionic and negativistic individuals. Finally, Prifitera and Ryan used the two scales to classify their sample into low and high narcissism and found that the instruments agreed on the classification 74% of the time.

In a similar study done with undergraduates, Auerbach (1984) showed a statistically significant correlation of .55 between the Narcissistic scale of the MCMI and the NPI. Auerbach found it troublesome, however, that the coefficient of homogeneity for the MCMI Narcissistic scale was low, thus suggesting that the scale may be measuring more than one concept in the case of college students. Moreover, neither the Narcissistic scale nor the NPI correlated significantly with the Marlowe–Crowne Social Desirability scale (Crowne & Marlowe, 1964), possibly pointing out that the concept of narcissism may not be related to a wish to be perceived as being socially desirable.

Using the NPI and clinical ratings to choose narcissistic patients, Chatham, Tibbals, and Harrington (1993) compared the narcissistic group with a control group of nonnarcissistic psychiatric patients. The study showed that the narcissistic respondents tended to score higher on the Histrionic, Narcissistic, and Antisocial personality scales and on the Paranoid, Hypomanic, and Drug Abuse scales of the MCMI–I. The findings characterized the narcissistic group as being more extraverted, aggressive, dramatizing, suspicious, and energetic than nonnarcissistic psychiatric patients (Chatham et al., 1993).

In their work with wife abusers, Beasley and Stoltenberg (1992) found the NPI to be less responsive than the MCMI–II to the narcissistic characteristics of their sample. They blamed their finding on the NPI having been developed to tap less extreme levels of narcissism than the MCMI–II.

The MCMI and Other Measures of the Borderline Personality

Lewis and Harder (1991) correlated the score of the Borderline scale of the MCMI–I with results obtained from Kernberg's (1977) Structural Interview, from the Diagnostic Interview for Borderline Personality Disorders (Gunderson & Singer, 1975), and from the Borderline Syndrome Index (Conte, Plutchik, Karasu, & Jerrett, 1980). The data showed the MCMI–I scale to have the most robust correlation with the other instruments.

The MCMI and the Defense Mechanism Inventory (DMI)

According to DMI data obtained by Whyne-Berman and McCann (1995), elevations on the Antisocial scale of the MCMI–II are associated with acting-out defenses. Obsessive–compulsive traits are found in individuals who use reaction formation as a defense, and paranoid tendencies are tied to projection. A negativistic style uses displacement. Finally, the Self-Defeating scale evokes the mechanism of devaluation. Although many significant correlations were found between these two instruments, the correlations tended to be modest (no higher than .38), indicating that the instruments measure different constructs.

The MCMI and the Defense Style Questionnaire (DSQ-40)

The DSQ-40 (Bond, 1995) is a 40-item self-report instrument measuring defense mechanisms at three levels of dysfunction: mature (sublimation, humor, anticipation, and suppression), neurotic (pseudoaltruism, idealization, reaction formation, and undoing), and immature (acting-out, denial, devaluation, displacement, dissociation, autistic fantasy, isolation, passive–aggression, projection, rationalization, somatization, and splitting). The personality disorders of the MCMI–II correlated positively with the immature defense style of the DSQ-40; the immature style explained 11% of the variance of the MCMI–II personality disorder scales (Sinha & Watson, 1999).

The MCMI and the COPE

The COPE is a 60-item self-report inventory designed to measure the frequency of habitual coping strategies (Carver, Scheier, & Weintraub, 1989). Data from this inventory led to the clustering of the MCMI–II personality scales into three groups according to the predominant coping strategy used. The first group, including the Aggressive, Narcissistic, Antisocial, Paranoid, and Histrionic scales, characterized individuals who typically cope with stress by venting emotions. The second group, containing the Negativistic, Borderline, and Self-Defeating scales, showed deficits of active coping and a tendency to disengage from goals, both mentally and behaviorally. Finally, the third group emphasized passivity, social withdrawal, and cognitive negativism as coping strategies. This group included the Schizotypal, Schizoid, and Compulsive scales (Vollrath, Alnaes, & Torgersen, 1994). COPE scores were used subsequently to predict change in the MCMI–II personality scale scores (Vollrath, Alnaes, & Torgersen, 1995).

The MCMI and Measures of Rationality and Self-Regard

The main focus of rational–emotive therapy is to help clients fight irrational thoughts that, according to A. Ellis (1977), have self-defeating consequences that interfere with their survival and happiness. Two studies examined the relationship of the MCMI–I and various experimental measures of rationality of thinking and positive self-regard. Results of both studies indicated that the Histrionic, Narcissistic, Antisocial, and Compulsive scales are correlated with rationality and positive self-regard, whereas most of the other MCMI scales tend to be correlated with irrationality. In both articles, the correlation found between the other personality scales (i.e., Schizoid, Avoidant, Dependent, Negativistic, Schizotypal, and Borderline) and irrational ways of thinking was noted (Hyer, Harrison, & Jacobsen, 1987; Leaf, Ellis, DiGiuseppe, Mass, & Alington, 1991).

The MCMI and Measures of Perfectionism

One study examined the MCMI–I and two obscure measures of perfectionism (Broday, 1988). This was a simple correlational study, somewhat limited by the modest sample size ($N = 91$). There were two interesting findings: The Passive–Aggressive scale was the most highly correlated with perfectionism, and the Compulsive scale was correlated inversely with perfectionism.

The MCMI and the Reciprocal Attachment Questionnaire (RAQ)

Elevations of the Dysthymia scale of the MCMI–I were used to distinguish a group of 42 depressed patients from a similar group of nondepressed patients. Five of the 11 scales of the RAQ (West, Sheldon, & Reiffer, 1987) were found to be significantly elevated for the depressed group (Pettem, West, Mahoney, & Keller, 1993).

The MCMI and the Minnesota Multiphasic Personality Inventory (MMPI)

The biggest competitor of the MCMI has been, of course, the MMPI. These two tests are used in the same settings and are both designed to measure broad-spectrum patterns of emotional disturbance. Research with previous versions of the MCMI and MMPI has shown significant similarities between the two tests (Chatham et al., 1993; Hyer, Woods, Summers, Boudewyns, & Harrison, 1990; McCann, 1989, 1991; McNiel & Meyer, 1990; Millon, 1987; Morey & Le Vine, 1988; Ownby, Wallbrown, Carmin, & Barnett, 1990, 1991; Schuler, Snibbe, & Buckwalter, 1994; Sexton et al., 1987; Sinha & Watson, 2001; Smith, Carroll, & Fuller, 1988; Ward, 1994; Wetzler et al., 1989; Wise, 1994a, 1996, 2001; Zarrella, Schuerger, & Ritz, 1990). Significant differences have also been noted (Blais, Benedict, & Norman, 1994; Marsh et al., 1988; McCann, 1992; Millon, 1987; Ownby et al., 1991; Schuler et al., 1994; Smith et al., 1988; Wise, 1994a; Zarrella et al., 1990). Comparing the diagnostic value of these two inventories, Libb, Murray, Thurstin, and Alarcon (1992) showed the MCMI–II achieving a higher hit rate (79% vs. 68% for the MMPI).

Looking at the validity scales, Morgan, Schoenberg, Dorr, and Burke (2002) compared the Modifier Indices of the MCMI–III with the validity measures of the MMPI–2. The MCMI–III Indices performed as expected and had high correlations with many of the MMPI–2 validity indicators (as high as .91). The researchers noted that the MCMI–III was much more tolerant of overreporting and remained valid until the MMPI–2 F scale approached a *T* score of 120. Because the MMPI–2 norms were compiled after any questionable cases were taken out of the pool (Butcher et al., 1989), however, it is just as likely that the MMPI–2 is too stringent in its designation of overreporting.

A different approach to that of examining the similarities between the MMPI and the MCMI has been to determine how these two inventories complement each other. A series of articles have suggested that the MCMI can add to the information derived from the MMPI (Antoni, Levine, Tischer, Green, & Millon, 1986, 1987; Antoni, Tischer, Levine, Green, & Millon, 1985a, 1985b; Levine, Tischer, Antoni, Green, & Millon, 1985).

Moving on to the present versions of these instruments, Millon (1994a) reported high convergence between only a few of the theoretically equivalent scales (e.g., .74 for the Avoidant scale of the MCMI–III and the Social Introversion scale of the MMPI–2; .71 for MCMI's Major Depression and

MMPI's Depression scales). In most cases the convergence between corresponding scales was modest (e.g., .63 between the MCMI Somatoform and the MMPI Hypochondriasis scales, .38 between the MCMI Delusional Disorder and the MMPI Paranoid scales). Moreover, many scales showed same-level correlations with a variety of scales of the other inventory (e.g., MCMI's Major Depression correlated .73 with MMPI's Psychasthenia, .67 with MMPI's Schizophrenia, .60 with MMPI's Hypochondriasis).

Although the MMPI did not originally have scales to measure personality disorders, Morey and his coworkers developed a set of such scales for the original version of the test (Morey, Waugh, & Blashfield, 1985). The Morey personality scales were updated for the MMPI–2 (Colligan, Morey, & Offord, 1994), and Somwaru and Ben-Porath (1995) developed another set of personality scales. With the exception of one scale, studies have generally shown reasonable convergent validity between the equivalent scales of the MCMI–III and the MMPI–2, with many correlations at the level of .70 or above (Hicklin & Widiger, 2000; Lindsay & Widiger, 2000). The exception has been the scales measuring the obsessive–compulsive personality, which led to a negative correlation (Hicklin & Widiger, 2000).

The MCMI and the Diagnostic Inventory of Personality (DIPS)

The DIPS (Vincent, 1985) is a psychiatric questionnaire containing 171 items designed to measure the greatest number of clinical syndrome (Axis I) groups (e.g., alcohol abuse, drug abuse, schizophrenia, paranoia, affective disorders, anxiety disorders). It has three scales tapping personality (Axis II) pathology (i.e., the Withdrawn Character, Immature Character, and Neurotic Character scales). The DIPS has been administered to psychiatric patients who also took the MCMI–I. The pattern of correlations showed the DIPS to measure the same clinical syndromes as those measured by the MCMI–I scales (Leroux, Vincent, McPherson, & Williams, 1990).

The MCMI and the Symptom Check List (SCL-90)

There also has been some interest in examining the SCL-90 (Derogatis, 1983) and the MCMI. According to Millon (1982b), only four of the SCL-90 scales are modestly related (correlations in the .60s) to scales of the

MCMI. Of these, the Depression scale is again noteworthy, having commonalities with the Psychotic Depression, Dysthymia, Negativistic, and Cyclothymia scales of the MCMI. Wetzler et al. (1989) found the Dysthymia scale of the MCMI and the Depression scale of the SCL-90 to be equally efficient in diagnosing major depressions.

Additionally, Millon (1982b) reported modest correlations between the SCL-90's Interpersonal Sensitivity scale and the Avoidant, Negativistic, Schizotypal, Cyclothymia, Psychotic Thinking, and Psychotic Depression scales of the MCMI. Anxiety, as measured by the SCL-90, seemed similar to the Anxiety, Psychotic Depression, and Cyclothymia scales of the MCMI. Finally, the Psychotic Thinking and Psychoticism scales were modestly related (Millon, 1982b). A factor analysis of both scales together has led to two interbattery factors thought to represent (a) anxious depression and emotionality and (b) paranoid thinking (Strauman & Wetzler, 1992).

The MCMI and the California Psychological Inventory (CPI)

Because the MCMI provides measures of personality styles, it should be related to other personality trait inventories such as the CPI (Gough, 1975). Holliman and Guthrie (1989) administered both the MCMI–I and the CPI to 237 college students. As expected, they reported a significant overlap in the variance between the two tests such that about 40% of the variance of either test could be accounted for by the other.

The measures of social withdrawal and detachment of the MCMI–I were predictably related to low scores on the interpersonal interaction scales of the CPI. Specifically, the Schizoid, Avoidant, and Dependent scales of the MCMI–I correlated negatively with the Class I scales of the CPI (i.e., the Dominance, Capacity for Status, Sociability, Social Presence, Social Acceptance, and Sense of Well-Being scales). The Histrionic, Narcissistic, and Antisocial scales, on the other hand, were positively correlated with these Class I scales of the CPI. Another significant finding was that the MCMI–I Compulsive scale was associated with higher scores on the Class II scales of the CPI (i.e., Responsibility, Socialization, Self-Control, Tolerance, Good Impression, and Communality). Holliman and Guthrie (1989) felt that the Compulsive scale might be a measure of good adjustment to some degree, at least with a college population. Finally, the Negativistic scale of the MCMI–I showed its highest correlations with scales related to delinquency and criminal behavior (negatively correlated with Responsibility, Socialization, Achievement via Conformance, and Intellectual Efficiency).

The MCMI and the Psychopathy Checklist—Revised (PCL–R)

When the MCMI and PCL–R (Hare, 1991) were given to convicts, the PCL–R total scores correlated most highly with the Antisocial scale of the MCMI–II. Significant associations also were found between the PCL–R total scores and the Narcissistic, Aggressive, Negativistic, Borderline, Paranoid, Drug Dependence, Thought Disorder, and Delusional Disorder scales (Hart et al., 1991).

The MCMI and the Profile of Mood States (POMS)

Correlations between the MCMI–I and the POMS (McNair, Loor, & Droppleman, 1971) also are available. For example, associations have been found between the Avoidant and Negativistic scales of the MCMI and the Depression and Confusion scales of the POMS (McMahon & Davidson, 1985a). The Anxiety, Dysthymia, and Psychotic Depression scales were found to be related to the Tension, Depression, Fatigue, and Confusion scales of the POMS (McMahon & Davidson, 1986a). All of the reported relationships, however, were modest; the best correlation was .56.

The MCMI and the Beck Depression Inventory (BDI)

A reasonable amount of agreement has been found between the BDI (Beck, Ward, Mendleson, Moug, & Erbaugh, 1961) and the Dysthymia scale of the MCMI–I (J. O. Goldberg et al., 1987; O'Callaghan, Bates, Jackson, Rudd, & Edwards, 1990).

The MCMI and the Alcohol Use Inventory (AUI)

Donat (1994) cluster analyzed results of alcoholic patients on the AUI (Horn, Wanberg, & Foster, 1986) scores and the MCMI–II. Using this method, he characterized five different groups on the basis of AUI and MCMI–II scores. The first group typically obtained one single elevation on the Gregarious scale of the AUI and tended to have elevations on the Histrionic and Narcissistic scales of the MCMI–II. These features, and the absence of high scores on other scales, suggest that drinking serves a social function for this group.

Despite the fact that these patients may be healthier emotionally than other groups, their reliance on alcohol to fulfill interpersonal needs may pose a problem in their recovery. There is the potential, however, for the productive use of social methods of recovery maintenance, such as Alcoholics Anonymous.

The second group was characterized by elevations on the marital scales of the AUI and no notable features on the MCMI–II. The findings suggested a vicious cycle in which the drinking aggravated existing marital problems, and the marital problems, in the patients' view, provoked them to drink. Because the quality of the marital relationship appeared to be tied to the drinking, consideration of the use of marital or couples therapy was recommended.

By contrast, the third cluster was represented by individuals who had low scores on the same marital scales of the AUI, but MCMI–II scores showed antisocial, aggressive, and drug-abusing tendencies. These patients were considered to be more self-directed and likely to place a high value on willpower and self-control. They typically were less concerned with the impact that their substance abuse might have on others and may have experienced caregivers as intrusive. For such patients, the treatment should emphasize the fact that the substance abuse interferes with their ability to obtain their personal goals. They must learn that in order to be in command of their lives, they must control their substance-abusing tendencies.

In contrast to the first group, the fourth group was characterized by low scores on the Gregarious scale and high scores on many of the other scales of the AUI (i.e., scales measuring compulsiveness, sustained drinking, loss of control, role maladaptation, and the experience of delirium and hangovers). MCMI–II scores showed elevations on the Avoidant, Antisocial, Negativistic, Self-Defeating, and Borderline scales. These profiles indicated high levels of emotional distress and few coping skills. The patients reported that they often drank alone and appeared to match the advanced stage of the traditional disease process of alcoholism. Therapy designed to manage the patients' social anxiety and depression was recommended.

Finally, the fifth group tended to be older and to have more women than the other groups. People in this group were characterized by low scores on the Gregarious scale and elevations on a scale indicating that the patients drink to manage their moods. The MCMI–II composite had an elevation on the Compulsive scale and relatively low scores on the Narcissistic, Antisocial, Aggressive, and Negativistic scales. Patients with such profiles tended to deny the presence of alcohol-related problems. The emphasis appeared to be one of maintaining strict control over emotions. The findings suggested that these individuals would drink alone in their struggle with emotional distress. Therapeutic interventions to help them deal with their distress also may be helpful with this group.

The MCMI and the Eating Disorder Inventory (EDI)

Lundholm (1989) gave the MCMI–I and the EDI (Garner & Olmsted, 1984) to a group of 135 undergraduate women. Findings showed that elevations of the Alcohol Abuse scale were associated with significantly higher scores on the Interoceptive Awareness, Ineffectiveness, Maturity Fears, Interpersonal Distrust, and Bulimia scales of the Eating Disorder Inventory.

The MCMI and Measures of Posttraumatic Stress Disorder

As measured by the Childhood Trauma Questionnaire (CTQ; D. P. Bernstein et al., 1994), lower scores on Emotional Neglect are associated with higher scores on the Histrionic and Narcissistic scales of the MCMI–III. Abuse and neglect (most prominently, the CTQ Sexual Abuse scale) were associated with higher scores on the Posttraumatic Stress Disorder, Somatization, Anxiety, and Dysthymia scales (Allen, Coyne, & Huntoon, 1998).

The MCMI and Projective Techniques

The author has often used the MCMI in conjunction with projective tests. Information about a particular person obtained from different sources can be used to either support some finding or add additional information about the patient. When scores on the Dysthymia scale of the MCMI are elevated, for instance, the clinician may search for other evidence of depression from other sources, such as presenting complaints involving affective symptoms, or markers of affective difficulties in the projective tests. The Rorschach Inkblot Test may be constricted and may show a repeated use of the blackness of the inkblot as a determinant, and the Thematic Apperception Test (TAT) stories may betray a preoccupation with problematic or depressing situations. Having such confirmation from several sources of information increases the clinician's level of confidence in the relevance of test findings and enables him or her to decide eventually, for instance, whether the patient meets *DSM–IV* criteria for a particular disorder.

The fact that projective tests can be used to gather evidence about the clinical syndromes is well known and needs no further discussion here. At one time the author strongly believed that the clients' personality styles were reflected in the way they performed on projective instruments. For example, in the first edition of this book, it was proposed that schizoid or avoidant personality styles would lead to signs of social detachment on the projective tests, such as a low number of human responses on the Rorschach or the portrayal of distant relationships on the TAT. A submissive and noncompetitive way of relating to others possibly could be shown in the TAT stories of dependent individuals. Histrionic individuals were expected to be superficial and have a great deal of color on the Rorschach, as well as to generate dramatic and interesting TAT stories. The grandiosity of narcissists and their arrogant style of relating theoretically should be apparent in the projective measures. The Rorschach of compulsive individuals undoubtedly would be too constricted and reveal a preoccupation with detail.

Intent on supporting some of our hypotheses, the author and his colleagues collected MCMI and Rorschach results on a group of 670 patients referred for emotional evaluations (Choca, Van Denburg, Mouton, & Shanley, 1992). We assembled eight groups representing individuals with schizoid, avoidant, dependent, histrionic, narcissistic, competitive/antisocial, compulsive, and negativistic personalities. The assignment to a particular group was made by an experienced clinician on the basis of both MCMI and historical data. Patients' personalities were further characterized with regard to their functional level as constituting personality traits, a personality style, or a personality disorder. Each respondent then was matched with a control patient who had the same primary Axis I psychopathology but a different personality makeup.

Having compiled the eight personality groups and the eight control groups with mixed personalities, we examined the effect that the personality had on Rorschach variables. We had at our disposal the 87 different variables and markers that are generated by the Hermann Rorschach computer program (Choca & Garside, 1992) and that include all the Exner scores and ratios. Because the personality groups were not large enough to support the use of all 87 variables, we selected the Rorschach variables to be used on theoretical grounds. The number of supportable variables and the variables selected varied from one personality group to another. For our schizoid group with 34 individuals, for instance, we selected the total number of responses (R), the number of unusual or minus form quality responses (FQu and FQ–), the number of whole human responses (H and [H]), and the number of responses that used the white section of the inkblot (S) as the variable to be compared. The histrionic group was larger ($n = 66$) and supported the selection of seven variables (R, FQu, FQ–, FC, CF, C, and W). The method was repeated for the other six personality styles.

Our findings showed almost no significant differences between the personality and control groups. This is not to say that some of the protocols were not casebook examples of what a particular personality should look like on the Rorschach. Some of our histrionic respondents, for example, did show the elevated number of whole and color responses that theoretically would be expected. The problem was that many other histrionic respondents did not show those signs and that the entire group was not different from its control. Although Rorschach experts routinely refer to this test as measuring personality variables, it is noteworthy that none of the personologists support the use of this test as a measure of personality style (e.g., see the section on problems in projective methods in McCrae & Costa, 1990).

In spite of our own findings, we still routinely use the Rorschach and think that the scores of this test give valuable clinical information. Our experience has taught us to remain a bit closer to the actual data than we would have in the past. An elevated number of whole responses, for instance, undoubtedly says something about the examinee and may even indicate that the person tends to have a global and superficial view of the world; the jump from that kind of interpretation to saying that the person is histrionic, however, is probably not warranted. On the basis of our findings, we strongly advise against interpreting negative Rorschach findings: It is too risky to assert that a person is not schizoid, compulsive, or negativistic because the Rorschach protocol is not what theoretically would be expected for that personality style.

That projective tests can be a good complement to the information obtained from psychiatric questionnaires such as the MCMI clearly can be seen by the fact that this combination represents the most popular clinical battery used with psychiatric patients. In such a battery, the Rorschach allows clinicians to evaluate the quality of patients' thought processes and their approaches to life. The psychiatric inventory typically provides a sophisticated way of looking at what patients think of themselves. TAT stories often signify life problems that the individuals are facing and the way those issues play out in their interpersonal relationships.

Determining what the usual personality style of a particular individual is can help clinicians decide which of the feasible interpretations of a particular marker in the projective techniques is the most valid. Constriction on the

Rorschach, for example, can be the result of personality traits or the reflection of an acute emotional state such as a depression. If patients who have a constricted Rorschach protocol are, according to the MCMI, highly compulsive, one would have to wonder about the degree to which the lack of determinants and the underproductivity were the result of their compulsive bent as opposed to a reflection of the lack of energy and enthusiasm that often accompanies a despondent mood. If the patients were to have almost any other personality style, however, the constriction of the protocol could be confidently seen as indicating depression.

Similar considerations can be applied to evaluating patients' contact with reality. Blatantly psychotic responses are, of course, pathological regardless of patients' personality styles. Milder forms of thought disturbances, however, are probably much more likely to be present with histrionic or negativistic individuals than with compulsive individuals. Thus, in our experience, the protocols of histrionic patients are bound to contain personal references, boundary problems in terms of mixing one response with another, and color or movement responses that are not carefully linked to the form of the inkblot. Thus, one may be more prone to disregard mild lapses in thought processes when patients have a histrionic personality style than another style.

Psychotherapy and the MCMI

Psychological assessment is most useful when it goes beyond the diagnosis and characterization of the individual and plays the important role it can play in the treatment process. Ideally, the determination of the diagnoses and attributes revealed by the testing should lead to the prescription of a distinct type of psychotherapeutic treatment that is specific to the particular individual.

The strength of the Millon Clinical Multiaxial Inventory (MCMI), especially in comparison with competitors like the Minnesota Multiphasic Personality Inventory (MMPI), has been its conceptualization of the personality makeup. Much of what has been written about therapy with the MCMI, as a result, has dealt with the treatment of personality disorders or with the consideration of the personality style in the treatment of clinical syndromes. Some information about therapeutic interventions was included in the personality style descriptions contained in chapter 6. This chapter will complement those recommendations by reviewing other information available about the use of the MCMI in treatment planning and therapy.

After discussing personality-informed supportive therapy, the chapter will look at the MCMI in the light of different orientations to psychotherapy and will review Millon's synergic treatment plan system. Finally, the chapter will cover what is known about the MCMI with respect to therapeutic modalities. It presents the author's ideas about personality-informed group therapy, as well as an example of what one such group was like. Finally, this chapter will review what is known about the MCMI and the treatment of specific syndromes, as well as the outcome of therapy.

MCMI-Informed Treatment Methods

Supportive Psychotherapy

The issue of whether psychotherapy must always be geared to changing the individual has been controversial. Most psychodynamic thinkers stress the need for change. Kernberg (1984b), for instance, held that patients benefit from an exploratory–expressive type of treatment and reserved supportive measures only for very extreme cases. Others, however, have argued that the vast majority of patients who seek psychotherapy are actually best served by supportive measures, because insight-oriented approaches are too anxiety provoking and expensive for most patients (e.g., Dewald, 1967, 1971; Werman, 1984).

This general controversy becomes even more of an issue when the problems addressed in therapy are characterological. McCrae and Costa (1990) argued persuasively that the personality of the individual is set in early adulthood and does not change through the person's life. Although the present author and his colleagues have shown that changes do occur (Choca, Van Denburg, Bratu, Meagher, & Updegrove, 1996; Dean & Choca, 2001), it is clear that the changes that do occur are small. Given that fact, the author has argued for treatment plans that accept the relative immutability of the personality makeup and attempt to work with it rather than change it (Choca, 1992).

One problem with the concept of supportive therapy is that the treatment is often unclear and poorly defined (Winston, Pinsker, & McCullough, 1986). What often is meant by *supportive therapy* is simply that the therapist will be making an effort to be understanding, conciliatory, sympathetic, compassionate, and nonconfrontational and that he or she will make no demands of the patient that the latter could find difficult. If those attributes are present in the relationship, it generally is thought, the relationship would feel comfortable to the client and would contribute to the reduction of tension. In spite of the merits of that general approach to therapy, the prescription of the same mode of interaction for every patient is simplistic and does not recognize the individual's uniqueness.

We know that the type of relationship that may feel most comfortable to one individual may be less than ideal to the next. Some clients find it easy to talk during the session and prefer for the therapist to be mostly a listener, whereas others are stressed by the expectation that they must talk during the session. Some patients may feel at home when the therapist behaves in an authoritative or parental way, and others may find such interactions offensive or demeaning. In the case of some noncompliant individuals, bringing an issue to a head and dictating strict external controls will have the effect of easing tensions and establishing a solid ground for the relationship. In contrast, other noncompliant persons need some slack and will escalate their rebelliousness or combativeness if the same approach were to be attempted.

How can therapists decide on the approach that would be most productive with a particular individual? The results of the MCMI can help the therapist revise his or her thinking by considering the client's personality style. Knowing the individual's basic life assumptions and the cluster of traits that make up his or her personality allows the practitioner to design an interpersonal environment that will be egosyntonic and productive for any particular client.

Table 9.1, taken from a training manual cowritten by Choca and Van Denburg (1996), offers interpersonal characteristics that theoretically lead to supportive therapeutic experiences with the different personality styles. This additional level of sophistication allows a good deal of flexibility. Looking at any particular type of intervention (e.g., confrontation), the consideration of the personality style would lead the practitioner to avoid the intervention with some individuals (e.g., avoidant or dependent clients) and to use it with others (e.g., competitive clients). With most clients, the issues become more complex than the table would lead one to believe, because most people have a combination of personality styles. Thus, the therapist would have to mix and integrate the recommendations given in the table to do justice to most patients.

Especially in the case of individuals whose personality traits are too extreme or too rigid and who may be considered to have a personality disorder, the therapist should take care not to emphasize the egosyntonic recommendations to the point of fostering further pathology. For the supportive relationship to remain beneficial, the therapist has to operate at the client's level so that the relationship is comfortable without being antitherapeutic. With dependent individuals, for instance, if the therapist were to take responsibility for tasks that the client can handle alone, the interventions would be seen as encouraging the individual to become more dependent than he or she already is, a regressive tactic.

From this viewpoint, the issue of supportive versus reconstructive therapy cannot involve the choice of one to the exclusion of the other. Most therapists adjust their treatment to fit patients' needs while attempting, at least to some degree, to increase the clients' understanding of their own functioning. The more capable, psychologically developed, functional, and

Table 9.1

Supportive Interventions for the Different Personality Styles

Personality style	Supportive interventions
1. Schizoid	Accept interpersonal distance Problem solve in practical matters Do not emphasize insight Do not emphasize relationships
2. Avoidant	Reassure Be careful with negative interpretations Be relaxed
3. Dependent	Be dominant Be protective
4. Histrionic	Allow patient to be center of attention Be emotionally demonstrative
5. Narcissistic	Allow patient to be dominant Be careful with negative interpretations
6. Antisocial	Accept competitive assumption Show how the client is not competing well in terms of psychological functioning Be firm when limits are tested
7. Compulsive	Be on time Be organized Accept a hierarchical view of the world
8. Negativistic	As much as possible, do not tell the patient what to do (any controls will be used as an issue by the patient) Tolerate and interpret moods

motivated the therapy candidate is, the more feasible it may be to emphasize the goal of raising their level of functioning or understanding. Whyne-Berman and McCann (1995) made the same point in terms of the sophistication of individuals' defense mechanisms, with the more primitive defenses calling for a more directive or supportive approach.

Personality-Based Treatment Course Issues

Knowledge of the client's personality style allows clinicians to foresee some aspects of the likely course of treatment, at least in the short run. Such awareness can be very useful in preventing pitfalls. Table 9.2 lists some treatment course issues for the different personality styles. While working

Table 9.2

Therapy Group Members' Scores on the Millon Clinical Multiaxial Inventory (MCMI–III)

Scale	Group members' Base Rate scores					
	A	B	C	D	E	F
Personality style scales						
1. Schizoid	17	60	66	5	35	79*
2A. Avoidant	39	85**	78*	5	48	50
3. Dependent	76*	86**	96**	15	65	40
4. Histrionic	93**	51	25	87**	73	59
5. Narcissistic	59	22	42	76*	74	76*
6A. Antisocial	62	24	61	93**	87**	66
7. Compulsive	13	74	30	61	32	94**
8A. Negativistic	53	60	65	5	85	60
Severe personality scales						
2B. Depressive	70	90**	81*	5	74	71
6B. Aggressive/Sadistic	17	36	44	5	75*	64
8B. Self-Defeating	60	73	80*	5	65	59
S. Schizotypal	36	56	96***	3	33	74
C. Borderline	67	62	73	3	93**	43
P. Paranoid	55	45	62	3	37	70
Clinical symptom scales						
A. Anxiety	57	96**	85**	3	13	89**
H. Somatic Preoccupations	64	75*	65	3	28	81*
N. Hypomania	73	24	55	63	54	40
D. Dysthymia	68	95**	73	3	69	76*
B. Alcohol Abuse	33	0	60	93**	73	68
T. Drug Abuse	41	0	55	98**	67	65
R. Posttraumatic Stress Disorder	64	70	62	3	42	70
Severe clinical syndromes						
SS. Psychotic Thinking	22	68	98**	3	30	66
CC. Psychotic Depression	51	105***	72	68	68	71
PP. Psychotic Delusion	58	60	55	12	70	55
Modifier Indices						
X. Disclosure	72	67	100***	60	76*	66
Y. Desirability	55	43	43	84*	64	84*
Z. Debasement	74	78*	87**	30	63	72
V. Validity	0	0	0	0	0	0

Note. Scores below the cutoff of 75 are shown without asterisks.
*Score elevation was between 75 and 84.
**Score elevation was between 85 and 94.
***Score elevation was between 95 and 105.

in a psychiatric ward, the author often made good use of such knowledge. The staff, for instance, can be prepared to deal with the isolative patient who may prove hard to engage, the antisocial individual who will test the limits of the ward rules, or the negativistic person who will pick a fight soon after admission. When given a chance to discuss the eventuality, the staff can plan and rehearse the optimal therapeutic intervention. Subsequently, when the issue arises, the prepared staff is able to react in a united, coherent, and well-reasoned manner.

Making predictions about the likely treatment course to the patient can be a powerful therapeutic tool. For instance, shortly after admission to the psychiatric ward, patients with a negativistic–antisocial personality style can be warned of the possibility that they will have a conflict with the staff and will then wish to terminate the treatment prematurely. Moreover, such patients can be cautioned that if the conflict occurs, they will be likely to focus only on the specific issue, arguing their point of view with tunnel vision, and will be incapable of appreciating the fact that the conflict is only one instance of a behavioral pattern they have established for themselves. Having prepared the patient in this manner, the therapist will have a better chance of helping such individuals examine their behavioral pattern, possibly preventing an early termination, and of intervening in their lives in an effective and productive manner.[1]

Traditional Treatment Approaches

To whatever degree the treatment plan calls for change in the individual, the therapist will need to have a way of understanding what changes are necessary and how to bring them about. Recognizing the need for a book linking the MCMI to the different psychotherapeutic approaches, Retzlaff (1995) asked MCMI followers to write chapters about their particular orientation. The resulting work, *Tactical Psychotherapy of the Personality Disorders,* outlines how to use the MCMI in therapy. In this book, approaches such

[1] Personality disorders are occasionally so pervasive and immutable that the author has unfortunately seen repeated cases when, in spite of all the preparation, the patient succeeded in doing exactly as predicted. Once these individuals had picked the issue upon which they would battle, they persisted with their tunnel vision to defeat any attempt to change the course of the vicious cycle and prevent the negative outcome. Such failures should not be taken as an indictment against the treatment plan. In other cases, when the patients were reminded of the prediction, it was as if a curtain had suddenly opened, and the individuals were able to see their self-defeating pattern for the first time in their lives.

as behavior therapy, self psychology, cognitive therapy, and object relations theory are applied to Millon's model. The various personality types are discussed from the point of view of the different theoretical models. Case examples are provided, along with MCMI–III findings, to integrate test results and treatment approaches. A review of the different approaches goes beyond the scope of the present book, but readers with a particular orientation are strongly encouraged to read the chapter that covers their particular approach in Retzlaff's book.

Millon's Integrative Approach

In contrast to the views advocated in the preceding section, Millon (1995) argued against the confinement of practitioners to one method of psychotherapy. Consistent with his emphasis on synergy, Millon has favored an integration of the different therapeutic approaches into a single treatment plan (Dorr, 1999; Millon, 1990, 1996, 1999a).

Millon divided his synergistic treatment plan into *strategic goals* and *tactical modalities.* The strategic goals are more general, whereas the tactical modalities constitute the more specific objectives to be reached. After the treatment plan is completed, Millon (1999a) prescribed different types of treatment and treatment modalities to be used in carrying out the treatment plan. The rest of this section will look at the process in more detail. The treatment for the histrionic personality will be used as an example to give the reader a sense of the system Millon proposed.

As discussed in chapter 2, each of the personality prototypes is seen as unbalanced in one or more of the polarities Millon used to explain the personality structure (see Table 2.1 for the specific details). The first of the strategic goals of the synergistic treatment plan is to balance polarities. Histrionics, for instance, are unbalanced in the adaptive mode polarity (i.e., they overuse the active mode at the expense of the passive) and in the replication strategy polarity (i.e., they are excessively strong in the other strategy and weak in the self). The treatment for such individuals needs to balance these polarities by "diminishing manipulative actions"—brought about by the excessive active mode—and "moderating the focus on others"—the excessive other strategy (Millon, 1999a, p. 408).

The second strategic goal is to counter perpetuations. Millon explained the immutability of the personality prototypes by noting elements in each of these prototypes that serve to keep the constellation of traits from changing. As explained in chapter 2, the histrionic focus on the external world translates into superficial social relationships and the repression of inner feelings. The resulting "empty shell" syndrome further drives the individual to seek the attention of others, closing the circle of the self-perpetuating process. To counter the histrionic perpetuating cycle, Millon pointed to the need to "reverse external preoccupations, kindle genuine social relationships, and acquire in-depth knowledge" of the inner self (Millon, 1999a, p. 408).

In order to develop the specific objectives, or tactical modalities, Millon advocates and examination of the disturbances that the personality prototype has in the clinical and structural domains (see chap. 2 and Table 2.3). In the case of the histrionic personality, the most salient disturbances involve the expressive behavior, interpersonal conduct, and cognitive style aspects of the functional domain and the mood aspect of the structural domain. The specific tactical modalities of the synergistic treatment plan then become to (a) reduce dramatic behaviors, (b) decrease interpersonal attention seeking, (c) reorient the flighty cognitive style, and (d) stabilize fickle moods (Millon, 1999a).

At this point the therapist selects and integrates the different kinds of treatment and treatment modalities that will be used to reach the objectives represented by the tactical modalities. In the case of the histrionic personality, for instance, Millon would prescribe training in relaxation, problem-solving strategies, and assertiveness. Transference issues and interpersonal disturbances can be addressed through individual, family, and group treatment modalities. Cognitive therapy will be needed to correct the histrionic client's diffuse cognitive style. Self-exploratory and logical cause-and-effect analysis is recommended to help the client build a stronger self-image that is apart from others. Intrapsychic techniques can be used to understand the familial origins of the histrionic client's desire to have "all of their needs met by a significant powerful other" (Millon, 1999a, p. 414). And, finally, pharmacologic intervention needs to be included when the mood symptoms are seen as biologically based.

The synergic arrangement, or integration of the different therapies and therapeutic modalities, is accomplished by considering which is the most urgent aspect of the person's maladjustment to be addressed at any particular time. In the case of the histrionic client, for instance, Millon saw the first therapeutic step as the need to curtail the patient's tendency to overemotionalize and thereby aggravate the level of distress. Relaxation training, as a result, is seen as the typical place to start (Millon, 1999a).

MCMI Personality Styles and the Therapeutic Relationship

Lovitt (1988) argued that "intensive study of each person's personality structure or coping style is necessary for a proper match between the patient and a treatment approach" (p. 518). Although that suggestion may be ideal, in most settings clinicians generally have to accept patients as they are referred or assigned. In either case, in theory, the MCMI results could help with the matching or at least indicate the kind of relationship that would result between two specific individuals on the basis of their particular personality styles.

Such a pragmatic, real-world model was suggested by Sweeney, Clarkin, and Fitzgibbon (1987). They supported the use of the MCMI as a test that could be used profitably in initial screenings to make treatment recommendations within an acute inpatient setting. Sweeney et al. called for a more focused problem-oriented assessment method that is economically practical and backed by empirical support.

Several researchers have explored the relation between single personality traits and treatment parameters. For instance, Fry (1975) found that a directive and controlling therapist produced more satisfaction for patients who looked outside of themselves for their locus of control. Canter's (1966, 1971) work indicated that the characteristic of authoritarianism was related to patients' preferences for different therapeutic approaches. The intraception trait on the Edwards Personal Preference Schedule (Edwards, 1959) has been correlated with an orientation toward insight in therapy (Birch, 1976; Gibeau, 1975). In addition, numerous researchers have examined the relation between "therapeutic behaviors" such as openness, empathy, and genuineness and the therapist's personality traits (S. Anderson, 1968; Bent, Putnam, Kiesler, & Nowicki, 1976; Beutler, Johnson, Neville, Workman, & Elkins, 1973; Brewer, 1974; Palmer, 1975; Wright, 1975).

It seems logical that an individual's personality style will significantly influence the quality of the interpersonal relationship that he or she establishes. In a pilot study conducted at our medical center (Choca, Silverman, & Gerber, 1980; J. T. Silverman, 1979), we examined the quality of relationship that patients established with their therapists in terms of strength, dominance, and conflictualness. As expected, the findings showed that schizoid individuals tended to establish relationships that were seen by the therapist as having low strength; an unpredicted significant correlation was found between Compulsive scale scores of the MCMI–I and the staff's strength rating. Our data suggested that histrionic and antisocial patients were inclined to play a more dominant role. Finally, the Antisocial and the Compulsive scale scores were significantly related to the amount of conflict that the patient perceived in the relationship.

In a well-designed study, Muran, Segal, Samstag, and Crawford (1994) looked at the relationship between pretreatment interpersonal variables and the therapeutic working alliance. The MCMI and Inventory of Interpersonal Problems were given to 32 patients before beginning brief (20-session) cognitive therapy. The patients then completed the Working Alliance Inventory after the third session of treatment. Positive correlations were found between measures of the working alliance and the interpersonal qualities of a friendly–submissive nature. Hostile–dominant problems were related negatively to the development of the working alliance.

Therapy for Posttraumatic Stress Disorder (PTSD)

The holistic assessment and treatment of PTSD proposed by Hyer and colleagues (Hyer, Davis, Woods, Albrecht, & Boudewyns, 1994; Hyer, Woods, & Boudewyns, 1991) starts with a lifestyle analysis that relies on patients' early recollections and family configuration; the private logic or beliefs that patients endorse also are taken into consideration. The system then investigates patients' personalities, typically with the help of the MCMI. Others have also emphasized the importance of taking into consideration characterological factors in the treatment of PTSD (e.g., Sherwood, Funari, & Piekarski, 1990). Finally, the PTSD symptoms are evaluated. The goal is to understand the symptoms that are informed by patients' lifestyles and their personalities.

In their writings, Hyer et al. (1991, 1994) offered many insights and advice in handling patients with different MCMI profiles. They characterized the general "traumatic personality" as a negativistic–avoidant style. These individuals are "oversensitive, fearful, self-preoccupied, disgruntled, uneasy, irritable . . . unsettled . . . anxious, complaining, and powerless" (Hyer et al., 1991, p. 176). Given this personality, the overall treatment approach must be one that emphasizes the increase of control as a therapeutic goal. This control would include attempts at "reduction of vacillating and self-defeating patterns" (Hyer, 1994, p. 237).

More specific advice also is available for the three personality subtypes that have been found. Individuals who have schizoid elements along with the negativistic–avoidant personality (the 8A2A1 code type) "appear cognitive and affectively confused" and experience themselves as "strange, lost and despairing" (Hyer et al., 1991, p. 178). A reasonable therapeutic approach is to respect the detachment and to build trust over time. By contrast, patients with benign but annoying dependent traits (the 8A2A13 code type) have a poor self-image and are submissive, a fact that tends to increase compliance. By far the most difficult patients are said to be those with an antisocial bent (the 8A2A16A code type). Their interpersonal distrust often makes the building of a working alliance difficult. In his later work, Hyer (1994) discussed how the self-defeating code-type added to the 8A2A1 negativistic–avoidant–schizoid profile "floods the avoidant and ambivalent character traits with a repetitive series of misfortunes" (p. 239). This group also "tends to increase problems and undermine progress in treatment" (Hyer, 1994, p. 239).

Hyer et al. (1994) also noted that elevations in any of the severe personality scales (e.g., Borderline), which occur in as many as 60% of these patients, further complicate the treatment and aggravate the prognosis. Although Hyer (1994) took pains to say that this material is best viewed as a "clinical taxonomy and represents anything but perfect classification" (p. 240), recent empirical work using the cluster analysis technique tended to support his assumptions (Hyer et al., 1994).

Everly and Lating (2003) advocated a two-pronged approach to the treatment of PTSD: (a) regulating the pathologically intense arousal that is typically part of the disorder and (b) assisting the patient in making intellectual sense of the traumatic experience. To accomplish those goals, the authors emphasized the need for a strong therapeutic alliance. They used Millon's theory and personality prototypes to emphasize aspects of treatment that need to be attended to, to provide the personologic alignment that would be needed to construct the therapeutic alliance. In one of the cases they presented, for example, they saw a need to build up the confidence of a narcissistic physician after a traumatic episode.

Therapy for Medical Patients

In a book titled *Personality-Guided Therapy in Behavioral Medicine,* Harper (2003) reviewed all of the personality disorders using a Millon perspective and described the theoretical implications of each personality in the treatment of medical problems.

Marital Therapy

As detailed in chapter 7, Craig and Olson (1995) used the MCMI–II to characterize four types of individuals who are likely to seek marital therapy.

The authors then considered the possible combinations of the four different types and the therapeutic interventions that might be useful. For example, the couple consisting of a narcissistic–aggressive–histrionic individual and a negativistic–aggressive–borderline individual is likely to have a conflictual marital relationship. These authors suggested that the therapist focus on the conflicts and attempt to decrease the frequency and intensity of the quarreling.

When the narcissistic–aggressive–histrionic individual is matched with either of the two dependent types, the theoretical result will be an overadequate–underadequate relationship, in which the dependent spouse may complain of the partner being too bossy and controlling. A similar overadequate–underadequate relationship can be expected to result from the marriage of a negativistic–aggressive–borderline individual with either of the two dependent types. In those cases, Craig and Olson (1995) contended that the dependent spouse needs to see how his or her own behaviors allow the other to be controlling, whereas the overadequate spouse needs to explore the effect that a more egalitarian relationship would have on his or her own self-esteem.

A different problem is foreseen with the marriage of two individuals with dependent personality styles. The difficulty of the resulting underadequate–underadequate relationship may be that each of the partners would want the other to take the lead. In those cases, Craig and Olson (1995) recommended individual therapy along with conjoint sessions designed to reduce the sensitivity to rejection and fear of making decisions.

Group Therapy

The group format offers great advantages for the treatment of personality disturbances. These advantages include economic factors, clients' ability to handle denial in a more effective manner, and the opportunity for role-playing new behaviors.

The treatment of personality issues typically involves a longer period of time than the treatment of more temporary clinical syndromes such as depression. Individual therapy, as a result, becomes an expensive proposition. Because the cost per session is less in a group, such treatment may be more feasible.

Personality attributes are often egosyntonic and feel so comfortable that the individual may be unaware of the way in which certain attributes may encumber his or her functioning. Although the sensitive and persistent individual therapist will eventually work with those defenses, a therapy group can be very powerful, especially when the perceptions of several group members coincide.

Another advantage of the group with respect to the treatment of personality attributes is its ability to provide modeling and training. In some cases people demonstrate traits at least in part because they lack the expertise it would take to act in a different manner. There are those shy individuals, for instance, who may find it useful to develop a few topics to use for conversations in a social situation.

The author developed a weekly group format that he successfully used for over 20 years. Although typically the group members had been first hospitalized with a clinical syndrome, the goal of this outpatient group was to manage the personality difficulties that were left after the clinical syndrome was in remission. A system of rolling admissions was established so that the composition of the group varied over time. The expectation, however, was that the incoming member would make a commitment to attend the meetings for at least 1 year.

In keeping with the author's view about the permanence of personality traits, the goal of the treatment was not to change the personality style. Rather, the goal was to help the group members make adjustments that would make their established personality style more effective, without changing the basic personality. In some cases these adjustments involved changes to the environment to improve the goodness of fit: Some members divorced or changed jobs during their time in the group. More often, the adjustment involved learning to behave in a slightly different manner or taking some beneficial action that the person had not been able to take before her or his participation in the group.

There were times when the therapist became very active in explaining or promoting a concept, and the session took on an instructional flavor. That amount of directiveness, however, was rare. More typically the therapist played the role of facilitator, engaging a group member who had been silent, helping a member reveal some sensitive material, or processing the feelings or reactions of the group about the presentation of a group member. The group was conducted in a way that emphasized the interaction among group members and encouraged members to be both open about their reactions and sensitive to the feelings of other members of the group.

The group work started with the introduction of a new individual into the group. As part of the intake, the MCMI was typically administered. The group process was then used to uncover the important elements of the individual's personality and the way in which those elements may have encumbered the person's adjustment. After achieving the necessary insights, the goal was to help the patient formulate ways of changing the environmental structure or modulating the characterological inclinations so that the behavior could become more adaptive and useful. The next section provides an example of how the process worked.

Therapy Example: A Group With Personality

During the years that the group was in operation, many people were group members for a period of time. The individuals described in this section were, in the author's mind, the most notable members. This section attempts to describe the individual, formulate the goals of the treatment, characterize the kind of interactions that the person had with the group, and describe the group interventions that may have helped the patient reach the treatment goals.

Mr. A

Mr. A was one of the founders of the group and the only one of the original group members who was still with the group at the end. As can be seen in Table 9.2, Mr. A had a histrionic personality with dependent elements. He suffered from a bipolar disorder and, in fact, joined the group after a fairly severe manic episode that resulted in the termination of his first marriage. He was on lithium carbonate when he joined the group; one of the goals of the treatment was to monitor his moods and provide feedback for the referring psychiatrist. Additionally, the group aspired to make Mr. A more aware of his overly dramatic tendencies and the way in which these tendencies exacerbated his mood instability and hampered his functioning.

Mr. A was a kingpin in the group. His good social skills allowed him to talk to everyone. His high energy level and search for attention meant that he could offer his thoughts or experience about almost anything that anyone else would bring up. He appeared to enjoy the group more than most and was absent only during the 3 weeks he was on vacation. When another histrionic and outspoken individual joined the group (Mr. D), Mr. A's leadership was questioned and challenged. Eventually an accommodation took place, with the apparent resolution that the two men would share the spotlight in the group.

The resolution to share the spotlight was forged only after heated controversies between the two men. During those controversies, both of these group members, insightful and adept at expressing themselves as they were, played a crucial role in enhancing each other's awareness of how they were seen by others. The enhanced awareness was also supported by many of the other group members, who might not have brought up the issue on their own but were quick to agree with the observations or insights of others. Through the years, Mr. A was able to use those insights to accept and moderate his own tendencies so as to function better. As a result, he was able to make changes in his life structure and to modify his own behavior.

Changes in life structure involved both the work setting and a second marriage. Mr. A had been working at a very traditional 9-to-5 job, where he was always in trouble for coming in late and not being structured enough. Recognizing these problems, he eventually found a job he loved that allowed him to be "self-employed." This job was structured so that he would be paid for any work he completed but was free to determine on his own when and how he would perform the service. It was a histrionic's dream job, with consistent interactions with the public in a situation where he was unlikely to have to deal with the same individual very frequently. Mr. A also found himself a new life partner whom he eventually married. His second wife was a no-nonsense individual with some compulsive traits who introduced a great deal of structure and stability in the patient's life.

As to his personal changes, Mr. A learned to appreciate the benefits of some punctuality. Although many parts of his life were structured in such a way that punctuality was not important, he became very aware that punctuality was imperative in other situations and would make whatever efforts he had to in order to comply with those requirements. Similarly, Mr. A learned of other instances where the histrionic mode of operation was counterproductive and his behavior had to be adjusted. He also was able to modify his level of energy and intensity, learning to gauge those times when he was "revving too fast" and needed to take a break from his activities, typically by going for a cup of coffee at a place where he could sit down and relax. At the end of the group Mr. A continued to have his emotive, ebullient, sociable, and dramatic personality, but he had refined his controls so that he could function at a much higher level.

Mr. B

A different set of issues was raised by Mr. B, another of the group founders. As can be seen from Table 9.2, Mr. B was a dependent–avoidant individual. His physical presentation was that of a shy, nervous, and inadequate person. Mr. B was also encumbered by a lifelong dysthymic disorder: He was one of those individuals who strongly believed that if he ever dropped toast, it would always land jelly-side down. At the time he joined the group, Mr. B had been hospitalized for an acute episode of depression with suicidal ideation.

A number of years prior to his hospitalization, Mr. B had left a job as an electronics technician in order to take care of ailing parents. The parents eventually died, first one and then the other, leaving the patient unemployed and with no suitable life structure. The home and modest funding Mr. B had inherited from his parents had provided for him up to the time of admission, but Mr. B was aware that he would eventually need to obtain gainful employment if he was to continue with the lifestyle to which he was accustomed.

At the time he joined the group, his characterological nervousness and feelings of inadequacy had been exacerbated by the lack of motivation and energy raised by his depression, to the extent that he was completely unable to search for a job. The goals for Mr. B obviously included supporting him in searching for a job, reducing the amount of anxiety he experienced in social situations, and increasing his level of socialization. The patient's dependent–avoidant personality was accepted, and the treatment plan called only for the modifications he needed to make to increase the functionality of this personality.

In contrast to Mr. A, Mr. B always looked uncomfortable in the group and remained fairly silent. When attempts were made to ask his opinion or draw him out, he always looked extremely uncomfortable and tended to respond with only brief comments or explanations. One beginning issue the group had with Mr. B was the fear that he would not return, because unlike other members, he did not appear to find the group sessions enjoyable. This issue was addressed from the start, and both the patient and the other group members committed to continue with the group for a year. When, in spite of this commitment, Mr. B started missing sessions, other group members took it on themselves to pick the patient up at his home and take him to the sessions. The fact that another person would be interested enough in him to make that kind of an effort was an eye-opener for Mr. B and cemented his group alliance, so that he renewed his commitment to attend the sessions on his own.

Eventually the same procedure was used to force Mr. B's hand in his job search. Another member of the group picked Mr. B up at his residence, drove him to an electronics repair shop with an advertised opening, and sat with Mr. B while he completed the application and talked to the shop manager. In this case, the procedure had an unintended result: Mr. B found it so embarrassing to have to be accompanied in this way while putting in an application that he started going out and completing applications on his own. The efforts eventually paid off when Mr. B was offered a reasonable technician job that he kept at least until he discontinued his participation in the group a number of years later.

With time, Mr. B became much more comfortable in the group, to the point of enjoying the group sessions and being an active participant, albeit in a serious and restrained manner. He was able to joke with other group members and accept their good-natured teasing. The interventions of the group were also helpful at other times. At one point, for instance, Mr. B was helped to reason through and turn down a position that would have involved more responsibility and other technicians reporting to him. The patient did not believe he could carry out the personnel responsibilities of the supervisory position, and the group supported him in being able to accept his limitations.

On another occasion, the group helped Mr. B negotiate an agreement with a new supervisor who felt that his work was too slow and that he needed to fix the equipment he was given in less time. Again at the group's insistence, the patient eventually renewed his membership in a chess club, an activity that he had found enjoyable during his younger years. After a chance encounter, he renewed the acquaintance of an old high school mate. This old acquaintance was a widow by now and eventually became the patient's "girlfriend." Even though Mr. B and his girlfriend always kept different residences, she was often at his home and used her influence in prompting Mr. B to repaint and modernize the house. As with Mr. A, Mr. B was considered a successful case in that the group appeared to have had a very favorable impact in his life.

Mr. C

In contrast, the effect of the group appeared to have been more limited with the next patient. Mr. C came to the group with the diagnosis of schizophrenia. After enlisting in the army and serving for 2 years, Mr. C became convinced that other soldiers in his barracks thought he was gay and would attack him sexually. He loaded his belongings into his car and was living in his car for a week before the authorities became aware of the problem. He was eventually taken to the hospital and later received a medical discharge and disability pension.

On his discharge, Mr. C went to a city that was near the base, rented a studio apartment, and stayed there for 2 years. One day, he had an accident while driving his car when he failed to yield the right-of-way while turning left in front of incoming traffic. Because he had failed to pay the insurance premium, he was uninsured at the time. After the accident, the patient put his belongings in storage, packed one bag with his clothes, and showed up at his parents' apartment in another city and state.

The patient's father, a diabetic, had lost both of his legs and had significant medical problems. The parents lived in a small apartment and did not have many resources. The patient slept on the living room couch and, at his mother's insistence, stored everything away when he was not sleeping. As a result, he was mostly living out of a suitcase. The arrangement was not to anyone's liking, but the patient would not seriously consider any other living accommodation.

Mr. C was a collector of old 78 and long-playing records, cassette cartridges, and music paraphernalia. Although he owned a turntable, the equipment was in storage in another state and was unavailable to him. Moreover, Mr. C liked to buy old 8-track cassettes, even though the players were no longer for sale, and he doubted that he would ever have the equipment necessary to play them. He was so addicted to his collection that he seemed incapable of staying out of the secondhand music stores. He spent every available dollar on adding items to his collection and storing them. Because he did not have any space in his parents' home, Mr. C leased some storage space shortly after coming into the area and had already been forced to move into a bigger space.

Although he still believed he had been at risk of being sexually attacked when he was in the military, Mr. C did not have any other delusional beliefs and was thought to have mainly a character disorder. As can be seen in Table 9.2, he had a schizotypal personality with self-defeating, dependent, and avoidant elements. It is noteworthy that the Psychotic Thinking scale was elevated, in spite of the fact that the patient was no longer psychotic. (The elevations on the Disclosure and Debasement scales were to be expected with an individual who had shown fairly severe pathology.)

Mr. C was fairly peculiar in his appearance. Even though he was in his 20s, he wore clothes more typical of a much older person. Unless the group insisted that he take off his winter coat, he kept it on for the entire session. He had somewhat unusual facial mannerisms when he talked. Like Mr. B, Mr. C seemed shy and inhibited at first, but unlike Mr. B, this patient could talk in an animated manner for reasonable periods of time, especially when he talked about one of his areas of interest.

Mr. C was able to get some odd jobs around his neighborhood, part-time jobs that had no benefits or security. At the group's instigation, he made considerable efforts to obtain a more acceptable position. The work of the group included some role-playing of job interviews, because the patient had been inclined to reveal all kinds of details about his history that would have scared off any prospective employer. For example, the patient learned that, without lying, he could state that his military service had been "fine" and not volunteer the details of how it had ended. He also received training from the Department of Occupational Rehabilitation. In spite of these efforts, Mr. C was never able to obtain full-time employment.

The group's efforts to moderate the patient's addiction to old music paraphernalia were also fairly unsuccessful. Mr. C could not be moved even into resolving in some manner the issue of the belongings he had left stored in the city where he had lived after being discharged from the military. Because he spent all of his available money in supporting his addiction to music paraphernalia, he did not have the funds he would have needed to find reasonable living space. In other words, in spite of the group's efforts, Mr. C was not able to improve any aspects of his life structure.

In fact, at the time the group ended, the accomplishments of Mr. C seemed very modest in comparison with those of some other group members. Nevertheless, the group represented the only relationships that Mr. C had been able to establish outside of the home. He attended the group sessions religiously and appeared to enjoy them, especially when they focused on him. The neuroleptic medication the patient had taken before his admission had been discontinued because it did not seem to have any effect, and there had been no recurrence of the delusional system the patient had at one time. It seemed that the group, at best, had provided a maintenance system, but it failed to bring about any productive changes.

Mr. D

Another member, Mr. D, was a middle-aged man who was the epitome of a salesman. Mr. D had sold insurance and real estate and was now selling used cars. He liked to talk about the schemes he had come up with at his different jobs to make more money. At his present job, for instance, he was trying to combine his previous occupation as an insurance salesman with the used car business. Mr. D was trying to negotiate an insurance policy that a used car buyer could purchase that would cover any major mechanical problems the car would develop during the first year of ownership. Although Mr. D had been able to put some of his creations into operation at one time or another, none of them had been as financially rewarding as he thought they would be.

Mr. D tended to present himself in slightly grandiose terms, as one would have expected from his MCMI scores (see Table 9.2), and he was diagnosed with a bipolar affective disorder at one time. The patient had also been an alcoholic and cocaine abuser. Perhaps because of his substance abuse, his life history was fairly checkered, and he had been fired from a number of jobs. He was living alone after his third divorce. He had two daughters and a son from his first marriage and two teenage children from his second marriage.

Mr. D served a brief jail term for cocaine possession, driving under the influence (DUI), and driving without a license (after his license had been suspended on a previous DUI conviction). For an individual like Mr. D, who thought of himself as a bit more competent and resourceful than others, facing the jail term was a wakeup call. He was then able to see his life as a string of failures, in spite of some undeniable talents and successes.

More than any of the other patients, Mr. D came into the group with a clear idea of what he wanted to accomplish. He interviewed the therapist before joining the group to assure himself that the group could meet the goals he had in mind. For one thing, the patient disagreed with the bipolar affective disorder diagnosis he was given by a psychiatrist after a 1-hour interview. He felt that the high energy level and attentional problems he had at that time were due to the cocaine he had been using; the patient disagreed with the psychiatrist's assessment that he was grandiose. Following similar reasoning, the patient saw his recurrent depressions as resulting from his substance abuse and the times he had ruined his life with his "drinking and drugging," as opposed to his having a "chemical imbalance." He wanted the group to assist with the appropriate assessment of that diagnosis in order to determine with confidence whether he was or was not suffering from bipolar mood fluctuations. The patient also wanted some help in recovering his driver's license and reestablishing his life on a more solid footing.

Mr. D became very dominant in the group from the start. He immediately challenged the leadership of the other dominant member by noting the way the members related to Mr. A and pointing out some of Mr. A's failures. Eventually, these two individuals made their own adjustments and shared the leadership role. Mr. D proved to be smart and insightful and was able to look at angles that no one else had noticed. Even though he was able to appreciate complexity, he favored crisp thinking and liked it when he could map out issues in fairly black-and-white ways. His tireless search for instances of denial, which he reassured the group was "more than a river in Egypt," often placed him in conflict with other group members but represented a significant contribution to the group.

Mr. D continued his commitment to remaining sober and drug free throughout his participation in the group. He was also participating in Alcoholics Anonymous meetings, where he became a sponsor and a bit of a leader as well. He was able to recover his driver's license and continued to make a living selling cars. When the Internal Revenue Service (IRS) tracked him down and threatened to put him in jail for years of unpaid taxes, the patient gained some significant insights about himself. As he told the story, while he was talking to an IRS agent and demanding some kind of adjustment, the agent stopped him and asked, "Who do you think you are, anyway?" With that question, the patient came to the realization that others are not likely to see him through the somewhat grandiose eyes with which he saw himself. To this agent, Mr. D was nothing more than a delinquent taxpayer who needed to be pressured into paying his back taxes, even if he had to be incarcerated in order to force compliance. After achieving this great discovery, Mr. D was able to negotiate a payment plan that would have him paying a fixed amount every quarter for what would probably be the rest of his life.

During his stay in the group, Mr. D was also able to reestablish his child support for his teenage children and arrange for the first of many outings with them. All of his negotiations benefited from feedback from the group, which tended to moderate the competitiveness and sense of entitlement that were associated with his personality inclinations. Mr. D was taken off his medication and had remained symptom free at the time the group ended.

Ms. E

So as not to leave the reader with the impression that the group had no failures, the case of Ms. E provides one such example. This patient had a borderline personality with antisocial and negativistic elements (see Table 9.2). In contrast to most of the other group members, who had suffered from a clinical syndrome at one time or another, Ms. E had never had any symptoms outside of her personality problems and had never been in the hospital. She had a few individual sessions with the therapist and was moved into the group as a way of continuing her treatment.

Ms. E's history was very typical for a borderline personality. The patient had gone from one job to another and from one relationship to the next in what appeared to be a sequence of unfulfilling and unproductive interactions. Her jobs typically ended when she had a fight with her supervisor and accused the supervisor of being unfair to her in one way or another. Although suicidal inclination had not been much of a problem for her, the history included many instances of behavioral acting-out in ways that were unproductive or dangerous. The incident that precipitated her treatment, for example, was her being charged with public indecency when she was caught in the men's bathroom of a singles bar performing oral sex on a male bar patron.

The goals of treatment in Ms. E's case were to make her aware of her predilection for acting out in ways that compromised her well-being. It was hoped, for instance, that Ms. E would be more in touch with her mood changes and how those changes typically led to the fights that ended her jobs or relationships.

During her participation in the group, Ms. E was often in conflict with the group. During the first week or two, for instance, she explained that she was "between jobs" and did not have enough money to get to the end of the month. After that session ended, several of the group members took up a collection so that she would have food to eat. When a group member observed her spending the money at a nearby store on popcorn and chocolates, the members of the group felt they had been taken and shared their feelings with her. As was typical, she became defensive and argued that the popcorn and chocolates were "nutritious" and that they had no right to dictate what she should be eating.

The group had a modicum of success in helping Ms. E look at the pattern of her life and accept the undeniable trend of going from one crisis to the next. At times during those early sessions, Ms. E made very encouraging progress. The insights were unfortunately possible only when Ms. E was not in the midst of an incident. While involved in an incident, she could never see what was happening. When she was arrested for shoplifting at a department store, for instance, she argued that she had been the victim of circumstances. From her point of view, it was the girl she was with who had been the real culprit. Ms. E argued that she had never shoplifted before, or almost never; that it was the girlfriend who talked her into going into the store and hiding the merchandise; and that one of the objects she was caught with was actually for the girlfriend rather than for herself.

Shortly after joining the group, Ms. E obtained a job as a retail clerk at a bakery. She lived a block away from this bakery and agreed to "split her shift": She worked in the morning, when the bakery was busy with the delivery of restaurant orders, and in the late afternoon, when people stopped to buy bread on their way home. At first Ms. E spoke with great fondness of the owner, a middle-aged lady who was quickly becoming Ms. E's mentor.

Later on, Ms. E started developing her own ideas about how to do the work better; when some of these ideas were not accepted, the relationship between Ms. E and the bakery owner began to shift. Eventually Ms. E took up the issue of her salary. The split shift, she argued, merited more pay, because many people would not be able or willing to work such peculiar hours. Besides, with all of her suggestions, she had already become a bit of a manager at the bakery. The entire group could see the process unfolding: In the span of just 3 months, the patient had gone from unemployment, to being the favored employee who brought bread into group sessions so that the members could try the products of "her" bakery, to placing herself on the brink of being fired. The patient, however, had no insight and was convinced she was too important to be fired. The day a new clerk was hired and Ms. E was told her services were no longer needed, she was hurt and angry, as if a great injustice had been done to her. When the group members were unsympathetic and reminded her about the concerns they had voiced in the previous weeks, the patient bolted from the group session and could not be convinced to return. Eventually she refused to talk even to the therapist. Two months later, when the therapist saw her elsewhere in the medical center, Ms. E looked the other way and refused to acknowledge his greeting.

The failure of the group with Ms. E was the topic of discussions in the group and of a peer review session the therapist had with his colleagues. The fact that the patient was a woman, and the other group members were men, was seen as an issue, as was her being younger than many of the other group members. In the therapist's mind, however, the main issue was the defense mechanism that could not be altered. In spite of the group's success in having Ms. E acknowledge the overall pattern of her behavior, she could not be helped to see how any one instance fit the pattern while she was living through it. This was unfortunate, because if she could have seen the role played by the instance, then she could have moved on to monitor her own behavior and emotions and make the adjustments that worked so well with many of the other group members.

Mr. F

In the final case, the process of insight, monitoring, and personality adjustments was much more successful. In his younger days Mr. F was an Olympic track athlete. He won a bronze metal and, for a brief period of time, held the world record for one of the events. For a farm boy from Nebraska, this had been the experience of a lifetime. He had never imagined being in the position of fending off news reporters, being the subject of feature articles written about him and his farming family, or seeing his picture in the paper every other day. Shortly after the Olympics, however, he "wrecked his knee" and was never again the athlete he had once been. He was still able to represent well the top-notch university where he had a track scholarship, but he was no longer one of the top runners of the world.

After obtaining his bachelor's degree, Mr. F went to another top-notch university to pursue a master's degree in political science. To make a living, he accepted a job in a federal agency. A hard and conscientious worker, Mr. F was rapidly promoted to a position that offered a reasonable salary. The schooling then began to lose its appeal. Mr. F took one semester off, and then another, and eventually abandoned his studies altogether. This was the source of much regret later on in his life, because he saw his studies as a way in which he could have possibly recovered some of the prominence of his athletic career. He had intended to use his political science background to become a professional politician, ambassador, or elected official. Although Mr. F did very well with the federal government and had more than 40 years of a productive career as a supervisor, he saw this accomplishment as mundane and unremarkable.

Mr. F never married and had always lived by himself. He had many friends and acquaintances from his years at work and from his neighborhood. He did not see himself as having any social problems, even though he maintained a certain distance from others. An athlete at heart, he had kept fit his entire life by doing calisthenics and swimming. He associated the depression from which he had been suffering with the medical problems he was having for the first time in his life. He explained that he had "stayed at the age of 40 until [he] became 70," at which time he "aged 30 years." What had happened was that the patient "pinched" his sciatic nerve. One day he could not move enough to reach the phone and call for help. Following that incident, the patient was in pain for an extended period of time. While he was seeing doctors for the sciatic nerve, a number of other medical problems were discovered. None of his problems were life threatening or even very serious, but they signaled to the patient that he had become an elderly person.

Mr. F had a compulsive personality with schizoid elements, as can be seen in Table 9.2. In his case, the elevation of the Desirability scale was just a product of his perfectionistic tendencies and did not suggest any problem with the validity of the scores. The compulsive personality played a role in the patient's depression. It was clear, as he talked to the group, that he had lived "right" all of his life: He had no vices, ate the right kinds of food, and exercised every day except for Sunday when he rested. The exercise was well proportioned, with the right kind of schedules and activities. It was a well-designed exercise program, informed by all of the sports books Mr. F read and the experts he had consulted. Having lived right, he did not expect to be stricken by the bothersome aspects of aging. Being an intelligent and well-educated man, Mr. F knew that all humans die. However, he sort of expected to be problem free until the age of 99 and then to pass on in his sleep. He had worked all of his life so as not to become prematurely elderly and perhaps partially disabled at the age of 70. The experience of medical problems had been especially hard for Mr. F because it shattered his basic assumption in life—that if one worked hard and avoided making mistakes, nothing negative would happen.

Mr. F became an active group member and seemed to derive much benefit from the group sessions. Through the eyes of the other members, he learned to see his own life as more productive and fulfilling than he had at first. He eventually connected his own personality attributes to his reactions to the medical problems he was facing. The group discussions served to validate his philosophy of life as a worthwhile philosophy, in spite of the fact that it did not always hold. Like any philosophy of life, Mr. F learned to appreciate that being compulsive and doing the right thing cannot always prevent some malady from happening. He was, nevertheless, reassured that it worked so much of the time that it provided a good guide to follow. As he worked on these issues and his medical problems improved, the depression lifted, and the patient showed considerable symptomatic improvement.

Although anecdotal and obviously colored by the author's biased recollections, the above descriptions were designed to offer the reader a therapist's view of what a personality-informed therapy group can accomplish. In the next section the book will review the empirical evidence available about treatment outcome in personality-oriented therapy.

Treatment Outcome Studies

The measurement of treatment outcome is a difficult and problematic task. For one thing, a good design would call for the comparison of treated individuals with a particular malady to a control group of similar individuals who were not treated. In most cases it is not possible to carry out such a design, because it is unethical to deny treatment to an individual who may benefit from it. It is possible to compare one type of treatment with another, but such a design leaves one with an incomplete picture, because there is no way of knowing if the same outcomes could have been obtained with no treatment at all.

Seligman (1995) specified procedures for evaluating the effectiveness of psychotherapy under real-life circumstances. Seligman's system calls for (a) the selection of a sample that truly reflects the population of individuals suffering from a particular disorder, (b) the collection of data regarding the type and duration of the treatment received, and (c) the repeated assessment of symptomatology and level of functioning through standard measures. Although the standard measures should ideally go beyond a self-report inventory, the MCMI has been repeatedly used successfully as a standard measure of outcome.

The MCMI–I was used in several studies to assess possible changes in personality that might occur as a result of using various treatment modalities. Clinical populations studied have included alcoholics and drug abusers (Calsyn, Wells, Fleming, & Saxon, 2000; McMahon, Flynn, & Davidson, 1985a), private psychiatric inpatients (Piersma, 1986b, 1989a), Vietnam veterans with posttraumatic stress disorder (PTSD; Hyer et al., 1989), and spouse abusers (Hamberger & Hastings, 1988b). A consistent finding across these studies is that regardless of whether there was clinical improvement, personality style scale results remained fairly stable from pre- to posttest assessments and were more stable than symptom scale results (e.g., level of anxiety, depression).

Three other studies using the MCMI touched on the use of this instrument in treatment contexts. Cantrell and Dana (1987) used the MCMI–I as a screening instrument with patients at a community mental health center. They demonstrated that the MCMI–I was poor at predicting premature termination of treatment.

McMahon and Davidson (1986b) used the MCMI–I to examine depressed and nondepressed alcoholics treated in a Veterans Administration inpatient unit. Patients were originally divided into the two groups on the basis of their scores on the Dysthymia scale. They demonstrated that these two groups could be differentiated on the basis of having a detached (schizoid or avoidant) personality style or suffering from disorganized or distracted mentation (Schizotypal and Psychotic Thinking scales). Because the depressed alcoholics also had a longer history of alcohol abuse and more physical and psychological symptoms, McMahon and Davidson (1986b) recommended that this subgroup "would benefit most from an intensive, comprehensive, and long-term therapeutic program" (p. 183).

From a biological perspective, Joffe and Regan (1989a) examined patients who did and did not respond to tricyclic antidepressant treatment to determine whether there were personality differences between the two groups. The MCMI–I, Beck Depression Inventory, Hamilton Rating Scale for Depression, and Schedule for Affective Disorders and Schizophrenia were administered. In the remission phase, there were no significant differences between responders and nonresponders on the MCMI–I. In the depressed phase, responders scored higher on the Antisocial and Paranoia scales. The MCMI–I tended to overdiagnose personality disorders in the depressed phase. There was no difference in frequency of personality disorders between responders and nonresponders. The findings of this study are limited because of the relatively small sample ($N = 42$).

Studies documenting improvement with a heterogeneous psychiatric group have been done with the MCMI–I (McMahon et al., 1985b; Piersma, 1986d), the MCMI–II (Piersma, 1989b; Piersma & Boes, 1997c), and the MCMI–III (Piersma & Boes, 1997a). Improvement with depressed individuals in treatment has been shown with the MCMI–II (Piersma & Smith, 1991) and the MCMI–III (Piersma & Boes, 1997b). Fals-Stewart and Lucente (1993) used the MCMI–II to demonstrate that obsessive–compulsive personality disorders with milder character pathology or with dependent and compulsive features did best in behavioral treatment.

The outcome of treatment for substance abuse has been studied with the MCMI–I (McMahon et al., 1985b). With decreases on various MCMI scales, outcome studies typically show an increase on the Histrionic, Narcissistic, and Compulsive scales (e.g., Piersma & Boes, 1997b), which have generally proved to be healthy personality indicators (see the Personality Theory section in chap. 2 for more details).

Moving on to the study of treatment modalities, the Anxiety, Dysthymia, and Major Depression scales of the MCMI–I were used to show the benefits of short-term cognitive therapy (Safran, Segal, Vallis, Shaw, & Wallner Samstag, 1993). The MCMI–I showed a change toward extraversion in the case of morbidly obese patients who received gastric stapling surgery and lost weight (Chandarana, Conlon, Holliday, Deslippe, & Field, 1990). Martin, Langone, Dole, and Wiltrout (1992) showed the benefits of deprogramming with the MCMI–I of former cult members. Piersma and Boes (1997a) used the MCMI–III to show that a psychiatric day hospital program was just as effective as inpatient care in reducing psychopathology. They argued in support of day hospitals because the cost of treatment is much lower than that of inpatient care. Peniston and Kulkosky (1990) compared the effect of alpha–

theta brain-wave relaxation training with the use of group therapy and lectures in the treatment of alcoholics. The findings indicated that the group treated with the relaxation technique decreased their MCMI–I scores on 13 of the 20 scales. By contrast, the respondents receiving only group therapy and lectures obtained significant decreases on 2 scales and showed an increase in Compulsive scale scores.

The trend of MCMI score reduction after treatment, however, was not always found. Judging from MCMI–I results, intense inpatient treatment of veterans with PTSD does not lead to a reduction in the symptomatology (Funari, Piekarski, & Sherwood, 1991; Hyer et al., 1989). Although improvement with dissociative identity disorders was initially shown with the MCMI–II (Ellason & Ross, 1996, 1997; Ellason et al., 1995), the changes were later shown to have been of questionable magnitude (Powell & Howell, 1998; Ross & Ellason, 1999).

A very practical approach to the study of treatment outcome is to investigate individual variables that may be associated with better or worse outcomes. In terms of predictor variables, higher scores on the Histrionic and Narcissistic scales of the MCMI–I and MCMI–II have been found to be associated with better outcomes (Chambless, Renneberg, Goldstein, & Gracely, 1992; Leaf, Ellis, Mass, DiGiuseppe, & Alington, 1990; Vaglum et al., 1990), except in the treatment of chronic pain (Elliott, Jackson, Layfield, & Kendall, 1996). Higher levels of schizoid, avoidant, and schizotypal traits have been associated with poorer outcomes (Chambless et al., 1992; Leaf, Ellis, et al., 1990; Vaglum et al., 1990). Elevations on the Schizoid, Histrionic, and Dysthymia scales of the MCMI–I have been related to poorer outcomes of pain patients receiving a lumbar laminectomy (Herron, Turner, & Weiner, 1986).

In spite of the failure of Craig's (1984) early attempt to predict treatment dropout of substance abusers with the MCMI–I, others have reported significant findings. Fals-Stewart (1992) found two substance abuse subtypes that respond poorly to treatment in a drug-free therapeutic community. The first of these subtypes was characterized by a single elevation on the Antisocial scale of the MCMI–I. Members of this group were thought to have little regard for social rules and proved more likely than others to be expelled from treatment as a result of program rule violations. The second substance abuse subtype with a poor prognosis was characterized by elevations on the Schizoid and Avoidant scales. Such individuals were thought to experience great discomfort in a milieu emphasizing interpersonal interactions and to become "self-critical, discouraged, and socially withdrawn"

(Fals-Stewart, 1992, p. 524). Both of the poor prognostic groups stayed fewer days in the program and remained alcohol or drug free for a shorter time. Finally, McMahon, Kelley, and Kouzekanani (1993) documented the same trend with cocaine-abusing men on the MCMI–II. Their data showed that "a fiercely independent orientation with manipulative, exploitive, and confrontive interpersonal features" (McMahon, Kelley, & Kouzekanani, 1993, p. 153) led to a lack of toleration of the kind of pressure for change that is typically a part of community-oriented treatment. Similar findings have been reported by others (Haller, Miles, & Dawson, 2002; Simonsen, Haslund, Larsen, & Borup, 1992).

With a narrower sample of drug abusers, Stark and Campbell (1988) reported that patients staying in treatment had a higher score on six of the MCMI–I scales than did immediate dropouts. Because four of these scales (i.e., the Paranoid, Psychotic Thinking, Psychotic Depression, and Psychotic Delusion) measure the most severe areas of pathology, the authors concluded that chronically mentally ill patients become dependent on the clinic for their basic psychological needs and tend to remain longer. However, the means reported all were at subclinical levels (58–61), hovered around the average for psychiatric patients (Base Rate score of 60), and were not indicative of psychopathology. An alternate explanation would be that the immediate-dropout group included patients in at least partial denial who endorsed fewer symptoms than the average psychiatric patient. If this turns out to be the case, it would then be signs of denial on the MCMI that would be predictive of early dropout from treatment.

McMahon, Davidson, and Flynn (1986) found that high-social-functioning alcoholics made significantly greater gains on the MCMI–I as a result of behaviorally oriented therapeutic community treatment than did the low-social-functioning alcoholics. Although their findings may be plagued by the problem of distinguishing between the severity of the alcoholism and the level of social functioning, these authors saw their data as indicating that lower-functioning alcoholics may need social skills training in addition to the conventional treatment for alcoholism.

Elevations on the Dysthymia scale of the MCMI–I were associated with poor outcome in the treatment of women with bulimia nervosa (Garner et al., 1990). Several of the MCMI scales showed significant improvement after treatment, including the Avoidant, Negativistic, Anxiety, and Dysthymia scales. In keeping with other outcome studies, a tendency to have elevated scores on the Compulsive scale during treatment also was reported with this group. Sansone and Fine (1992) found that women with eating disorders who obtained elevated Borderline scale scores on the MCMI–I showed greater psychopathology 3 years later and had less life satisfaction than similar patients without the borderline characteristics.

Low therapist ratings of therapeutic response to inpatient treatment for PTSD were found to be associated with elevations on the Hypomania scale of the MCMI–I. The inventory, however, failed to predict treatment dropout (Munley, Bains, Frazee, & Schwartz, 1994).

Looking at the completion of a treatment program for the prevention of partner abuse, Faulkner, Cogan, Nolder, and Shooter (1991) were unable to find significant MCMI–I predictors. The characteristics of recidivists after spouse abuse abatement counseling also have been investigated. The data show that elevations on the substance abuse scales of the MCMI–I are associated with continued abuse even after completion of a treatment program. This finding is explainable in terms of the obvious link between substance abuse, the loss of control, and the lowering of inhibitions in many individuals. It is recommended that such individuals be involved in treatment for their substance abuse in addition to the treatment for partner abuse. Recidivists also scored significantly higher on the Histrionic and the Narcissistic scales. Perhaps individuals with such elevations have more difficulty, because of their narcissistic needs, in appreciating the partner's perspective and have more trouble seeing themselves as being in need of change (Hamberger & Hastings, 1990).

10 The Interpretive Process

By now this book has covered all of the groundwork that a clinician would need in order to interpret the MCMI appropriately. This chapter takes the reader through the steps experienced clinicians follow in formulating their interpretations of MCMI profiles. The process starts with the assessment of the validity of the protocol and continues with the assessment of the personality disorders and styles (Axis II) and of the clinical syndromes (Axis I). The task then turns to integrating the findings, first from the personality and clinical syndromes and then from other instruments. Ideally the process would lead to a thorough understanding of the individual, from which a diagnostic formulation would follow. That understanding and the diagnostic formulation, in turn, should inform recommendations that constitute a logical outgrowth of the entire process.

Some of these tasks will be broken up into several steps, so the interpretive process proposed in this chapter is made up of 11 steps. The assessment of the validity of the protocol, for instance, involves 4 steps: (1) the assessment of inattentive responding, (2) the assessment of guardedness, (3) the assessment of exaggeration of psychopathology, and (4) the issue of interpreting invalid profiles. The assessment of personality starts with (5) the interpretation of severe personalities and continues with (6) the characterization of basic personality styles. After (7) assessing the clinical syndromes, the job becomes (8) to integrate the personality and the clinical syndrome findings. Next, the clinician needs (9) to integrate the MCMI findings with other sources of information. The mark of the good clinician is the ability to go beyond these 9 steps (10) to develop a diagnostic formulation, a vivid understanding of what the examinee is all about. This understanding, in turn, should lead to (11) the generation of treatment recommendations that are well informed and useful.

Assessing Validity

Inattentive Responding

The evaluation of every report should start with a look at the Validity scale. A Validity score of anything but 0 should be of concern to the examiner. A score of more than 1 strongly suggests that the examinee was not reading or understanding the items in a meaningful manner and that the test findings may not be clinically useful. Individuals who claim to have crossed the Atlantic 30 times in the last year or not to have seen a car in 10 years clearly cannot be trusted to give meaningful information through the other test items.

Some profiles with a Validity score of 1 may be valid. The examiner once tested a controversial elected official whose picture had indeed been on the front page of several magazines during the last year, which explained why that individual had marked that item in the "wrong" direction. Some examinees may give the wrong response to a Validity item if they think it is a trick item that requires an unusual response. It is useful, whenever possible, to take a look at the Validity items (items 65, 110, and 157) to determine if any sense can be made of the individual endorsing the item as he or she did. It is also useful to ask the individual about those items before determining how meaningful the rest of the test may be.

Patient A in Table 10.1 was a 36-year-old White man who was readmitted to a psychiatric ward after taking an overdose of medication with suicidal intent. The patient was found to be mentally retarded. The profile did point to some of the patient's problems, such as his dependent and self-defeating nature, the presence of anxiety and depression, and his occasional alcohol abuse. Nevertheless, the Validity score of 3 pointed to his inability to answer questions in a meaningful manner and makes it impossible to be confident about any of the scores.

Guardedness

In assessing the trustworthiness of the profile, there are two tendencies that the clinician needs to be watchful for: guardedness and exaggeration of psychopathology. In extreme cases, these tendencies distort the results

Table 10.1

Examples of MCMI–III Profiles

Scale	Patients' Base Rate scores			
	A	B	C	D
Personality style scales				
1. Schizoid	60	63	97**	35
2A. Avoidant	80*	66	105***	70
3. Dependent	65	72	99**	69
4. Histrionic	48	67	14	84*
5. Narcissistic	61	66	38	48
6A. Antisocial	85**	49	99**	75
7. Compulsive	26	90**	12	74
8A. Negativistic	80*	47	115***	67
Severe personality scales				
2B. Depressive	81*	48	100***	83*
6B. Aggressive	78*	54	115***	70
8B. Self-Defeating	78*	47	100***	72
S. Schizotypal	67	64	98**	49
C. Borderline	84*	58	100***	93**
P. Paranoid	74	67	115***	69
Clinical symptom scales				
A. Anxiety	80*	19	115***	53
H. Somatic Preoccupations	74	65	85**	74
N. Hypomania	60	53	72	64
D. Dysthymia	78*	37	115***	98**
B. Alcohol Abuse	83*	45	71	89**
T. Drug Abuse	67	39	115***	73
R. Posttraumatic Stress Disorder	45	27	115***	10
Severe clinical syndromes				
SS. Psychotic Thinking	67	44	100***	0
CC. Psychotic Depression	72	41	115***	62
PP. Psychotic Delusion	71	57	78*	60
Modifier Indices				
X. Disclosure	73	25	100***	56
Y. Desirability	47	82*	0	71
Z. Debasement	71	42	98**	61
V. Validity, raw score	3	0	0	0

Note. Scores below the cutoff of 75 are shown without asterisks.
*Score elevation was between 75 and 84.
**Score elevation was between 85 and 94.
***Score elevation was between 95 and 105.

enough that the score profile obtained may be quite meaningless and may not offer any real information about the examinee.

The first of the invalidating tendencies is the tendency to be guarded and unrevealing. Some individuals answer the test questions with a conscious intent to cover up problem areas. In other cases individuals may truthfully believe that they represent the epitome of mental health and may not be aware of their own difficulties. In either case, however, the MCMI findings may be misleading.

To look for signs of guardedness, the clinician should first direct attention to the Modifying Indices. The guarded profile is characterized by an elevation on the Desirability scale, when neither the Disclosure nor the Debasement scale is elevated. In the case of the Disclosure scale, the reader is reminded that this is the one scale that can be interpreted when it is low. The Disclosure scale may be low in the case of guarded profiles.

In some cases a guarded profile may show no elevation at all on any of the clinical scales. Raw scores for the different scales of 0 indicate that the examinee would not acknowledge even the milder items of the scale. If there are no elevated scores (> 75), that fact by itself is a good indication of guardedness, because it occurs in only about 3% of the nonpsychiatric population.

As detailed in chapter 5, many individuals trying to portray themselves in a positive light do have elevated scores on some of the scales; the literature cites elevations on the Dependent, Narcissistic, and Compulsive scales. When one of those scales has an elevated score, the interpretation of the profile becomes much more difficult. In such cases the clinician has to judge whether the elevation is portraying a true characteristic of the individual, the patient's defensiveness, or both. The differentiation between these two possibilities typically has to be made on the basis of nontest information, which would include behavioral observations, characterization by individuals who know the examinee, and historical information. In the case of an individual with a history of a compulsive personality who demonstrates compulsive behaviors during the testing, for instance, the guardedness would be interpreted as part of that personality and would not be seen as a factor contributing to the invalidity of the report.

Patient B in Table 10.1 was a 19-year-old single White man who was admitted to a psychiatric ward because he talked to himself and seemed to be psychotic. The patient was very guarded and defensive during the interview. The profile showed an expected pattern, with an elevation on the Desirability scale and a low score on the Disclosure index. The only scale that was elevated outside of the Modifier Indices was the Compulsive scale.

Exaggeration of Psychopathology

The other problem leading to invalidity of a profile is when the examinee, consciously or unconsciously, exaggerates emotional problems while answering the questionnaire. The expected profile in this case would be the opposite of the guarded profile. In terms of the Modifier Indices, for example, the exaggerated profile would be expected to show elevations on the Disclosure and Debasement scales, as well as a lack of elevation on the Desirability scale. In sharp contrast to the guarded profiles described above, the exaggerated profile typically shows many elevations, particularly in the scales measuring the more exuberant symptoms, such as the Paranoid and Thought Disorder scales. In some cases the MCMI profile, if taken at face value, would indicate a person with practically every imaginable psychiatric disorder, including disorders that are unlikely to coexist in the same individual (e.g., disorders reflecting insecurity, such as an anxiety disorder, with disorders suggesting aggressiveness and projection, such as paranoia).

The diagnostic uncertainty with possibly exaggerated profiles is raised in cases where the individual has a history of severe mental illness. In the case of a chronically disturbed individual, the profile may very well follow the pattern being described but constitutes an honest reflection of what the patient experiences.

Patient C in Table 10.1 was a 30-year-old single White woman who was admitted to the psychiatric ward with suicidal ideation. The patient's history showed signs of a borderline personality disorder with instability of moods, unstable interpersonal relationships, impulsiveness, and recurrent suicidal behavior. The projective tests and the clinical observations were consistent with the presence of an anger-prone histrionic personality makeup behind the dysfunctional borderline personality. The affective symptoms were seen as part of the mood instability of the borderline personality. The poor quality of her Rorschach responses raised concerns about the possible presence of a psychotic core. The MCMI showed the typical fake-bad pattern with elevations on the Disclosure and Debasement scales, as well as a multitude of elevations on the personality and clinical scales. This profile can be seen as a "cry for help" of an individual with a borderline personality disorder.

Clinical Interpretations of Invalid Profiles

Invalid profiles raise two clinical issues. The first is that of understanding what may be behind the invalidity problems. In the case of the elected official mentioned above, what appeared at first to be a validity problem turned out to be an item that did not perform well with that particular individual. More typically, however, elevations on the Validity scale are a sign of inattention. In some cases the examiner has to decide whether the inattention is due to an altered mental status on the part of the examinee (e.g., schizophrenia, low intellectual ability, attention deficit disorder). In other cases the examiner may decide that the person was not invested in doing a good job and was responding to the test in a random manner, endorsing items without reading them.

In the case of a guarded profile from a noncompulsive individual, the examiner must consider possible reasons for the examinee wanting to place himself or herself in the best possible light. One typical reason is a psychiatric patient's desire to show that he or she is emotionally healthy and can be discharged from the hospital. Some situations may encourage guardedness, such as that of a parent being evaluated as part of a custody battle or an employee who is being evaluated because of difficulties with his or her performance at work.

Exaggerated reports may be obtained from acutely distressed patients who see themselves as more disturbed than they really are. Such reports may represent a "cry for help," or be fueled by a conscious or unconscious wish by examinees to present themselves in the worst possible light. Exaggerated reports are often an issue in litigation cases, workers' compensation cases, applications for admission to a psychiatric program, or any case where a person would benefit from looking more disturbed than he or she really is.

Beyond examining the reasons for the validity problems, the examiner has to decide whether the obtained profile is interpretable. Some moments of inattention leading to a Validity scale score of 1, for instance, do not necessarily mean that the rest of the data are of no value. In such cases, one way of assessing the usefulness of the data is to determine how well the profile fits the patient's history and clinical observations. Commonly enough, examinees who were not able to sustain a good level of attention throughout the questionnaire were, nevertheless, able to respond appropriately to enough of the test items that the resulting profile is still an accurate depiction of the individual's personality. The examiner can go on to interpret the clinical profile, even after acknowledging and interpreting the validity issues.

Assessing Personality

Severe Personality Scales

The evaluation of the examinee's personality should start with an examination of the more severe personality scales. These severe patterns are so prominent and problematic that the personality elements will tend to fade into the background. Consider, for instance, an individual with an elevation on the Schizotypal scale who also obtained an elevation on the Schizoid scale. That individual's schizoid traits (e.g., social detachment, emotional blandness) will be completely subsumed under the schizotypal description, because the schizotypal prototype includes all of the schizoid traits at a possibly more severe level. Even if the elevation on the Schizotypal scale is accompanied by an elevation on a scale that has less in common with it, such as the Dependent scale, the schizotypal makeup, being as it is a bit of a mild schizophrenic pattern, will appear clinically as a more prominent and dysfunctional aspect of the individual than the more benign pattern of dependency on others.

Included among the more severe personality types to be considered first are the three personality scales labeled as severe patterns by Millon (Schizotypal, Paranoid, and Borderline). The system advocated here is to add to those three scales two scales that are not listed among the severe personality patterns by Millon, namely the Aggressive and Self-Defeating scales. Whenever either of the latter scales is elevated, the examinee invariably shows fairly severe personality pathology that, together with the Millon-recognized severe personality patterns, must be considered ahead of the other personality prototypes. The depressive personality is not considered by the *DSM–IV* to be a personality prototype (Axis II). To be consistent with *DSM–IV,* the reader is encouraged to consider elevations on that scale as indicating a mood disorder rather than a personality pattern.

Thus, to reiterate, whenever any of the five severe personality scales are elevated, that finding should be considered first. When such is the case, the author typically starts with a narrative attached to that scale and feeds into that description other elevations on personality scales. Let us take a profile showing an elevation of the Borderline and Histrionic personality scales, as shown for Patient D on Table 10.1. The author typically starts with the description of the borderline personality offered in chapter 6 and then alters that description to take into account some of the traits that are highlighted by the patient's elevation on the Histrionic scale. The final narrative may read something like the following:

> The indications from the testing were that the examinee suffers from a borderline personality disorder with histrionic and antisocial elements. The borderline personality can explain some of the symptoms the patient had been experiencing, such as the intense anger, mood fluctuations, and even substance abuse. Her having this kind of personality disorder is not surprising, given her childhood history of an alcoholic mother,

> unstable nuclear family relationships, and a sexually abusive father figure.
>
> The test results indicate that the patient experiences a pervasive instability in terms of her moods, interpersonal relationships, and self-image. The scores describe her as typically responding in an impulsive and overemotional way so that her affective response tends to be labile, at times showing apathy and numbness and at other times demonstrating an excessive amount of intensity or involvement. Sadness, hopelessness, and aimlessness are often underlying the more obvious emotional response. Similar individuals have significant problems with authority and resent any controls that are placed on them. They can be aggressive, angry, or even cruel and are plagued by destructive ideas, which may be directed toward themselves or toward others. The anger may be temporarily displaced by bothersome feelings of guilt or remorse. The patient's self-image is also problematic, as she is likely to feel worthless and to be encumbered by self-doubt while, at the same time, feeling used by others. The Rorschach pointed to a chronic state of stimulus overload, which impairs her capacity for control and makes her vulnerable to impulsiveness and disorganization.
>
> Individuals with similar test profiles like to be the center of attention. They tend to be somewhat emotional and dramatic and enjoy being in social situations. They are colorful and lively but can be seen as somewhat superficial and not serious enough in their approach to the world. They have a tendency to get bored easily, so that sometimes they go on to other enterprises before finishing something that they were working on.

Thus, in the above narrative, the author starts with a characterization of the borderline personality, adding a few comments to take into account the histrionic element. The same procedure would be followed for both the Schizotypal and the Paranoid scales.

When the Self-Defeating or Aggressive scales are elevated, however, further interpretive adjustments have to be made, because these are not acceptable *DSM–IV* personality prototypes. In the case of the Self-Defeating scale, an elevation on that scale typically indicates the presence of a dependent personality disorder. The narrative can follow the usual procedure of taking the narrative from the Self-Defeating personality and adjusting it to reflect the other elevations that may be present. Usually the final product should be geared to describe what is basically a dependent personality disorder. The following description may be a good example of such a narrative:

> Mrs. __ has a dependent personality and tends to feel less important or capable than most other people. Similar individuals are easily led by others and relate in a submissive and dependent manner. They are made uncomfortable by highly competitive situations. They are unconceited

> and try to be as congenial as possible to the people around them. Often they are afraid of being rejected by others and, as a result, feel some discomfort when relating to others. Individuals with similar MCMI scores have such a poor self-image that they are uncomfortable when they are treated nicely and seem to seek out situations where they will be hurt or rejected. It is as if they have come to expect mistreatment and routinely have, almost by design, the type of interpersonal interactions that would bring about the abuse. Even though she is inclined to put herself down, the indications are that she is just as likely to devalue others. Similar people show their resentment in a somewhat insulting way of interacting. This, in return, creates the ill will that activates the person's own resentment in frustrating vicious cycle.

Finally, in the case of an elevation on the Aggressive scale, the clinician has to evaluate what other personality disorder the examinee may fit. Often enough the individual may have an antisocial personality disorder. There are some cases, however, when an elevation on the Aggressive personality scale reflects not a personality disorder but a clinical syndrome, such as the intermittent explosive disorder.

Basic Personality Scales

If there are no elevations on the severe personality scales, the clinician assesses the personality on the basis of the eight personality style scales. The process of interpreting those scales was detailed in chapter 6. The more difficult diagnostic issue is to decide whether the personality pattern represents a functional normal personality or a personality disorder. As has been argued (see chap. 7), that distinction requires a clinical judgment after taking the person's history into consideration and cannot be made on the basis of test scores alone.

That is not to say that the elevated scores should not be taken into consideration. Obviously, the more elevated the score is, the more extreme the traits can be expected to be. Some people are able to function, or even function well, in spite of (or even because of) personality traits that are out of the ordinary. The clinician's job is to take a look at the history and decide how functional the personality has been.

In making the determination of a personality diagnosis, the clinician needs to consider the kind of personality the examinee has and the type of problems he or she has had in life. If the person has had periods when he or she has functioned well, that history would argue against the presence of a personality disorder. Personality disorders are, by definition, lifelong dysfunctions.

To make matters more complicated, a person may suffer from a lifelong disorder that is not intrinsically related to his or her personality. Take, for instance, the schizophrenic who has shown disorganized thinking, paranoid delusions, and auditory hallucinations throughout life. The MCMI–III may show a narcissistic personality for that individual. Although the patient has had a chronic mental health problem, the history may indicate that the narcissism has not directly caused the dysfunction, which has been more directly associated with the psychotic symptomatology. In that case, the person would be seen as having a narcissistic personality but not a personality disorder.

An even more difficult diagnostic issue is posed by the schizophrenic individual with a schizoid personality. In this case, the social detachment and isolation that may be the prominent symptoms of the schizophrenia may be difficult to distinguish from the personality makeup. Questions to be asked in such a case include whether the schizoid tendencies predated the onset of the schizophrenic disorder and whether the schizoid tendencies improve considerably when the schizophrenic symptoms go into remission.

To sum up, a good personality assessment should address two issues: (a) the kind of personality the person has and (b) whether that personality is dysfunctional and constitutes a personality disorder or should be seen as the individual's personality style. The MCMI–III can be useful in addressing both of these issues. However, the clinician will need to rely on the individual's history in deciding how dysfunctional his or her personality may be.

Assessing Clinical Syndromes

The assessment of clinical syndromes is more straightforward than that of the other aspects of personality covered in this chapter. Part of this simplicity comes from the different ways in which clinicians look at the personality and clinical syndromes. In spite of the fact that the *DSM–IV* allows for the diagnosis of more than one personality type or disorder, clinicians generally see the individual as having only one personality. This personality may be made up of different elements, but the clinician's bias is to see the personality as a unitary construct. Consequently, part of the clinician's job in interpreting a test like the MCMI is to integrate the different personality scale elevations into one personality description.

In contrast, the prevailing attitude among clinicians is that the clinical syndromes can just be added to one another. An alcoholic who also suffers from depression is seen as suffering from two different disorders, rather than one disorder made up of two elements. That kind of conceptualization is, of course, simplistic: Clinical syndromes also interact with each other, and depressed alcoholism is a very different syndrome from schizophrenic alcoholism. Nevertheless, the simplistic conceptualization makes interpretation of the MCMI–III clinical syndrome scales relatively easy, because the examiner only has to add the information learned from one scale elevation to the information learned from the next.

There are two exceptions to that method on the MCMI–III. Often the clinician needs to integrate findings from more than one depression scale elevation or from the substance abuse scales. With the depression scales, for instance, typically more than one scale is elevated, and the clinician has to take the findings from the elevated scales and fit them into one of the two disorders recognized by the *DSM–IV* (Dysthymia or Major Depression). In many cases the issue of bipolarity has to be addressed, even when the Bipolar Manic scale is not elevated, because depressed bipolar individuals would not be expected to have elevated scores on that scale. Because many examinees have elevated scores on both of the substance abuse scales, the clinician must integrate both of those scales.

Integrating Personality and Clinical Syndrome Findings

The distinction between the Axis I clinical syndromes and the Axis II personalities is made mostly for the sake of convenience, and as discussed in chapter 2, all of these elements are highly interrelated. The next task an examiner should perform is to integrate, however tentatively, the personality and clinical syndrome findings.

It should be clear that all areas measured by the MCMI–III influence each other. A depression, for instance, can be expected to exacerbate certain personality aspects such as dependency, social isolation, and mood instability. In the case of a depressed individual, as a result, the scores obtained on the Schizoid, Avoidant, Dependent, or Borderline scales may have been pulled up by the person's depressive state.

On the other hand, it is also undeniable that personality styles serve to color the presentation of certain clinical syndromes. The depression of a dependent individual, for instance, may include guilt feelings and can be expected to emphasize the limitations and failures of the individual. In contrast, the depression of a narcissistic person may be colored by the perception of mistreatment, of a world that has denied the individual the resources he or she was entitled to have. The substance abuse of the antisocial person may be flavored by the approach of living for the moment, whereas an avoidant's substance abuse may be colored by the person's discomfort in social relations.

Thus, after describing both the personality and the clinical syndrome, the diagnostician should consider the possible interactions of all the areas described. One case may merit comments about the difficulty of diagnosing a histrionic–narcissistic personality makeup on a hypomanic person; another case may require a discussion of the interaction between borderline elements and the oppositional defiant disorder of a young adult.

Integrating Other Sources of Information

The findings of any test are best when they are not interpreted in isolation. The importance of having accurate historical information has already been highlighted. Additionally, findings from other psychological tests are often invaluable in arriving at a useful understanding of the individual. To cite but one example, thought disorder or schizophrenic scales in personality questionnaires are notoriously invalid with many schizophrenics due to the person's denial or lack of awareness of his or her own symptoms. An examination of the quality of the person's thought process through a projective test such as the Rorschach is often the only way to investigate the extent of a person's psychotic thinking. Findings from other tests can be used to add information to the data gathered through the MCMI–III or to modify the MCMI–III findings through the consideration of information from other sources.

Chapter 8 reviewed what is known about the MCMI and many other instruments. The author has found that narrowband tests can be very useful when administered in conjunction with the MCMI–III. Studies where the MCMI was administered with the Alcohol Use Inventory or the Eating Disorder Inventory, to mention only two examples, can help the diagnostician provide a deeper conceptualization of what is going on with a client.

Developing a Psychological Formulation

A psychological formulation of the individual includes more than the assignment of diagnoses to the different axes of the *DSM–IV*. Although such assignments should be part of the end product, the psychological formulation goes beyond those assignments and requires an understanding of what the individual is all about and how the person came to a particular point in his or her life.

Take, for instance, the character of Melvin Udall in the film *As Good as It Gets* (Johnson, Zea, & Brooks, 1998). As he is presented at the beginning of the film, Mr. Udall is a narcissistic–schizoid–negativistic individual, with no feelings for anyone else, who suffers from an obsessive–compulsive disorder. One way of understanding this fictional character is to analyze what happens to him when he becomes attracted to a waitress in the neighborhood restaurant where he has breakfast every morning.

Diagnostic formulations are typically guided by the different psychological theories. In his last book, *Paradigms of Personality Assessment,* Wiggins (2003) proposed that five paradigms (the psychodynamic, interpersonal, personological, multivariate [factor analytic], and empirical paradigms) constitute the foundations of all psychological assessments.[1]

If one were to apply the interpersonal paradigm to Mr. Udall's case, for instance, he could be seen as struggling with the attraction he was developing for the waitress and the vulnerability of venturing out of the very restrictive and dysfunctional life he has been leading. The possibility of the relationship has a curative effect on him. With the pull of this positive influence, Mr. Udall becomes extremely generous, first with his money, then with his time, and eventually with his personal space. By the end of the movie, the interpersonal changes are beginning to transfer into symptom reduction, as he no longer has to avoid the cracks of the sidewalk and abandons the repeated rechecking of the locks on the door. Although the use of Wiggins's paradigms may allow the clinician to structure his or her thinking and produce predictable interpretations, the fact remains that the diagnostic formulation is the most creative of the interpretative tasks and the hardest to accomplish well.

Generating Treatment Recommendations

The different kinds of recommendations that can be offered include (a) dispositional recommendations, (b) recommendations for medical treatment including medications, (c) clinical syndrome recommendations,

[1] Wiggins focused on other theorists and did not discuss Millon's theory. However, Millon's theory would best fit the personological paradigm, although it has psychodynamic and interpersonal elements.

(d) personologic recommendations, and (e) recommendations derived from the psychological formulation. Examples of dispositional recommendations include a recommendation for placement in the case of a dysfunctional individual who has not been able to make it in an independent living situation and recommendations for increased or decreased supervision of a chronically mentally ill person. Although MCMI findings can occasionally be used to support a dispositional recommendation, these recommendations are typically based on historical data.

In the course of evaluating a patient, psychologists often hear complaints of a medical nature. In those cases, the reports include recommendations for further evaluation or treatment of the medical symptoms. MCMI findings may show that the person is suffering from a clinical syndrome that may be helped by a psychotropic medication. In cases of depression or schizophrenia, for instance, consideration should be given to a trial of an appropriate psychotropic drug. Especially when the referral came from a physician, the clinician has to be careful to phrase the recommendation in an appropriate manner. Suggesting a particular medication, for instance, is typically uncalled for.

Recommendations for treatment of the clinical syndrome should not be limited to considering medication. Many depressed individuals, for instance, would benefit from some type of psychotherapy. The examiner may also have other recommendations. In the case of a depressed patient who is spending most of the time in bed, the examiner may recommend the introduction of scheduled activities. The treatment of many clinical syndromes (e.g., posttraumatic stress disorder, eating disorder, substance abuse disorders) calls for specific treatment plans that can be included in the testing report.

A unique contribution of the MCMI is the information it offers about the individual's personality. Knowledge of the personality makeup should allow the clinician to make specific recommendations for the individual that could not be offered otherwise. Some of the possible recommendations are included as part of the personality narratives in chapter 6. In the case of the dependent personality, for instance, the narrative might include the following comments:

> In the light of this personality style, such individuals can be expected to form a quick alliance with any therapist willing to play a benevolent parental role. An approach in which they are given guidance in an affectionate and understanding manner would be experienced as supportive. It may be difficult if part of the treatment plan is to move clients toward more independence or increase their ability to compete

> assertively or effectively. If that is the case, these clients may feel vulnerable and threatened and may respond with maladaptive behaviors.

The recommendations for the antisocial personality might be as follows:

> In the light of this personality style, the establishment of a therapeutic alliance may be somewhat difficult. Clients are not inclined to see psychotherapy as valuable unless it offers a tangible material benefit, such as a way out of a jam. One approach to establishing an alliance in spite of this difficulty may be to accept, at least temporarily, the same competitive outlook that the clients favor. The therapist then may be in the position to help them explore the behaviors and attitudes that get in the way of their being a "winner."

Going beyond those recommendations offered in chapter 6, the examiner can use information reviewed in chapter 9 to offer more treatment suggestions, especially for individuals who are found to have a personality disorder. Finally, the examiner should use the richness of the psychological formulation in order to further guide the treatment of the individual. Mr. Udall's psychiatrist in *As Good as It Gets* apparently relied mostly on medications and was fairly insensitive to the patient's needs when Mr. Udall came to see him without an appointment. A more responsive clinician could have explored the great sense of vulnerability that the patient may have been experiencing and could have helped him to understand what was going on inside. Switching to a psychodynamic mode, developing an understanding of the historical antecedents of the patient's characterological problems could have been helpful to him. In any event, the point is that the clinician's understanding of the patient's psychological dynamics should obviously be informing the treatment plan.

Case Reports

This chapter offers a brief introduction to report writing and provides four examples of testing reports using the MCMI–III. The reports aim to exemplify how the MCMI–III can be integrated with historical information and data obtained from projective tests into descriptive and useful narratives. Although the test data are reported without any alterations, all of the identifying information has been changed in order to protect the clients' confidentiality.

Each case report contains a thorough review of the history and a discussion of the findings. A review of the logical steps taken in interpreting the MCMI–III data follows each case report. Finally, raw data are presented for each case so that readers may conduct their own analyses. For the raw data presented, the Rorschach Inkblot Test (Rorschach, 1921) results were done with the help of the Hermann computer program sold by Multi-Health Systems (Choca & Garside, 1992). The Thematic Apperception Test (TAT; Murray, 1943) results were taped at the time of administration and were transcribed thereafter.

Regrettably, the writing of test reports has been neglected in the training of clinical psychologists. A recent survey showed a median number of less than one MCMI–III report written by students in graduate or professional schools (Stedman, Hatch, & Schoenfeld, 2001). This is a very unfortunate practice, because the test report is typically the only part of the diagnostic work that others see. A poorly written or uninformative report is a disservice not only to the client but to the field as well, because it discourages further use of psychological instruments.

Organizational Schemes for Report Discussions

In writing reports, it often is useful to have a scheme around which to organize them. This idea has been described in detail elsewhere (Choca & Van Denburg, 1996; Kvaal, Choca, & Groth-Marnat, 2003) and involves the use of one of four different organizational strategies, labeled *personality*, *developmental*, *motivational*, and *diagnostic*.

The typical report using a personality scheme begins with a description of the individual's basic personality style. Once the personality has been described, the rest of the data can be presented as they relate to the personality. If there was a clear precipitant to the onset of the symptomatology, the importance of that event could be discussed in terms of the values and assumptions of the individual's personality. Using this model, the psychopathology can be explained as exaggerations of the basic personality style, as maladjustments caused by the interaction between that personality style and the environment, or as some reflection of the personality traits.

The common thread in the different parts of the report in the developmental scheme is the tracing of the client's history to explain how the client developed the way he or she did. This scheme may involve speculations about the etiological underpinnings of the personality style, a description of the personality style per se, and a review of the effect that the personality style might have had during the different stages of development to bring about the experiences that the individual had at that stage. The psychopathology then is understood in terms of a failure to complete successfully developmental tasks along the way.

The motivational scheme is particularly useful when the client's life has revolved around striving toward a particular conscious or unconscious goal. In such cases, the report can be organized around the client's striving. The personality then may be seen as resulting from such a striving (e.g., the person who resolved early in life that he or she would avoid making mistakes and developed a compulsive personality style) or as influencing the different attempts that the client has made to reach his or her goal. The psychopathology then can be explained as reactions the person had to difficulties in striving for the goal.

Finally, with patients presenting a difficult differential diagnosis question, it may be useful to follow a diagnostic organizational scheme. Such a report would revolve around the issues involved in the differential diagnosis, perhaps discussing the different criteria for the diagnoses under consideration and offering the evidence that the testing has provided in support of or against each of the criteria. This system may be used for the Axis I syndromes first and then repeated for the Axis II personality structure.

These schemes should be thought of as a way of conceptualizing and organizing the report and should not inhibit readers from developing some of their own. In addition, the manner of presentation can be varied for any one of the schemes; in other words, a report following the personality scheme does not always need to begin with a description of the personality, as suggested earlier, because one could do it just as well in the reverse order. The schemes also could be intermixed (e.g., the report of a schizophrenic using the diagnostic organizational scheme could switch, at some point, into the developmental scheme and discuss how the psychotic episodes have prevented the individual from accomplishing various developmental tasks in his or her life).

The cases that follow were chosen to represent the different kinds of pathology rather than to exemplify the different diagnostic schemes, but clinicians may be able to see more than one organization being used in the reports.

Case Study 1: Thought Disturbance in a Schizoid Personality Disorder

Referral Information

Donald Green was a 26-year-old Black man who was admitted to the psychiatric unit while he was in a psychotic state. Mr. Green had come to believe that he could control the weather with his thoughts. He placed tapes across his chest in response to the request of the voices he heard. Four days before admission, Mr. Green shaved his head because he believed there were "things" living in his head and that he could get rid of them by doing that. He admitted feeling that he was "more than one person" and could hear "two voices," one male and one female, when he spoke. He also tended to be somatically preoccupied: He reportedly had been suffering from headaches and abdominal pain for some time and was complaining of a cracking noise in his left shoulder.

A psychological evaluation was requested to help with the differential diagnosis. In particular, the issue was whether Mr. Green was suffering from a schizophrenic disorder. At the time of the testing, Mr. Green was being treated with Stelazine.

Psychiatric History

This was the first time that the patient had received psychiatric treatment. Mr. Green denied abusing alcohol or drugs and knew of no family member who had a history of psychiatric problems.

Medical History

Mr. Green was hospitalized at a medical hospital in July 1985 with complaints of headaches and abdominal pain. That was the only other time he had been in the hospital. During the current admission, a computed tomography scan of the brain and an electroencephalogram were taken and found to be within normal limits.

Family History

Mr. Green had considerable difficulty detailing his history. He often claimed not to know what different members of the family did for a living or other important pieces of information. At other times, his answers were confusing, and it took great effort to clarify what he was trying to say.

Mr. Green was born in New York City and was raised in the Brooklyn area. He was the oldest of six children who were raised together, but he had three younger stepsisters who were not raised with him. Mr. Green was born out of wedlock. His biological father was a 53-year-old machinist whom the patient saw annually. His father left the relationship with Mr. Green's mother early on, married someone else, and had three daughters from that marriage.

Mr. Green's mother was a 51-year-old woman employed by a hospital in Brooklyn. He described her as being very religious and seemed to have positive feelings toward her. She married when Mr. Green was young but is now divorced.

The ex-husband, Mr. Green's stepfather, was in his 50s. Mr. Green referred to this man as his "father" because he was the male figure in the home throughout most of Mr. Green's childhood. The stepfather had worked as a mail carrier but had quit his job some time ago and moved out of state. Mr. Green therefore did not see him frequently.

The patient was the oldest of his siblings and was followed by William. A 25-year-old single man, William did not have a place to live and had been living in the streets. Gwen was Mr. Green's 24-year-old sister, who was single and lived with him. He characterized her as a "pain" because she had a "big mouth." Gwen worked at the same Brooklyn hospital as their mother. David was a 22-year-old Marine stationed elsewhere. A 21-year-old brother, Rodney, obtained a college degree on a football scholarship and lived in California. Brenda, age 9, was the last of the siblings raised together. She was still living with her mother.

Mr. Green was married in 1983. The marriage lasted 2 years. His ex-wife was still single, and they saw each other fairly often. She was characterized as being straightforward. They had a 2-year-old daughter who was not a problem.

Mr. Green readily admitted that he had no friends. For social enjoyment, he went out dancing but picked different partners and did not have a steady companion.

Educational History

While he was in high school in Brooklyn, Mr. Green worked just hard enough to get by. He was never placed in a special education program, but he always was a below-average student. The patient attended a technical school for 2 years, but he ended up feeling "wiped out" and dropped out to go to work.

Occupational History

Mr. Green worked at a freight company for 9 years until that company was purchased by a trucking company. For the previous 6 months, he had been employed as a dispatcher by the latter company and apparently had had no problems with his job.

Mental Status Examination

At the time of this evaluation, Mr. Green was alert, oriented, verbal, and coherent. His speech and language functions were intact. The other intellectual functions examined (e.g., memory, figure reproductions, mental control, abstractions) also were within normal limits. His ability to perform calculations could not be tested because he refused to cooperate: He stated that he never calculated anything and would not make the necessary effort. His thought processes were jumbled at times, and his thought content was marked by delusions and auditory hallucinations. He was evasive and superficial. Affective responses often were inappropriate in that he sometimes joked constantly and refused to take the testing seriously. At other times, he seemed angry with the examiner. His mood was within normal limits, and he had a good range of emotions. Anger, however, was prevalent in his comments and sarcastic remarks. There was no suicidal or homicidal ideation.

He was mildly restless and needed to stand up or walk around several times during the testing. Although he tried to appear relaxed, he seemed tense and apprehensive about the testing. He had no insight and claimed that there was nothing wrong with him, even when he spoke of fairly severe psychiatric symptoms. Mr. Green was only minimally cooperative; he often tried to avoid having to give information and completed the entire procedure rapidly.

Discussion

Unfortunately, all the data obtained were consistent with the presence of a schizophrenic process. About the only requirement that did not appear to be met for a schizophrenic disorder was that of duration: Mr. Green had not been in a psychotic state for 6 months at the time of the evaluation.

Specifically, Mr. Green showed a defective contact with reality, which was clinically obvious in his auditory hallucinations, deluded thinking, and possible somatic delusions. His Rorschach results, on the other hand, uncovered vague and confused thinking as well as occasional illogical reasoning (see Exhibit 11.1). As seen on this test, his communications often were so egocentric that they seemed not to be intended to share information: His thinking frequently could be understood only after repeated questioning to clarify all of the steps in the chain of associations that he had not communicated.

Mr. Green seemed bizarre, both inside and outside of the testing. This effect often was created by the content of his responses, as was the case when he made several inappropriate sexual responses on the Rorschach. At other times, the bizarre quality was produced by the lability of the affect and by the defenses that he was using. The lability left the examiner off balance, not knowing what to expect next. On the Rorschach, a constriction and an inability to share his feelings and use his psychic resources were intermixed with an uncontrolled expression of emotions. On the surface, the mood lability materialized in the following manner: It seemed as if Mr. Green first attempted to deny troublesome thoughts through humor. He repeatedly made humorous discounting remarks about the testing or to the examiner, not taking the diagnostic procedure seriously. This defense did not last long, and he eventually projected his discomfort through sarcasm or a mildly insulting comment about the procedure or the examiner.

Exhibit 11.1

Donald Green's Rorschach Test Results

Rorschach Protocol

1. Card I | Reaction time: 16 s
   SCORE: W oF | o | A | P | 1.0
   Bee
   INQUIRY: prongs, wings
2. Card I | Reaction time: 19 s
   SCORE: W vF | o | Art | | 1.0
   Blotches on a blot folded in half
   INQUIRY: just the way they looked
3. Card I | Reaction time: 39 s
   SCORE: W oF | o | A | (P)PSV | 1.0
   Bat
   INQUIRY: same thing, wing
4. Card I | Reaction time: 9 s
   SCORE: W vF | v | Art
   Somebody sat in some ink or something
   INQUIRY: it just looks like the mark that would be left if you sat on some paint
5. Card II | Reaction time: 333 s
   SCORE: D oF | o | Ad
   Butterfly
   INQUIRY: tail end, long tail sticking out, something doesn't make sense
   LOCATION: Bottom central detail
6. Card II | Reaction time: 201 s
   SCORE: Dd oF | o | Ls | PER
   Positions, church steeple
   INQUIRY: I've seen church steeples shaped like that
   LOCATION: midcenter
7. Card II | Reaction time: 57 s
   SCORE: D oM | ao | (2)(H) | P | 3.0
   Two ladies beating the drums; the titties are together, though.
   Two ladies or two men, I don't know
   INQUIRY: Heads, breasts, kettle; mixing ups some kind of potion
   Two witches

continued

Exhibit 11.1

Donald Green's Rorschach Test Results *Continued*

Rorschach Protocol *Continued*

8. Card II Reaction time: 12 s
   SCORE: D oF o Cg
   Bow tie
   INQUIRY: looks like one
9. Card II Reaction time: 5 s
   SCORE: D oF u (2)An INC1.DV1 3.0
   Two hearts joined together
   INQUIRY: shape
   I don't understand why you are showing me such pictures
10. Card IV Reaction time: 4 s
   SCORE: W om pu Hh 2.0
   A bell
   INQUIRY: The Liberty Bell. Shape, little hanger in the middle. It's hung by here
11. Card IV Reaction time: 61 s
   SCORE: W oM.FD p- H.Sx P 2.0
   A guy laying on his back with his feet up and his dick between his legs
   INQUIRY: laughs
   Laying on his back? you are looking at his feet first
12. Card V Reaction time: 5 s
   SCORE: W oF o A P
   A bat
   INQUIRY: wings
13. Card VI Reaction time: 19 s
   SCORE: D oFC' - Hh.Bl (P)CONTAM 2.5
   A blood stain on a fur rug, a bear skin rug
   INQUIRY: the whole thing could be a bloodstain rug? the way it looks Bl? this spot here (darker cn)
   LOCATION: bottom D
14. Card VI Reaction time: 24 s
   SCORE: Rejected
   Blood stain
   INQUIRY: part of Number 13, does not want by itself.

continued

Exhibit 11.1

Donald Green's Rorschach Test Results *Continued*

Rorschach Protocol *Continued*

15. Card VII   Reaction time: 4 s
SCORE: W vF   v   Art   2.5
Black ink spot
INQUIRY: just the way it looks

16. Card VIII   Reaction time: 15 s
SCORE: D oF   o   (2)A   P
Pair of lions, like the Lowenbrau bottle with the two lions on it
INQUIRY: two cats on side

17. Card IX   Reaction time: 29 s
SCORE: DW vm   -   Fi
A solar flare
INQUIRY: Shooting out. It can reach way over here too (expanding the gray D on top to W)

18. Card X   Reaction time: 4 s
SCORE: DW vCF   -   An.Sx   DV
Picture of the ovaries and stuff like that
INQUIRY: Two blue spots reminds me of a picture I drew in grammar school. I saw three levels, too.
? (can't explain)
LOC? wants W

19. Card X   Reaction time: 5 s
SCORE: D oF   o   Ls
Could be the Eiffel Tower too.
INQUIRY: the shape

Rorschach Score Sequence

Card	No.	Time (seconds)	Scoring					
I	1	46	W	oF	o	A	P	1.0
I	2	19	W	vF	o	Art		1.0
I	3	39	W	oF	o	A	(P)PSV	1.0
I	4	9	W	vF	v	Art		

continued

Exhibit 11.1

Donald Green's Rorschach Test Results *Continued*

Rorschach Score Sequence *Continued*

Card	No.	Time (seconds)	Scoring					
II	5	333	D	oF	o	Ad		
II	6	201	Dd	oF	o	Ls	PER	
II	7	57	D	oM	ao	(2)(H)	P	3.0
II	8	12	D	oF	o	Cg		
II	9	5	D	vF	v	(2)An	INC1.DV1	3.0
IV	10	4	W	vm	pu	Hh		2.0
IV	11	61	W	oM.FD	p-	H.Sx	P	2.0
V	12	5	W	oF	o	A	P	
VI	13	19	D	oFC'	-	Hh.Bl	(P)CON	2.5
VI	14	24	Rejected					
VII	15	4	W	vF	v	Art		2.5
VIII	16	15	D	oF	o	(2)A	P	
IX	17	29	DW	vm	-	Fi		
X	18	4	DW	vCF	-	An.Sx	DV1	
X	19	5	D	oF	o	Ls		

Rorschach Structural Summary

Global	n	%	Location	n	%	Determinants	n	%	Contents	n	%	Quality	n	%
R	18		W	8	44	M	2	11	CONT	10		OF ALL		
Rejects	1		D	7	39	FM	0	0				+	0	0
			Dd	1	6	m	2	11	H	1	5	o	10	56
P	5	28	DW	2	11	FT	0	0	(H)	1	5	v	4	22
(P)	2	11	S	0	0	TF	0	0	Hd	0	0	-	4	22
						T	0	0	(Hd)	0	0			
(2)	3	17				FY	0	0	A	4	18	OF F		
Fr	0	0	POSITION			YF	0	0	(A)	0	0	+	0	0
rF	0	0	▲	18	100	Y	0	0	Ad	1	5	o	9	75
3r+(2)		17	►	0	0	FV	0	0	(Ad)	0	0	v	3	25
			◄	0	0	VF	0	0	Ab	0	0	-	0	0

continued

Exhibit 11.1

Donald Green's Rorschach Test Results *Continued*

Rorschach Structural Summary *Continued*

Global	*n*	%	Location	*n*	%	Determinants	*n*	%	Contents	*n*	%	Quality	*n*	%
RT Ach	23		▼	0	0	V	0	0	Al	0	0			
RT Ch	74					FC′	1	5	An	2	9			
						C′F	0	0	Art	3	14	DV1	2	12
AFR		29	DEV QUAL			C′	0	0	Ay	0	0	DV2	0	0
			+	0	0	FC	0	0	Bl	1	5	INC1	1	6
			v/+	0	0	CF	1	5	Bt	0	0	INC2	0	0
			o	11	61	C	0	0	Cg	1	5	DR1	0	0
Zf	10		v	7	39	Cn	0	0	Cl	0	0	DR2	0	0
ZSum	18					FD	1	5	Ex	0	0	FAB1	0	0
						F	12	63	Fi	1	5	FAB2	0	0
									Fd	0	0	ALOG	0	0
						Blends	1		Ge	0	0	CON	1	6
									Hh	2	9	AB	0	0
			RATIOS			RATIOS			Ls	2	9	CP	0	0
			W	8		a	1	6	Na	0	0	AG	0	0
			M	2		p	2	11	Sc	0	0	MOR	0	0
									Sx	3	14	CFB	0	0
			W	8		M	2		Vo	0	0	PER	1	6
			D	7		wtd C	1.0		Xy	0	0	COP	0	0
												PSV	1	6
						M+wtd C	3							
						FM+m	2							
						Y+T+V+C′	1		RATIOS					
									H+HD	2				
						ΣFMmYTVC′	3		A+AD	5				
						FC	0		H+A	6				
						CF+C	1		HD+AD	1				
									A%	23				

Almost all his MCMI pathology scale scores were elevated, showing that, even by his own assessments, Mr. Green was having many emotional problems and functioning poorly (see Table 11.1). In fact, the scores were so elevated that they probably constituted a "cry for help," an attempt on Mr. Green's part to communicate that things were not going well with him.

Table 11.1

Donald Green's MCMI Test Results

Scale	Base Rate Score
Modifying Indices	
X. Disclosure	85**
Y. Desirability	65
Z. Debasement	95**
V. Validity (raw score)	0
Personality style scales	
1. Schizoid	99**
2A. Avoidant	92**
3. Dependent	88**
4. Histrionic	69
5. Narcissistic	64
6A. Antisocial	65
7. Compulsive	30
8A. Negativistic	105**
Severe personality scales	
2B. Depressive	83*
6B. Aggressive	45
8B. Self-Defeating	61
S. Schizotypal	85**
C. Borderline	81*
P. Paraphrenic	108**
Clinical syndrome scales	
A. Anxiety	109**
H. Somatoform	81*
N. Bipolar: Manic	119**
D. Dysthymia	94**
B. Alcohol Dependence	94**
T. Drug Dependence	97**
R. Posttraumatic Stress Disorder	76*
Severe clinical syndrome scales	
SS. Thought Disorder	101**
CC. Major Depression	88**
PP. Delusional Disorder	114**

Note. Scores below the cutoff of 75 are shown without asterisks.
*Score elevation was between 75 and 84.
**Score elevation was 85 or above.

As far as his personality structure was concerned, Mr. Green's scores have to be taken with caution. The elevations he obtained showed negativistic, schizoid, avoidant, and dependent components in his personality. It is possible that some of these traits had been acutely exacerbated by the patient's psychotic state, because he might have become more isolated, distrusting, and resentful as a result of his psychosis. As a result, the validity of the personality findings will remain questionable until the acute episode goes into remission. Even if the personality style revealed by the MCMI remains after remission, Mr. Green probably should not be seen as suffering from a personality disorder, because no characterological problems were reported before the onset of the psychotic episode.

If the personality style remains as shown by the MCMI after remission, the patient would be seen as having a resentful, introversive, and insecure personality. Individuals with similar styles tend to be moody and to change their overall feelings without any obvious reason. At times, they may be friendly and engaging; they then become angry and resentful; later yet, they may feel guilty and contrite. The cycle is completed when they again become friendly and cooperative. A different substyle of the same basic personality makeup can be observed in individuals who vent their resentment through obstructionistic maneuvers that allow them to dissipate their anger without threatening their interpersonal support.

Most of these individuals have considerable feelings of insecurity. They tend to feel that others are more gifted, more capable, or more worthy. They feel, however, that if others got to know them, they would recognize these individuals' lack of value and reject them. Such individuals also tend to be nervous and uncomfortable when relating to others; they often feel that the other person does not really like them and that they are imposing. They frequently avoid some of the discomfort of relating by avoiding social relationships altogether. As a result, these people tend to lead lonely lives, being fairly distant from others, whom they view as untrustworthy and judgmental.

Individuals with similar MCMI scores are sensitive people. They would like to be appreciated by others and wish they could relate better than they do. They are caught, however, between wanting to depend on others but feeling that if they trust others, they will be hurt in the end. The emotional changes and other possible maladaptive developments are simply the surface behaviors that their basic conflict brings about.

All of Mr. Green's personality findings were consistent with what was known about his premorbid functioning. For example, Mr. Green admitted having no friends, and his mother apparently described him as a "sensitive" individual who was "a loner, given to daydreaming." Thus, he seemed to have a schizoid personality disorder that preceded the psychotic episode.

The psychological strengths uncovered by the evaluation included the absence of a cognitive or memory impairment and at least average intellectual abilities. The patient also had a good work history and seemed to function, even if at a marginal level, before the onset of the psychosis. Therefore, it is possible that when the patient recovers from his psychotic episode, he may be able to return to his previous level of functioning.

Mr. Green's stories on the TAT were varied and did not suggest that he was preoccupied with any interpersonal issue (see Exhibit 11.2). As a result, it was difficult to identify any troublesome situations in his life. The findings that he had several inappropriate sexual responses on the Rorschach and that the story evoked by the heterosexual intercourse card of the TAT involved the murder of the woman probably indicate difficulty with that kind of sexual intimacy.

Diagnostic Assignments and Recommendations

I. Schizophreniform disorder (295.40)
II. Schizoid personality disorder (301.20)
III. No known contributing medical problems

Recommendations

Continued evaluation for the use of psychotropic medications seems indicated. In addition, the formation of a therapeutic alliance would be beneficial. The problem with the latter recommendation is that any kind of close relationship will be threatening to Mr. Green and therefore difficult to establish.

MCMI Interpretive Logic

Because the Validity index score was 0, one could assume that the examinee read and understood the test items. The elevations on the Disclosure and Debasement scales suggest a tendency to exaggerate the symptomatology, which is further supported by the numerous elevations on the severe symptom scales. The finding is interpreted as a "cry for help" in the discussion. An 812 personality profile was obtained. Because the personality elevations might have been aggravated by the acute psychotic symptomatology, a note of caution is included in the report. Because there were no signs of characterological dysfunction before the onset of the clinical syndrome, however,

Exhibit 11.2

Donald Green's Thematic Apperception Test Stories

1. A little boy sitting in a dark room wishing he had a violin, and according to the picture he has got his violin and now he has to learn to read the music. I don't see no future there.

2. I see a girl going to school, and she is watching her parents fixing the yard or planting seeds for next summer. (Oh, there are two ladies.) One is going to school, and one is watching the man work. The horse and the man be serious. I hope he will get good crops.

3BM. It looks like someone is praying, or either hurting, in pain, or they are looking for their keys and they are right by their foot and they don't see them. The lady is sitting in an awkward position hoping that she can find her keys, and they are right next to her feet and she hasn't found them yet, but according to this picture she should see them.

4. I see a man and a woman standing outside of a doorway or a window. He is fixing to go get in some trouble he ain't got no business getting into, and she is saying, "Baby, will you please wait and think about it?" He just froze there, so he didn't go.

6BM. I don't see nothing in this one, just a lady and a man. The woman is looking out of the window; the guy is grabbing his hat or something, I don't know. It looks like half of this part was cut out. Maybe somebody died and they are both sad about it.

7BM. Father and son—the son is trying to do what he wants to do, and the father is saying, "Look, would you listen? I got the gray hair here." Hopefully the guy will get wise.

8BM. It looks like somebody got shot, and the doctor is trying to remove the bullet and the woman is walking away with the gun. I wouldn't come near; I don't know, he might die.

10. A mother and daughter—I couldn't tell you what is happening in this picture. It looks like they are knee-deep in trouble for sure. It looks like she is whispering in her ear. I don't know what will happen.

12M. I can't tell if her eyes are open or closed. Are her eyes open or closed? Someone is laying on the bed, and somebody came and knelt beside them in the bed; maybe he is trying to hypnotize her and showing his right hand. I don't know. The outcome of that is she should wake up.

13MF. Well, it looks like she did not wake up. He just killed her. Now he is upset at what he has done. The outcome of that is straight to jail. Do not pass go. Do not collect $200.

16. Spades. Those who went bowling before would have wished they hadn't. This reminds me of space because the paper is blank, or a full moon because the paper is blank, that is about it.

continued

Exhibit 11.2

Donald Green's Thematic Apperception Test Stories *Continued*

17BM. It looks like somebody is climbing a rope. They are coming down a rope and looking somewhere else as they do it. It is a fireman coming down a rope, and he is trying to get to the squad before it becomes more than just a one-alarm fire, so he is in a hurry. He forgot his clothes though. He was in a real hurry.

18BM. This I couldn't tell you nothing about. It looks like a fat man with a nice jacket. He has got hands all in his back. Somebody is grabbing him from behind. It looks like he is trying to get shook up real good there. No, maybe he is going to jail. He is handcuffed, and the cops got their hands on him, taking him away.

the personality structure is not seen as constituting a personality disorder. The numerous elevations on the clinical syndrome scales, especially on the more severe syndrome scales, are consistent with the presence of a psychotic state.

Case Study 2: Affective Disorder With a Dependent Personality Style

Referral Information

Paul D'Angelo was a 32-year-old White man admitted to the psychiatric ward after becoming paranoid at his job. The patient explained that when a wallet belonging to another employee was stolen, a supervisor threatened to fire all the employees unless the wallet was found. Even though he had nothing to do with the incident, he felt the need to openly deny that he had done anything wrong and thought that others were talking about him behind his back. He became tense and somewhat agitated and was not able to sleep well. He became insecure and indecisive and believed that he was unable to cope with the demands of his daily life.

On admission into the unit, Mr. D'Angelo was described as guarded and agitated and was said to be preoccupied with his genitals. Flight of ideas and ideas of reference also were noted. He was diagnosed as having an agitated depression. At the time of the testing, he was on Navane and Norpramine.

Psychiatric History

Mr. D'Angelo was seen by a physician on consultation during a medical hospitalization in August 1986. At the time he complained of labile emotions and mood swings that had been bothering him for several months. The physician felt that the patient was depressed and prescribed antidepressants. Mr. D'Angelo received follow-up treatment from another physician and was kept on antidepressants. According to the patient, his emotional difficulties began after his wife and his mother quarreled; he had taken his wife's side and had not been on speaking terms with his mother before this admission. Mr. D'Angelo admitted having a problem with excessive drinking in the past but said he had had only an occasional beer since he was put on medication last August.

The family history was remarkable in that Mr. D'Angelo's father reportedly had a bipolar affective disorder. His mother and three of his brothers were alleged to be alcoholics.

Medical History

The patient's medical history was unremarkable except for a bout of pneumonia that required hospitalization when he was 15 years old. A medical evaluation by a physician at a hospital the previous August led to negative findings. A computed tomography scan of the brain taken during this latest admission also was within normal limits.

Family History

Mr. D'Angelo was born and raised in the Los Angeles area, the youngest of five siblings in a Catholic Italian family. His 65-year-old father was in and out of hospitals all of his life. The father was a building inspector and had worked for the city until 4 years previously. His father was characterized as a mild-mannered individual, a "weak" person needing to take direction from the patient's mother. One of the issues that led to the falling out with his mother was Mr. D'Angelo's disapproval of her decision to put his father in a nursing home. In spite of the patient's feeling that the nursing home was the best place for his father, he resented that the decision was made only on the basis that the mother was "tired of him." The father had been in the nursing home since the previous July.

Mr. D'Angelo's mother (age 57 years) used to be a clerk at a community center but was not currently employed. The patient talked about her as a "good mother" in spite of her drinking six beers every day. He characterized all family members as inclined to ignore their problems. It was apparently this characteristic that led to the fight between his wife and his mother a year ago: His wife reportedly confronted her mother-in-law about the fact that many of the siblings were drinking excessively, an issue that the mother allegedly did not want to face.

The oldest of the siblings was Tom (age 39). Tom was an alcoholic and an inpatient in the psychiatric ward at the same hospital; Tom was in detox at the time of the testing. A plumber, Tom had difficulty finding work during the past 5 years, perhaps because of his alcohol abuse. Tom was married and had two children. As an adult, the patient had been closer to Tom than to any of the other brothers. The frequency of their contacts, however, varied considerably depending on whether their wives were getting along well.

The second brother was 38-year-old Danny. Danny lived in Texas with his new wife. He was an epileptic on anticonvulsant medication and also was thought to be an alcoholic. Danny was a driver for a major beer company.

Frank (age 37) was disabled with a left-sided partial hemiparesis. He was hurt when he dove into the shallow end of a swimming pool. Frank never married and was cared for by his mother.

The brother immediately preceding the patient was Tony, a 35-year-old handyman who lived in Montana. Tony was married and had two children. One of the children had a defect in the spinal cord that caused paralysis of the lower extremities.

Mr. D'Angelo married his current wife, a 33-year-old housewife, 9 years ago. She was characterized as a beautiful woman who was outgoing, straightforward, and energetic and was thought to be very good to him. The D'Angelos have two children. Tiffany was 7 years old, and Chip was 5. Both were doing well and had presented no problems.

Educational History

Mr. D'Angelo went to a Catholic elementary school and graduated from a public high school in Los Angeles. He was an "average" student and never had any significant difficulties in school.

Occupational History

After his high school graduation, Mr. D'Angelo went to work for a car dealership. He was first employed unloading new cars but was able to learn repair work and became an assistant mechanic. He had worked for that employer for 12 years, was very satisfied with his current position, and felt that his supervisor was happy with his work.

Mental Status Examination

At the time of the evaluation, the patient was alert, oriented, verbal, and coherent. His speech and language functions were intact. The other intellectual functions examined—including memory, calculations, figure reproductions, mental control, and abstractions—also were within normal limits. His thought process was orderly and effective. The thought content was unremarkable. The presence of paranoid delusions, ideas of reference, and preoccupation with his genitals was noted on admission. His affective responses always were appropriate. Mood was within normal limits and demonstrated a good range of emotions, but this apparently constituted a change from his previous dysphoria. There was no suicidal or homicidal ideation. Psychomotor activity was within normal limits at the time of the testing, although the patient reportedly was originally in an agitated state.

Mr. D'Angelo was anxious, asked how he was doing on several occasions, and showed a fine hand tremor when he was required to draw figures. He associated this tremor with his being tense and claimed that he did not have it the rest of the time. He was friendly and cooperative and posed no problems during the test administration.

Discussion

The scores that Mr. D'Angelo obtained on the MCMI indicated that he has a dependent personality (see Table 11.2). Individuals with similar personalities assume that they are not very capable of taking care of themselves and must find someone who is benevolent and dependable and would support them, at least emotionally. They tend to form strong attachments to people who would then take a dominant role in decision making. They are followers rather than leaders and often are submissive in interpersonal affairs, shying away from highly competitive situations. Concerned with losing friends, they hide their feelings, especially when such feelings are aggressive or objectionable. These are unconceited people who try to be as congenial as possible to the people around them. Mr. D'Angelo is probably well liked but may be occasionally considered wishy-washy because he never takes a strong position on controversial issues. Similar individuals could be criticized for their inclination to be submissive, their lack of self-esteem, and their constant looking outside themselves for help.

Table 11.2

Paul D'Angelo's MCMI Test Results

Scale	Base Rate Score
Modifying Indices	
X. Disclosure	60
Y. Desirability	65
Z. Debasement	26
V. Validity (raw score)	0
Personality style scales	
1. Schizoid	51
2A. Avoidant	60
3. Dependent	80*
4. Histrionic	65
5. Narcissistic	28
6A. Antisocial	18
7. Compulsive	64
8A. Negativistic	24
Severe personality scales	
2B. Depressive	78*
6B. Aggressive	0
8B. Self-Defeating	61
S. Schizotypal	72
C. Borderline	78*
P. Paraphrenic	22
Clinical syndrome scales	
A. Anxiety	84*
H. Somatoform	92**
N. Bipolar: Manic	4
D. Dysthymia	84*
B. Alcohol Dependence	70
T. Drug Dependence	49
R. Posttraumatic Stress Disorder	57
Severe clinical syndrome scales	
SS. Thought Disorder	58
CC. Major Depression	47
PP. Delusional Disorder	9

Note. Scores below the cutoff of 75 are shown without asterisks.
*Score elevation was between 75 and 84.
**Score elevation was 85 or above.

Mr. D'Angelo has been able to establish himself well, both socially and occupationally, and leads a fairly independent life. As a result, his personality style cannot be considered dysfunctional or to constitute a personality disorder. Nevertheless, the dependent personality style can explain the kind of stress that Mr. D'Angelo has been under. It seems that his mother was the all-powerful figure in his childhood home, the stronghold of the family on whom the patient had learned to depend. Although his loyalties have shifted to his wife and his acquired family, it seems that he still needs the support of his mother to feel comfortable. Thus, when the quarrel ensued between his mother and wife, Mr. D'Angelo's insecurities increased, and he started having emotional problems. It is interesting that the issues at work revolved around the possible loss of support from another authority figure, a supervisor, and that the patient strongly wished to reassure everyone of his innocence so that there would be no chance that this support also would be compromised.

At the time of testing, Mr. D'Angelo was not actively psychotic. Nevertheless, several of his Rorschach responses showed faulty reality contact (see Exhibit 11.3). Although the number of such responses was not extreme, it was significantly higher than the normal range. In addition, the patient often saw "eyes" as an important part of his responses and was reminded of a "mask" on many of the cards, both of which are thought to be associated with paranoid defenses.

The presence of anxiety and depression was repeatedly observed throughout the testing. For example, most of the TAT stories revolved around negative or depressive events such as a car accident, a man who is about to leave his wife, a son who leaves his mother, a dying father, a man who is emotionally distressed after having sex with a prostitute, and so on (see Exhibit 11.4). In keeping with the preoccupation with his genitals that he demonstrated at the beginning of the hospitalization, his MCMI scores also indicated the presence of somatic concerns. Finally, there were indications that Mr. D'Angelo abuses alcohol as a way of defending against his anxieties.

On the positive side, there were no signs of cognitive deficits in the mental status examination. The impression was that Mr. D'Angelo has average intellectual capacities. That he also has achieved all of the major developmental milestones of the past is impressive. Thus, Mr. D'Angelo has established himself independently, has a good family and a good job, and has no great conflicts in his life. Once he has been able to reconstitute the sources of support that he needs, he may be able to return to his premorbid level of functioning.

Exhibit 11.3

Paul D'Angelo's Rorschach Test Results

Rorschach Protocol

1. Card I — Reaction time: 0 s
   SCORE=> W oF o A P 1.0
   Wasp or bee
   INQUIRY: Tail, wide wing span
2. Card I — Reaction time: 22 s
   SCORE=> W SoFT o (Ad) 1.0
   Mask
   INQUIRY: Of a wolf, outline, two sets of eyes, whiskers (?) shaggy outline; face of a wolf
3. Card I — Reaction time: 7 s
   SCORE=> W om ai Hh
   Glider plane
   INQUIRY: Flying over. They build them in such weird shapes these days
4. Card II — Reaction time: 4 s
   SCORE=> D oFC o (2)H P 3.0
   Two women, old
   INQUIRY: In black dress and red faces. They could be two chickens, too, with the beaks
5. Card II — Reaction time: 3 s
   SCORE=> D SvFC' o Hh 4.5
   A night light in the blackness.
   INQUIRY: Imprint of a lampshade in the middle of the dark
   LOCATION: black and white center
6. Card II — Reaction time: 10 s
   SCORE=> D oFM ao (2)(A) (P) 3.0
   Two chickens touching hands
   INQUIRY: Looking at each other, from a cartoon
7. Card III — Reaction time: 10 s
   SCORE=> D oF - Ad 3.0
   Two people looking at each other
   INQUIRY: The looks. Some kind of animal face or something
   At a distance; nostrils, eyes
   LOCATION: the usual P including orange cn D. Patient is seeing only two faces

continued

Exhibit 11.3

Paul D'Angelo's Rorschach Test Results *Continued*

Rorschach Protocol *Continued*

8. Card III — Reaction time: 3 s
   SCORE=> D oM — ao — H — P
   Two women
   INQUIRY: the way they look
9. Card III — Reaction time: 4 s
   SCORE=> D oF — v — (Ad)
   Two eyes in a mask
   INQUIRY: Mask of a wasp or something, face. It's a very ugly creature. Head of a wasp
10. Card IV — Reaction time: 15 s
    SCORE=> W oF — o — (A) — P
    A giant monster with a long tail hanging down the middle. Two big feet, two small claws
    INQUIRY: Head, pinhead
11. Card V — Reaction time: 5 s
    SCORE=> W oFC' — o — A — INC1 — 1.0
    Butterfly with a woman's face, maybe
    INQUIRY: In the fine blackness you can see two eyes and a nose.
12. Card V — Reaction time: 1 s
    SCORE=> D oM — po — (2)Hd — 2.5
    Two heads looking down
    INQUIRY: Forehead, nose and mouth
13. Card VI — Reaction time: 9 s
    SCORE=> W vm — o — (A) — 2.5
    A cat flattened out on the pavement after it got run down by a steamroller
14. Card VI — Reaction time: 5 s
    SCORE=> D oM — o — (2)Hd.Cg — 6.0
    Two opposing faces looking out
    INQUIRY: King with a crown, long beard, nose
15. Card VI — Reaction time: 41 s
    SCORE=> W vF — v — An — 2.5
    The inside anatomy of something
    INQUIRY: The amoebas or something, like that in somebody's body

continued

Exhibit 11.3

Paul D'Angelo's Rorschach Test Results *Continued*

Rorschach Protocol *Continued*

16. Card VII　　Reaction time:　4 s
SCORE=> D oM　　po　(2)Hd　　P　　3.0
Two women looking at each other
INQUIRY: Faces, hats

17. Card VII　　Reaction time:　4 s
SCORE=> D oFM　　po　(2)(Ad)　　3.0
Two pigs looking away from each other
INQUIRY: Round nose, something you might see in a cartoon, eye

18. Card VII　　Reaction time:　2 s
SCORE=> D oFM　　po　A　　1.0
Upside-down butterfly
INQUIRY: Body, wings spread out
LOCATION: bm D

19. Card VIII　　Reaction time:　6 s
SCORE=> DdS-F　　-　(Ad)　　4.0
Mask of a wasp or something
INQUIRY: I see a face in here somewhere
LOCATION: circular area taking the cn part of both of the top Ds (green and blue)

20. Card VIII　　Reaction time:　7 s
SCORE=> D -F　　-　Hd.Cg　　3.0
Face of a man with a hat
LOCATION: top and cn D (green and blue)

21. Card VIII　　Reaction time:　2 s
SCORE=> Dd om　　po　(2)Hd
Maybe a couple of legs fused together
INQUIRY: Couldn't find at first
LOCATION: tiny projections at cn bm of blue D

22. Card IX　　Reaction time:　12 s
SCORE=> W -F　　-　Ad　　▶　　5.5
Some kind of insect's face, upside-down
INQUIRY: Eyes, stinger, nose

continued

Exhibit 11.3

Paul D'Angelo's Rorschach Test Results *Continued*

Rorschach Protocol *Continued*

23. Card IX Reaction time: 20 s
SCORE=> Dd vF v Na
Map of river with tributaries
INQUIRY: Lake, river, and tributaries
LOCATION: inside darker edge of orange D

24. Card IX Reaction Time: 5 s
SCORE=> Dd oM po (2)Hd 4.5
Two faces looking away on the green part
INQUIRY: Nose, eyes
LOCATION: outside edge

25. Card X Reaction time: 7 s
SCORE=> D S+F + Hd
Two faces, one on bottom, one on top
INQUIRY: Eyes (yellow), nose (green cn), mustache (green)
LOCATION: white space with defined by pink in bm

26. Card X Reaction time: 3 s
SCORE=> D oFM ao (2)A P 4.5
Two crabs meeting at top
INQUIRY: claws (green)
LOCATION: blue D

27. Card X Reaction time: 13 s
SCORE=> DdS oF - (Hd) 6.0
Face
INQUIRY: eyes (tiny circular s defined by blue D in cn and pink D
LOCATION: circular area bound by the pink D, the wishbone on top and the green D on bm

28. Card X Reaction time: 3 s
SCORE=> Dd oF o Hd
Three sets of eyes
LOCATION: tiny details in three different places of the blot

29. Card X Reaction time: 11 s
SCORE=> D oFM ao (2)A 4.0
Butting heads here (top gray)
INQUIRY: like two animals butting heads

continued

Exhibit 11.3

Paul D'Angelo's Rorschach Test Results *Continued*

Rorschach Score Sequence

Card	No.	Time (seconds)	Scoring					
I	1	0	W	oF	o	A	P	1.0
I	2	22	W	SoFT	o	(Ad)		1.0
I	3	7	W	om	ao	Hh		
II	4	4	D	oFC	o	(2)H	P	3.0
II	5	3	D	SvFC'	o	Hh		4.5
II	6	10	D	oFM	ao	(2)(A)	(P)	3.0
III	7	10	D	-F	-o	Ad		3.0
III	8	3	D	oM	ao	H	P	
III	9	4	D	vF	v	(Ad)		
IV	10	15	W	oF	o	(A)	P	
V	11	5	W	oFC'	o	A	INC1	1.0
V	12	1	D	oM	po	(2)Hd		2.5
VI	13	9	W	vm	o	(A)		2.5
VI	14	5	D	oM	o	(2)Hd.Cg		6.0
VI	15	41	W	vF	v	An		2.5
VII	16	4	D	oM	po	(2)Hd	P	3.0
VII	17	4	D	oFM	po	(2)(Ad)		3.0
VII	18	2	D	oFM	po	A		1.0
VIII	19	6	DdS	vF	-	(Ad)		4.0
VIII	20	7	D	vF	-	Hd.Cg		3.0
VIII	21	2	Dd	om	po	(2)Hd		
IX	22	12	W	-F	-	Ad	Ú	5.5
IX	23	20	Dd	vF	v	Na		
IX	24	5	Dd	oM	po	(2)Hd		4.5
X	25	7	D	S+F	+	Hd		
X	26	3	D	oFM	ao	(2)A	P	4.5
X	27	13	DdS	-F	-	(Hd)	6.0	
X	28	3	Dd	oF	o	Hd		
X	29	11	D	oFM	ao	(2)A		4.0

continued

Exhibit 11.3

Paul D'Angelo's Rorschach Test Results *Continued*

Rorschach Structural Summary

Global	n %	Location	n %	Determinants	n %	Contents	n %	Quality	n %
R	29	W	8 28	M	5 17	CONT	6	OF ALL	
Rejects	0	D	15 52	FM	5 17			+	1 3
		Dd	6 21	m	3 10	H	2 6	o	20 69
P	6 21	DW	0 0	FT	1 3	(H)	0 0	v	3 10
(P)	1 3	S	5 17	TF	0 0	Hd	8 26	-	5 17
				T	0 0	(Hd)	0 0		
(2)	10 34			FY	0 0	A	6 19	OF F	
Fr	0 0	POSITION		YF	0 0	(A)	3 10	+	1 8
rF	0 0	▲	28 97	Y	0 0	Ad	2 6	o	3 25
3r+(2)	34	►	0 0	FV	0 0	(Ad)	4 13	v	3 25
		◄	0 0	VF	0 0	Ab	0 0	-	5 42
RT Ach	10	▼	1 3	V	0 0	Al	0 0		
RT Ch	7			FC′	2 7	An	1 3		
				C′F	0 0	Art	0 0	DV1	0 0
AFR	61	DEV QUAL		C′	0 0	Ay	0 0	DV2	0 0
		+	1 3	FC	1 3	Bl	0 0	INC1	1 3
		v/+	0 0	CF	0 0	Bt	0 0	INC2	0 0
		o	18 62	C	0 0	Cg	2 6	DR1	0 0
Zf	22	v	10 34	Cn	0 0	Cl	0 0	DR2	0 0
ZSum	72			FD	0 0	Ex	0 0	FAB1	0 0
				F	12 41	Fi	0 0	FAB2	0 0
						Fd	0 0	ALOG	0 0
				Blends	0	Ge	0 0	CON	0 0
						Hh	2 6	AB	0 0
		RATIOS		RATIOS		Ls	0 0	CP	0 0
		W	8	a	5 17	Na	1 3	AG	0 0
		M	5	p	6 21	Sc	0 0	MOR	0 0
						Sx	0 0	CFB	0 0
		W	8	M	5	Vo	0 0	PER	1 6
		D	15	wtd C	.5	Xy	0 0	COP	0 0
								PSV	1 6
				M+wtd C	6				
				FM+m	8				
				Y+T+V+C′	3	RATIOS			
						H+HD	10		
				ΣFMmYTVC′	11	A+AD	15		
				FC	1	H+A	11		
				CF+C	0	HD+AD	14		
						A%	48		

Exhibit 11.4

Paul D'Angelo's Thematic Apperception Test Stories

1. This is a little boy looking at a violin. He looks kind of sad. The violin could be broken or something. It looks like before he wanted to play the violin, and now that he has got the violin, he doesn't know if he can play it. In the future he will be a great violinist.

2. This looks like a guy plowing the field, getting ready to plow some corn with the fork. It could have been the winter snows. There is a lady looking on with a book. It looks like it is going to be a good harvest in the future, although he is doing it by hand. It is like winter, and now it is spring where the guy is plowing the field, and in the fall it will be a good harvest.

3BM. This is a picture of a man or woman sobbing over something. It looks like I see a set of keys lying on the floor. Maybe she was in a car accident or something and she is crying about what happened, but in the future she will learn not to drink and drive. Maybe she was drunk when she was driving, caused an accident. She will quit drinking from the picture.

4. It kind of reminds me of a old Navy World War II movie star and actress. They are all talking on the porch, maybe before they were in dancing or something. It looks like maybe she said something to make him mad, and he is getting ready to leave. He will be leaving her. She is trying to hold him back. It looks like she said something to make him mad and he is leaving, either that or he is going off to war or something.

Diagnostic Assignments and Recommendations

I. Major depression with psychotic features (296.34)
II. Dependent personality style with no personality disorder
III. No known contributing medical problem

Recommendations

Continued evaluation for the use of psychotropic medications to control the symptomatology seems indicated. In addition, Mr. D'Angelo may benefit from psychotherapy. Given his personality style, he will obtain support from a therapeutic relationship that is protective and guiding in a parentlike manner.

MCMI Interpretive Logic

Because the Validity scale score was 0, the test gave no indications of the patient having difficulties understanding or responding appropriately to the items. The Modifying Indices all were unremarkable. The personality profile (300) indicated a dependent personality, and the history showed that the patient had been highly functional and did not point to the presence of a personality disorder. Other elevations showed the patient to be depressed, anxious, and somatically preoccupied. The mild elevation of the Borderline scale was seen as resulting from mood instability rather than from any of the other aspects associated with the borderline personality disorder.

Case Study 3: Substance Abuse in a Borderline Personality Disorder

Referral Information

Janet Olsen was a 35-year-old woman who was admitted to a chemical abuse program for detoxification and treatment. The patient stated that in addition to her drinking, she had been feeling lonely and isolated and had been having crying spells. She felt abused by her family members and feared that she "couldn't trust anybody." Finally, she felt that she was "falling apart" and was "losing control" of her life.

Among the recent stressors that might have been associated with the presenting complaints was that the family had moved into their present area recently, and the patient felt that she did not have any good friends. Mrs. Olsen had heard rumors that her husband was having an affair and explained that her husband was an amphetamine abuser. She had had trouble controlling her 15-year-old daughter and was concerned about facial scars that her 13-year-old daughter had received in an accident. The family had financial difficulties and was still involved in a legal suit to recover their losses from the accident in which the daughter was injured.

The course of treatment during the current admission was marked by obvious symptoms of alcohol withdrawal during the first few days, including hand tremors. The current evaluation was requested to learn more about the patient, particularly whether she was suffering from an affective disorder.

Psychiatric History

This was the second psychiatric admission for Mrs. Olsen. The first admission took place when she was 20 years old. At the time, she spent 2 weeks at a hospital in Nashville, Tennessee. The patient recalled that in 1978, she had attempted to kill herself and her children by turning on the gas but then changed her mind and received no treatment for her depression. Mrs. Olsen had been drinking continuously for the previous 8 months, during which time she had had amnesic episodes and two blackouts. There was also weekly abuse of marijuana and cocaine. Before admission, she had been on Elavil and Xanax, which were given to her the preceding April by a general practitioner.

Her family history was remarkable in that her mother had suffered from a psychiatric disorder and was in an institution for 6 years. Her father was an abusive alcoholic, a problem that one of her brothers and one of her sisters also had. In addition, the same sister was said to have emotional problems and to be under psychiatric care.

Medical History

Mrs. Olsen had never had any major medical problems or serious accidents. She had a dilation and curettage procedure about 8 years ago.

Social History

Mrs. Olsen was born and raised in Nashville. Both parents reportedly abused the children physically, and she was sexually abused by her father and two of her brothers. She remembers her childhood as being difficult and traumatic. Her father, who was referred to as a "jerk" and was an alcoholic, died of liver failure when the patient was an adult. Her mother had to be psychiatrically hospitalized for 6 years when Mrs. Olsen's father went into the military and was said to have lived a "rough" life. The mother lived with the youngest sister in Nashville and was apparently dying of complications associated with her diabetes.

Mrs. Olsen was the fourth of five children. Her older sister died of diabetes before the age of 40. The rest of the siblings still lived in Nashville. Her older brother, Joe, was in his 40s and worked as a plumber. He was married to a nonsighted and physically challenged woman. David (age 37) was an alcoholic who abused his wife. Mrs. Olsen came next and was followed by Nancy (age 27), an alcoholic with other emotional problems. Nancy's boyfriend killed her children when "they would not stop wetting the bed."

Mrs. Olsen moved to Kentucky 14 years previously while she was still married to her first husband. She married him when she was 18 years old to get out of her parents' home. She claimed that the first husband physically abused her. Her first hospitalization took place, however, when they were not getting along and he had sent her back to Tennessee. The couple were apart for perhaps a year, during which time Mrs. Olsen had a boyfriend and lived in Virginia. She eventually went back to her first husband, but the marriage ended in divorce 9 years ago.

After separating from her first husband, Mrs. Olsen went to live with her current husband and his girlfriend. It was at that time that she tried to kill herself and the children. Three years ago, however, after the girlfriend left, Mrs. Olsen married her present husband.

Her husband, Kevin, was a 35-year-old appliance salesperson. He was an outgoing man who seemed to love being the center of attention when he was in public, but he was quiet at home. The husband was reportedly bothered by Mrs. Olsen's inability to "carry on an intelligent conversation," something that suggested to her that she was not the "right" woman for him, and this made her feel guilty. She thought about going back to school as a way to remedy the situation. The husband was addicted to amphetamines and recently had changed jobs.

Mrs. Olsen has a 15-year-old daughter from her first husband. Eleanor was described as "confused" and occasionally suicidal. She recently went into a hospital emergency room stating that she had been raped. There had been conflicts between the patient and Eleanor because Mrs. Olsen disapproved of Eleanor's friends. Other problems included her poor school performance and her being injured when she was struck by a car.

The second of Mrs. Olsen's daughters, Cathy, was born from the relationship the patient had with a boyfriend during her first marriage. Cathy was 13 years old and had been a poor student. She was hurt 4 months earlier when a store's plate glass window shattered as she was standing next to it waiting for a bus, and she was left with facial scars. The family hoped to obtain plastic surgery for Cathy with money from their lawsuit against the store owner.

Angela (age 11) was fathered by the patient's first husband during the period when they were reconciled. Angela was a quiet child. She was involved in church activities and was doing better in school than her siblings. However, Angela had experienced emotional problems, perhaps as a result of her feeling responsible for her parents' divorce. She had seen a psychiatrist at a mental health center.

Finally, Mrs. Olsen had a fourth child by her current husband. Donald was born before the couple was married and had another last name. He had a difficult time in school and was currently in special education. In addition, he had allergies and had to take a medication that tended to make him lethargic.

Educational and Occupational History

Mrs. Olsen finished 8th grade before dropping out of school. She explained that she "failed a few years" and was told that she read at a 4th-grade level. The patient had been a housewife most recently but had been employed as a file clerk intermittently throughout her adult life.

Mental Status Examination

At the time of the evaluation, this right-handed individual was alert, oriented, verbal, and coherent. Her speech and language functions were intact. Most of the other intellectual functions examined showed only mild deficits. However, her memory was somewhat impaired (e.g., the patient could remember only one out of three words after a 5-min delay). She had trouble doing simple subtractions, even when she was allowed to use paper and pencil; she was never able to accurately do simple multiplications. She had trouble thinking of different meanings for the same word, and proverb interpretations were concrete. The figure reproductions were within normal limits.

Her thought processes were disordered, confused, and circumstantial. Mrs. Olsen often experienced blocking, such that she would not offer information unless asked directly. At times, she talked as if she took for granted that the examiner knew something that she had not yet disclosed. There also were several instances in which she stated that she did not want to talk about something or seemed uncomfortable and asked questions about who would have access to that information. No delusions or hallucinations seemed to be present. Her affective responses always were appropriate. Her mood was within normal limits, and she demonstrated a good range of emotions. There was no suicidal or homicidal ideation. Her psychomotor activity and anxiety levels were within normal limits. The patient was friendly and cooperative.

Discussion

Mrs. Olsen appeared to suffer from a borderline personality disorder. Her history, for instance, showed affective instability, the tendency to act out sexually, an inclination to attempt suicide as a way to solve her problems, and difficulties with self-image. Those symptoms are the hallmarks of this disorder according to the fourth edition of the *Diagnostic and Statistical Manual of Mental Disorders* (*DSM–IV*).

In keeping with the borderline diagnosis, the MCMI described Mrs. Olsen as showing a pervasive instability in terms of moods, interpersonal relationships, and self-image (see Table 11.3). Her scores indicated that she typically responds in an impulsive and overemotional way and that her affective response tends to be labile, at times showing apathy and numbness or demonstrating excessive intensity or involvement. Sadness, hopelessness, and aimlessness often were underlying the more obvious emotional responses.

Underneath the borderline surface is a personality makeup consisting of introversiveness, a fear of rejection, and inadequate, self-defeating tendencies. Her MCMI scores suggest that she wants to be liked by others but expects that her social approaches will be rejected. As a result, Mrs. Olsen is likely to be apprehensive. Probably perceived as a nervous individual, she tends to feel uncomfortable in social situations. This type of person often is caught in a bind: She would like to interact with others and to be liked and appreciated, but she tends to avoid social situations to avoid the anxiety that these situations evoke.

At times, Mrs. Olsen may appear to be dependent and submissive. People with similar personality profiles usually underestimate themselves: When they compare themselves with others, they feel that they are less capable or less worthy. In fact, the indications are that the patient has such a poor self-image that she feels uncomfortable when she is treated nicely and may seek out situations in which she will be hurt or rejected. It is as if she has come to expect mistreatment and routinely has, almost by design, the type of interpersonal interactions that could be expected to bring about the abuse. When abuse has taken place, it might have been provoked, at least partly, by the resentments that Mrs. Olsen commonly harbors. Even though she is inclined to put herself down, the indications are that she is just as likely to devalue others. Similar people show their resentment in a somewhat insulting or even hostile way of interacting and appear to derive some pleasure from humiliating others. This, in return, creates ill will from others, which activates the person's own resentment in an angry and frustrating vicious cycle.

The testing was most informative because it offered a rare glimpse of the dynamics that possibly were connected with the borderline personality disorder. She appeared to feel unappreciated by either of her parents and to have a poor relationship with all of her siblings. Her self-esteem was not

Table 11.3

Janet Olsen's MCMI Test Results

Scale	Base Rate Score
Modifying Indices	
X. Disclosure	50
Y. Desirability	65
Z. Debasement	55
V. Validity (raw score)	0
Personality style scales	
1. Schizoid	115**
2A. Avoidant	109**
3. Dependent	96**
4. Histrionic	0
5. Narcissistic	26
6A. Antisocial	54
7. Compulsive	62
8A. Negativistic	87**
Severe personality scales	
2B. Depressive	103**
6B. Aggressive	42
8B. Self-Defeating	76*
S. Schizotypal	63
C. Borderline	92**
P. Paraphrenic	60
Clinical syndrome scales	
A. Anxiety	107**
H. Somatoform	87**
N. Bipolar: Manic	70
D. Dysthymia	112**
B. Alcohol Dependence	78*
T. Drug Dependence	59
R. Posttraumatic Stress Disorder	65
Severe clinical syndrome scales	
SS. Thought Disorder	81*
CC. Major Depression	73
PP. Delusional Disorder	72

Note. Scores below the cutoff of 75 are shown without asterisks.
*Score elevation was between 75 and 84.
**Score elevation was 85 or above.

enhanced by her school experiences either, because her intellectual abilities were low enough that she was seen as "retarded." The one area in which she probably felt wanted was sexually. Unfortunately, she was abused sexually by her father and brothers, which caused her to be conflicted and confused. Ultimately, she became "ashamed" of her lack of education and human potential and obtained gratification in life primarily through her ability to please men sexually. In what seemed like a replay of her childhood home situation, the picture she has of herself is negative and unrewarding.

In keeping with all of these dynamics, two themes were prevalent in the TAT stories (see Exhibit 11.5). These themes were the theme of shame, which often was associated with a lack of education, and the theme of difficulties in her romantic relationships.

The shame theme started on the first TAT card, with the boy afraid to "take that chance of trying to learn how to play [the violin]." It continued with the following comments obtained on card 2: "It is quite possible that she is ashamed of her mother. Maybe her mother is not well educated, and she is getting more proper education. Look at the difference of clothing. Look at how nice she looks, and look at mama." Although her response to card 2 betrays a concern that her children are ashamed of her, the most prevalent preoccupation involved her husband and the way he felt ashamed of the wife. It was noteworthy that the issue was often deeper than abandonment. It is not just that the men leave her after they have sex, but that they abuse her again: Her men have a need to bolster their own self-esteem by denigrating hers.

The theme of being taken advantage of in her romantic relationships was recurrent. The "husband" on card 3GF was said to be an "alcoholic" and possibly "cheating" on his wife. In response to card 4, she stated that the husband "can't even look her in the face," that he is a "jerk" who will "end up leaving her." Finally, on a card that portrays two people in a gentle embrace, it was striking how far Mrs. Olsen had to distance herself from the two people. She first placed them in a group different from her own, and she minimized the emotional ties by making them into distant friends.

The patient's low self-esteem and shame probably date back to a childhood sense of deprivation, as suggested in the following excerpt:

> It reminds me of me. But I never had any dolls. I never had nice clothes either. . . . You know what they used to say . . . because I was quiet and shy and I wasn't doing any good in school? They told my mother that I was retarded, deformed in the mind. . . . The little girl is in pain. She has, like, buried herself.

Exhibit 11.5

Janet Olsen's Thematic Apperception Test Stories

1. This reminds me of a young boy looking at a violin. He is trying to figure out, Can I play it? or Should I take that chance of trying to learn how to play it? The way his eyes look, it doesn't look like he really wants to learn how to play according to his eyes, because they look awfully uninterested in it. They look sad and down, and his mouth looks sad. It doesn't look like he wants to play it.

2. This reminds me of farmers living out in the country. It looks like a man is plowing, fixing the field for corn, and this looks like the mother leaning against the tree. This looks like the daughter looking back at her mother. It looks like she is going to school or to church, the way she is dressed. It looks like that to me. That could be a Bible, or it could be a schoolbook of some kind. It looks like the woman is pregnant with child, unless she is overweight. It just looks like a family, a farmer. It looks like there is water out in the back. That's what it looks like to me. If you look at it from my point of view, I'd like to be where they are. I envy them, I honestly do, because it doesn't look like they are really pleased by their mouths. This woman looks like she is contented. He looks like he is strong. He is healthy, but she doesn't look too happy the way her mouth is, down. It is quite possible that she is ashamed of her mother. Maybe her mother is not well educated, and she is getting more proper education. Look at the difference of clothing. Look at how nice she looks, and look at mama. Mother doesn't have her hair fixed up nicely, and you can see that mama is plain, but it looks like the daughter has some makeup on. It looks like to me she is just going to take off and leave her mother.

3GF. It looks like she is crying. It looks like she is upset. She is trying to decide if she should walk out of that door, or shouldn't I? Should I go get help, or shouldn't I? She looks very unhappy, very unhappy, and as for myself the way she is trying to force herself out, I think she will make it. She could be unhappy about anything. She could find that her husband is an alcoholic. She could find out that her husband is cheating on her. It looks like to me, she wants to go and get help.

4. It looks like she is really in love with him, and he is turning away from her. He is turning his head away. He can't even look her in the face, look her in the eye. That is terrible. What a jerk. Look at the love in her face. He is going to end up leaving her, and she is going to have a broken heart, and she is going to cry.

continued

Exhibit 11.5

Janet Olsen's Thematic Apperception Test Stories *Continued*

6GF. It looks like they are having some kind of discussion or something. He said something, and she looked back. He is looking at her and saying, "Do you understand what I am saying?" and her eyes are going, I understand what he is saying, but I don't really want to tell him how I feel because if I tell him how I feel, it is just going to cause problems, and why should I do that? She just keeps it to herself.

7GF. That doesn't remind me of a mother; it looks like a housemaid. It is a child, and the child looks lonely. She is holding a little doll. The woman looks sad. She wants to communicate with the child because she can tell the child is, you know. You know what that reminds me of? But I never had any dolls. It reminds me of me. But I never had any dolls. I never had nice clothes either. You know what they used to say about me, my sisters and brothers, because I was quiet and shy and I wasn't doing good in school? They told my mother that I was retarded, deformed in the mind. It wasn't that. It was just that it did no good to speak out. It did no good. That is what it reminds me of. The little girl is in pain. She has, like, buried herself. I hope that woman can reach her. She has a book in her hand. Maybe she is trying to read something to the child. Maybe communication wasn't doing too good, so she got a book to read to the child to see if she could communicate with the child like that, or maybe the child is supposed to be listening—you know, you could look at this at a different angle, honestly, if you think about it. Maybe my mind was just in a depressing way, right. Because it is possible that the woman, she is no mother, I can see that according to her clothing, and maybe she is trying to help the child with remembering things. She could be reading to the child. Like myself, if someone reads to me or if I read out loud, I remember better.

9GF. It looks like they are at the beach, the ocean, trees, water, waves. It looks like this young woman is going down the beach and this one is, like, spying on her, watching her. This one isn't quite as pretty as this one. This one looks more intelligent. This one looks more prettier. Maybe she envies her because she is prettier. The problem does not get solved. The women do not really communicate to understand why they have these feelings towards each other. They will stay away from each other.

continued

Exhibit 11.5

Janet Olsen's Thematic Apperception Test Stories *Continued*

10. It looks like someone is hugging somebody. It looks like a father hugging his son. It sure don't look like no woman, no young girl. You know how I've seen on TV, I've also seen it here, you know how a priest leans over and kisses the forehead of a woman. Catholic people, that's what it reminds me of too. It looks like they are showing caringness, you know, feelings. You know how even though you don't love that person, you just want to hug them as a friend.

13MF. You know what this reminds me of. He just had sex with her, and after he is done he is ashamed of her, and he is hiding. "Aw, I'm ashamed of you." It's done and over. I got what I wanted. I'm not trying to be nasty, but I got to tell you what is on my mind. That's the reason it aggravates me about men, honestly, because you know, that irritates me, it really aggravates me. Everything is fine and dandy until after they have sex, and then they are done with the woman. They say, I'm ashamed of you. They get what they wanted. So rather than deal with saying goodbye, they say, I'm ashamed of you.

16. I can tell you right away, because this is what I want. I want it bad. I want to go visit Florida and see the white sand, the beautiful waves, the sailboats, people surfing, and way out there, see, Pensacola is a Navy town, and when you look way, way out, well way back, well, it has been years. I don't know if they have the ships out in the Gulf again. That's what I see. I see Pensacola Beach on the Gulf side. I go back not so much to visit my friends, but I want to visit the town because the town then I disliked because it has too many memories. I want to go back and see it as something beautiful, something I can say, yes, it has changed. I see happiness. I don't have to look at Pensacola as something ugly and disgusting.

17GF. This is like a bridge of some kind. That could be the sun or the moon. This is the water and the boats. This is like a shed of some kind. This woman is looking down at the water. It looks like fishermen. Not really, not fishermen. It looks like they are carrying some heavy packages of some kind. Have you ever seen those old-fashioned potato sacks? Well, that is what it reminds me of, some kind of grain of some kind. I don't really see a story, to tell you the truth. It is a young girl just looking down in the water, watching the people. Well, she was all alone, and now she is happy they are back so she won't have to be alone anymore.

In addition to the characterological problems discussed so far, the testing generated concerns about the presence of other kinds of psychopathology. Mrs. Olsen, for example, had significant problems with her thinking processes, which was evident in the faulty reality contact on her Rorschach responses and the disturbed thought processes observed during the interview (see Exhibit 11.6). Given that she apparently has never been delusional, these problems could be blamed on the combination of the borderline personality disorder and low intellectual abilities. However, the indications would be that she has some propensity toward thought disturbances as part of the borderline syndrome.

The presence of alcohol abuse also was indicated. Substance abuse frequently has been found with individuals having Mrs. Olsen's combination of borderline, schizoid, avoidant, and dependent personality elements. Similar people have been described as being anxious and depressed and demonstrating widespread and severe maladjustment. They are thought to be typically caught between feelings of loneliness and social apprehension. Their drinking may serve to alleviate social anxiety to a level that produces self-assurance and permits social contact. Participation in treatment programs is especially difficult for this type of alcoholic.

Finally, there were signs that she experienced periods of despondency and depression and a high level of anxiety. At least at the time of the testing, neither of these problems seemed pronounced enough to constitute a separate disorder. Rather, these problems were seen as part of the borderline character pathology that has been described already.

Diagnostic Assignments and Recommendations

I. Alcohol intoxication, alcohol abuse disorder
II. Borderline personality disorder
III. No known contributing medical problems

Recommendations

Mrs. Olsen needs to take her drinking problem seriously and to commit herself to actively participating in Alcoholics Anonymous. That her husband also is a substance abuser presents additional difficulties; an effort probably should be made to have the two of them treated during the same period if permanent gains are to be made. The use of family therapy to evaluate and improve the relationships at home also is recommended.

Exhibit 11.6

Janet Olsen's Rorschach Test Results

Rorschach Protocol

1. Card I Reaction time: 0 s
   SCORE=> D -F - (2)A
   Butterfly
   INQUIRY: flares out, four butterflies
   LOCATION: top outside D and the outside D
2. Card I Reaction time: 5 s
   SCORE=> D -F - (2)A
   (Second set of butterflies from Response 1)
3. Card I Reaction time: 5 s
   SCORE=> W -F - A 1.0
   Like the nest of bats, queen and family, getting closed in for protection or food. This one is saying I'm the king, I'm under control. Vampire, because I saw a vampire movie last night.
   INQUIRY: we would kill them when we were kids
4. Card II Reaction time: 6 s
   SCORE=> D M a (2)H P 3.0
   This is kind of silly. Reminds me of a cartoon, clapping hands, dancing. Could be regular dancers too.
5. Card III Reaction time: 3 s
   SCORE=> D M a (2)H P 3.0
   Reminds me of waiters for some reason. It's like they are wearing tuxedos. They are holding their hats. It looks like they are gentlemen (laughs). It could also be dancers because of the heels and the different positions.
6. Card IV Reaction time: 28 s
   SCORE=> W F (A) P 2.0
   Monster, something evil. I don't like this one at all. Makes me feel fear. I do not like it.
   INQUIRY: tail
7. Card V Reaction time: 6 s
   SCORE=> W F A P 1.0
   Butterfly
   INQUIRY: wings and body

continued

Exhibit 11.6

Janet Olsen's Rorschach Test Results *Continued*

Rorschach Protocol *Continued*

8. Card V Reaction time: 5 s
SCORE=> W M p H.Cg 1.0
A dancer in Vegas wearing a costume.
INQUIRY: the dancer is here in the middle and this is the costume. Is got the arms spread out like this.

9. Card V Reaction time: 18 s
SCORE=> Dd F Hd PER
Reminds me of something ugly. It looks like my mother because she was. . . . I don't want to look at it.
INQUIRY: the face. The face she used to look at me. (Talks about the last time she saw her mother.)
LOCATION: face in Dd cn top below the "ears"

10. Card VI Reaction time: 13 s
SCORE=> W vma u Na 2.5
Earthquake, ground is cracking, earth is opening up.

11. Card VI Reaction time: 4 s
SCORE=> W vma u Na.Ex 2.5
Could be a volcano.
INQUIRY: this part over here and here is the lava coming out

12. Card VI Reaction time: 6 s
SCORE=> W vma u Fi 2.5
Fourth of July with flares going up

13. Card VI Reaction time: 2 s
SCORE=> Dd vF u Hd
Evil face
LOCATION: top cn inner detail

14. Card VII Reaction time: 7 s
SCORE=> W vMa (2)H.Hh (P) 2.5
Oh, goodness. Seesaw in the park with ponytails. That's cute.
INQUIRY: two girls here

15. Card VII Reaction time: 23 s
SCORE=> D vFMp u A.Hh PER 1.0
We have dogs. They really surprise you. Dogs: Sandy and Bandit on top of the picnic table.
INQUIRY: Picnic Table with our dogs
LOCATION: picnic table = bm D; dogs = mid D; top D not included

continued

Exhibit 11.6

Janet Olsen's Rorschach Test Results *Continued*

Rorschach Protocol *Continued*

16. Card VII Reaction time: 21 s
SCORE=> D M a (2)Hd Ag 3.0
Two people staring at each other, like a contest of outstaring. Or full of anger.
LOCATION: top D, head only

17. Card VIII Reaction time: 33 s
SCORE=> W vCF u Na PER 4.5
Oh, at least this one has some color, more cheerful. Like Christmas colors. Tree with birds on the side of the tree. I love going into the forest preserve. I only see nice things on this.

18. Card IX Reaction time: 11 s
SCORE=> W vma u Hh 5.5
Fountain, middle part shooting up. Water going in separate directions

19. Card IX Reaction time: 4 s
SCORE=> D Ma (2)(H) 4.5
Sword fighting up here
INQUIRY: two creatures fighting with swords
LOCATION: orange D

20. Card X Reaction time: 13 s
SCORE=> D F (2)A
Clams or crabs, different kinds of fish
INQUIRY: it looks like a clam with something sticking out
LOCATION: side brown D

21. Card X Reaction time: 2 s
SCORE=> D F (2)A PER
Goldfish
INQUIRY: we used to have a couple of aquariums.
LOCATION: yellow D with red circle in midfield

22. Card X Reaction time: 5 s
SCORE=> D -F - A
Lobster
INQUIRY: it looks like one
LOCATION: blue D

23. Card X Reaction time: 17 s
SCORE=> D F (2)A
Worms. Pretty colors, a pleasure to look at, no fear
LOCATION: green bm

continued

Exhibit 11.6

Janet Olsen's Rorschach Test Results *Continued*

Rorschach Score Sequence

Card	No.	Time (seconds)	Scoring					
I	1	0	D	-F	-	(2)A		
I	2	5	D	-F	-	(2)A		
I	3	5	W	-F	-	A		1.0
II	4	6	D	M	a	(2)H	P	3.0
III	5	3	D	M	a	(2)H	P	3.0
IV	6	28	W	F		(A)	P	2.0
V	7	6	W	F		A	P	1.0
V	8	5	W	M	p	H.Cg		1.0
V	9	18	Dd	F		Hd	PER	
VI	10	13	W	vm	au	Na		2.5
VI	11	4	W	vma	u	Na.Ex		2.5
VI	12	6	W	vma	u	Fi		2.5
VI	13	2	Dd	vF	u	Hd		
VII	14	7	W	vMa		(2)H.Hh	(P)	2.5
VII	15	23	D	vFMp	u	A.Hh	PER	1.0
VII	16	21	D	Ma		(2)Hd	Ag	3.0
VIII	17	33	W	vCF	u	Na	PER	4.5
IX	18	11	W	vma	u	Hh		5.5
IX	19	4	D	Ma		(2)(H)		4.5
X	20	13	D	F		(2)A		
X	21	2	D	F		(2)A	PER	
X	22	5	D	-F	-	A		
X	23	17	D	F		(2)A		

Rorschach Structural Summary

Global	n %	Location	n %	Determinants	n %	Contents	n %	Quality	n %
R	23	W	10 43	M	6 26	CONT	7	OF ALL	
Rejects	0	D	11 48	FM	1 4			+	0 0
		Dd	2 9	m	4 17	H	4 15	o	12 52
P	4 17	DW	0 0	FT	0 0	(H)	1 4	v	7 30

continued

Exhibit 11.6

Janet Olsen's Rorschach Test Results *Continued*

Rorschach Structural Summary *Continued*

Global	n	%	Location	n	%	Determinants	n	%	Contents	n	%	Quality	n	%
(P)	1	4	S	0	0	TF	0	0	Hd	3	11	-	4	17
						T	0	0	(Hd)	0	0			
(2)	10	43				FY	0	0	A	9	33	OF F		
Fr	0	0	POSITION			YF	0	0	(A)	1	4	+	0	0
rF	0	0	▲	23	100	Y	0	0	Ad	0	0	o	6	55
3r+(2)		43	►	0	0	FV	0	0	(Ad)	0	0	v	1	9
			◄	0	0	VF	0	0	Ab	0	0	-	4	36
RT Ach	10		▼	0	0	V	0	0	Al	0	0			
RT Ch	10					FC′	0	0	An	0	0			
						C′F	0	0	Art	0	0	DV1	0	0
AFR		44	DEV QUAL			C′	0	0	Ay	0	0	DV2	0	0
			+	0	0	FC	0	0	Bl	0	0	INC1	0	0
			o	11	48	CF	1	4	Bt	0	0	INC2	0	0
			v	8	35	C	0	0	Cg	1	4	DR1	0	0
Zf	17		-	4	17	Cn	0	0	Cl	0	0	DR2	0	0
ZSum	46					FD	0	0	Ex	1	4	FAB1	0	0
						F	11	48	Fi	1	4	FAB2	0	0
									Fd	0	0	ALOG	0	0
						Blends	0		Ge	0	0	CON	0	0
									Hh	3	11	AB	0	0
			RATIOS			RATIOS			Ls	0	0	CP	0	0
			W	10		a	9	39	Na	3	11	AG	1	4
			M	6		p	1	4	Sc	0	0	MOR	0	0
									Sx	0	0	CFB	0	0
			W	10		M	6		Vo	0	0	PER	4	17
			D	11		wtd C	1.0		Xy	0	0	COP	0	0
												PSV	0	0
						M+wtd C	7							
						FM+m	5							
						Y+T+V+C′	0		RATIOS					
									H+HD	8				
						ΣFMmYTVC′	5		A+AD	10				
						FC	0		H+A	15				
						CF+C	1		HD+AD	3				
									A%	37				

Mrs. Olsen would benefit from individual psychotherapy. It would be helpful if she could gradually learn to develop closeness and positive feelings for another person. An exploration of her low sense of self and her feeling of being abused by others could lead to growth-producing insights.

MCMI Interpretive Logic

The Validity scale and Modifying Indices were all unremarkable and can be disregarded. The elevations on severe personality scales indicate that the patient has a personality disorder. The elements of this disorder are organized in the narrative under the umbrella of the borderline personality. In keeping with the seriousness of the personality disorder, the discussion uses more pejorative terms (e.g., self-defeating) in addition to the milder terms that can be used to describe particular personality traits (e.g., submissive). Given this personality disorder and the patient's history, the elevations on the mood disorder scales (i.e., Depressive Personality and Dysthymia) are interpreted to be part of the borderline syndrome.

Case Study 4: Anxiety Disorder in an Avoidant Personality

Referral Information

Brenda Wolcott is a 62-year-old single White woman admitted to the psychiatric ward with complaints of intense anxiety, panic attacks, and depression. The patient had been sleeping and eating poorly, was experiencing a low energy level and a lack of motivation, and was anhedonic. She was unable to stay home alone or function independently. Ms. Wolcott also had several somatic complaints such as a strange feeling on the back of her neck, shortness of breath, a tingling sensation in the head, and stomachaches. Among the stressors noted was the death of her mother a month earlier, her being withdrawn from the chronic use of a minor tranquilizer, and a lack of social contacts.

The course of treatment during the hospitalization was marked by many requests from the patient to be placed back on Ativan. Sinequan was given for a day or so, but it was discontinued when the patient complained about the amount of sedation she experienced. At the time of the testing, Ms. Wolcott was kept on Tolectin and Buspar.

Psychiatric History

Ms. Wolcott explained she has been "nervous" all of her life. She was admitted to the medical ward of a hospital 20 years previously, and it was at that time that she was placed on benzodiazepam. She had only recently stopped taking this drug as prescribed by her family physician. Last November, already suffering from the problems that led to the current admission, Ms. Wolcott spent a week in a medical ward at the same hospital she had been in 20 years before. A history of psychiatric problems in the family was denied.

Medical History

Ms. Wolcott had a tonsillectomy at the age of 9 and had gallbladder surgery 6 years previously. Laboratory tests during the current admission were said to indicate subclinical hypothyroidism.

Family History

Ms. Wolcott was born and raised in Madison, Wisconsin. Her father died 15 years ago at the age of 72. He worked for a heating and air conditioning company and was characterized as a wonderful man who was liked by everyone. Ms. Wolcott always had a good relationship with him.

As close as Ms. Wolcott was to her father, she had an even closer relationship with her mother. The patient explained that she had lived with her mother all of her life and that when her mother had to be placed in a nursing home before her death, her absence left the patient feeling lonely. The mother worked for 20 years as a bookkeeper in an office supply store. She is remembered as "the best," but the patient recalled how her mother unfortunately tried to shelter her too much from the world.

Ms. Wolcott never married. She was the youngest of two siblings. Her 66-year-old brother was an aerospace engineer. He had recently accepted a job at the University of Louisville and moved to Kentucky. Her brother was married and had a daughter. He was expected to live with the patient temporarily until he could find a place for himself and his family.

Ms. Wolcott explained that she had always been shy and "never went out to make friends." In fact, the patient admitted that she seldom went out with anyone outside the family. As long as she was employed, she had a group of acquaintances at work. However, she lost those contacts when she retired and had been very isolated, especially after her mother went into the nursing home.

Educational History

Ms. Wolcott recalled that after graduating from grammar school, she was sent to a boarding school for 2 years. She went to the boarding school on the advice of her grammar school principal, who felt that she needed to be "away from the home." She apparently never adjusted to the boarding school and felt lonely and homesick. Thus, at the end of 2 years, she was allowed to return home and continued her studies in a local business school. Ms. Wolcott was an average student and never presented any academic difficulties.

Occupational History

The patient retired 4 years ago from the company where she did bookkeeping work for 37 years. She explained that at the end of her tenure there, she was expected to do tasks (e.g., moving files from one room to another) that she was not physically able to do anymore. Up until that time, however, she had apparently performed her functions well. Because her mother became sick right after the patient's retirement and had since died, Ms. Wolcott had not enjoyed her retirement. She currently felt she needed to create some activities and some way to structure her life.

Mental Status Examination

At the time of the evaluation, the patient was alert, oriented, verbal, and coherent. Her speech and language functions were intact; the other intellectual functions examined also were within normal limits. These functions included memory, calculations, figure reproductions, mental control, and abstractions. Her thought process was orderly and effective. Her thought content was remarkable only in that she was originally preoccupied with the fear that she would not be given her medication on time. She talked about the death of her mother several times but did not seem unduly preoccupied with that loss. There were no indications of delusions or hallucinations.

The affective responses always were appropriate. Although her mood was within normal limits, it tended to be serious. There was no verbalized suicidal or homicidal ideation. The psychomotor activity and anxiety levels were within normal limits. Ms. Wolcott was very anxious at the beginning, repeatedly asking questions while taking the paper-and-pencil questionnaire and wondering whether she could do an adequate job on the testing. As time went on, however, she seemed to become more comfortable and relaxed. She was friendly and cooperative throughout.

Discussion

The test results were consistent with the presence of a generalized anxiety disorder. In addition, the indications were that Ms. Wolcott was mildly depressed. Her Rorschach responses, for instance, were somewhat unproductive and constricted (see Exhibit 11.7), and her TAT stories often alluded to the death of someone in the family (see Exhibit 11.8), as in the following story obtained on Card 3GF:

> It looks like somebody is in the depths of despair. Looks like she is crying, very sad about something. She could have been happy before this happened. I'd say someone close to her died, and in her future she will get over her grief.

Among the other stories with similar depressive themes, the one that is noteworthy is her response to Card 14, on which the protagonist thinks of committing suicide by jumping out a window.

Judging from her MCMI scores, at the basis of Ms. Wolcott's problems is a personality style with schizoid, avoidant, dependent, and compulsive components (see Table 11.4). The indications from the history were that the patient met criteria for an avoidant personality disorder. This type of personality is prevalent among individuals with an anxiety disorder, the "anxious" cluster of the *DSM–IV* personality prototypes. Although it was possible that the acute anxiety episode had aggravated the patient's personality traits, the history pointed to the lifelong prevalence of these tendencies.

Individuals with similar MCMI scores tend to have low self-esteem; they see others as being more capable or valuable than they are. They are followers rather than leaders, often taking a passive role in interpersonal affairs. They would like to seek the emotional support and protection of others, but with that wish, they experience discomfort in social situations.

The discomfort comes from the assumption that if others got to know them as well as they know themselves, they would develop the same uncomplimentary views that these individuals hold of themselves. Similar people try to put their best foot forward and have a tendency to cover up their true feelings, especially when these feelings are aggressive or otherwise objectionable. They may seem tense, nervous, and distant. Because they feel ill at ease in social situations, they often avoid such affairs and frequently are lonely and isolated.

Exhibit 11.7

Brenda Wolcott's Rorschach Test Results

Rorschach Protocol

1. Card I Reaction time: 2 s
   SCORE=> W o FMa.FC' O A P 1.0
   butterfly
   Flying bat, more than a butterfly
   INQUIRY: It's black. Wing spread, the body and the feet
2. Card II Reaction time: 4 s
   SCORE=> W o vFMa.FC u A 4.5
   Oh my God, two colors! Could be a flying insect but it's so big. Here is the body and these are the wings
   INQUIRY: wings, two different colors, this glow is like the end lights up.
3. Card III Reaction time: 9 s
   SCORE=> D o Ma O (2)H P 3.0
   Two people stirring up a pot
   INQUIRY: repeats
4. Card III Reaction time: 3 s
   SCORE=> D o FC O A CONT
   a butterfly between them
   INQUIRY: the wings, the color, the shape
5. Card IV Reaction time: 8 s
   SCORE=> W o F O (A) P 2.0
   Oh my! Some kind of a monster from a creepy show
   INQUIRY: Big feet, floppy arms. Like King Kong.
6. Card V Reaction time: 7 s
   SCORE=> W o F O A P 1.0
   They are all very similar, they would have to be.
   Some kind of butterfly, the legs sticking out
   INQUIRY: the wings, the legs, the thing coming out on top.
7. Card VI Reaction time: 8 s
   SCORE=> W vF u (2)(A) 2.5
   These are all very similar. Wings sticking out. Some kind of a creepy character. Some kind of a monster. Head there, there are a couple of eyes there.
   INQUIRY: I don't know what kind of a monster would have two sets of wings.

continued

Exhibit 11.7

Brenda Wolcott's Rorschach Test Results *Continued*

Rorschach Protocol *Continued*

8. Card VII Reaction time: 5 s
SCORE=> D o F O (2)Ad 1.0
That don't look like nothing. Too much space in between. There is a face on each one of these.
INQUIRY: two faces on each side. The eye, the nose, the mouth. The ear and the snout.
LOCATION: 2nd D from top, below the usual girl's face

9. Card VII Reaction time: 9 s
SCORE=> D o F O A 1.0
butterfly
INQUIRY: the wings with the body in the middle
LOCATION: bottom D

10. Card VII Reaction time: 10 s
SCORE=> D v F u A Ú 1.0
a long tail
INQUIRY: a tail, a body and the head. It's kind of an animal.
LOCATION: top D with card upside down

11. Card VIII Reaction time: 18 s
SCORE=> D o F O (2)A P 3.0
This is different. I see two rats on each side.
INQUIRY: long tail, head

12. Card VIII Reaction time: 3 s
SCORE=> D o FC O A
butterfly
INQUIRY: the wings, the color, the body.
LOCATION: bottom D

13. Card VIII Reaction time: 2 s
SCORE=> D v FMa u (2)A 3.0
two insects
INQUIRY: they are getting together.
LOCATION: uppermost green D

14. Card IX Reaction time: 7 s
SCORE=> D o F O A 2.5
They get worse. That looks like a big butterfly.
INQUIRY: the wings and the body
LOCATION: midsection

continued

Exhibit 11.7

Brenda Wolcott's Rorschach Test Results *Continued*

Rorschach Protocol *Continued*

15. Card IX Reaction time: 10 s
SCORE=> Rejected
The line going down the middle makes you think that it is the body of an insect. Maybe more than one kind because of the different colors.
INQUIRY: (cannot find and rejects)

16. Card X Reaction time: 7 s
SCORE=> D o F O A P 4.0
An animal with a lot of feet
INQUIRY: the feet. It's a crab or something
LOCATION: upper blue D

17. Card X Reaction time: 6 s
SCORE=> D o FC O (2)A
two rats
INQUIRY: black rats. There are two of them
LOCATION: top gray D

18. Card X Reaction time: 6 s
SCORE=> Dd v F v Xy 4.0
An X-ray of the inside of a body.
INQUIRY: this part coming down here
LOCATION: center bottom up to the blue D

Rorschach Score Sequence

Card	No.	Time (seconds)	Scoring					
I	1	2	W	FM.FC'	a	A	P	1.0
II	2	4	W	vFM.FC	au	A		4.5
III	3	9	D	M	a	(2)H	P	3.0
III	4	3	D	FC		A		
IV	5	8	W	F		(A)	P	2.0
V	6	7	W	F		A	P	1.0
VI	7	8	W	vF	u	(2)(A)		2.5
VII	8	5	D	F		(2)Ad		1.0
VII	9	9	D	F		A		1.0

continued

Exhibit 11.7

Brenda Wolcott's Rorschach Test Results *Continued*

Rorschach Score Sequence *Continued*

Card	No.	Time (seconds)	Scoring					
VII	10	10	D	vF	u	A	Ú	1.0
VIII	11	18	D	F		(2)A	P	3.0
VIII	12	3	D	FC		A		
VIII	13	2	D	vFM	au	(2)A		3.0
IX	14	7	D	F		A		2.5
X	16	7	D	F		A	P	4.0
X	17	6	D	FC		(2)A		
X	18	6	Dd	vF	u	Xy		4.0

Rorschach Structural Summary

Global	*n* %	Location	*n* %	Determinants	*n* %	Contents	*n* %	Quality	*n* %
R	17	W	5 29	M	1 5	CONT	3	OF ALL	
Rejects	0	D	11 65	FM	3 16			+	0 0
		Dd	1 6	m	0 0	H	1 6	o	12 71
P	6 35	DW	0 0	FT	0 0	(H)	0 0	v	5 29
(P)	0 0	S	0 0	TF	0 0	Hd	0 0	-	0 0
				T	0 0	(Hd)	0 0		
(2)	6 35			FY	0 0	A	12 71	OF F	
Fr	0 0	POSITION		YF	0 0	(A)	2 12	+	0 0
rF	0 0	▲	16 94	Y	0 0	Ad	1 6	o	7 70
3r+(2)	35	►	0 0	FV	0 0	(Ad)	0 0	v	3 30
		◄	0 0	VF	0 0	Ab	0 0	-	0 0
RT Ach	7	▼	1 6	V	0 0	Al	0 0		
RT Ch	6			FC′	1 5	An	0 0		
				C′F	0 0	Art	0 0	DV1	0 0
AFR	70	DEV QUAL		C′	0 0	Ay	0 0	DV2	0 0
		+	0 0	FC	4 21	Bl	0 0	INC1	0 0
		o	12 71	CF	0 0	Bt	0 0	INC2	0 0
		v	5 29	C	0 0	Cg	0 0	DR1	0 0

continued

Exhibit 11.7

Brenda Wolcott's Rorschach Test Results *Continued*

Rorschach Structural Summary *Continued*

Global	*n*	%	Location	*n*	%	Determinants	*n*	%	Contents	*n*	%	Quality	*n*	%
Zf	14		-	0	0	Cn	0	0	Cl	0	0	DR2	0	0
ZSum	34					FD	0	0	Ex	0	0	FAB1	0	0
						F	10	53	Fi	0	0	FAB2	0	0
									Fd	0	0	ALOG	0	0
						Blends	2		Ge	0	0	CON	0	0
									Hh	0	0	AB	0	0
			RATIOS			RATIOS			Ls	0	0	CP	0	0
			W	5		a	4	24	Na	0	0	AG	0	0
			M	1		p	0	0	Sc	0	0	MOR	0	0
									Sx	0	0	CFB	0	0
			W	5		M	1		Vo	0	0	PER	0	0
			D	11		wtd C	2.0		Xy	1	6	COP	0	0
												PSV	0	0
						M+wtd C	3							
						FM+m	3							
						Y+T+V+C′	1		RATIOS					
									H+HD	1				
						ΣFMmYTVC′	4		A+AD	15				
						FC	4		H+A	15				
						CF+C	0		HD+AD	1				
									A%		88			

Exhibit 11.8

Thematic Apperception Test Stories

1. That looks like a boy studying his lesson. He looks like 5 or 6 years old and that would be before his school days, I would say. Well, he will go on to have a career in his life, whatever he wants to do in his life.

2. This looks like a farm. A man is working with a horse. This might be his wife and daughter. He's probably been a farmer all his life. His daughter is going to school, and his wife is standing here and he's working with a plow horse. The girl looks like she is going to school with books in her hand. She will go on to do better things too. If she continues with her studies she will make something out of her life.

3GF. It looks like somebody is in the depths of despair, looks like she's crying, very sad about something. She could have been happy before this happened. I'd say somebody close to her died, and in her future she will get over her grief. Just like me when my mother died.

4. Looks like two movie stars in two movies that I saw not too long ago. These people remind me of a musical I saw. They fell in love with each other. He left her and never came back to her. Looks like he's pulling away from her. He's a riverboat gambler, but he left her and finally came back after he found out she had a child and it was his.

6GF. This woman is talking to a man standing behind her and turning around. The look on her face, he must have startled her. Well, she might have been married and is falling in love with him, both nice-looking people and that's what will happen in the future.

7GF. That's a mother talking to her daughter who is holding a doll, both sitting on a couch talking about something. She looks like she's got a book in her hand. She must be reading to her but she doesn't look like she is paying any attention to her. If she was paying any attention to her mother she would get something out of it. They are all cooking out there.

9GF. This girl is running away for some reason. This one is standing behind a tree with something in her hand. I can't make it out. She is watching her run away wondering where she is going but she looks frightened. This is water, maybe she sees someone in the water that needs help and she is running to help that person. See, she's got a towel in her arms and she will save the person that needs help.

10. This is two middle-aged people that have been married for a long time, and they still love each other. He is kissing her on the forehead. It looks like they are married for almost 50 years and will be married for the rest of their life.

13MF. The man is in despair over the death of his wife. She is not already gone. She will die, and that will be it.

continued

Exhibit 11.8

Thematic Apperception Test Stories *Continued*

14. It looks like he's ready to jump out the window. A small picture, looks like somebody is jumping out the window in a dark room. Either he's thinking about doing himself in or trying to escape from something. Whoever is bothering him or whatever is bothering him, maybe despondent over something.

15. Looks like a man in the graveyard, he's praying for something he's buried there. It's an old gravestone. He came to visit somebody's grave and he's praying for them. Nothing can happen if the person is dead there, then nothing can happen.

17GF. This looks like a house, but there's some people outside the house, or one person at least. It looks like there's other people too. There is somebody on the roof, another building here and the sun is shining. There's a boat here. They are getting out of the boat, in the water. Somebody's looking down on them. There's a high wall around the house, high windows. They can get out of the boat right there. The sun shining down and somebody's looking down. It almost looks like they are up to no good to me. They are brining something to this house on the rafters by boat. This looks like a woman here and these are men. They look like smugglers and might hide it in this house here, and if they get caught they will get thrown in jail.

18GF. This looks like a very sad woman. She is holding her daughter in her arms, and she must be very ill. That's why she looks so sad, because her daughter is so ill. There is a staircase here. I don't know if somebody fell down the stairs and got hurt. She was laying there and she picked her up in her arms and she could have died or be seriously injured in the fall. Hopefully, she will recover if she is still living. You always hope for something better.

One way in which Ms. Wolcott defends against the insecurity that her low self-esteem may bring is by counting on the guidance and protection of others. The second defense mechanism she uses is thinking that if she manages to avoid making a mistake, she always can expect the outcome to be a positive one. Individuals with a similar compulsive bent are orderly and plan for the future. They prepare in a conscientious manner and do their work on schedule. They try to be efficient, dependable, industrious, and persistent. These individuals often relate in an overly respectful and ingratiating manner. They may be somewhat perfectionistic and self-disciplined. They tend to be indecisive, especially when they have to make a decision by themselves. The compulsive inclination also may serve to

Table 11.4

Brenda Wolcott's MCMI Test Results

Scale	Base Rate Score
Modifying Indices	
X. Disclosure	55
Y. Desirability	57
Z. Debasement	37
V. Validity (raw score)	0
Personality style scales	
1. Schizoid	85**
2A. Avoidant	85**
3. Dependent	94**
4. Histrionic	3
5. Narcissistic	24
6A. Antisocial	35
7. Compulsive	95**
8A. Negativistic	7
Severe personality scales	
2B. Depressive	73
6B. Aggressive	32
8B. Self-Defeating	52
S. Schizotypal	80*
C. Borderline	53
P. Paraphrenic	74
Clinical syndrome scales	
A. Anxiety	76*
H. Somatoform	84*
N. Bipolar: Manic	0
D. Dysthymia	75*
B. Alcohol Dependence	35
T. Drug Dependence	0
R. Posttraumatic Stress Disorder	66
Severe clinical syndrome scales	
SS. Thought Disorder	68
CC. Major Depression	44
PP. Delusional Disorder	70

Note. Scores below the cutoff of 75 are shown without asterisks.
*Score elevation was between 75 and 84.
**Score elevation was 85 or above.

strengthen the feelings of inadequacy that are beneath it in that whenever bad events take place, Ms. Wolcott will be inclined to look for what mistakes she made that might have led to the undesirable outcome.

The extent to which this dependent, anxiously shy, and compulsive personality style was caused by an overprotective mother is debatable. What seems undeniable, however, is that it fits well with the relationship that the patient had with her mother. The mother was the protective figure and was the only real, safe relationship that she had.

Perhaps as a result of this good fit, the indications were that the patient's personality style was exaggerated enough to be dysfunctional. Her MCMI scores suggested that she is isolated and has few real relationships. Individuals obtaining similar scores are somewhat eccentric. They may have a rich fantasy life and may mix their own personal idiosyncrasies with other material in their conversations; they appear anxious and apprehensive and may have a flat affect.

Finally, her responses to the projective measures depict a fairly immature and infantile individual who is not well developed psychologically. The impression was that the personality structure was impaired enough to constitute a personality disorder. Encumbered with this personality disorder, Ms. Wolcott has been able to make only a marginal adjustment in her adult life. She was never able to establish significant relationships outside of the family and seemed to cope psychologically only with the help of her family; even with that support, she became dependent on tranquilizers as the only way to control the anxieties she experienced. The loss of her job a few years before the testing further jeopardized the kind of adjustment that she was able to make.

Regarding psychological strengths, Ms. Wolcott is very personable and shows no evidence of intellectual or memory deficits. She also has some insight into her problems and seemed well motivated.

Diagnostic Assignments

I. Generalized anxiety disorder, benzodiazepine dependence, uncomplicated bereavement

II. Avoidant personality disorder with schizoid, dependent, and compulsive elements

III. No known contributing medical problems

Recommendations

Continued evaluation for the use of psychotropic medications to reduce the patient's anxiety is indicated. In addition, Ms. Wolcott may benefit from a period of psychotherapy. Given her personality style, she can be expected to experience as supportive a relationship in which the therapist has a benevolent and protective attitude toward her. Feeling that the therapist is a powerful expert who will advise and guide her appropriately will be reassuring for Ms. Wolcott. The patient's fear of rejection may require frequent reaffirmation and promise of support.

MCMI Interpretive Logic

The Validity and Modifying Indices all are at an acceptable level and can be disregarded. The elevation of the schizotypal personality raises the question of her having a personality disorder. After a review of the items endorsed, it is evident that most of the items dealt with the patient's social isolation; the elevations on the Schizoid and Avoidant scales give further support to this personality structure, and the history meets criteria for the avoidant personality disorder. The discussion also works to blend in the compulsive aspects. Finally, the elevations of clinical syndrome scales, with the support of information from other sources, served to arrive at the diagnosis of a generalized anxiety disorder.

References

Abraham, K. (1927). The influence of oral eroticism on character formation. In D. Bryan & A. Strachey (Trans.), *Selected papers on psychoanalysis* (pp. 393–406). London: Hogarth. (Original work published 1924)

Ackerman, M. J., & Ackerman, M. C. (1996). Child custody evaluation practices: A 1996 survey of psychologists. *Family Law Quarterly, 30,* 565–586.

Adams, W., & Clopton, J. (1990). Personality and dissonance among Mormon missionaries. *Journal of Personality Assessment, 54,* 684–693.

Adler, A. (1956). The style of life. In H. L. Ansbacher & R. R. Ansbacher (Eds.), *The individual psychology of Alfred Adler* (pp. 172–203). New York: Basic Books.

Ahrens, J., Evans, R., & Barnett, R. (1990). Factors related to dropping out of school in an incarcerated population. *Educational and Psychological Measurement, 50,* 611–617.

Alden, L. E., Wiggins, J. S., & Pincus, A. L. (1990). Construction of the circumplex scales for the Inventory of Interpersonal Problems. *Journal of Personality Assessment, 55,* 521–536.

Alexander, G. E., Choca, J. P., Bresolin, L. B., DeWolfe, A. S., Johnson, J. E., & Ostrow, D. G. (1987, May). *Personality styles in affective disorders: Trait components of a state disorder.* Paper presented at the convention of the Midwestern Psychological Association, Chicago.

Alexander, G. E., Choca, J. P., DeWolfe, A. S., Bresolin, L. B., Johnson, J. E., & Ostrow, D. G. (1987, August). *Interaction between personality and mood in unipolar and bipolar patients.* Paper presented at the 95th Annual Convention of the American Psychological Association, New York.

Alexander, P. C. (1993). The differential effects of abuse characteristics and attachment in the prediction of long term effects of sexual abuse. *Journal of Interpersonal Violence, 8,* 346–362.

Allen, J. G., Coyne, L., & Huntoon, J. (1998). Complex posttraumatic stress disorder in women from a psychometric perspective. *Journal of Personality Assessment, 70,* 277–298.

Allen, J. G., Huntoon, J., & Evans, R. B. (1999). Complexities in complex posttraumatic stress disorder in inpatient women: Evidence from a cluster analysis of MCMI–III personality disorder scales. *Journal of Personality Assessment, 73,* 449–471.

Allport, G. W., & Odbert, H. S. (1936). Trait names: A psycho-lexical study. *Psychological Monographs, 47* (1, Whole No. 211).

Alnaes, R., & Torgersen, S. (1990). MCMI personality disorders among patients with major depression with and without anxiety disorders. *Journal of Personality Disorders, 4,* 141–149.

Alnaes, R., & Torgersen, S. (1991). Personality and personality disorders among patients with various affective disorders. *Journal of Personality Disorders, 5,* 107–121.

American Psychiatric Association. (1980). *Diagnostic and statistical manual of mental disorders* (3rd ed.). Washington, DC: Author.

American Psychiatric Association. (1987). *Diagnostic and statistical manual of mental disorders* (3rd ed., rev.). Washington, DC: Author.

American Psychiatric Association. (1994). *Diagnostic and statistical manual of mental disorders* (4th ed.). Washington, DC: Author.

Anderson, S. (1968). Effects of confrontation by high and low-functioning therapists. *Journal of Counseling Psychology, 15,* 411–416.

Anrig, G. R. (1987). "Golden Rule": Second thoughts. *APA Monitor, 18,* p. 3.

Antoni, M., Levine, J., Tischer, P., Green, C., & Millon, T. (1986). Refining personality assessments by combining MCMI high-point profiles and MMPI codes, Part IV: MMPI 89/98. *Journal of Personality Assessment, 50,* 65–72.

Antoni, M., Levine, J., Tischer, P., Green, C., & Millon, T. (1987). Refining personality assessments by combining MCMI high-point profiles and MMPI codes, Part V: MMPI 78/87. *Journal of Personality Assessment, 51,* 375–387.

Antoni, M., Tischer, P., Levine, J., Green, C., & Millon, T. (1985a). Refining personality assessments by combining MCMI high-point profiles and MMPI codes, Part I: MMPI 28/82. *Journal of Personality Assessment, 49,* 392–398.

Antoni, M., Tischer, P., Levine, J., Green, C., & Millon, T. (1985b). Refining personality assessments by combining MCMI high-point profiles and MMPI codes, Part III: MMPI 24/42. *Journal of Personality Assessment, 49,* 508–515.

Auerbach, J. S. (1984). Validation of two scales for narcissistic personality disorder. *Journal of Personality Assessment, 48,* 649–653.

Bagby, R. M., Gillis, J. R., & Dickens, S. (1990). Detection of dissimulation with the new generation of objective personality measures. *Behavioral Sciences and the Law, 8,* 93–102.

Bagby, R. M., Gillis, J. R., & Rogers, R. (1991). Effectiveness of the Millon Clinical Multiaxial Inventory validity index in the detection of random responding. *Psychological Assessment, 2,* 285–287.

Bagby, R. M., Gillis, J. R., Toner, B. B., & Goldberg, J. (1991). Detecting fake-good and fake-bad responding on the Millon Clinical Multiaxial Inventory–II. *Psychological Assessment, 3,* 496–498.

Bagby, R. M., Joffe, R. T., Parker, J. D. A., & Schuller, D. R. (1993). Reexamination of the evidence for the DSM–III personality disorder clusters. *Journal of Personality Disorders, 7,* 320–328.

Baile, W., Gibertini, M., Scott, L., & Endicott, J. (1993). Prebiopsy assessment of patients with suspected head and neck cancer. *Journal of Psychosocial Oncology, 10,* 79–91.

Baker, J. D., Capron, E. W., & Azorlosa, J. (1996). Family environment characteristics of persons with histrionic and dependent personality disorders. *Journal of Personality Disorders, 10,* 82–87.

Baldessarini, R. J., Finklestein, S., & Arana, G. W. (1983). The predictive power of diagnostic tests and the effect of prevalence of illness. *Archives of General Psychiatry, 40,* 569–573.

Bard, L., & Knight, R. (1987). Sex offender subtyping with the MCMI. In C. Green (Ed.), *Conference on the Millon inventories* (pp. 133–137). Minneapolis, MN: National Computer Systems.

Bartsch, T. W., & Hoffman, J. J. (1985). A cluster analysis of Millon Clinical Multiaxial Inventory (MCMI) profiles: More about a taxonomy of alcoholic subtypes. *Journal of Clinical Psychology, 41,* 707–713.

Baumeister, R. F. (1989). The optimal margin of illusion. *Journal of Social and Clinical Psychology, 8,* 176–189.

Beasley, R., & Stoltenberg, C. D. (1992). Personality characteristics of male spouse abusers. *Professional Psychology: Research and Practice, 23,* 310–317.

Beattie, M. (1986). *Codependent no more.* New York: Harper/Hazelden.

Beck, A. T. (1983). Cognitive therapy of depression: New perspectives. In P. Clayton & J. E. Barrett (Eds.), *Treatment of depression: Old controversies and new approaches* (pp. 265–290). New York: Raven Press.

Beck, A. T., Ward, C. H., Mendelson, M., Mock, J. E., & Erbaugh, J. K. (1961). An inventory for measuring depression. *Archives of General Psychiatry, 4,* 561–571.

Belter, R. W., & Piotrowski, C. (1999). Current status of the master's level training in psychological assessment. *Journal of Psychological Practice, 5,* 1–5.

Bender, D. S., Farber, B. A., & Geller, J. D. (2001). Cluster B personality traits and attachment. *Journal of the American Academy of Psychoanalysis, 29,* 551–563.

Benjamin, L. S. (1974). Structural analysis of social behavior. *Psychological Review, 81,* 392–495.

Benjamin, L. S. (1984). Principles of prediction using Structural Analysis of Social Behavior (SASB). In R. A. Zucker, J. Aronoff, & A. J. Rabin (Eds.), *Personality and the prediction of behaviors* (pp. 121–173). New York: Guilford Press.

Benjamin, L. S. (1993). *Interpersonal diagnosis and treatment of personality disorders.* New York: Guilford Press.

Benjamin, L. S. (1995). *Interpersonal diagnosis and treatment of personality disorders* (2nd ed.). New York: Guilford Press.

Ben-Porath, Y. S., Shondrick, D. D., & Stafford, K. P. (1995). MMPI–2 and race in a forensic diagnostic sample. *Criminal Justice & Behavior, 22,* 19–32.

Ben-Porath, Y., & Waller, N. (1992a). Five big issues in clinical assessment: A rejoinder to Costa and McCrae. *Psychological Assessment, 4,* 23–25.

Ben-Porath, Y., & Waller, N. (1992b). "Normal" personality inventories in clinical assessment: General requirements and the potential for using the NEO Personality Inventory. *Psychological Assessment, 4,* 14–19.

Bent, R., Putnam, D., Kiesler, D., & Nowicki, S. (1976). Correlates of successful and unsuccessful psychotherapy. *Journal of Consulting and Clinical Psychology, 44,* 149.

Bernstein, D. P., Fink, L., Handelsman, L., Foote, J., Lovejoy, M., Wenzel, K., Sapareto, E., & Ruggiero, J. (1994). Initial reliability and validity of a new retrospective measure of child abuse and neglect. *American Journal of Psychiatry, 151,* 1132–1136.

Bernstein, E., & Putnam, F. (1986). Development, reliability, and validity of a dissociation scale. *Journal of Nervous and Mental Disease, 174,* 727–735.

Bersoff, D. N. (1988). Should subjective employment devices be scrutinized? It's elementary, my dear Ms. Watson. *American Psychologist, 12,* 1016–1018.

Beutler, L., Johnson, D., Neville, C., Workman, S., & Elkins, D. (1973). The A–B–therapy–type distinction, accurate empathy, nonpossessive warmth and therapist genuineness in psychotherapy. *Journal of Abnormal Psychology, 82,* 273–277.

Birch, W. (1976). The relationship between personality traits and treatment outcome in a therapeutic environment. *Dissertation Abstracts International, 37,* A3508.

Birtchnell, J. (1991). The measurement of dependence by questionnaire. *Journal of Personality Disorders, 5,* 281–295.

Bishop, D. R. (1993). Validity issues in using the Millon–II with substance abusers. *Psychological Reports, 73,* 27–33.

Black, C. (1981). *"It will never happen to me!"* New York: Ballantine.

Blackburn, R. (1975). An empirical classification of psychopathic personality. *British Journal of Psychiatry, 127,* 456–460.

Blackburn, R. (1986). Patterns of personality deviation among violent offenders: Replication and extension of an empirical taxonomy. *British Journal of Criminology, 26,* 254–269.

Blackburn, R. (1996). Replicated personality disorder clusters among mentally disordered offenders and their relation to dimensions of personality. *Journal of Personality Disorders, 10,* 68–81.

Blais, M. A., Benedict, K. B., & Norman, D. K. (1994). Associations among the MCMI–II clinical syndrome scales and the MMPI–2 clinical scales. *Assessment, 1,* 407–413.

Blatt, S. J., & Auerbach, J. S. (1988). Differential cognitive disturbances in three types of borderline patients. *Journal of Personality Disorders, 2,* 198–211.

Blount, C., Evans, C., Birch, S., Warren, F., & Norton, K. (2002). The properties of self-report research measures: Beyond psychometrics. *Psychology and Psychotherapy: Theory, Research and Practice, 75,* 151–164.

Bonato, D. P., Cyr, J. J., Kalpin, R. A., Prendergast, P., & Sanhueza, P. (1988). The utility of the MCMI as a DSM–III Axis I diagnostic tool. *Journal of Clinical Psychology, 44,* 867–875.

Bond, M. P. (1995). The development and properties of the Defense Style Questionnaire. In H. R. Conte & R. Plutchik (Eds.), *Ego defenses: Theory and measurement* (pp. 202–220). Oxford, England: John Wiley & Sons.

Bornstein, R. F. (1995). Sex differences in objective and projective tests: A meta-analytic review. *Assessment, 2,* 319–331.

Borum, R., & Grisso, T. (1995). Psychological test use in forensic evaluations. *Professional Psychology: Research and Practice, 26,* 465–473.

Boyle, G. J., & Le Déan, L. (2000). Discriminant validity of the Illness Behavior Questionnaire and Millon Clinical Multiaxial Inventory–III in a heterogeneous sample of psychiatric outpatients. *Journal of Clinical Psychology, 56,* 779–791.

Braver, M., Bumberry, J., Green, K., & Rawson, R. (1992). Childhood abuse and current psychological functioning in a university counseling center population. *Journal of Counseling Psychology, 39,* 252–257.

Brewer, B. (1974). Relationships among personality, empathic ability and counselor effectiveness. *Dissertation Abstracts International, 35,* A6449.

Broday, S. (1988). Perfectionism and Millon basic personality patterns. *Psychological Reports, 63,* 791–794.

Bronisch, T., & Klerman, G. (1991). Personality functioning: Change and stability in relationship to symptoms and psychopathology. *Journal of Personality Disorders, 5,* 307–317.

Brown, H. P. (1992). Substance abuse and the disorders of the self: Examining the relationship. *Alcoholism Treatment Quarterly, 9,* 1–27.

Bryer, J. B. (1990). Inpatient psychiatric outcome: A research program and initial findings for adults. *Psychiatric Hospital, 21,* 79–88.

Bryer, J. B., Martines, K. A., & Dignan, M. (1990). Millon Clinical Multiaxial Inventory Alcohol Abuse and Drug Abuse scales and the identification of substance abuse patients. *Personality Assessment, 2,* 438–441.

Bryer, J. B., Nelson, B. A., Miller, J. B., & Krol, P. A. (1987). Childhood sexual and physical abuse as factors in adult psychiatric illness. *American Journal of Psychiatry, 144,* 1426–1430.

Busby, D. M., Glenn, E., Steggell, G. L., & Adamson, D. W. (1993). Treatment issues for survivors of physical and sexual abuse. *Journal of Marital and Family Therapy, 19,* 377–391.

Buss, A. (1989). Personality as traits. *American Psychologist, 44,* 1378–1388.

Butcher, J. N. (1999). *A beginner's guide to the MMPI–2.* Washington, DC: American Psychological Association.

Butcher, J. N., Braswell, L., & Raney, D. (1983). A cross-cultural comparison of American Indian, Black and White inpatients on the MMPI and presenting symptoms. *Journal of Consulting and Clinical Psychology, 51,* 587–594.

Butcher, J. N., Dahlstrom, W. G., Graham, J. R., Tellegen, A., & Kaemmer, B. (1989). *MMPI–2: Minnesota Multiphasic Personality Inventory—2. Manual for administration and scoring.* Minneapolis: University of Minnesota Press.

Butcher, J., & Owen, P. (1978). Objective personality inventories: Recent research and some contemporary issues. In B. Wolman (Ed.), *Clinical diagnoses of mental disorders: A handbook* (pp. 475–546). New York: Plenum.

Butcher, J. N., & Rouse, S. V. (1996). Personality: Individual differences and clinical assessment. *Annual Review of Psychology, 47,* 87–111.

Butler, S. F., Gaulier, B., & Haller, D. (1991). Assessment of Axis II personality disorders among female substance abusers. *Psychological Reports, 68,* 1344–1346.

Butters, M., Retzlaff, P., & Gibertini, M. (1986). Non-adaptability to basic training and the Millon Clinical Multiaxial Inventory. *Military Medicine, 151,* 574–576.

Calsyn, D. A., & Saxon, A. J. (1990). Personality disorder subtypes among cocaine and opioid addicts using the Millon Clinical Multiaxial Inventory. *International Journal of Addictions, 25,* 1037–1049.

Calsyn, D. A., Saxon, A. J., & Daisy, F. (1990). Validity of the MCMI Drug Abuse Scale with drug abusing and psychiatric samples. *Journal of Clinical Psychology, 46,* 244–246.

Calsyn, D. A., Saxon, A. J., & Daisy, F. (1991). Validity of the MCMI Drug Abuse Scale varies as a function of drug choice, race, and Axis II subtypes. *American Journal of Drug and Alcohol Abuse, 17,* 153–159.

Calsyn, D. A., Wells, E. A., Fleming, C., & Saxon, A. J. (2000). Changes in Millon Clinical Multiaxial Inventory scores among opiate addicts as a function of retention in methadone maintenance and recent drug abuse. *American Journal of Drug and Alcohol Abuse, 26,* 297–309.

Camera, W., Nathan, J., & Puente, A. (1998). *Psychological test usage in professional psychology: Report to the APA Practice and Science Directorates.* Washington, DC: American Psychological Association.

Campbell, B. K., & Stark, M. J. (1991). Psychopathology and personality characteristics in different forms of substance abuse. *International Journal of the Addictions, 25,* 1467–1474.

Campbell, D. T., & Stanley, J. C. (1963). *Experimental and quasi-experimental design for research.* Chicago: Rand McNally.

Campbell, N. B., Franco, K., & Jurs, S. (1988). Abortion in adolescence. *Adolescence, 23,* 813–823.

Cannon, D., Bell, W., Fowler, D., Penk, W., & Finkelstein, A. (1990). MMPI differences between alcoholics and drug abusers: Effect of age and race. *Psychological Assessment, 2,* 51–55.

Canter, F. (1966). Personality factors related to participation in treatment of hospitalized male alcoholics. *Journal of Clinical Psychology, 22,* 114–116.

Canter, F. (1971). Authoritarian attitudes, degree of pathology and preference for structured versus unstructured psychotherapy in hospitalized mental patients. *Psychological Reports, 28,* 231–234.

Cantrell, J. D., & Dana, R. H. (1987). Use of the Millon Clinical Multiaxial Inventory (MCMI) as a screening instrument in a community mental health center. *Journal of Clinical Psychology, 43,* 366–375.

Carver, C. S., Scheier, M. F., & Weintraub, J. K. (1989). Assessing coping strategies: A theoretically based approach. *Journal of Personality and Social Psychology, 56,* 267–283.

Cash, T. F., Mikulka, P. J., & Brown, T. A. (1989). Validity of Millon's computerized interpretation system for the MCMI: Comment on Moreland and Onstad. *Journal of Consulting and Clinical Psychology, 57,* 311–312.

Cattell, R. B. (1946). *The description and measurement of personality.* New York: World Book.

Cattell, R. B. (1965). *The scientific analysis of personality.* Chicago: Aldine.

Cattell, R. B. (1986). *Manual for the Sixteen Personality Factor Questionnaire.* Savoy, IL: Institute for Personality and Ability Testing.

Cattell, R. B., Ever, H. W., & Tatsuoka, M. M. (1970). *Handbook for the 16PF.* Campaign, IL: Institute for Personality and Ability Testing.

Caudill, B. D., Flynn, P. M., Hamilton, J. G., & Hoffman, J. A. (1992, August). *Psychopathology and substance use in crack addicts entering cocaine abuse treatment.* Paper presented at the 100th Annual Convention of the American Psychological Association, Washington, DC.

Cermak, T. L. (1986). *Diagnosing and treating codependence.* Minneapolis: Johnson Institute.

Chambless, D. L., Renneberg, B., Goldstein, A., & Gracely, E. J. (1992). MCMI diagnosed personality disorders among agoraphobic outpatients: Prevalence and relationship to severity and treatment outcome. *Journal of Anxiety Disorders, 6,* 193–211.

Chandarana, P. C., Conlon, P., Holliday, R. L., Deslippe, T., & Field, V. A. (1990). A prospective study of psychosocial aspects of gastric stapling surgery. *Psychiatric Journal of the University of Ottawa, 15,* 32–35.

Chantry, K., & Craig, R. J. (1993). Psychological screening of violent offenders with the MCMI. *Journal of Clinical Psychology, 50,* 430–435.

Chantry, K., & Craig, R. J. (1994). MCMI typologies of criminal sexual offenders. *Sexual Addiction and Compulsivity, 1,* 215–226.

Charter, R. A., & Lopez, M. N. (2002). Millon Clinical Multiaxial Inventory (MCMI–III): The inability of the validity conditions to detect random responders. *Journal of Clinical Psychology, 58,* 1615–1617.

Chatham, P., Tibbals, C., & Harrington, M. (1993). The MMPI and the MCMI in the evaluation of narcissism in a clinical sample. *Journal of Personality Assessment, 60,* 239–251.

Chick, D., Martin, S. K., Nevels, R., & Cotton, C. R. (1994). Relationship between personality disorders and clinical symptoms in psychiatric inpatients as measured by the Millon Clinical Multiaxial Inventory. *Psychological Reports, 74,* 331–336.

Chick, D., Sheaffer, C. I., Goggin, W., & Sison, G. F. (1993). The relationship between MCMI personality scales and clinician-generated DSM–III–R personality disorder diagnosis. *Journal of Personality Assessment, 61,* 264–276.

Childs, R. A., & Eyde, L. D. (1999, August). *Assessment training in clinical psychology doctoral programs: An analysis of curriculum and course content.* Paper presented at the 107th Annual Convention of the American Psychological Association, Boston.

Choca, J. (1992, August). *Treatment plan and supportive psychotherapy training with the MCMI.* Paper presented at the 100th Annual Convention of the American Psychological Association, Washington, DC.

Choca, J. P. (1997, August–September). *Millon personality polarities and the MCMI–III.* Paper presented at the 95th Annual Convention of the American Psychological Association, Chicago.

Choca, J. P. (1999). Evolution of Millon's personality prototypes. *Journal of Personality Assessment, 72,* 353–364.

Choca, J., Bresolin, L., Okonek, A., & Ostrow, D. (1988). Validity of the Millon Clinical Multiaxial Inventory in the assessment of affective disorders. *Journal of Personality Assessment, 53,* 96–105.

Choca, J., & Garside, D. (1992). Hermann: A Rorschach administrator and scoring assistant (2nd ed.) [Computer program]. Toronto, Ontario, Canada: Multi-Health Systems.

Choca, J. P., Gibeau, P. M., Craig, R. J., & Van Denburg, E. (2000, August). *Diagnostic efficiency of the Millon Clinical Multiaxial Inventory–III.* Paper presented at the 108th Annual Convention of the American Psychological Association, Washington, DC.

Choca, J. P., Greenblatt, R., Tobin, D., Shanley, L., & Van Denburg, E. (1989, August). *Factor analytic structure of the MCMI items.* Paper presented at the 97th Annual Convention of the American Psychological Association, New Orleans, LA.

Choca, J. P., Peterson, C. A., & Shanley, L. A. (1986a). Factor analysis of the Millon Clinical Multiaxial Inventory. *Journal of Consulting and Clinical Psychology, 54,* 253–255.

Choca, J., Peterson, C., & Shanley, L. (1986b, August). *Racial bias and the MCMI.* Paper presented at the 94th Annual Convention of the American Psychological Association, Washington, DC.

Choca, J., Retzlaff, P., Strack, S., Mouton, A., & Van Denburg, E. (1996). Factorial elements of the MCMI–II personality scales. *Journal of Personality Disorders, 10,* 377–383.

Choca, J., Shanley, L. A., Peterson, C. A., & Van Denburg, E. (1990). Racial bias and the MCMI. *Journal of Personality Assessment, 54,* 479–490.

Choca, J., Shanley, L. A., Van Denburg, E., Agresti, A., Mouton, A., & Uskokovic, L. (1992). Personality disorder or personality style: That is the question. *Journal of Counseling and Development, 70,* 429–431.

Choca, J., Silverman, J., & Gerber, J. (1980). *The effect of the patient's personality style on the therapeutic relationship and therapy outcome ratings.* Unpublished manuscript.

Choca, J., & Van Denburg, E. (1996). *Manual for clinical psychology trainees* (3rd ed.). New York: Brunner/Mazel.

Choca, J. P., Van Denburg, E., Bratu, M. E., Meagher, S., & Updegrove, A. (1996, March). *Personality changes of psychiatric patients with aging.* Paper presented at the midwinter meeting of the Society for Personality Assessment, Denver, CO.

Choca, J. P., Van Denburg, E., Mouton, A., & Shanley, L. (1992). *The Rorschach: A test with no personality.* Unpublished manuscript.

Claridge, G. (1994). Psychobiological models and issues. In S. Strack & M. Lorr (Eds.), *Differentiating normal and abnormal personality* (pp. 137–157). New York: Springer.

Clarkin, J. F., Widiger, T. A., Frances, A., Hurt, S. W., & Gilmore, M. (1983). Prototypic typology and the borderline personality disorder. *Journal of Abnormal Psychology, 92,* 263–275.

Clemence, A. J., & Handler, L. (2001). Psychological assessment on internship: A survey of training directors and their expectations for students. *Journal of Personality Assessment, 76,* 18–47.

Cloninger, C. R. (1987). A systematic method for clinical description and classification of personality variants. *Archives of General Psychiatry, 44,* 573–588.

Cloninger, C. R., & Svrakic, D. M. (1994). Differentiating normal and deviant personality by seven-factor personality model. In S. Strack & M. Lorr (Eds.), *Differentiating normal and abnormal personality* (pp. 3–25). New York: Springer.

Cohen, J. (1988). *Statistical power analysis for the behavioral sciences* (2nd ed.) Hillsdale, NJ: Erlbaum.

Colligan, R., Morey, L., & Offord, K. (1994). The MMPI/MMPI–2 personality disorder scales: Contemporary norms for adults and adolescents. *Journal of Clinical Psychology, 43,* 366–375.

Conte, H. R., Plutchik, R., Karasu, T. B., & Jerrett, I. (1980). A self-report borderline scale: Discriminate validity and preliminary norms. *Journal of Nervous and Mental Disease, 168,* 428–435.

Coolidge, F. L., & Merwin, M. M. (1992). Reliability and validity of the Coolidge Axis II Inventory: A new inventory for the assessment of personality disorders. *Journal of Personality Assessment, 59,* 223–238.

Corbisiero, J. R., & Reznikoff, M. (1991). The relationship between personality type and style of alcohol use. *Journal of Clinical Psychology, 47,* 291–298.

Costa, P. T., & McCrae, R. R. (1985). *The NEO Personality Inventory manual.* Odessa, FL: Psychological Assessment Resources.

Costa, P. T., & McCrae, R. R. (1990). Personality disorders and the five-factor model of personality. *Journal of Personality Disorders, 4,* 362–371.

Costa, P., & McCrae, R. (1992a). Normal personality assessment in clinical practice: The NEO Personality Inventory. *Psychological Assessment, 4,* 5–13.

Costa, P., & McCrae, R. (1992b). Reply to Ben-Porath and Waller. *Psychological Assessment, 4,* 20–22.

Costa, P., & Widiger, T. (1994). *Personality disorders and the Five Factor Model of personality.* Washington, DC: American Psychological Association.

Costello, R. M., Fine, H. J., & Blau, B. I. (1973). Racial comparisons on the Minnesota Multiphasic Personality Inventory. *Journal of Clinical Psychology, 29,* 63–65.

Costello, R. M., Tiffany, D. W., & Gier, R. H. (1972). Methodology issues and racial (Black–White) comparisons on the MMPI. *Journal of Consulting and Clinical Psychology, 38,* 161–168.

Craig, R. J. (1984). Can personality tests predict treatment dropouts? *International Journal of Addictions, 19,* 665–674.

Craig, R. J. (1988). A psychometric study of the prevalence of DSM–III personality disorders among treated opiate addicts. *International Journal of Addictions, 23,* 115–124.

Craig, R. J. (1993a). Contemporary trends in substance abuse. *Professional Psychology: Research and Practice, 24,* 182–189.

Craig, R. J. (1993b). *Psychological assessment with the Millon Clinical Multiaxial Inventory (II): An interpretative guide.* Odessa, FL: Psychological Assessment Resources.

Craig, R. J. (1995). Clinical diagnoses and MCMI codetypes. *Journal of Clinical Psychology, 51,* 352–360.

Craig, R. J. (1997). Sensitivity of the MCMI–III scales T (drugs) and B (alcohol) in detecting substance abuse. *Substance Use and Misuse, 32,* 1385–1393.

Craig, R. J. (1999a). Overview and current status of the Millon Clinical Multiaxial Inventory. *Journal of Personality Assessment, 72,* 390–406.

Craig, R. J. (1999b). Testimony based on the Millon Clinical Multiaxial Inventory: Review, commentary and guidelines. *Journal of Personality Assessment, 73,* 290–304.

Craig, R. J. (2000). Prevalence of personality disorders among cocaine and heroin addicts. *Substance Abuse, 21,* 87–94.

Craig, R. J. (2003). Use of the Millon Clinical Multiaxial Inventory in the psychological assessment of domestic violence: A review. *Aggression and Violent Behavior, 8,* 235–243.

Craig, R. J., & Bivens, A. (2000). MCMI–III scores on substance abusers with and without histories of suicide attempts. *Substance Abuse, 21,* 155–161.

Craig, R. J., Bivens, A., & Olson, R. (1997). MCMI–III-derived typological analysis of cocaine and heroin addicts. *Journal of Personality Assessment, 69,* 583–595.

Craig, R. J., Kuncel, R., & Olson, R. E. (1994). Ability of drug abusers to avoid detection of substance abuse on the MCMI–II. *Journal of Social Behavior and Personality, 9,* 95–106.

Craig, R. J., & Olson, R. E. (1990). MCMI comparisons of cocaine abusers and heroin addicts. *Journal of Clinical Psychology, 46,* 230–237.

Craig, R. J., & Olson, R. E. (1992). Relationship between MCMI–II scales and normal personality traits. *Psychological Reports, 71,* 699–705.

Craig, R. J., & Olson, R. E. (1995). MCMI–II profiles and typologies for patients seen in marital therapy. *Psychological Reports, 76,* 163–170.

Craig, R. J., & Olson, R. (1997). Assessing PTSD with the Millon Clinical Inventory–III. *Journal of Clinical Psychology, 53,* 943–952.

Craig, R. J., & Olson, R. (1998). Stability of the MCMI–III in a substance-abusing inpatient sample. *Psychological Reports, 83,* 1273–1274.

Craig, R. J., & Olson, R. (2001). Adjectival descriptions of personality disorders: A convergent validity study of the MCMI–III. *Journal of Personality Assessment, 77,* 259–271.

Craig, R. J., & Olson, R. E. (2002). *On the decline of MCMI-based research.* Unpublished manuscript.

Craig, R. J., Verinis, J. S., & Wexler, S. (1985). Personality characteristics of drug addicts and alcoholics on the Millon Clinical Multiaxial Inventory. *Journal of Personality Assessment, 49,* 156–160.

Craig, R. J., & Weinberg, D. (1992a). Assessing alcoholics with the Millon Clinical Multiaxial Inventory: A review. *Psychology of Addictive Behaviors, 6,* 200–208.

Craig, R. J., & Weinberg, D. (1992b). Assessing drug abusers with the Millon Clinical Multiaxial Inventory: A review. *Journal of Substance Abuse Treatment, 9,* 249–255.

Cronbach, L. J. (1975). Five decades of public controversy over mental testing. *American Psychologist, 30,* 1–14.

Crowne, D., & Marlowe, D. (1964). *The approval motive.* New York: Wiley.

Curtis, J., & Cowell, D. (1993). Relation of birth order and scores on measures of pathological narcissism. *Psychological Reports, 72,* 311–315.

Daubert, S. D., & Metzler, A. E. (2000). The detection of fake-bad and fake-good responding on the Millon Clinical Multiaxial Inventory III. *Psychological Assessment, 12,* 418–424.

Davis, R. D. (1999). Millon: Essentials of his science, theory, classification, assessment, and therapy. *Journal of Personality Assessment, 72,* 330–352.

Davis, R. D., Wenger, A., & Guzman, A. (1997). Validation of the MCMI–III. In T. Millon (Ed.), *The Millon inventories: Clinical and personality assessment* (pp. 327–359). New York: Guilford Press.

Davis, S. E., & Hays, L. W. (1997). An examination of the clinical validity of the MCMI–III Depressive Personality Scale. *Journal of Clinical Psychology, 53,* 15–23.

Davis, W. E., Beck, S. J., & Ryan, T. A. (1973). Race-related and educationally-related MMPI profile differences among hospitalized schizophrenics. *Journal of Clinical Psychology, 29,* 478–479.

Davis, W. E., & Greenblatt, R. (1990). Age differences among psychiatric inpatients on the MCMI. *Journal of Clinical Psychology, 46,* 770–774.

Davis, W. E., Greenblatt, R., & Choca, J. (1990). *Racial bias and the MCMI–II.* Unpublished manuscript.

Davis, W. E., Greenblatt, R. L., & Pochyly, J. M. (1990). Test of MCMI Black norms for five scales. *Journal of Clinical Psychology, 46,* 175–178.

Dean, K. J., & Choca, J. (2001, August). *Psychological changes of emotionally disturbed men with age.* Paper presented at the 109th Annual Convention of the American Psychological Association, San Francisco, CA.

DeJong, C. A. J., van den Brink, W., Jansen, J. A. M., & Schippers, G. M. (1989). Interpersonal aspects of the DSM–III Axis II: Theoretical hypotheses and empirical findings. *Journal of Personality Disorders, 3,* 135–146.

DeLamatre, J. E., & Schuerger, J. M. (1992). Personality disorder concept scales and 16 PF dimensions. *Psychological Reports, 70,* 839–849.

del Rosario, P. M., McCann, J. T., & Navarra, J. W. (1994). The MCMI–II diagnosis of schizophrenia: Operating characteristics and profile analysis. *Journal of Personality Assessment, 63,* 438–452.

Denton, L. (1988, August). Board votes to oppose Golden Rule technique. *APA Monitor, 19,* p. 7.

Derogatis, L. (1983). *The Symptom Checklist–90 Manual II.* Towson, MD: Clinical Psychometric Research.

Dewald, P. (1967). Therapeutic evaluation and potential: The psychodynamic point of view. *Comprehensive Psychiatry, 8,* 284–298.

Dewald, P. (1971). *Psychotherapy: A dynamic approach.* New York: Basic Books.

DeWolfe, A. S., Larson, J. K., & Ryan, J. J. (1985). Diagnostic accuracy of the Millon test computer reports for bipolar affective disorder. *Journal of Psychopathology and Behavioral Assessment, 7,* 185–189.

DiGiuseppe, R., Robin, M., Szeszko, P. R., & Primavera, L. H. (1995). Cluster analysis of narcissistic personality disorders on the MCMI–II. *Journal of Personality Disorders, 9,* 304–317.

Divac-Jovanovic, M., Svrakic, D., & Lecic-Tosevski, D. (1993). Personality disorders: Model for conceptual approach and classification: I. General model. *American Journal of Psychotherapy, 47,* 558–571.

Dohrendwend, B. S., & Dohrendwend, B. P. (1981). Life stress and illness: Formulation of the issues. In B. S. Dohrendwend & B. P. Dohrendwend (Eds.), *Stressful life events and their contexts* (pp. 1–27). New York: Prodist.

Donat, D. C. (1988). Millon Clinical Multiaxial Inventory (MCMI) clusters for alcohol abusers: Further evidence for validity and implications for medical psychotherapy. *Medical Psychotherapy, 1,* 41–50.

Donat, D. C. (1994). Empirical groupings of perceptions of alcohol use among alcohol dependent persons: A cluster analysis of the Alcohol Use Inventory (AUI) scales. *Assessment, 1,* 103–110.

Donat, D., Geczy, B., Helmrich, J., & LeMay, M. (1992). Empirically derived personality subtypes of public psychiatric patients: Effect on self-reported symptoms, coping inclinations, and evaluation of expressed emotion in caregivers. *Journal of Personality Assessment, 58,* 36–50.

Donat, D., Walters, J., & Hume, A. (1991). Personality characteristics of alcohol dependent inpatients: Relationship of MCMI subtypes to self-reported drinking behavior. *Journal of Personality Assessment, 57,* 335–344.

Donat, D., Walters, J., & Hume, A. (1992). MCMI differences between alcoholics and cocaine abusers: Effect of age, sex, and race. *Journal of Personality Assessment, 58,* 96–104.

Dorr, D. (1999). Approaching psychotherapy of the personality disorders from the Millon perspective. *Journal of Personality Assessment, 72,* 407–425.

Dorr, D., Barley, W., Gard, B., & Webb, C. (1983). Understanding and treating borderline personality organization. *Psychotherapy: Theory, Research and Practice, 20,* 397–404.

Dougherty, R. J., & Lesswing, N. L. (1989). Inpatient cocaine abusers: An analysis of psychological and demographic variables. *Journal of Substance Abuse Treatment, 6,* 45–47.

Dubro, A. F., Wetzler, S., & Kahn, M. W. (1988). A comparison of three self-report questionnaires for the diagnosis of the DSM–III personality disorders. *Journal of Personality Disorders, 2,* 256–266.

Duthie, B., & Vincent, K. R. (1986). Diagnostic hit rates of high point codes for the Diagnostic Inventory of Personality and Symptoms using random assignment, base rates, and probability scales. *Journal of Clinical Psychology, 42,* 612–614.

Dutton, D. C. (1994). The origin and structure of the abusive personality. *Journal of Personality Disorders, 8,* 181–191.

Dwyer, C. A. (1996). Cut scores and testing: Statistics, judgment, truth and error. *Psychological Assessment, 8,* 360–362.

Dyce, J. A., & O'Connor, B. P. (1998). Personality disorders and the five-factor model: A test of facet-level predictions. *Journal of Personality Disorders, 12,* 31–45.

Dyce, J. A., O'Connor, B. P., Parkins, S. Y., & Janzen, H. L. (1997). Correlational structure of the MCMI–III personality disorder scales and comparison with other data sets. *Journal of Personality Assessment, 69,* 568–582.

Dyer, F. J. (1984). *Gordon Personality Profile Inventory: An interpretive guide.* San Antonio, TX: Psychological Corporation.

Dyer, F. J. (1994). Factorial trait variance and response bias in MCMI–II personality disorder scale scores. *Journal of Personality Disorders, 8,* 121–130.

Dyer, F. J. (1997). Application of the Millon inventories in forensic psychology. In T. Millon (Ed.), *The Millon inventories: Clinical and personality assessment* (pp. 327–359). New York: Guilford Press.

Dyer, F. J. (1999). *Psychological consultation in parental rights cases.* New York: Guilford Press.

Dyer, F. J., & McCann, J. T. (2000). The Millon clinical inventories, research critical of their forensic application, and Daubert criteria. *Law and Human Behavior, 24,* 487–497.

Edwards, A. L. (1959). *Edwards Personal Preference Schedule.* San Antonio, TX: Psychological Corporation.

Ellason, J. W., & Ross, C. A. (1996). Millon Clinical Multiaxial Inventory–II follow-up of patients with dissociative identity disorder. *Psychological Reports, 78,* 707–716.

Ellason, J. W., & Ross, C. A. (1997). Two year follow-up of inpatients with dissociative identity disorder. *American Journal of Psychiatry, 154,* 832–839.

Ellason, J. W., Ross, C. A., & Fuchs, D. L. (1995). Assessment of dissociative identity disorder with the Millon Clinical Multiaxial Inventory–II. *Psychological Reports, 76,* 895–905.

Elliott, T. R., Jackson, W. T., Layfield, M., & Kendall, D. (1996). Personality disorders and response to outpatient treatment of chronic pain. *Journal of Clinical Psychology in Medical Settings, 3,* 219–234.

Ellis, A. (1977). The basic clinical theory of rational–emotive therapy. In A. Ellis & R. Grieger (Eds.), *Handbook of rational–emotive therapy* (pp. 3–34). New York: Springer.

Ellis, T. E., Rudd, M. D., Rajab, M. H., & Wehrly, T. E. (1996). Cluster analysis of MCMI scores of suicidal psychiatric patients: Four personality profiles. *Journal of Clinical Psychology, 52,* 411–422.

Embretson, S. E. (1996). The new rules of measurement. *Psychological Assessment, 8,* 341–349.

Endler, N. S., & Edwards, J. M. (1988). Personality disorders from an interactional perspective. *Journal of Personality Disorders, 2,* 326–333.

Endler, N. S., & Magnusson, D. (1976). Toward an interactional psychology of personality. *Psychological Bulletin, 83,* 956–974.

Everly, G. S., & Lating, J. M. (2003). *On the nature of personality and posttraumatic stress disorder.* Washington, DC: American Psychological Association.

Eysenck, H. J. (1947). *Dimensions of personality.* London: Routledge & Kegan Paul.

Eysenck, H. J. (1994). Normality–abnormality and the three-factor model of personality. In S. Strack & M. Lorr (Eds.), *Differentiating normal and abnormal personality* (pp. 3–25). New York: Springer.

Eysenck, H. J., & Eysenck, S. B. G. (1975). *The Eysenck Personality Questionnaire.* San Diego, CA: Educational and Industrial Testing Service.

Fals-Stewart, W. (1992). Personality characteristics of substance abusers: An MCMI cluster typology of recreational drug users treated in a therapeutic community and its relationship to length of stay and outcome. *Journal of Personality Assessment, 59,* 515–527.

Fals-Stewart, W. (1995). The effect of defensive responding by substance-abusing patients on the Millon Clinical Multiaxial Inventory. *Journal of Personality Assessment, 64,* 540–551.

Fals-Stewart, W., & Lucente, S. (1993). An MCMI cluster typology of obsessive–compulsives: A measure of personality characteristics and its relationship to treatment. *Journal of Psychiatric Research, 27,* 139–154.

Farmer, R., & Nelson-Gray, R. (1990). Personality disorders and depression: Hypothetical relations, empirical findings, and methodological considerations. *Clinical Psychology Review, 10,* 453–476.

Faulkner, K. K., Cogan, R., Nolder, M., & Shooter, G. (1991). Characteristics of men and women completing cognitive/behavioral spouse abuse treatment. *Journal of Family Violence, 6,* 243–254.

Fink, D., & Golinkoff, D. (1990). MPD, borderline personality disorder and schizophrenia: A comparative study of clinical features. *Dissociation, 8,* 127–134.

Finn, S. E. (1982). Base rates, utilities, and the DSM–III: Shortcomings of fixed rule systems of psychodiagnosis. *Journal of Abnormal Psychology, 91,* 294–302.

Flynn, P. M., McCann, J. T., & Fairbank, J. A. (1995). Issues in the assessment of personality disorder and substance abuse using the Millon Clinical Multiaxial Inventory (MCMI–II). *Journal of Clinical Psychology, 51,* 415–421.

Flynn, P. M., McCann, J. T., Luckey, J. W., Rounds-Bryant, J. L., Theisen, A. C., Hoffman, J. A., et al. (1997). Drug dependence scale in the Millon Clinical Multiaxial Inventory. *Substance Use & Misuse, 32,* 733–748.

Flynn, P. M., & McMahon, R. C. (1983a). Indicators of depression and suicidal ideation among drug abusers. *Psychological Reports, 52,* 784–786.

Flynn, P. M., & McMahon, R. C. (1983b). Stability of the drug misuse scale of the Millon Clinical Multiaxial Inventory. *Psychological Reports, 52,* 536–538.

Flynn, P. M., & McMahon, R. C. (1984a). An examination of the factor structure of the Millon Clinical Multiaxial Inventory. *Journal of Personality Assessment, 48,* 308–311.

Flynn, P. M., & McMahon, R. C. (1984b). Stability of the Drug Abuse scale of the Millon Clinical Multiaxial Inventory. *International Journal of the Addictions, 19,* 459–468.

Fry, D. (1975). Interaction between locus of control, level of inquiry and subject control in the helping process: A lab analogue study. *Journal of Counseling Psychology, 22,* 280–287.

Funari, D. J., Piekarski, A. M., & Sherwood, R. J. (1991). Treatment outcomes of Vietnam veterans with posttraumatic stress disorder. *Psychological Reports, 68,* 571–578.

Gabrys, J. B., Utendale, K. A., Schumph, D., Phillips, N., Peters, K., Robertson, G., et al. (1988). Two inventories for the measurement of psychopathology: Dimensions and common factorial space on Millon's clinical and Eysenck's general personality scales. *Psychological Reports, 62,* 591–601.

Gallucci, N. T. (1990). On the synthesis of information from psychological tests. *Psychological Reports, 67,* 1243–1260.

Ganellen, R. J. (1996). Comparing the diagnostic efficiency of the MMPI, the MCMI–II, and the Rorschach: A review. *Journal of Personality Assessment, 67,* 219–243.

Garner, D. M. (1991). *Eating Disorder Inventory–2.* Odessa, FL: Psychological Assessment Resources.

Garner, D. M., & Olmsted, M. P. (1984). *Eating Disorder Inventory manual.* Odessa, FL: Psychological Assessment Resources.

Garner, D. M., Olmsted, M. P., Davis, R., Rockert, W., Goldbloom, D., & Eagle, M. (1990). The association between bulimic symptoms and reported psychopathology. *International Journal of Eating Disorders, 9,* 1–15.

Genther, R. W., & Graham, J. R. (1976). Effect of short-term public hospitalization for both Black and White patients. *Journal of Consulting and Clinical Psychology, 44,* 118–124.

Gibeau, E. (1975). An exploratory study of selected relationships among counseling orientations, theoretical orientations, personality and counselor effectiveness. *Dissertation Abstracts International, 36,* A1303–A1304.

Gibertini, M., Brandenburg, N. A., & Retzlaff, P. D. (1986). The operating characteristics of the Millon Clinical Multiaxial Inventory. *Journal of Personality Assessment, 50,* 554–567.

Gibertini, M., & Retzlaff, P. D. (1988a). Factor invariance of the Millon Clinical Multiaxial Inventory. *Journal of Psychopathology and Behavioral Assessment, 10,* 65–74.

Gibertini, M., & Retzlaff, P. D. (1988b, August). *Personality and alcohol use patterns among inpatient alcoholics.* Paper presented at the 96th Annual Convention of the American Psychological Association, Atlanta, GA.

Gilbride, T. V., & Hebert, J. (1980). Pathological characteristics of good and poor interpersonal problem-solvers among psychiatric outpatients. *Journal of Clinical Psychology, 36,* 121–127.

Glass, M., Bieber, S., & Tkachuk, M. (1996). Personality styles and dynamics of Alaska Native and nonnative incarcerated men. *Journal of Personality Assessment, 66,* 583–603.

Goldberg, J. O., Segal, Z. V., Vella, D. D., & Shaw, B. F. (1989). Depressive personality: Millon Clinical Multiaxial Inventory profiles of sociotropic and autonomous subtypes. *Journal of Personality Disorders, 3,* 193–198.

Goldberg, J. O., Shaw, B. F., & Segal, Z. V. (1987). Concurrent validity of the Millon Clinical Multiaxial Inventory depression scales. *Journal of Consulting and Clinical Psychology, 55,* 785–787.

Goldberg, L. R. (1992). The development of markers of the Big-Five factor structure. *Psychological Assessment, 4,* 26–42.

Gondolf, E. W. (1999). MCMI–III results for batterer program participants in four cities: Less pathological than expected. *Journal of Family Violence, 14,* 1–17.

Gough, H. B. (1975). *Manual for the California Psychological Inventory* (Rev. ed.) Palo Alto, CA : Consulting Psychologists Press.

Green, C. J. (1982). The diagnostic accuracy and utility of MMPI and MCMI computer interpretive reports. *Journal of Personality Assessment, 46,* 359–365.

Green, S. B., & Kelley, C. K. (1988). Racial bias in prediction with the MMPI for a juvenile delinquent population. *Journal of Personality Assessment, 52,* 263–275.

Greenblatt, R. L., & Davis, W. E. (1992). Accuracy of MCMI classification of angry and psychotic Black and White patients. *Journal of Clinical Psychology, 48,* 59–63.

Greenblatt, R. L., & Davis, W. E. (1993). The MCMI in the diagnosis and assessment of schizophrenia. In R. J. Craig (Ed.), *The Millon Clinical Multiaxial Inventory: A clinical research information synthesis* (pp. 93–109). Hillside, NJ: Erlbaum.

Greenblatt, R. L., Mozdzierz, G. J., Murphy, T. J., & Trimakas, K. (1986, March). *Nonmetric multidimensional scaling of the MCMI.* Paper presented at the conference on the Millon Clinical Inventories, Miami, FL.

Greenblatt, R. L., Mozdzierz, G. J., Murphy, T. J., & Trimakas, K. (1992). A comparison of non-adjusted and bootstrapped methods: Bootstrapped diagnosis might be worth the trouble. *Educational and Psychological Measurement, 52,* 181–187.

Grossman, L. S., & Craig, R. J. (1994). Comparison of the MCMI–II and 16PF validity scales. *Journal of Personality Assessment, 64,* 384–389.

Guilford, J. P. (1952). When not to factor analyze. *Psychological Bulletin, 49,* 26–37.

Gunderson, J. G., & Singer, M. T. (1975). Defining borderline patients: An overview. *American Journal of Psychiatry, 132,* 1–9.

Gunsalus, A. C., & Kelly, K. R. (2001). Korean cultural influences on the Millon Clinical Multiaxial Inventory III. *Journal of Mental Health Counseling, 23,* 151–161.

Gynther, M. D. (1972). White norms and Black MMPIs: A prescription for discrimination? *Psychological Bulletin, 78,* 386–402.

Gynther, M. D. (1981). Is the MMPI an appropriate assessment device for Blacks? *Journal of Black Psychology, 7,* 67–75.

Gynther, M. D. (1989). MMPI comparisons of Blacks and Whites: A review and commentary. *Journal of Clinical Psychology, 45,* 878–883.

Gynther, M. D., & Green, S. B. (1980). Accuracy may make a difference, but does a difference make for accuracy? A response to Pritchard and Rosenblatt. *Journal of Consulting and Clinical Psychology, 48,* 268–272.

Haller, D. L., Miles, D. R., & Dawson, K. S. (2002). Psychopathology influences treatment retention among drug-dependent women. *Journal of Substance Abuse Treatment, 23,* 431–436.

Halon, R. L. (2001). The Millon Clinical Multiaxial Inventory–III: The normal quartet in child custody cases. *American Journal of Forensic Psychology, 19,* 57–75.

Hamberger, L. K., & Hastings, J. E. (1986). Personality correlates of men who abuse their partners: A cross-validation study. *Journal of Family Violence, 1,* 323–341.

Hamberger, L. K., & Hastings, J. E. (1987, April). *The male batterer and alcohol abuse: Differential personality characteristics.* Paper presented at the meeting of the Western Psychological Association, Long Beach, CA.

Hamberger, L. K., & Hastings, J. E. (1988a). Characteristics of male spouse abusers consistent with personality disorders. *Hospital and Community Psychiatry, 39,* 763–770.

Hamberger, L. K., & Hastings, J. E. (1988b). Skills training for treatment of spouse abusers: An outcome study. *Journal of Family Violence, 3,* 121–130.

Hamberger, L. K., & Hastings, J. E. (1990). Recidivism following spouse abuse abatement counseling: Treatment program implications. *Violence and Victims, 5,* 157–170.

Hamberger, L. K., & Hastings, J. E. (1991). Personality correlates of men who batter and nonviolent men: Some continuities and discontinuities. *Journal of Family Violence, 6,* 131–147.

Hamberger, L. K., & Hastings, J. (1992). Racial differences on the MCMI in an outpatient clinical sample. *Journal of Personality Assessment, 58,* 90–95.

Hare, R. D. (1991). *The Hare Psychopathy Checklist—Revised.* Toronto, Canada: Multi-Health Systems.

Harkness, A. R., & McNulty, J. L. (1994). The personality psychopathology five (PSY–5): Issue from the pages of a diagnostic manual instead of a dictionary. In S. Strack & M. Lorr (Eds.), *Differentiating normal and abnormal personality* (pp. 291–315). New York: Springer.

Harper, R. G. (2003). *Personality guided therapy in behavioral medicine.* Washington, DC: American Psychological Association.

Hart, S. D., Dutton, D. G., & Newlove, T. (1993). The prevalence of personality disorder among wife assaulters. *Journal of Personality Disorders, 7,* 329–341.

Hart, S., Forth, A., & Hare, R. (1991). The MCMI–II and psychopathy. *Journal of Personality Disorders, 5,* 318–327.

Hastings, J. E., & Hamberger, L. K. (1988). Personality characteristics of spouse abusers: A controlled comparison. *Violence and Victims, 3,* 31.

Hastings, J. E., & Hamberger, L. K. (1994). Psychosocial modifiers of psychopathology for domestically violent and nonviolent men. *Psychological Reports, 74,* 112–114.

Hathaway, S. R., & McKinley, J. C. (1967). *Minnesota Multiphasic Personality Inventory manual.* New York: Psychological Corporation.

Head, S., Baker, J., & Williamson, D. (1991). Family environment characteristics and dependent personality disorder. *Journal of Personality Disorders, 5,* 256–263.

Head, S. B., & Williamson, D. A. (1990). Association of family environment and personality disturbances in bulimia nervosa. *International Journal of Eating Disorders, 9,* 667–674.

Helmes, E. (1989). Stability of the internal structure of the Millon Clinical Multiaxial Inventory. *Journal of Psychopathology and Behavioral Assessment, 11,* 327–338.

Helmes, E., & Barilko, O. (1988). Comparison of three multiscale inventories in identifying the presence of psychopathological symptoms. *Journal of Personality Assessment, 52,* 74–80.

Herron, L., Turner, J., & Weiner, P. (1986). A comparison of the Millon Clinical Multiaxial Inventory and the Minnesota Multiphasic Personality Inventory as predictors of successful treatment by lumbar laminectomy. *Clinical Orthopaedics and Related Research, 203,* 232–238.

Hess, A. K. (1985). Review of Millon Clinical Multiaxial Inventory. In J. V. Mitchell, Jr. (Ed.), *Ninth mental measurement yearbook* (pp. 984–986). Lincoln, NE: Buros Institute.

Hibbard, S. (1989). Personality and object relational pathology in young adult children of alcoholics. *Psychotherapy, 26,* 504–509.

Hibbs, B. J., Kobos, J. C., & Gonzalez, J. C. (1979). Effects of ethnicity, sex and age on MMPI profiles. *Psychological Reports, 45,* 591–597.

Hicklin, J., & Widiger, T. A. (2000). Convergent validity of alternative MMPI–2 personality disorder scales. *Journal of Personality Assessment, 75,* 502–518.

Hills, H. A. (1995). Diagnosing personality disorders: An examination of the MMPI–2 and the MCMI–II. *Journal of Personality Assessment, 65,* 21–34.

Himmelfarb, N., Strack, S., & Amanat, E. (1993, August). *Assessing combat-related PTSD with the MCMI–II in Hispanic veterans.* Paper presented at the 101st Annual Convention of the American Psychological Association, Toronto, Ontario, Canada.

Hippocrates. (1950). The sacred disease. In J. Chadwich & W. N. Mann (Trans.), *The medical works of Hippocrates* (pp. 179–193). Springfield, IL: Charles C Thomas. (Original work ca. 460–357 B.C.)

Hirschfeld, R. M. A. (1993). Personality disorders: Definition and diagnosis. *Journal of Personality Disorders, 7,* 9–17.

Hirschfeld, R. M. A., Klerman, G. L., Clayton, P. J., Keller, M. P., McDonald-Scott, P., & Larkin, B. H. (1983). Assessing personality: Effects of the depressive state on trait measurement. *American Journal of Psychiatry, 140,* 695–699.

Hogg, B., Jackson, H., Rudd, R., & Edwards, J. (1990). Diagnosing personality disorders in recent-onset schizophrenia. *Journal of Nervous and Mental Disease, 178,* 194–199.

Holcomb, W. R., & Adams, N. (1982). Racial influences on intelligence and personality measures of people who commit murder. *Journal of Clinical Psychology, 38,* 793–796.

Holliman, N. B., & Guthrie, P. C. (1989). A comparison of the Millon Clinical Multiaxial Inventory and the California Psychological Inventory in assessment of a nonclinical population. *Journal of Clinical Psychology, 45,* 373–382.

Horn, J. L., Wanberg, H. W., & Foster, F. M. (1986). *The Alcohol Use Inventory (AUI).* Minneapolis, MN: National Computer Systems.

Horowitz, L. M., Rosenberg, S. E., Baer, B. A., Ureño, G., & Villaseñor, V. S. (1988). Inventory of Interpersonal Problems: Psychometric properties and clinical applications. *Journal of Consulting and Clinical Psychology, 56,* 885–892.

Hsu, L. M. (2002). Diagnostic validity statistics and the MCMI–III. *Psychological Assessment, 14,* 410–422.

Hull, J. S., Range, L. M., & Goggin, W. C. (1992). Suicide ideas: Relationship to personality disorders on the MCMI. *Death Studies, 16,* 371–375.

Hunt, C., & Andrews, G. (1992). Measuring personality disorder: The use of self-report questionnaires. *Journal of Personality Disorders, 6,* 125–133.

Hyer, L. (Ed.). (1994). *Trauma victim: Theoretical issues and practical suggestions.* Muncie, IN: Accelerated Development Incorporated.

Hyer, L., & Boudewyns, P. A. (1987). The 8-2 MCMI code in a PTSD typology. *Center for Stress Recovery Newsletters, 4,* 7–8.

Hyer, L., Boyd, S., Stanger, E., Davis, H., & Walters, P. (1997). Validation of the MCMI–III PTSD scale among combat veterans. *Psychological Reports, 80,* 720–722.

Hyer, L., Carson, M., Nixon, D., Tamkin, A., & Saucer, R. T. (1987). Depression among alcoholics. *International Journal of Addiction, 22,* 1235–1241.

Hyer, L., Davis, H., Woods, G., Albrecht, J. W., & Boudewyns, P. (1992). Relationship between the Millon Clinical Multiaxial Inventory and the Millon II: Value of scales for aggressive and self-defeating personalities in posttraumatic stress disorder. *Psychological Reports, 71,* 867–879.

Hyer, L., Davis, H., Woods, G., Albrecht, W., & Boudewyns, P. (1994). Cluster analysis of MCMI and MCMI–II on chronic PTSD victims. *Journal of Clinical Psychology, 50,* 502–515.

Hyer, L., Harrison, W. R., & Jacobsen, R. H. (1987). Later-life depression: Influences of irrational thinking and cognitive impairment. *Journal of Rational–Emotive Therapy, 5,* 43–48.

Hyer, L., Woods, M., & Boudewyns, P. A. (1991). A three tier evaluation of PTSD among Vietnam combat veterans. *Journal of Traumatic Stress, 4,* 165–195.

Hyer, L., Woods, M. G., Boudewyns, P. A., Bruno, R., & O'Leary, W. (1988). Concurrent validation of the Millon Clinical Multiaxial Inventory among Vietnam veterans with posttraumatic stress disorder. *Psychological Reports, 63,* 271–278.

Hyer, L., Woods, M., Boudewyns, P., Harrison, W., & Tamkin, A. (1990). MCMI and 16PF with Vietnam veterans: Profiles and concurrent validation of the MCMI. *Journal of Personality Disorders, 4,* 391–401.

Hyer, L., Woods, M., Bruno, R., & Boudewyns, P. (1989). Treatment outcomes of Vietnam veterans with PTSD and the consistency of the MCMI. *Journal of Clinical Psychology, 45,* 547–552.

Hyer, L., Woods, M. G., Summers, M. N., Boudewyns, P., & Harrison, W. R. (1990). Alexithymia among Vietnam veterans with posttraumatic stress disorder. *Journal of Clinical Psychiatry, 51,* 243–247.

Hyler, S. E., Rieder, R. O., Williams, J. W. B., Spitzer, R. L., Hendler, J., & Lyons, M. (1988). The Personality Diagnostic Questionnaire: Development and preliminary results. *Journal of Personality Disorders, 2,* 229–237.

Ibsen, H. (1879). A doll's house. In *Eleven plays of Henrik Ibsen* (pp. 3–92). New York: Random House.

Immelman, A. (1993). The assessment of political personality: A psychodiagnostically relevant conceptualization and methodology. *Political Psychology, 14,* 725–741.

Immelman, A. (1998). The political personalities of 1996 U.S. presidential candidates Bill Clinton and Bob Dole. *Leadership Quarterly, 9,* 335–366.

Inch, R., & Crossley, M. (1993). Diagnostic utility of the MCMI–I and MCMI–II with psychiatric outpatients. *Journal of Clinical Psychology, 49,* 358–366.

Jackson, H. J., Gazis, J., Rudd, R. P., & Edwards, J. (1991). Concordance between two personality disorder instruments with psychiatric inpatients. *Comprehensive Psychiatry, 32,* 252–260.

Jackson, H. J., Rudd, R., Gazis, J., & Edwards, J. (1991). Using the MCMI–I to diagnose personality disorders in inpatients: Axis I/Axis II associations and sex differences. *Australian Psychologist, 26,* 37–41.

Jackson, J. J., Greenblatt, R. L., Davis, W. E., Murphy, T. J., & Trimakas, K. (1991). Assessment of schizophrenic inpatients with the MCMI. *Journal of Clinical Psychology, 47,* 505–510.

Jaffe, L. T., & Archer, R. P. (1987). The prediction of drug use among college students from MMPI, MCMI, and Sensation Seeking scales. *Journal of Personality Assessment, 51,* 243–253.

Jay, G. W., Grove, R. N., & Grove, K. S. (1987). Differentiation of chronic headache from non-headache pain patients using the Millon Clinical Multiaxial Inventory (MCMI). *Headache, 27,* 124–129.

Jensen, A. R. (1980). *Bias in mental testing.* New York: Free Press.

Joffe, R. T., & Regan, J. J. (1988). Personality and depression. *Journal of Psychiatric Research, 22,* 279–286.

Joffe, R., & Regan, J. (1989a). Personality and response to tricyclic antidepressants in depressed patients. *Journal of Nervous and Mental Disease, 177,* 745–749.

Joffe, R., & Regan, J. (1989b). Personality and suicidal behavior in depressed patients. *Comprehensive Psychiatry, 30,* 157–160.

Joffe, R. T., & Regan, J. J. (1991). Personality and family history of depression in patients with affective illness. *Journal of Psychiatric Research, 25,* 67–71.

Joffe, R. T., Swinson, R. P., & Regan, J. J. (1988). Personality features of obsessive–compulsive disorder. *American Journal of Psychiatry, 145,* 1127–1129.

Johnson, B., & Zea, K. (Producers) & Brooks, J. L. (Director). (1998). *As good as it gets* [Motion picture]. United States: TriStar Pictures.

Josiassen, R. C., Shagass, C., & Roemer, R. (1988). Somatosensory evoked potential correlates of schizophrenic subtypes identified by the Millon Clinical Multiaxial Inventory. *Psychiatric Research, 23,* 209–219.

Jung, C. G. (1971). Psychology typology. In *Psychological types* (Rev. ed.; R. F. C. Hull, Trans.). Princeton, NJ: Princeton University Press. (Original work published 1936.)

Kelln, B. R. C., Dozois, D. J. A., & McKenzie, I. E. (1998). An MCMI–III discriminant function analysis of incarcerated felons: Prediction of subsequent institutional misconduct. *Criminal Justice & Behavior, 25,* 177–189.

Kendall, R. E. (1983). DSM–III: A major advance in psychiatric nosology. In A. L. Spitzer, J. B. W. Williams, & A. E. Skodol (Eds.), *International perspectives on DSM–III* (pp. 55–68). Washington, DC: American Psychiatric Press.

Kennedy, S. H., McVey, G., & Katz, R. (1990). Personality disorders in anorexia nervosa and bulimia nervosa. *Journal of Psychiatric Research, 24,* 259–269.

Kernberg, O. F. (1975). *Borderline conditions and pathological narcissism.* Northvale, NJ: Jason Aronson.

Kernberg, O. F. (1977). The structural diagnosis of borderline personality organization. In P. Hartocoullis (Ed.), *Borderline personality disorder* (pp. 87–121). Madison, CT: International Universities Press.

Kernberg, O. (1984a). *Severe personality disorders.* New Haven, CT: Yale University Press.

Kernberg, O. F. (1984b). *Treatment of severe personality disorders: Psychotherapeutic strategies.* New Haven, CT: Yale University Press.

Kiesler, D. J. (1983). The interpersonal circle: A taxonomy for complementarity in human transactions. *Psychological Review, 90,* 184–214.

Kiesler, D. J. (1986). The 1982 interpersonal circle: An analysis of DSM–III personality disorders. In T. Millon & G. Klerman (Eds.), *Contemporary issues in psychopathology* (pp. 1–23). New York: Guilford Press.

King, A. R. (1998). Relations between the MCMI–II personality variables and measures of academic performance. *Journal of Personality Assessment, 71,* 253–268.

King, R. E. (1994). Assessing aviators for personality pathology with the Millon Clinical Multiaxial Inventory (MCMI). *Aviation, Space, and Environmental Medicine, 65,* 227–231.

Klein, M. H., Benjamin, L. S., Rosenfeld, R., Treece, C., Husted, J., & Greist, J. H. (1993). The Wisconsin Personality Disorders Inventory: Development, reliability, and validity. *Journal of Personality Disorders, 7,* 285–303.

Klein, M. H., Wonderlich, S., & Shea, M. T. (1993). Models of relationships between personality and depression: Toward a framework for theory and research. In M. H. Klein, D. J. Kupfer, & M. T. Shea (Eds.), *Personality and depression* (pp. 1–54). New York: Guilford Press.

Kristensen, H., & Torgersen, S. (2001). MCMI–II personality traits and symptom traits in parents of children with selective mutism: A case-control study. *Journal of Abnormal Psychology, 110,* 640–652.

Krug, S. E., & Laughlin, J. E. (1977). Second order factors among normal and pathological primary personality traits. *Journal of Consulting Psychology, 45,* 575–582.

Kvaal, S. A., Choca, J. P., & Groth-Marnat, G. (2003). The integrated psychological report. In L E. Beutler and G. Groth-Marnat (Eds.), *Integrative assessment of adult personality* (2nd ed., pp. 398–433). New York: Guilford Press.

Lall, R., Bongar, B., Johnson, W. B., Jain, V. K., & Mittauer, M. W. (1999). Efficacy of the Millon Clinical Multiaxial Inventory–II in disciminating mental health patients with or without suicide ideation. *Military Psychology, 11,* 423–432.

Lambert, N. M. (1981). Psychological evidence in *Larry P. v. Wilson Riles. American Psychologist, 36,* 937–952.

Lampel, A. K. (1999). Use of the Millon Clinical Multiaxial Inventory–III in evaluating child custody litigants. *American Journal of Forensic Psychology, 17,* 10–31.

Langevin, R., Lang, R., Reynolds, R., Wright, P., Garrels, D., Marchese, V., et al. (1988). Personality and sexual anomalies: An examination of the Millon Clinical Multiaxial Inventory. *Annals of Sex Research, 1,* 13–32.

Lanyon, R. I. (1984). Personality assessment. *Annual Review of Psychology, 35,* 667–701.

Leaf, R. C., Alington, D. E., Ellis, A., DiGiuseppe, R., & Mass, R. (1992). Personality disorders, underlying traits, social problems, and clinical syndromes. *Journal of Personality Disorders, 6,* 134–152.

Leaf, R., Alington, D., Mass, R., DiGiuseppe, R., & Ellis, A. (1991). Personality disorders, life events, and clinical syndromes. *Journal of Personality Disorders, 5,* 264–280.

Leaf, R. C., DiGiuseppe, R., Ellis, A., Mass, R., Backx, W., Wolfe, J., et al. (1990). "Healthy" correlates of MCMI Scales 4, 5, 6, and 7. *Journal of Personality Disorders, 4,* 312–328.

Leaf, R. C., Ellis, A., DiGiuseppe, R., Mass, R., & Alington, D. E. (1991). Rationality, self-regard and the "healthiness" of personality disorders. *Journal of Rational–Emotive and Cognitive–Behavior Therapy, 9,* 3–37.

Leaf, R. C., Ellis, A., Mass, R., DiGiuseppe, R., & Alington, D. E. (1990). Countering perfectionism in research on clinical practice: II. Retrospective analysis of treatment progress. *Journal of Rational–Emotive and Cognitive–Behavior Therapy, 8,* 203–220.

Leary, T. (1957). *Interpersonal diagnosis of personality.* New York: Ronald Press.

Leary, T., & Coffey, H. (1955). Interpersonal diagnosis: Some problems of methodology and validation. *Journal of Abnormal and Social Psychology, 50,* 110–124.

Lees-Haley, P. R. (1992). Efficacy of MMPI–2 validity scales and MCMI–II modifier scales for detecting spurious PTSD claims: F, F K, Fake Bad scale, Ego Strength, Subtle Obvious subscales, DIS, and DEB. *Journal of Clinical Psychology, 48,* 681–689.

Lemkau, J. P., Purdy, R. R., Rafferty, J. P., & Rudisill, J. R. (1988). Correlates of burnout among family practice residents. *Journal of Medical Education, 63,* 682–691.

Leroux, M. D., Vincent, K. R., McPherson, R. H., & Williams, W. (1990). Construct validity of the Diagnostic Inventory of Personality and Symptoms: External correlates. *Journal of Clinical Psychology, 46,* 285–291.

Levine, J., Tischer, P., Antoni, M., Green, C., & Millon, T. (1985). Refining personality assessments by combining MCMI high-point profiles and MMPI codes, Part II: MMPI 27/72. *Journal of Personality Assessment, 49,* 501–507.

Lewis, S. J., & Harder, D. W. (1991). A comparison of four measures to diagnose DSM–III–R borderline personality disorder in outpatients. *Journal of Nervous and Mental Disease, 179,* 329–337.

Libb, J. W., Murray, J., Thurstin, H., & Alarcon, R. D. (1992). Concordance of the MCMI–II, the MMPI, and Axis I discharge diagnosis in psychiatric inpatients. *Journal of Personality Assessment, 58,* 580–590.

Libb, J. W., Stankovic, S., Freeman, A., Sokol, R., Switzer, P., & Houck, C. (1990). Personality disorders among depressed outpatients as identified by the MCMI. *Journal of Clinical Psychology, 46,* 277–284.

Libb, J. W., Stankovic, S., Sokol, R., Freeman, A., Houck, C., & Switzer, P. (1990). Stability of the MCMI among depressed psychiatric outpatients. *Journal of Personality Assessment, 55,* 209–218.

Lindsay, K. A., & Widiger, T. A. (1995). Sex and gender bias in self-report personality disorder inventories: Item analyses of the MCMI–II, MMPI, and PDQ–R. *Journal of Personality Assessment, 65,* 1–20.

Lindsay, K. A., Sankis, L. M., & Widiger, T. A. (2000). Gender bias in self-report personality disorder inventories. *Journal of Personality Disorders, 14,* 218–232.

Litman, L. C., & Cernovsky, Z. Z. (1993). An MCMI–II taxonomy of substance abusers. *Research Communications in Psychology, Psychiatry and Behavior, 18,* 67–72.

Livesley, W. J., Jackson, D. N., & Schroeder, M. L. (1989). A study of the factorial structure of personality pathology. *Journal of Personality Disorders, 3,* 292–306.

Livesley, W. J., Jackson, D. N., & Schroeder, M. L. (1992). Factorial structure of traits delineating personality disorders in clinical and general population samples. *Journal of Abnormal Psychology, 101,* 432–440.

Llorente, M. D., Currier, M. B., Norman, S. E., & Mellman, T. A. (1992). Night terrors in adults: Phenomenology and relationship to psychopathology. *Journal of Clinical Psychiatry, 53,* 392–394.

Locke, K. D. (2000). Circumplex scales of interpersonal values: Reliability, validity and applicability to interpersonal problems and personality disorders. *Journal of Personality Assessment, 75,* 249–267.

Lohr, J. M., Hamberger, L. K., & Bonge, D. (1988). The nature of irrational beliefs in different personality clusters of spouse abusers. *Journal of Rational–Emotive and Cognitive–Behavior Therapy, 6,* 273–285.

Lorr, M., & McNair, D. M. (1963). An interpersonal behavior circle. *Journal of Personality and Social Psychology, 67,* 68–75.

Lorr, M., Retzlaff, P. D., & Tarr, H. C. (1989). An analysis of the MCMI–I at the item level. *Journal of Clinical Psychology, 45,* 884–890.

Lorr, M., & Strack, S. (1990). Profile clusters of the MCMI–II personality disorder scales. *Journal of Clinical Psychology, 46,* 606–612.

Lorr, M., Strack, S., Campbell, L., & Lamnin, A. (1990). Personality and symptom dimensions of the MCMI–II: An item factor analysis. *Journal of Clinical Psychology, 46,* 749–754.

Loughead, T. A., Spurlock, V. L., & Ting, Y. (1998). Diagnostic indicators of codependence: An investigation using the MCMI–II. *Journal of Mental Health Counseling, 20,* 64–76.

Lovitt, R. (1988). Current practice of psychological assessment: Response to Sweeney, Clarkin, and Fitzgibbon. *Professional Psychology: Research and Practice, 19,* 516–521.

Lumsden, E. A. (1986, March). *Internal structure validation of the MCMI: Correlations among unshared scale items.* Paper presented at the Conference of the Millon Clinical Inventories, Miami, FL.

Lumsden, E. A. (1988). The impact of shared items on the internal structure validity of the MCMI. *Educational and Psychological Measurement, 49,* 669–678.

Lundholm, J. K. (1989). Alcohol use among university females: Relationship to eating disordered behavior. *Addictive Behaviors, 14,* 181–185.

Lundholm, J. K., Pellegreno, D. D., Wolins, L., & Graham, S. L. (1989). Predicting eating disorders in women: A preliminary measurement study. *Measurement and Evaluation in Counseling and Development, 22,* 23–30.

Luteijn, F. (1990). The MCMI in the Netherlands: First findings. *Journal of Personality Disorders, 4,* 297–302.

Machiavelli, N. (1931). *The prince* (W. Marriott, Trans.). London: J. M. Dent. (Original work published 1532)

Malec, J. F., Romsaas, E. P., Messing, E. M., Cummings, K. C., & Trump, D. L. (1990). Psychological and mood disturbance associated with the diagnosis and treatment of testis cancer and other malignancies. *Journal of Clinical Psychology, 46,* 551–557.

Malec, J., Wolberg, W., Romsaas, E., Trump, D., & Tanner, M. (1988). Millon Clinical Multiaxial Inventory (MCMI) findings among breast clinic patients after initial evaluation and at 4- or 8-month follow-up. *Journal of Clinical Psychology, 44,* 175–180.

Marlowe, D. B., Festinger, D. S., Kirby, K. C., Rubenstein, D. F., & Platt, J. J. (1998). Congruence of the MCMI–II and the MCMI–III in cocaine dependence. *Journal of Personality Assessment, 7,* 15–28.

Marlowe, D. B., Husband, S. D., Bonieskie, L. M., Kirby, K. C., & Platt, J. J. (1997). Structured interview versus self-report test vantages for the assessment of personality pathology in cocaine dependence. *Journal of Personality Disorders, 11,* 177–190.

Marlowe, D. B., & Wetzler, S. (1994). Contributions of discriminant analysis to differential diagnosis by self-report. *Journal of Personality Assessment, 62,* 320–331.

Marsella, A. J., Sanaborn, K. O., Kameoka, V., Shizuru, L., & Brennan, J. (1975). Cross-validation of self-report measures of depression among normal populations of Japanese, Chinese, and Caucasian ancestry. *Journal of Clinical Psychology, 31,* 281–287.

Marsh, D. T., Stile, S. A., Stoughton, N. L., & Trout-Landen, B. L. (1988). Psychopathology of opiate addiction: Comparative data from the MMPI and MCMI. *American Journal of Drug and Alcohol Abuse, 14,* 17–27.

Martin, P., Langone, M., Dole, A., & Wiltrout, J. (1992). Post-cult symptoms as measured by the MCMI before and after residential treatment. *Cultic Studies Journal, 9,* 219–251.

Matano, R. A., & Locke, K. D. (1995). Personality disorder scales as predictors of interpersonal problems of alcoholics. *Journal of Personality Disorders, 9,* 62–67.

Matano, R. A., Locke, K. D., & Schwartz, K. (1994). MCMI personality subtypes for male and female alcoholics. *Journal of Personality Assessment, 63,* 250–264.

May, B, & Bos, J. (2000). Personality characteristics of ADHD adults assessed with the Millon Clinical Multiaxial Inventory–II: Evidence of four distinct subtypes. *Journal of Personality Assessment, 75,* 236–248.

Mayer, G. S., & Scott, K. J. (1988). An exploration of heterogeneity in an inpatient male alcoholic population. *Journal of Personality Disorders, 2,* 243–255.

McAllister, H. A., Baker, J. D., Mannes, C., Stewart, H., & Sutherland, A. (2002). The optimal margin of illusion hypothesis: Evidence from the self-serving bias and personality disorders. *Journal of Social and Clinical Psychology, 21,* 414–426.

McCann, J. T. (1989). MMPI personality disorder scales and the MCMI: Concurrent validity. *Journal of Clinical Psychology, 45,* 365–369.

McCann, J. T. (1990a). Bias and Millon Clinical Multiaxial Inventory (MCMI–II) diagnosis. *Journal of Psychopathology and Behavioral Assessment, 12,* 17–26.

McCann, J. T. (1990b). A multitrait–multimethod analysis of the MCMI–II clinical syndrome scales. *Journal of Personality Assessment, 55,* 465–476.

McCann, J. T. (1991). Convergent and discriminant validity of the MCMI–II and MMPI personality disorder scales. *Psychological Assessment, 3,* 9–18.

McCann, J. T. (1992). A comparison of two measures for obsessive–compulsive personality disorder. *Journal of Personality Disorders, 6,* 18–23.

McCann, J. T. (2002). Guidelines for forensic application of the MCMI–III. *Journal of Forensic Psychology Practice, 2,* 55–70.

McCann, J. T., & Dyer, F. J. (1996). *Forensic assessment with the Millon inventories.* New York: Guilford Press.

McCann, J. T., Flynn, P. M., & Gersh, D. M. (1992). MCMI–II diagnosis of borderline personality disorder: Base rates versus prototypic items. *Journal of Personality Assessment, 58,* 105–114.

McCann, J., & Gergelis, R. (1990). Utility of the MCMI–II in assessing suicide risk. *Journal of Clinical Psychology, 46,* 764–770.

McCann, J., & Suess, J. (1988). Clinical applications of the MCMI: The 1-2-3-8 codetype. *Journal of Clinical Psychology, 44,* 181–186.

McCrae, R. (1991). The five factor model and its assessment in clinical settings. *Journal of Personality Assessment, 57,* 399–414.

McCrae, R., & Costa, P. (1985). Updating Norman's "adequate taxonomy": Intelligence and personality dimensions in natural language and in questionnaires. *Journal of Personality and Social Psychology, 49,* 710–721.

McCrae, R., & Costa, P. (1986). Clinical assessment can benefit from recent advances in personality psychology. *American Psychologist, 41,* 1001–1003.

McCrae, R. R., & Costa, P. T. (1990). *Personality in adulthood.* New York: Guilford Press.

McCreary, C., & Padilla, E. (1977). MMPI differences among Black, Mexican-American and White male offenders. *Journal of Clinical Psychology, 33,* 171–177.

McDermott, W. F. (1987). The diagnosis of post-traumatic stress disorder using the Millon Clinical Multiaxial Inventory. In C. Green (Ed.), *Conference of the Millon Clinical Inventories (MCMI, MBHI, MAPI)* (pp. 257–262). Minneapolis, MN: National Computer Systems.

McGill, J. C. (1980). MMPI score differences among Anglo, Black and Mexican American welfare recipients. *Journal of Consulting and Clinical Psychology, 36,* 147–171.

McMahon, R., Applegate, B., Kouzekanani, K., & Davidson, R. (1990, August). *Confirmatory factor analysis of the Millon Clinical Multiaxial Inventory.* Paper presented at the 98th Annual Convention of the American Psychological Association, Boston.

McMahon, R., & Davidson, R. (1985a). An examination of the relationship between personality patterns and symptom/mood patterns. *Journal of Personality Assessment, 49,* 552–556.

McMahon, R., & Davidson, R. (1985b). Transient versus enduring depression among alcoholics in inpatient treatment. *Journal of Psychopathology and Behavioral Assessment, 7,* 317–328.

McMahon, R., & Davidson, R. (1986a). Concurrent validity of the clinical symptom scales of the Millon Multiaxial Inventory. *Journal of Clinical Psychology, 42,* 908–912.

McMahon, R., & Davidson, R. (1986b). An examination of depressed vs. nondepressed alcoholics in inpatient treatment. *Journal of Clinical Psychology, 42,* 177–184.

McMahon, R. C., & Davidson, R. S. (1988, August). *Factor structure of the Millon Clinical Multiaxial Inventory in an alcohol abusing population.* Paper presented at the 96th Annual Convention of the American Psychological Association, Atlanta, GA.

McMahon, R., & Davidson, R. (1989, August). *A comparison of continuous and episodic drinkers using the MCMI, MMPI, and ALCEVAL–R.* Paper presented at the 97th Annual Convention of the American Psychological Association, New Orleans, LA.

McMahon, R. C., Davidson, R. S., & Flynn, P. M. (1986). Psychosocial correlates and treatment outcomes for high and low social functioning alcoholics. *International Journal of Addictions, 21,* 819–835.

McMahon, R. C., Davidson, R. S., Gersh, D., & Flynn, P. (1991). A comparison of continuous and episodic drinkers using the MCMI, MMPI, and ALCEVAL–R. *Journal of Clinical Psychology, 47,* 148–159.

McMahon, R. C., Flynn, P. M., & Davidson, R. S. (1985a). The personality and symptom scales of the Millon Clinical Multiaxial Inventory: Sensitivity to posttreatment outcomes. *Journal of Clinical Psychology, 41,* 862–866.

McMahon, R. C., Flynn, P. M., & Davidson, R. S. (1985b). Stability of the personality and symptom scales of the Millon Clinical Multiaxial Inventory. *Journal of Personality Assessment, 49,* 231–234.

McMahon, R. C., Gersh, D., & Davidson, R. S. (1989). Personality and symptom characteristics of continuous vs. episodic drinkers. *Journal of Clinical Psychology, 45,* 161–168.

McMahon, R. C., Kelley, A., & Kouzekanani, K. (1993). Personality and coping styles in the prediction of dropout from treatment for cocaine abuse. *Journal of Personality Assessment, 61,* 147–155.

McMahon, R., Kouzekanani, K., & Bustillo, S. (1991, August). *Factor structure of the Millon Clinical Multiaxial Inventory–II.* Paper presented at the 99th Annual Convention of the American Psychological Association, San Francisco, CA.

McMahon, R. C., Malow, R. M., & Penedo, F. J. (1998). Substance abuse problems, psychiatric severity, and HIV risk in Millon Clinical Multiaxial Inventory–II personality subgroups. *Psychology of Addictive Behaviors, 12,* 3–13.

McMahon, R. C., & Richards, S. K. (1996). Profile patterns, consistency, and change in the Millon Clinical Multiaxial Inventory–II in cocaine abusers. *Journal of Clinical Psychology, 52,* 75–79.

McMahon, R., Schram, L., Davidson, R. (1993). Negative life events, social support, and depression in three personality types. *Journal of Personality Disorders, 7,* 241–254.

McMahon, R., & Tyson, D. (1989). *Transient versus enduring depression among alcoholic women.* Paper presented at the 97th Annual Convention of the American Psychological Association, New Orleans, LA.

McMahon, R., & Tyson, D. (1990). Personality factors in transient versus enduring depression among inpatient alcoholic women: A preliminary analysis. *Journal of Personality Disorders, 4,* 150–160.

McNair, D. M., Lorr, M., & Droppleman, L. F. (1971). *Profile of Mood States, manual.* San Diego, CA: Educational and Industrial Testing Service.

McNiel, K., & Meyer, R. (1990). Detection of deception on the Millon Clinical Multiaxial Inventory (MCMI). *Journal of Clinical Psychology, 46,* 755–764.

Meehl, P. E., & Rosen, A. (1955). Antecedent probability and the efficiency of psychometric signs, patterns, or cutting scores. *Psychological Bulletin, 52,* 194–216.

Messina, N., Wish, E., Hoffman, J., & Nemes, S. (2001). Diagnosing personality disorder among substance abusers: The SCID versus the MCMI–II. *American Journal of Drug and Alcohol Abuse, 27,* 699–717.

Miller, C., Knapp, S., & Daniels, C. (1968). MMPI study of Negro mental hygiene clinic patients. *Journal of Abnormal Psychology, 73,* 168–173.

Miller, C., Wertz, C., & Counts, S. (1961). Racial differences on the MMPI. *Journal of Clinical Psychology, 17,* 159–160.

Miller, H. R., Goldberg, J. O., & Streiner, D. L. (1993). The effects of the modifier and correction indices on MCMI–II profiles. *Journal of Personality Assessment, 60,* 477–485.

Miller, H. R., Streiner, D. L., & Parkinson, A. (1992). Maximum likelihood estimates of the ability of the MMPI and MCMI personality disorder scales and the SIDP to identify personality disorders. *Journal of Personality Assessment, 59,* 1–13.

Miller, T. W., Martin, W., & Shapiro, K. (1991). Traumatic stress disorder: Diagnostic and clinical issues in former prisoners of war. *Comprehensive Psychiatry, 30,* 139–148.

Millon, C., Salvato, F., Blaney, N., Morgan, R., Montero-Atienza, E., Klimas, N., et al. (1989). A psychological assessment of chronic fatigue syndrome/chronic Epstein–Barr virus patients. *Psychology and Health, 3,* 131–141.

Millon, T. (1969). *Modern psychopathology: A biosocial approach to maladaptive learning and functioning.* Philadelphia: W. B. Saunders.

Millon, T. (1973). A biosocial-learning approach. In T. Millon (Ed.), *Theories of psychopathology and personality* (pp. 492–502). Philadelphia: W. B. Saunders.

Millon, T. (1977). *Millon Clinical Multiaxial Inventory.* Minneapolis, MN: National Computer Systems.

Millon, T. (1981). *Disorders of personality: DSM–III Axis II.* New York: Wiley.

Millon, T. (1982a). *Millon Behavioral Health Inventory manual.* Minneapolis, MN: National Computer Systems.

Millon, T. (1982b). *Millon Clinical Multiaxial Inventory manual* (2nd ed.). Minneapolis, MN: National Computer Systems.

Millon, T. (1983). *Millon Clinical Multiaxial Inventory manual* (3rd ed.). Minneapolis, MN: National Computer Systems.

Millon, T. (1984). *Millon Clinical Multiaxial Inventory manual supplement.* Minneapolis: MN: National Computer Systems.

Millon, T. (1985). The MCMI provides a good assessment of DSM–III disorders: The MCMI–II will prove even better. *Journal of Personality Assessment, 49,* 379–391.

Millon, T. (1986). The MCMI and DSM–III: Further commentaries. *Journal of Personality Assessment, 50,* 205–207.

Millon, T. (1987). *Manual for the MCMI–II* (2nd ed.). Minneapolis, MN: National Computer Systems.
Millon, T. (1990). *Toward a new personology: An evolutionary model.* New York: Wiley.
Millon, T. (1994a). *Manual for the MCMI–III.* Minneapolis, MN: National Computer Systems.
Millon, T. (1994b). *Millon Index of Personality Scales manual.* San Antonio, TX: Psychological Corporation.
Millon, T. (1995). Foreword. In P. D. Retzlaff (Ed.), *Tactical psychotherapy of the personality disorders: An MCMI–III based approach* (pp. ix–xi). Boston: Allyn & Bacon.
Millon, T. (1996). *Disorders of personality: DSM–IV and beyond.* New York: Wiley.
Millon, T. (1997). *Manual for the MCMI–III* (2nd ed.). Minneapolis, MN: National Computer Systems.
Millon, T. (1998). Discussion. In S. Strack (Chair), *Millon theory: Data and treatment suggestions.* Symposium conducted at the 106th Annual Convention of the American Psychological Association, San Francisco, CA.
Millon, T. (1999a). *Personality-guided therapy.* New York: Wiley.
Millon, T. (1999b). Reflections on psychosynergy: A model for integrating science, theory, classification, assessment, and therapy. *Journal of Personality Assessment, 72,* 437–456.
Millon, T. (2002). Assessment is not enough: The SPA should participate in constructing a comprehensive science of personality. *Journal of Personality Assessment, 78,* 209–218.
Millon, T., & Davis, R. (1996). An evolutionary theory of personality disorders. In J. Clarkin & M. Lenzenweger (Eds.), *Major theories of personality disorder* (pp. 221–346). New York: Guilford Press.
Millon, T., & Davis, R (1997). The MCMI–III: Present and future directions. *Journal of Personality Assessment, 68,* 69–85.
Millon, T., Davis, R., & Millon, C. (1998). *Corrections report user's guide.* Minneapolis, MN: National Computer Systems.
Millon, T., & Millon, R. (1974). *Abnormal behavior and personality.* Philadelphia: W. B. Saunders.
Millon, T., Weiss, L., Millon, C., & Davis, R. D. (1994). *MIPS: Millon Index of Personality Styles.* San Antonio, TX: Psychological Corporation.
Mischel, W. (1968). *Personality assessment.* New York: Wiley.
Mischel, W. (1973). Toward a cognitive social learning reconceptualization of personality. *Psychological Review, 80,* 252–283.
Montag, I., & Comrey, A. L. (1987). Millon MCMI scales analyzed and correlated with MMPI and CPS scales. *Multivariate Behavioral Research, 22,* 401–413.
Moreland, K. (1992). If it's personality patterns you're interested in . . . *Journal of Personality Assessment, 58,* 438–440.
Moreland, K. L., & Onstad, J. A. (1987). Validity of Millon's computerized interpretation system for the MCMI: A controlled study. *Journal of Consulting and Clinical Psychology, 55,* 113–114.
Morey, L. C. (1985). An empirical comparison of interpersonal and DSM–III approaches to classification of personality disorders. *Psychiatry, 48,* 358–364.
Morey, L. C. (1986). A comparison of three personality disorder assessment approaches. *Journal of Psychopathology and Behavioral Assessment, 8,* 25–30.
Morey, L. C., & Le Vine, D. J. (1988). A multitrait–multimethod examination of Minnesota Multiphasic Personality Inventory (MMPI) and Millon Clinical Multiaxial Inventory (MCMI). *Journal of Psychopathology and Behavioral Assessment, 10,* 333–344.
Morey, L. C., Waugh, M. H., & Blashfield, R. K. (1985). MMPI scales for the DSM–III personality disorders: Their derivation and correlates. *Journal of Personality Assessment, 49,* 245–251.
Morgan, C. D., Schoenberg, M. R., Dorr, D., & Burke, M. J. (2002). Overreport on the MCMI–III: Concurrent validation with the MMPI–2 using a psychiatric inpatient sample. *Journal of Personality Assessment, 78,* 288–300.

Mortensen, E. L., & Simonsen, E. (1990). Psychometric properties of the Danish MCMI–I translation. *Scandinavian Journal of Psychology, 31,* 149–153.

Munley, P. H., Bains, D. S., Bloem, W. D., Busby, R. M., & Pendziszewski, S. (1995). Posttraumatic stress disorder and the MCMI–II. *Psychological Reports, 76,* 939–944.

Munley, P. H., Bains, D. S., Frazee, J., & Schwartz, L. T. (1994). Inpatient PTSD treatment: A study of pretreatment measures, treatment dropout, and therapist ratings of response to treatment. *Journal of Traumatic Stress, 7,* 319–325.

Muran, J., Segal, Z., Samstag, L., & Crawford, C. (1994). Patient pretreatment interpersonal problems and therapeutic alliance in short-term cognitive therapy. *Journal of Consulting and Clinical Psychology, 62,* 185–190.

Murphy, C. M., Meyer, S. L., & O'Leary, K. D. (1993). Family of origin violence and MCMI–II psychopathology among partner assaultive men. *Violence and Victims, 8,* 165–176.

Murphy, T. J., Greenblatt, R. L., Mozdzierz, G. J., & Trimakas, K. A. (1990). Stability of the Millon Clinical Multiaxial Inventory among psychiatric inpatients. *Journal of Psychopathology and Behavioral Assessment, 12,* 143–150.

Murray, H. A. (1943). *Thematic Apperception Test.* Cambridge, MA: Harvard University Press.

Nakao, K., Gunderson, J., Phillips, K., Tanaka, N., Yorifuji, K., Takaishi, J., et al. (1992). Functional impairment in personality disorders. *Journal of Personality Disorders, 6,* 24–33.

Nazikian, H., Rudd, R. P., Edwards, J., & Jackson, H. J. (1990). Personality disorder assessment for psychiatric inpatients. *Australian and New Zealand Journal of Psychiatry, 24,* 37–46.

Nerviano, V., & Gross, W. (1983). Personality types of alcoholics in objective inventories. *Journal of Studies on Alcohol, 44,* 837–851.

Norman, D., Blais, M., & Herzog, D. (1993). Personality characteristics of eating-disordered patients as identified by the Millon Clinical Multiaxial Inventory. *Journal of Personality Disorders, 7,* 1–9.

O'Callaghan, T., Bates, G. W., Jackson, H. J., Rudd, R. P., & Edwards, J. (1990). The clinical utility of the Millon Clinical Multiaxial Inventory Depression subscales. *Australian Psychologist, 25,* 45–61.

O'Connor, B. P., & Dyce, J. A. (1998). A test of models of personality disorder configuration. *Journal of Abnormal Psychology, 107,* 3–16.

Offer, D., & Sabshin, M. (1991). Introduction. In D. Offer & M. Sabshin (Eds.), *The diversity of normal behavior* (pp. xi–xxi). New York: Basic Books.

Oldham, J., Clarkin, J., Appelbaum, A., Carr, A., Kernberg, P., Lotterman, A., et al. (1985). A self-report instrument for borderline personality organization. In T. H. McGlashan (Ed.), *The borderline: Current empirical research* (pp. 1–18). Washington, DC: American Psychiatric Press.

Overholser, J. C. (August, 1989). *Temporal stability of the MCMI personality disorder scales.* Paper presented at the 97th Annual Convention of the American Psychological Association, New Orleans, LA.

Overholser, J. C. (1991). Categorical assessment of the dependent personality disorder in depressed inpatients. *Journal of Personality Disorders, 5,* 243–255.

Overholser, J. C., Kabakoff, R., & Norman, W. H. (1989). The assessment of personality characteristics in depressed and dependent psychiatric inpatients. *Journal of Personality Assessment, 53,* 40–50.

Ownby, R. L., Wallbrown, F., Carmin, C., & Barnett, R. W. (1990). A combined factor analysis of the Millon Clinical Multiaxial Inventory and the MMPI in an offender population. *Journal of Clinical Psychology, 46,* 89–96.

Ownby, R. L., Wallbrown, F. H., Carmin, C., & Barnett, R. (1991). A canonical analysis of the Millon Clinical Multiaxial Inventory and the MMPI for an offender population. *Journal of Personality Disorders, 5,* 15–24.

Page, R. D., & Bozlee, S. (1982). A cross-cultural MMPI comparison of alcoholics. *Psychological Reports, 50,* 639–646.

Palmer, C. (1975). Characteristics of effective counselor–trainees. *Dissertation Abstracts International, 36,* A2031.

Papciak, A. S., & Feuerstein, M. (1991). Psychological factors affecting isokinetic trunk strength testing in patients with work related chronic low back pain. *Journal of Occupational Rehabilitation, 1,* 95–104.

Patrick, J. (1988). Concordance of the MCMI and the MMPI in the diagnosis of three DSM–III Axis I disorders. *Journal of Clinical Psychology, 44,* 186–191.

Patrick, J. (1990). Assessment of narcissistic psychopathology in the clergy. *Pastoral Psychology, 38,* 173–180.

Patrick, J. (1993). Validation of the MCMI–I Borderline Personality Disorder scale with a well-defined criterion sample. *Journal of Clinical Psychology, 49,* 28–32.

Pendleton, L., Tisdale, M., & Marler, M. (1991). Personality pathology in bulimics versus controls. *Comprehensive Psychiatry, 32,* 516–520.

Penedo, F. J., Malow, R. M., McMahon, R. C., & Kouzekanani, K. (1996, August). *Substance abuse problems in MCMI–II personality subtypes.* Paper presented at the 104th Annual Convention of the American Psychological Association, Toronto, Canada.

Peniston, E. G., & Kulkosky, P. J. (1990). Alcoholic personality and alpha–theta brainwave training. *Medical Psychotherapy, 3,* 37–45.

Peterson, G., Clark, A., & Bennet, B. (1989). The utility of the MMPI subtle, obvious scales for detecting fake good and fake bad response sets. *Journal of Clinical Psychology, 45,* 575–582.

Petrovic, M., Vandierendonck, A., Mariman, A., van Maele, G., Afschrift, M., & Pevernagie, D. (2002). Personality traits and socio-epidemiological status of hospitalized elderly benzodiazepine users. *International Journal of Geriatric Psychiatry, 17,* 733–738.

Pettem, O., West, M., Mahoney, A., & Keller, A. (1993). Depression and attachment problems. *Journal of Psychiatry and Neuroscience, 18,* 78–81.

Pfohl, B., Stangl, D., & Zimmerman, M. (1983). *Structured Interview for DSM–III personality disorders* (2nd ed.) Unpublished manuscript, University of Iowa, Iowa City, IA.

Piekarski, A. M., Sherwood, R., & Funari, D. J. (1993). Personality subgroups in an inpatient Vietnam veteran treatment program. *Psychological Reports, 72,* 667–674.

Piersma, H. L. (1986a, August). *Computer-generated diagnoses: How do they compare to clinical judgment?* Paper presented at the 94th Annual Convention of the American Psychological Association, Washington, DC.

Piersma, H. L. (1986b). The factor structure of the Millon Clinical Multiaxial Inventory (MCMI) for psychiatric inpatients. *Journal of Personality Assessment, 50,* 578–584.

Piersma, H. L. (1986c). The Millon Clinical Multiaxial Inventory (MCMI) as a treatment outcome measure for psychiatric inpatients. *Journal of Clinical Psychology, 42,* 493–499.

Piersma, H. L. (1986d). The stability of the Millon Clinical Multiaxial Inventory for psychiatric inpatients. *Journal of Personality Assessment, 50,* 193–197.

Piersma, H. L. (1987a). The MCMI as a measure of DSM–III Axis II diagnoses: An empirical comparison. *Journal of Clinical Psychology, 43,* 478–483.

Piersma, H. L. (1987b). Millon Clinical Multiaxial Inventory (MCMI) computer-generated diagnoses: How do they compare to clinical judgment? *Journal of Psychopathology and Behavioral Assessment, 9,* 305–312.

Piersma, H. L. (1987c). The use of the Millon Clinical Multiaxial Inventory in the evaluation of seminary students. *Journal of Psychology and Theology, 15,* 227–233.

Piersma, H. L. (1989a). The MCMI–II as a treatment outcome measure for psychiatric inpatients. *Journal of Clinical Psychology, 45,* 87–93.

Piersma, H. L. (1989b). The stability of the MCMI–II for psychiatric inpatients. *Journal of Clinical Psychology, 45,* 781–785.

Piersma, H. L. (1991). The MCMI–II depression scales: Do they assist in the differential prediction of depressive disorders? *Journal of Personality Assessment, 56,* 478–486.

Piersma, H. L., & Boes, J. L. (1997a). Comparison of psychiatric day hospital patient and inpatient scores on the MCMI–III. *Journal of Clinical Psychology, 53,* 629–634.

Piersma, H. L., & Boes, J. L. (1997b). MCMI–III as a treatment outcome measure for psychiatric inpatients. *Journal of Clinical Psychology, 53,* 825–831.

Piersma, H. L., & Boes, J. L. (1997c). The relationship of length of stay to MCMI–II and MCMI–III change scores. *Journal of Clinical Psychology, 53,* 535–542.

Piersma, H. L., Ohnishi, H., Lee, D. J., & Metcalfe, W. E. (2002). An empirical evaluation of Millon's dimensional polarities. *Journal of Psychopathology and Behavioral Assessment, 24,* 151–158.

Piersma, H. L., & Smith, A. Y. (1991). Individual variability in self-reported improvement for depressed psychiatric inpatients on the MCMI–II. *Journal of Clinical Psychology, 47,* 227–232.

Pincus, A. L. (1994). The interpersonal circumplex and the interpersonal theory: Perspectives on personality and its pathology. In S. Strack & M. Lorr (Eds.), *Differentiating normal and abnormal personality* (pp. 114–136). New York: Springer.

Piotrowski, C., & Keller, J. W. (1989). Psychological testing in outpatient mental health facilities: A national study. *Professional Psychology: Research and Practice, 20,* 423–425.

Piotrowski, C., & Lubin, B. (1989). Assessment practices of Division 38 practitioners. *Health Psychologist, 11,* 1.

Piotrowski, C., & Lubin, B. (1990). Assessment practices of health psychologists: Survey of APA Division 38 clinicians. *Professional Psychology: Research and Practice, 21,* 99–106.

Platt, J. J., & Spivack, G. (1975). *Manual for the Means–Ends–Problem-Solving Procedure (MEPS): A measure of interpersonal problem-solving skills.* Philadelphia, PA: Hahnemann Medical College.

Plemons, G. (1977). A comparison of the MMPI scores of Anglo and Mexican-American psychiatry patients. *Journal of Consulting and Clinical Psychology, 45,* 149–150.

Pochyly, J. M., Greenblatt, R. L., & Davis, W. E. (1989, August). *The effect of race on MCMI clinical scales.* Paper presented at the 97th Annual Convention of the American Psychological Association, New Orleans, LA.

Pollack, D., & Shore, J. H. (1980). Validity of the MMPI with Native Americans. *American Journal of Psychiatry, 137,* 946–950.

Porcerelli, J. H., Cogan, R., & Hibbard, S. (1998). Cognitive and affective representations of people and the MCMI–II personality pathology. *Journal of Personality Assessment, 70,* 535–540.

Powell, R. A., & Howell, A. J. (1998). Effectiveness of treatment for dissociative identity disorder. *Psychological Reports, 83,* 483–490.

Prifitera, A., & Ryan, J. J. (1984). Validity of the Narcissistic Personality Inventory (NPI) in a psychiatric sample. *Journal of Clinical Psychology, 40,* 140–142.

Raskin, R. N., & Hall, C. S. (1979). A narcissistic personality inventory. *Psychological Reports, 45,* 590.

Reich, J. (1985). Measurement of DSM–III Axis II. *Comprehensive Psychiatry, 26,* 352–363.

Reich, J. (1989). Update on instruments to measure DSM–III and DSM–III–R personality disorders. *Journal of Nervous and Mental Disease, 177,* 366–370.

Reich, J. (1990). The effect of personality on placebo response in panic patients. *Journal of Nervous and Mental Disease, 178,* 699–702.

Reich, J., Noyes, R., & Troughton, E. (1987). Dependent personality disorder associated with phobic avoidance in patients with panic disorder. *American Journal of Psychiatry, 144,* 323–326.

Reich, J., & Troughton, E. (1988). Comparison of DSM–III personality disorders in recovered depressed and panic disorder patients. *Journal of Nervous and Mental Disease, 176,* 300–304.

Reich, W. (1949). *Character analysis.* New York: Noonday Press.

Renneberg, B., Chambless, D. L., Dowdall, D. J., Fauerbach, J. A., & Gracely, E. J. (1992). The Structured Clinical Interview for the DSM–III–R and the Millon Clinical Multiaxial Inventory: A concurrent validity study of personality disorders among anxious outpatients. *Journal of Personality Disorders, 6,* 117–124.

Repko, G. R., & Cooper, R. (1985). The diagnosis of personality disorder: A comparison of MMPI profile, Millon inventory, and clinical judgment in a workers' compensation population. *Journal of Clinical Psychology, 41,* 867–881.

Retzlaff, P. D. (1991, August). *MCMI–II scoring challenges: Multi-weight items and site specific algorithms.* Paper presented at the 99th Annual Convention of the American Psychological Association, San Francisco, CA.

Retzlaff, P. (Ed.). (1995). *Tactical psychotherapy of the personality disorders.* Boston: Allyn & Bacon.

Retzlaff, P. (1996). MCMI–III validity: Bad test or bad validity study? *Journal of Personality Assessment, 66,* 431–437.

Retzlaff, P. D., & Bromley, S. (1991). A multi-test alcoholic-taxonomy: Canonical coefficient clusters. *Journal of Clinical Psychology, 47,* 299–309.

Retzlaff, P., & Cicerello, A. (1995). Compensation and pension evaluations: Psychotic, neurotic, and post-traumatic stress disorder Millon Clinical Multiaxial Inventory II profiles. *Military Medicine, 160,* 493–496.

Retzlaff, P., & Deatherage, T. (1993). Air Force mental health consultation: A six-year retention follow-up. *Military Medicine, 158,* 338–340.

Retzlaff, P., & Gibertini, M. (1987). Air Force pilot personality: Hard data on "the right stuff." *Multivariate Behavioral Research, 22,* 383–399.

Retzlaff, P. D., & Gibertini, M. (1988). Objective psychological testing of U. S. Air Force officers in pilot training. *Aviation, Space, and Environmental Medicine, 59,* 661–663.

Retzlaff, P., Lorr, M., Hyer, L., & Ofman, P. (1991). An MCMI–II item–level component analysis: Personality and clinical factors. *Journal of Personality Assessment, 57,* 323–334.

Retzlaff, P., Ofman, P., Hyer, L., & Matheson, S. (1994). MCMI–II high-point codes: Severe personality disorder and clinical syndrome extensions. *Journal of Clinical Psychology, 50,* 228–234.

Retzlaff, P. D., Sheehan, E. P., & Fiel, A. (1991). MCMI–II report style and bias: Profile and validity scales analyses. *Journal of Personality Assessment, 56,* 466–477.

Retzlaff, P. D., Sheehan, E. P., & Lorr, M. (1990). MCMI–II scoring: Weighted and unweighted algorithms. *Journal of Personality Assessment, 55,* 219–223.

Retzlaff, P. D., Stoner, J., & Kleinsasser, D. (2002). The use of the MCMI–III in the screening and triage of offenders. *International Journal of Offender Therapy and Comparative Criminology, 46,* 319–332.

Reynolds, C. R. (1982). The problem of bias in psychological assessment. In C. R. Reynolds & T. B. Gutkin (Eds.), *The handbook of school psychology* (pp. 178–208). New York: Wiley.

Reynolds, C. R. (1983). Test bias: In God we trust; all others must have data. *Journal of Special Education, 17,* 241–260.

Ritzler, B. (1996, Spring/Summer). Personality assessment and research: The state of the Union. *SPA Exchange, 6,* 15.

Robbins, S. B., & Patton, M. J. (1986). Procedures for construction of scales for rating counselor outcomes. *Measurement and Evaluation in Counseling and Development, 19,* 131–140.

Robert, J. A., Ryan, J. J., McEntyre, W. L., McFarland, R. S., Lips, O. J., & Rosenberg, S. (1985). MCMI characteristics of DSM–III: Posttraumatic stress disorder in Vietnam veterans. *Journal of Personality Assessment, 49,* 226–230.

Rogers, R., Salekin, R. T., & Sewell, K. W. (1999). Validation of the Millon Clinical Multiaxial Inventory for Axis II disorders: Does it meet the Daubert standard? *Law and Human Behavior, 23,* 425–443.

Rogers, R., Salekin, R. T., & Sewell, K. W. (2000). The MCMI and the Daubert standard: Separating rhetoric from reality. *Law and Human Behavior, 24,* 501–506.

Rorer, L. G., & Dawes, R. M. (1982). A base-rate bootstrap. *Journal of Consulting and Clinical Psychology, 50,* 419–425.

Rorschach, H. (1921). *Psychodiagnostics.* Bern, Switzerland: Hans Huber Publishers.

Ross, C. A., & Ellason, J. (1999). Comment on the effectiveness of treatment for dissociative identity disorder. *Psychological Reports, 84,* 1109–1110.

Ross, C., Ryan, L., Voigt, H., & Eide, L. (1991). High and low dissociators in a college student population. *Dissociation, 4,* 147–151.

Rubino, I., Saya, A., & Pezzarossa, B. (1992). Percept–genetic signs of repression in histrionic disorder. *Perceptual and Motor Skills, 74,* 451–464.

Rudd, M. D., & Orman, D. T. (1996). Millon Clinical Multiaxial Inventory profiles and maladjustment in the military: Preliminary findings. *Military Medicine, 161,* 349–351.

Sabshin, M. (1989). Normality and the boundaries of psychopathology. *Journal of Personality Disorders, 3,* 259–273.

Safran, J. D., Segal, Z. V., Vallis, T. M., Shaw, B. F., & Wallner Samstag, L. (1993). Assessing patient suitability for short-term cognitive therapy with an interpersonal focus. *Cognitive Therapy and Research, 17,* 23–38.

Sansone, R. A., & Fine, M. A. (1992). Borderline personality as a predictor of outcome in women with eating disorders. *Journal of Personality Disorders, 6,* 176–186.

Schinka, J. A., & Borum, R. (1993). Readability of adult psychopathology inventories. *Psychological Assessment, 5,* 384–386.

Schmidt, J. P., Sanders, A. U., Burdick, T. H., & Lohr, J. M. (1991, August). *Bulimia symptoms and personality characteristics: A cluster analysis comparison.* Paper presented at the 99th Annual Convention of the American Psychological Association, San Francisco, CA.

Schoenberg, M., Dorr, D., & Morgan, C. D. (2003). The ability of the Millon Clinical Multiaxial Inventory—Third Edition to detect malingering. *Psychological Assessment, 15,* 198–204.

Schuler, C. E., Snibbe, J. R., & Buckwalter, J. G. (1994). Validity of the MMPI Personality Disorder scales (MMPI-PD). *Journal of Clinical Psychology, 50,* 220–227.

Schuller, D. R., Bagby, R. M., Levitt, A. J., & Joffe, R. T. (1993). A comparison of personality characteristics of seasonal and nonseasonal major depression. *Comprehensive Psychiatry, 34,* 360–362.

Schutte, J. M. (2001). Using the MCMI–III in forensic evaluations. *American Journal of Forensic Psychology, 19,* 5–20.

Schwartz, M. A., Wiggins, O. P., & Norko, M. A. (1989). Prototypes, ideal types and personality disorders: The return to classical psychiatry. *Journal of Personality Disorders, 3,* 1–9.

Seligman, M. E. P. (1995). The effectiveness of psychotherapy: The *Consumer Reports* study. *American Psychologist, 50,* 965–974.

Sexton, D. L., McIlwraith, R., Barnes, G., & Dunn, R. (1987). Comparison of the MCMI and the MMPI–168 as psychiatric inpatient screening inventories. *Journal of Personality Assessment, 51,* 388–398.

Sherwood, R. J., Funari, D. J., & Piekarski, A. M. (1990). Adapted character styles of Vietnam veterans with posttraumatic stress disorder. *Psychological Reports, 66,* 623–631.

Shipley, W. C. (1986). *Shipley Institute of Living Scale.* Los Angeles: Western Psychological Services.

Shure, G. H., & Rogers, M. S. (1965). Note of caution on the factor analysis of the MMPI. *Psychological Bulletin, 63,* 14–18.

Siddall, J. W., & Keogh, N. J. (1993). Utility of computer interpretive reports based on counselors' ratings of the Diagnostic Inventory of Personality and Symptoms. *Psychological Reports, 72,* 347–350.

Siever, L. & Davis, K. (1991). A psychobiological perspective on the personality disorders. *American Journal of Psychiatry, 148,* 1647–1658.

Silverman, J. S., & Loychik, S. (1990). Brain-mapping abnormalities in a family with three obsessive compulsive children. *Journal of Neuropsychiatry, 2,* 319–322.

Silverman, J. T. (1979). *The effect of personality variables on the patient–therapist relationship in psychotherapy.* Unpublished doctoral dissertation, Boston College, Boston.

Sim, J. P., & Romney, D. M. (1990). The relationship between a circumplex model of interpersonal behaviors and personality disorders. *Journal of Personality Disorders, 4,* 329–341.

Simonsen, E., Haslund, J., Larsen, A., & Borup, C. (1992). Personality pattern in first time admitted alcoholics. *Nordic Journal of Psychiatry, 46,* 175–179.

Simonsen, E., & Mortensen, E. L. (1990). Difficulties in translation of personality scales. *Journal of Personality Disorders, 4,* 290–296.

Sinha, B. K., & Watson, D. C. (1999). Predicting personality disorder traits with the Defense Style Questionnaire in a normal sample. *Journal of Personality Disorders, 13,* 281–286.

Sinha, B. K., & Watson, D. C. (2001). Personality disorder in university students: A multitrait–multimethod matrix study. *Journal of Personality Disorders, 15,* 235–244.

Smith, D., Carroll, J., & Fuller, G. (1988). The Millon Clinical Multiaxial Inventory and the MMPI in a private outpatient mental health clinic population. *Journal of Clinical Psychology, 44,* 165–174.

Smith Silberman, C., Roth, L., Segal, D. L., & Burns, W. J. (1997). Relationship between the Millon Clinical Multiaxial Inventory–II and Coolidge Axis II Inventory in chronically mentally ill older adults: A pilot study. *Journal of Clinical Psychology, 53,* 559–566.

Snibbe, J. R., Peterson, P. J., & Sosner, B. (1980). Study of psychological characteristics of a worker's compensation sample using the MMPI and the Millon Clinical Multiaxial Inventory. *Psychological Reports, 47,* 959–966.

Soldz, S., Budman, S., Demby, A., & Merry, J. (1993a). Diagnostic agreement between the Personality Disorder Examination and the MCMI–II. *Journal of Personality Assessment, 60,* 486–499.

Soldz, S., Budman, S., Demby, A., & Merry, J. (1993b). Representation of personality disorders in circumplex and five factor space: Explorations with a clinical sample. *Psychological Assessment, 5,* 41–52.

Somwaru, D. P., & Ben-Porath, Y. S. (1995, March). *Development and reliability of MMPI–2 based personality disorder scales.* Paper presented at the Annual Workshop and Symposium on Recent Developments in Use of the MMPI–2 and MMPI–A, Saint Petersburg Beach, FL.

Sperling, M. B., Sharp, J. L., & Fishler, P. H. (1991). On the nature of attachment in a borderline population: A preliminary investigation. *Psychological Reports, 68,* 543–546.

Stankovic, S., Libb, J. W., Freeman, A., & Roseman, J. (1992). Post-treatment stability of the MCMI–II personality scales in depressed outpatients. *Journal of Personality Disorders, 6,* 82–89.

Stark, M. J., & Campbell, B. K. (1988). Personality, drug use, and early attrition from substance abuse treatment. *American Journal of Drug and Alcohol Abuse, 14,* 475–485.

Stedman, J. M., Hatch, J. P., & Schoenfeld, L. S. (2001). The current status of psychological assessment training in graduate and professional schools. *Journal of Personality Assessment, 77,* 398–407.

Stewart, A. E., Hyer, L., Retzlaff, P., & Ofman, P. (1995, August). *MCMI–II personality scales: Factors and latent traits.* Paper presented at the 103rd Annual Convention of the American Psychological Association, New York.

Stone, M. H. (1980). *The borderline syndromes.* New York: McGraw-Hill.

Strack, S. (1987). Development and validation of an adjective check list to assess the Millon personality types in a normal population. *Journal of Personality Assessment, 51,* 588–594.

Strack, S. (1990). *Manual for the Personality Adjective Check List (PACL).* Richland, WA: Pacific Psychological.

Strack, S. (1991a). Factor analysis of the MCMI–II and the PACL basic personality scales in a college sample. *Journal of Personality Assessment, 57,* 345–355.

Strack, S. (1991b, August). *Response bias and the MCMI–II: Clinical and research issues.* Paper presented at the 99th Annual Convention of the American Psychological Association, San Francisco, CA.

Strack, S. (1999). Millon's normal personality styles and dimensions. *Journal of Personality Assessment, 72,* 426–436.

Strack, S., Choca, J. P., & Gurtman, M. B. (2001). Circular structure of the MCMI–III personality disorder scales. *Journal of Personality Disorders, 15,* 263–274.

Strack, S., & Lorr, M. (1994). *Differentiating normal and abnormal personality.* New York: Springer.

Strack, S., & Lorr, M. (1997). The challenge of differentiating normal and disordered personality. *Journal of Personality Disorders, 11,* 105–122.

Strack, S., Lorr, M., & Campbell, L. (1989, August). *Similarities in Millon personality styles among normals and psychiatric patients.* Paper presented at the 97th Annual Convention of the American Psychological Association, New Orleans, LA.

Strack, S., Lorr, M., & Campbell, L. (1990). An evaluation of Millon's circular model of personality disorders. *Journal of Personality Disorders, 4,* 353–361.

Strack, S., Lorr, M., Campbell, L., & Lamnin, A. (1992). Personality disorder and clinical syndrome factors of MCMI–II scales. *Journal of Personality Disorders, 6,* 40–52.

Strauman, T. J., & Wetzler, S. (1992). The factor structure of SCL-90 and MCMI scale scores: Within measure and interbattery analyses. *Multivariate Behavioral Research, 27,* 1–20.

Streiner, D. L., Goldberg, J. O., & Miller, H. R. (1993). MCMI–II item weights: Their lack of effectiveness. *Journal of Personality Assessment, 60,* 471–476.

Streiner, D. L., & Miller, H. R. (1989). The MCMI–II: How much better than the MCMI? *Journal of Personality Assessment, 53,* 81–84.

Streiner, D., & Miller, H. (1990). Maximum likelihood estimates of the accuracy of four diagnostic techniques. *Educational and Psychological Measurement, 50,* 653–662.

Sullivan, H. S. (1953). *The interpersonal theory of psychiatry.* New York: Norton.

Sweeney, J. A., Clarkin, J. F., & Fitzgibbon, M. L. (1987). Current practice of psychological assessment. *Professional Psychology: Research and Practice, 18,* 377–380.

Swirsky-Sacchetti, T., Gorton, G., Samuel, S., Sobel, R., Genetta-Wadley, A., & Burleigh, B. (1993). Neuropsychological function in borderline personality disorder. *Journal of Clinical Psychology, 49,* 385–396.

Tamkin, A. S., Carson, M. F., Nixon, D. H., & Hyer, L. A. (1987). A comparison among some measures of depression in male alcoholics. *Journal of Studies on Alcohol, 48,* 176–178.

Tango, R. A., & Dziuban, C. D. (1984). The use of personality components in the interpretation of career indecision. *Journal of Student Personnel, 25,* 509–512.

Tellegen, A. (1985). Structures of mood and personality and their relevance to assessing anxiety, with an emphasis on self-report. In A. H. Tuma & J. D. Maser (Eds.), *Anxiety and the anxiety disorders* (pp. 681–706). Hillsdale, NJ: Erlbaum.

Terpylak, O., & Schuerger, J. M. (1994). Broad factor scales of the 16 PF Fifth Edition and Millon personality disorder scales: A replication. *Psychological Reports, 74,* 124–126.

Terry, C. (1990, December 30). Vaclav Havel's new role. *Chicago Tribune,* Section 13, p. 3.

Tisdale, M. J., Pendleton, L., & Marler, M. (1990). MCMI characteristics of DSM–III–R bulimics. *Journal of Personality Assessment, 55,* 477–483.

Tolman, R. M. (1989). The development of a measure of psychological maltreatment of women by their male partners. *Violence and Victims, 4,* 159–177.

Torgersen, S., & Alnaes, R. (1990). The relationship between the MCMI personality scales and the DSM–III Axis II. *Journal of Personality Assessment, 55,* 698–707.

Turley, B., Bates, G. W., Edwards, J., & Jackson, H. J. (1992). MCMI–II personality disorders in recent onset bipolar disorders. *Journal of Clinical Psychology, 48,* 320–329.

Tyrer, P. (1988). What's wrong with the DSM–III personality disorders? *Journal of Personality Disorders, 2,* 281–291.

Uomoto, J. M., Turner, J. A., & Herron, L. D. (1988). Use of the MMPI and the MCMI in predicting outcome of lumbar laminectomy. *Journal of Clinical Psychology, 44,* 191–197.

Vaglum, P., Friis, S., Irion, T., Johns, S., Karterud, S., Larsen, F., et al. (1990). Treatment response of severe and nonsevere personality disorders in a therapeutic community day unit. *Journal of Personality Disorders, 4,* 161–172.

Van Denburg, E., & Choca, J. P. (1997). Interpretation of the MCMI–III. In T. Millon (Ed.), *The Millon inventories* (pp. 41–58). New York: Guilford Press.

Van Gorp, W. G., & Meyer, R. G. (1986). The detection of faking on the Millon Clinical Multiaxial Inventory (MCMI). *Journal of Clinical Psychology, 42,* 742–747.

Vereycken, J., Vertommen, H., & Corveleyn, J. (2002). Authority conflicts and personality disorders. *Journal of Personality Disorders, 16,* 41–51.

Vincent, K. R. (1985). *Revised manual for the Diagnostic Inventory of Personality Symptoms.* Richland, WA: Pacific Psychological.

Vollrath, M., Alnaes, R., & Torgersen, S. (1994). Coping and MCMI–II personality disorders. *Journal of Personality Disorders, 8,* 53–63.

Vollrath, M., Alnaes, R., & Torgersen, S. (1995). Coping styles predict change in personality disorders. *Journal of Personality Disorders, 9,* 371–385.

Vorce, D. E., Jones, K. A., Helder, L. M., Pettibon, W. H., & Reiter, W. M. (1995, August). *Correcting MCMI–II subscale Base Rate scores for chronic fatigue syndrome (CFS) patients.* Paper presented at the 103rd Annual Convention of the American Psychological Association, New York.

Wakefield, H., & Underwager, R. (1993). Misuse of psychological tests in forensic settings: Some horrible examples. *American Journal of Forensic Psychology, 11,* 55–75.

Wall, T. L., Schuckit, M. A., Mungas, D., & Ehlers, C. L. (1990). EEG alpha activity and personality traits. *Alcohol, 7,* 461–464.

Ward, L. C. (1994). Correspondence of the MMPI–2 and MCMI–II in male substance abusers. *Journal of Personality Assessment, 64,* 390–393.

Watkins, C. E., Campbell, V. L., Nieberding, R., & Hallmark, R. (1995). Contemporary practices of psychological assessment by clinical psychologists. *Professional Psychology: Research and Practice, 26,* 54–60.

Watson, D. C., & Sinha, B. K. (1995). Dimensional structure of personality disorder inventories: A comparison of normal and clinical populations. *Personality and Individual Differences, 19,* 817–826.

Wechsler, D. (1997). *Wechsler Adult Intelligence Scale—Third Edition.* San Antonio, TX: The Psychological Corporation.

Weekes, J. R., & Morison, S. J. (1993). Offender typologies: Identifying treatment-relevant personality characteristics. *Forum on Corrections Research, 5,* 10–12.

Weekes, J. R., Morison, S. J., Millson, W. A., & Fettig, D. M. (1995). A comparison of Native, Métis, and Caucasian offender profiles on the MCMI. *Canadian Journal of Behavioral Science, 27,* 187–198.

Werman, D. (1984). *The practice of supportive psychotherapy.* New York: Brunner/Mazel.

West, M., Sheldon, A., & Reiffer, L. (1987). An approach to the delineation of adult attachment: Scale development and reliability. *Journal of Nervous and Mental Disease, 175,* 738–741.

Wetzler, S. (1990). The Millon Clinical Multiaxial Inventory (MCMI): A review. *Journal of Personality Assessment, 55,* 445–464.

Wetzler, S., & Dubro, A. (1990). Diagnosis of personality disorders by the Millon Clinical Multiaxial Inventory. *Journal of Nervous and Mental Disease, 178,* 261–263.

Wetzler, S., Kahn, R. S., Cahn, W., van Praag, H. M., & Asnis, G. M. (1990). Psychological test characteristics of depressed and panic patients. *Psychiatry Research, 31,* 179–192.

Wetzler, S., Kahn, R., Strauman, T., & Dubro, A. (1989). Diagnosis of major depression by self-report. *Journal of Personality Assessment, 53,* 22–30.

Wetzler, S., Khadivi, A., & Oppenheim, S. (1995). The psychological assessment of depression: Unipolars versus bipolars. *Journal of Personality Assessment, 65,* 557–566.

Wetzler, S., & Marlowe, D. (1990). "Faking bad" on the MMPI, MMPI–2 and Millon–II. *Psychological Reports, 67,* 1117–1118.

Wetzler, S., & Marlowe, D. (1993). The diagnosis and assessment of depression, mania, and psychosis by self-report. *Journal of Personality Assessment, 60,* 1–31.

Wheeler, D. S., & Schwarz, J. C. (1989). Millon Clinical Multiaxial Inventory (MCMI) scores with a collegiate sample: Long-term stability and self-other agreement. *Journal of Psychopathology and Behavioral Assessment, 11,* 339–352.

Whyne-Berman, S. M., & McCann, J. T. (1995). Defense mechanisms and personality disorders: An empirical test of Millon's theory. *Journal of Personality Assessment, 64,* 132–144.

Widiger, T. A. (1985). Review of Millon Clinical Multiaxial Inventory. In J. V. Mitchell, Jr. (Ed.), *Ninth mental measurement yearbook* (pp. 986–988). Lincoln, NE: Buros Institute.

Widiger, T. A. (1989). The categorical distinction between personality and affective disorders. *Journal of Personality Disorders, 3,* 77–91.

Widiger, T. A. (1992). Categorical versus dimensional classification: Implications from and for research. *Journal of Personality Disorders, 6,* 287–300.

Widiger, T. A. (1999). Millon's dimensional polarities. *Journal of Personality Assessment, 72,* 365–389.

Widiger, T. A., & Corbitt, E. M. (1994). Normal versus abnormal personality from the perspective of the DSM. In S. Strack & M. Lorr (Eds.), *Differentiating normal and abnormal personality* (pp. 158–175). New York: Springer.

Widiger, T. A., & Frances, A. (1987). Interviews and inventories for the measurement of personality disorders. *Clinical Psychology Review, 7,* 49–74.

Widiger, T. A., Frances, A., Spitzer, R. L., & Williams, J. B. (1988). The DSM–III–R personality disorders: An overview. *American Journal of Psychiatry, 145,* 786–795.

Widiger, T. A., Hurt, S. W., Frances, A., Clarkin, J. F., & Gilmore, M. (1984). Diagnostic efficiency and the DSM–III. *Archives of General Psychiatry, 41,* 1005–1012.

Widiger, T. A., & Kelso, K. (1983). Psychodiagnosis of Axis II. *Clinical Psychology Review, 3,* 491–510.

Widiger, T. A., & Sanderson, C. (1987). The convergent and discriminant validity of the MCMI as a measure of the DSM–III personality disorders. *Journal of Personality Assessment, 51,* 228–242.

Widiger, T. A., Trull, T. J., Clarkin, J. F., Sanderson, C., & Costa, P. T. (1994). A description of the DSM–III and DSM–IV personality disorders with the five-factor model of personality. In P. T. Costa & T. A. Widiger (Eds.). *Personality disorders and the five-factor model of personality* (pp. 41–57). Washington, DC: American Psychological Association.

Widiger, T. A., Williams, J. B. W., Spitzer, R. L., & Frances, A. (1985). The MCMI as a measure of DSM–III. *Journal of Personality Assessment, 49,* 366–378.

Widiger, T. A., Williams, J. B. W., Spitzer, R. L., & Frances, A. (1986). The MCMI and DSM–III: A brief rejoinder to Millon. *Journal of Personality Assessment, 50,* 198–204.

Wiederman, M. W., & Pryor, T. L. (1997). MCMI–II personality scale scores among women with anorexia nervosa or bulimia nervosa. *Journal of Personality Assessment, 69,* 508–516.

Wierzbicki, M. (1993a). The relationship between MCMI subtlety and severity. *Journal of Personality Assessment, 61,* 259–263.

Wierzbicki, M. (1993b). Use of MCMI subtle and obvious scales to detect faking. *Journal of Clinical Psychology, 49,* 809–814.

Wierzbicki, M. (1997). Use of subtle and obvious scales to detect faking on the MCMI–II. *Journal of Clinical Psychology, 53,* 421–426.

Wierzbicki, M., & Daleiden, E. L. (1993). The differential responding of college students to subtle and obvious MCMI subscales. *Journal of Clinical Psychology, 49,* 204–208.

Wierzbicki, M., & Goldade, P. (1993). Sex typing of the Millon Clinical Multiaxial Inventory. *Psychological Reports, 72,* 1115–1121.

Wierzbicki, M., & Gorman, J. L. (1995). Correspondence between students' scores on the Millon Clinical Multiaxial Inventory–II and Personality Diagnostic Questionnaire—Revised. *Psychological Reports, 77,* 1079–1082.

Wierzbicki, M., & Howard, B. J. (1992). The differential responding of male prisoners to subtle and obvious MCMI subscales. *Journal of Personality Assessment, 58,* 115–126.

Wiggins, J. S. (1979). A psychological taxonomy of trait-descriptive terms: The interpersonal domain. *Journal of Personality and Social Psychology, 37,* 395–412.

Wiggins, J. S. (1982). Circumplex models of interpersonal behavior in clinical psychology. In P. C. Kendall & J. N. Butcher (Eds.), *Handbook of research methods in clinical psychology* (pp. 183–222). New York: Wiley.

Wiggins, J. S. (2003). *Paradigms of personality assessment.* New York: Guilford Press.

Wiggins, J., & Pincus, A. (1989). Conceptions of personality disorders and dimensions of personality. *Psychological Assessment, 4,* 305–316.

Winston, A., Pinsker, H., & McCullough, L. (1986). A review of supportive psychotherapy. *Hospital and Community Psychiatry, 37,* 1105–1114.

Wise, E. A. (1994a). Managed care and the psychometric validity of the MMPI and MCMI personality disorder scales. *Psychotherapy in Private Practice, 13,* 81–97.

Wise, E. A. (1994b). Personality style codetype concordance between the MCMI and the MBHI. *Journal of Clinical Psychology, 50,* 367–380.

Wise, E. A. (1996). Comparative validity of the MMPI–2 and MCMI–II personality disorder classifications. *Journal of Personality Assessment, 66,* 569–582.

Wise, E. A. (2001). The comparative validity of the MCMI–II and the MMPI–2 personality disorder scales with forensic examinees. *Journal of Personality Disorders, 15,* 275–279.

Wise, E. A. (2002). Relationship of personality disorders with MMPI–2 malingering, defensiveness, and inconsistent response scales among forensic examinees. *Psychological Reports, 90,* 760–766.

Wolberg, W. H., Tanner, M. A., Romsaas, E. P., Trump, D. L., & Malec, J. F. (1987). Factors influencing options in primary breast cancer treatment. *Journal of Clinical Oncology, 5,* 68–74.

Wright, W. (1975). Counselor dogmatism: Willingness to disclose and client's empathy ratings. *Journal of Counseling Psychology, 22,* 390–394.

Yeager, R. J., DiGiuseppe, R., Resweber, P. J., & Leaf, R. (1992). Comparison of Millon personality profiles of chronic residential substance abusers and a general outpatient population. *Psychological Reports, 71,* 71–79.

Zarrella, K. L., Schuerger, J. M., & Ritz, G. H. (1990). Estimation of MCMI DSM–III Axis II constructs from MMPI scales and subscales. *Journal of Personality Assessment, 55,* 195–201.

Index

A

B

C

D

E

I

J

K

L

M

N

O

P

R

S

T

U

V

W

About the Author

James P. Choca, PhD, is the director of doctoral studies in the School of Psychology at Roosevelt University in Chicago. Dr. Choca serves as a diagnostic consultant in several school districts and as an attending psychologist in two private hospitals. He is the author of numerous articles and book chapters and has given presentations on different aspects of the Millon Clinical Multiaxial Inventory. His interest in the use of computers in psychology has also led to articles and presentations as well as to the development of two commercially available programs: one to administer the Category Test of the Halstead Reitan Battery and one to assist with the administration and scoring of the Rorschach Inkblot Test. More recently, he has been directing the development of a new computerized test to measure *Diagnostic and Statistical Manual of Mental Disorders* (4th ed.) entities and the Emotional Assessment System.